Access to **Maths**

PEARSON

We work with leading authors to develop the
strongest educational materials in maths,
bringing cutting-edge thinking and best learning
practice to a global market.

Under a range of well-known imprints, including
Prentice Hall, we craft high quality print and
electronic publications which help readers to
understand and apply their content,
whether studying or at work.

To find out more about the complete range of our
publishing, please visit us on the World Wide Web at:
www.pearsoned.co.uk

ACCESS TO
MATHS

Sheila Evans University of Derby

**Prentice Hall
is an imprint of**

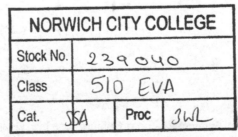
Harlow, England • London • New York • Boston • San Francisco • Toronto • Sydney • Singapore • Hong Kong
Tokyo • Seoul • Taipei • New Delhi • Cape Town • Madrid • Mexico City • Amsterdam • Munich • Paris • Milan

Pearson Education Limited

Edinburgh Gate

Harlow

Essex CM20 2JE

England

and Associated Companies throughout the world

Visit us on the World Wide Web at:
www.pearsoned.co.uk

First published 2009

© Pearson Education Limited 2009

ISBN 978-1-4058-5961-5

British Library Cataloguing-in-Publication Data
A catalogue record for this book is available from the British Library.

Library of Congress Cataloging-in-Publication Data
Evans, Sheila, 1960–
  Access to maths / Sheila Evans.
    p. cm.
  ISBN 978-1-4058-5961-5 (pbk.)
  1. Mathematics–Study and teaching (Secondary)–Great Britain.   2. General
Certificate of Secondary Education.   I. Title.
  QA14.G7E93 2009
  510–dc22
                                                       2009020711

10 9 8 7 6 5 4 3 2 1
13 12 11 10 09

Typeset in 9/12pt Helvetica by 35
Printed and bound in Great Britain by Ashford Colour Press Ltd, Gosport, Hampshire

The publisher's policy is to use paper manufactured from sustainable forests.

Contents

Chapter 2: Collecting, Recording and Analysing Data   135

Chapter 3: Shape, Space and Measurement   223

About This Book

This book is for anyone learning Maths on an Access course, or studying for an Adult Numeracy qualification or a GCSE.

It will also help those who may be studying on courses not normally thought of as 'mathematical', but where Maths plays a part, whether healthcare, hairdressing or events management.

Access to Maths is full of everyday practical applications for Maths, from diet and exercise to healthcare and holidays. It will provide you with a sound understanding of how Maths is relevant, interesting and informative. It may even help you avoid some common pitfalls encountered in totalling up shopping bills, working out percentages or building a straight wall!

The book is organised into four chapters to provide complete coverage of number work; collecting, recording and analysing data; shape, space and measurement; and algebra. Assignment questions at the end of each chapter will give you plenty of opportunity for consolidation work, bringing together different aspects of the chapter. The 'Mapping Out' flow charts are there to guide you through questions, however they may not always be the sole route through a problem, so don't think you have to stick rigidly to them. If your own method works, use it!

Acknowledgements

I'm indebted to the many students, friends and colleagues without whom this book could never have been written. I would like to thank Dave Bailey, Ian Woodley, Hugh Milner, Rachel Maynard, Kath Nolan, Pauline Bonner and Emma Dowse who kindly provided detailed background information for the case studies. I am particularly grateful to Gervaise McCarron, Helen Popplewell, Cheryl Lanyon, Claire Lambert, Barbara Marsh,

Rita Adair, Sylvia Evans and Nessie Stevenson, all who provided some great ideas for the book. I would like to especially thank Colin Billett, John Manson, Mukesh Patel, Janette Reynolds, Anna Smith, Janet Stanley and Hilary Walsh who took time out to evaluate the book when in its early stages. And lastly I would like to thank my family – Ken, George and Harry – for supporting and encouraging me throughout.

Sheila Evans

1 Number Work

Introduction

Figure it out

A man buys a £100 mobile phone. After he's paid he decides he actually wanted a different phone. The shop assistant takes back the first phone, gives him the new phone and asks for £100. 'That's ridiculous,' says the man. 'I've just paid you £100 and also given you a £100 phone – that makes £200 so we're quits!' He walks out, leaving the assistant scratching his head . . .

What should the shop assistant have said or done?

Paired worked

List five areas of everyday life where Maths is used.

A web discussion on the relevance of number work

> I hated Maths at school, never saw the point of it and still don't. Since leaving I've not used it once, not in my job, not at home and never out and about.

> What about checking your supermarket change?

> Well, I do give it a quick glance to make sure it's about right but I never add it up – it wouldn't make me too popular with other customers in the queue!

> Got you – that's maths – you're making a quick estimation of what your change should be.

> Mmm . . . maybe, but what about all that stuff we had to learn about percentages – I've never touched that again.

> Here is a recent attention grabbing headline from a national newspaper:
> '*Student dropouts increase by 50%.*'
> If you understood percentages you'd be asking the question '*That does sound a lot but how many used to drop out, ten or ten thousand?*' That would make the difference between the headline being really sensational or true news.

> OK, but what about negative numbers – I've got **you** there. We did loads of the stuff at school and I certainly don't feel I've been deprived by not using them since.

> Have you never been overdrawn? Knowing how much you need to pay back over the year to get you back into the black is a very practical use of negative numbers.

> Mmm . . . well on that note I think I'll see if I can improve my bank balance with some online poker – only kidding – I do know about negative returns.

1.1 Place Value

The place a **digit** sits within a number determines its value.

Key term

Digit:
Figures 0–9, used to form numbers, e.g. the number 2 563 contains four digits.

Example

Write down the value of 4 in the following numbers:

a. 240
b. 2 427
c. 842 136
d. 4 937 002

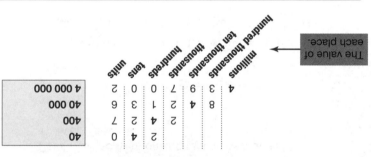

Each place is 10× bigger than the previous →

	millions	hundred thousands	ten thousands	thousands	hundreds	tens	units	
	4	9	3	7	0	0	2	**4 000 000**
		8	4	2	1	3	6	**40 000**
				2	4	2	7	**400**
					2	4	0	**40**

The value of each place. ←

Work it out

1. Write down the value of **6** in the following numbers:
   a. 2 **6**35
   b. 7**6** 803
   c. **6** 921 320
   d. 54 3**26**
   e. 1 **6**82 341
   f. **6**52 003

2. Use these digits to write down the largest and smallest possible number:
   a. 0, 4, 5, 3
   b. 1, 7, 9, 7

3. In the number 73 452, what single digit represents the:
   a. hundreds?
   b. ten thousands?

4. In the number 23 504 729, what single digit represents the:
   a. millions?
   b. hundred thousands?

5. Copy the line and write:
   • 6 in the hundreds place
   • 3 in the ten thousands place
   • 0 in the units place
   • 2 in the thousands place
   • 7 in the hundred thousands place
   • 9 in the tens place

   ___ ___ ___ ___ ___ ___

When is seven not worth seven?
When it is in the middle of a number, e.g. in the number 370 the 7 is worth seventy.

6. Copy the line and write:

- 7 in the millions place
- 5 in the tens place
- 1 in the thousands place
- 4 in the hundred thousands place
- 0 in the units place
- 0 in the ten thousands place
- 3 in the hundreds place

___ ___ ___ ___ ___ ___ ___ ___

7. Which is bigger:

a.   23 045 or 23 054

b.   539 928 or 540 989

c.   1 905 393 or 1 905 387

d.   7 349 002 or 7 349 200

Keeping score in a TV quiz

8. The producer of a games show has come up with a unique method of scoring. Contestants are asked eight questions at each of the five scoring levels. The winner is the person with the most points.

a.   What is the total number of questions each contestant is asked?

Points gained from one correct answer at the:

1st level: 1

2nd level: 10

3rd level: 100

4th level: 1 000

5th level: 10 000

From level to level the difficulty of the questions remains the same.

These are the results of two players:

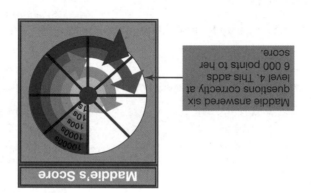

Maddie's Score

Maddie answered six questions correctly at level 4. This adds 6 000 points to her score.

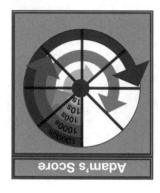

Adam's Score

b.   What is Maddie's score?

c.   What is Adam's score?

d.   What is the problem with this method of scoring?

e.   Think up a more exciting way of keeping the score, but still using the concept of levels.

9. Jim has completed one game of pinball and is in the middle of a second. The diagrams show the two games.

Pinball is a game where a player scores points by manipulating a metal ball to hit targets. The aim of the game is to score as many points as possible. In this version of the game each target can be hit a maximum of three times, after which hits do not change the scoreline.

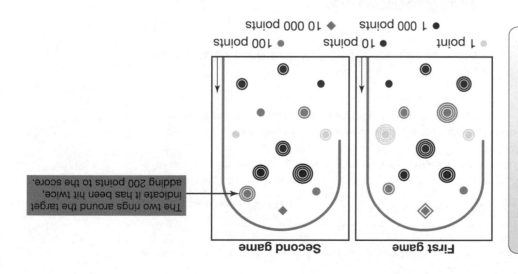

First game   **Second game**

The two rings around the target indicate it has been hit twice, adding 200 points to the score.

● 1 point   ● 10 points   ● 100 points
● 1 000 points   ◆ 10 000 points

a. What is the most any player can score in one game?
b. Work out how many points Jim has scored in the first game.
c. Before the second game ends Jim hits three more targets, none of them a 10 000-point target. What is the most he can score?
d. In a third game Jim scores 11 325, but didn't hit any of the 1000-point targets. Draw a diagram of the situation.

Using place value in sums

10. Use the digits in the bottom part of each diagram and any combination of pluses and minuses to obtain the answer in the top section. The digits can be combined to make a larger number but must appear in order in the sum. The first one has been done for you:

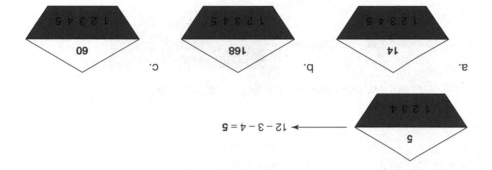

5 / 1 2 3 4 → $12 - 3 - 4 = 5$

a. 14 / 1 2 3 4 5
b. 168 / 1 2 3 4 5
c. 60 / 1 2 3 4 5

Reading and writing numbers in words

Here is some information about wind turbines:

> **Wind turbines in the UK**
>
> A wind turbine produces enough electricity to supply **1 203** homes. There are currently **one thousand**, **eight hundred and seventy six** wind turbines in the UK, producing enough electricity to supply the equivalent of **2 256 828** homes. They reduce CO_2 emissions by an estimated **four million**, **nine hundred and fifty two thousand**, **three hundred and sixty six** tonnes.

The figures in the article can be written in words:

1 203:

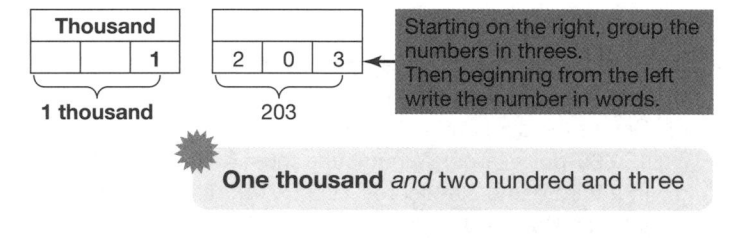

One thousand *and* two hundred and three

2 256 828:

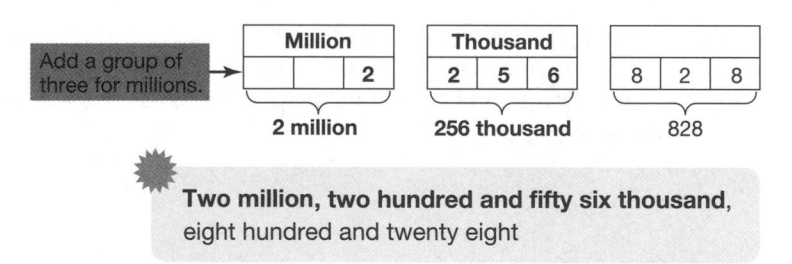

Two million, two hundred and fifty six thousand, eight hundred and twenty eight

The words in the article can be written as figures:

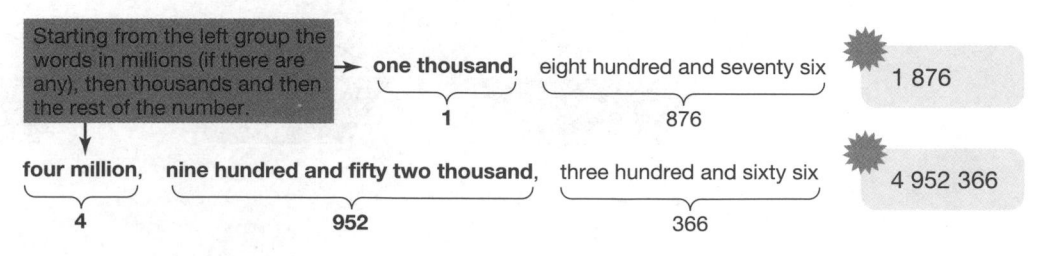

> ## Work it out

1. Write the following figures in words:
    a. 236   b. 89
    c. 23 090   d. 4 506 820.

2. Write the following words in figures:
    a. thirty seven
    b. five hundred and thirty four
    c. forty two thousand, five hundred and eighty three
    d. seven million, three hundred and seven thousand, nine hundred and ninety nine.

3. There are websites that provide a snap shot in numbers of the world around us. Here are a few of the figures:

a. Average number of seconds before there is a death in a Will Smith movie	117
b. The number of people who aren't doctors but play them on TV	Sixty eight
c. The number of people who aren't doctors but play them in hospitals	1 280
d. The number of people who didn't turn up for their own wedding this year	14 073
e. The number of dust mites sharing your bed	Five hundred and seventy eight thousand, two hundred and seven
f. The number of people sharing their heads with lice	3 209 362
g. The number of men who have written letters proposing marriage to Angelina Jolie	Seven thousand, five hundred and eighty
h. The number of people who believe the figures in this question are trustworthy	Fifty three thousand, four hundred and eight
i. The number of people who believe in leprechauns	Fifty three thousand, four hundred and eight

Convert the numbers into words and vice versa.

4. Why is S. Evans not happy with this cheque?

		Date: 28/06/09
Pay S. Evans		
Amount one hundred and twenty thousand,	£ 12,300 —	
Three hundred pounds only		
		P.Pearson

The ancient Egyptians used numbers in many areas of life from building the pyramids and measuring the flood levels of the Nile to calculating taxes and measuring time. They used symbols, known as hieroglyphics to represent numbers:

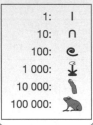

1:	I
10:	∩
100:	℮
1 000:	⚲
10 000:	⌇
100 000:	🐸

Investigation – Egyptian numbers

Here is a document that lists the gifts given at a wedding in ancient Egypt:

> IIII guests each bring ∩∩∩III bushels of barley
>
> IIIII chariots each containing ∩ barrels of wine
>
> ⚲∩∩∩II clay pots of frankincense
>
> IIIIII guests each bring ℮℮III pieces of silk each
>
> ⚲⚲℮℮II royal cubits of land
>
> This all costs well over 🐸🐸🐸II denarii

1. Replace all the Egyptian symbols with ordinary numbers.

2. Write in hieroglyphics the total number of:
   a. bushels of barley given
   b. barrels of wine given
   c. pieces of silk given.

3. What is the big disadvantage of the Egyptian number system?

Multiplying and dividing by 10, 100, 1 000 etc.

A house worth £25 000 30 years ago now commands an asking price ten times this value. What is the current price of the house?

25 000 × 10 = **£250 000**   ⟵   Adding a zero means the number becomes ten times bigger.

Example

This diagram shows some distances relative to the distance between London and New York.

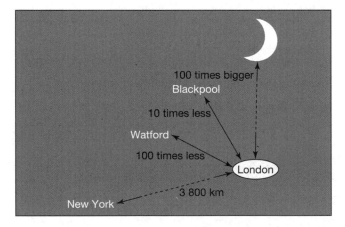

What is the distance between London and Blackpool?

 3 80Ø ÷ 10 = **380 kilometres**   ← Removing a zero means the number becomes ten times smaller.

What is the distance between London and Watford?

 3 8ØØ ÷ 100 = **38 kilometres**   ← Removing two zeros means the number becomes one hundred times smaller.

What is the distance between the earth and the moon?

 3 840 × 100 = **384 000 kilometres**   ← Adding two zeros means the number becomes one hundred times bigger.

Work it out

> **Multiplying (add)/ dividing (remove) by:**
>
> *Add/remove*
> 10 → 1 zero
> 100 → 2 zeros
> 1 000 → 3 zeros
> 10 000 → 4 zeros
> and so on.
>
> This method only works when there are no decimal points in the question or the answer.

1. Work out:
   a. $5 \times 1\,000$
   b. 3×100
   c. $45 \times 10\,000$
   d. $234 \times 1\,000$

2. Copy and fill in the missing figures:
   a. $4 \times \square = 400$
   b. $8 \times 10 = \square$
   c. $23 \times \square = 2\,300$
   d. $\square \times 1\,000 = 540\,000$

3. Work out:
   a. $600 \div 10$
   b. $7\,200 \div 100$
   c. $4\,320\,000 \div 10\,000$
   d. $43\,000 \div 100$

4. Copy and fill in the missing figures:
   a. $520 \div \square = 52$
   b. $8\,000 \div 100 = \square$
   c. $67\,000 \div \square = 670$
   d. $\square \div 1\,000 = 730$

1.2 Number Types

Key terms

Negative number
Number less than zero.

Integer or whole number
A positive or negative number with no fractional parts.

Natural number
A positive whole number.

Factor
A number that divides exactly into another number, e.g. 1, 2, 3, 4 and 6 are all factors of 12.

Prime number
An integer greater than one that can only be divided by itself and one. It has two factors.

Prime factor
Factor of a number that is also a prime e.g. 3 and 5 are both prime factors of 15.

Numbers can be classified according to their characteristics.

Integers	$\{\ldots, -3, -2, -1, 0, 1, 2, 3, \ldots\}$
Natural numbers	$\{1, 2, 3, \ldots\}$
Prime numbers	$\{2, 3, 5, 7, 11, 13, \ldots\}$

Example 1

A furniture designer wants to make a spice rack that can hold 12 spice jars. He draws three possible arrangements:

6 by 2   4 by 3   12 by 1

The jars have been arranged using the **factors** of 12: 6, 2, 4, 3, 12 and 1.
The prime factors of 12 are 2 and 3.

Example 2

Use a **prime factor** tree to work out how 60 can be written as a product of its prime factors:

A prime factor tree:

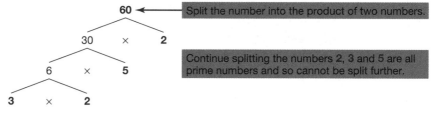

The prime factors of 60 are 2, 3 and 5.
60 as a product of primes is $3 \times 2 \times 5 \times 2$.

Example 3

The furniture designer now wants to make two DVD racks, one that will hold 126 DVDs and the other 84. For ease of construction he wants both to have the same number of

DVD slots in each column. What is the maximum number of DVDs that can fit in one column?

Here are the prime factor trees of the two numbers:

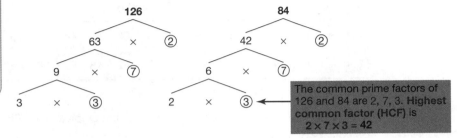

Key term

Highest common factor (HCF)
The highest number that divides exactly into two or more numbers, e.g. 6 is the highest common factor of 12 and 18.

The common prime factors of 126 and 84 are 2, 7, 3. **Highest common factor (HCF) is 2 × 7 × 3 = 42**

Each column in both DVD racks will hold 42 DVDs.
One rack will be 3 columns wide (3 × 42 = 126), the other 2 (2 × 42 = 84).

Example 4

What are the first three **multiples** of 7?

$1 \times 7 = \mathbf{7}$,
$2 \times 7 = \mathbf{14}$,
$3 \times 7 = \mathbf{21}$

Key terms

Multiples (of a number)
The number multiplied by any other whole number.

Lowest common multiple (LCM)
The smallest common multiple of two or more numbers.

Example 5

What is the **lowest common multiple (LCM)** of 6 and 8?

Multiples of 6 are: 6 12 18 **24** 30 36 42 **48** 54 60 66 **72**...
Multiples of 8 are: 8 16 **24** 32 40 **48** 56 64 **72** 80...

24, 48 and 72 are common multiples but 24 is the lowest: **LCM = 24**

Example 6

A construction company has built two new homes and now wants them decorated. They have asked three firms to quote for the job. All came back with similar estimates but the time to do the job varied considerably:

Sunnyside Decorators   5 days
G.B. Gibson and Sons Ltd   4 days
Deluxe Interiors   6 days

▶

The company decided that to get the decorating done fast they will employ all three decorators at the same time.

How long will the job take?

Find the lowest common multiple of 5, 4 and 6:

Multiples of 5:	5	10	15	20	25	30	35	40	45	50	55	**60**	65	70	
Multiples of 4:	4	8	12	16	20	24	28	32	36	40	44	48	52	56	**60**
Multiples of 6:	6	12	18	24	39	36	42	48	54	**60**	66	72			

LCM is **60**

Number of equivalent jobs each decorator could complete in **60** (the LCM) days:

> Using the LCM here means we do not need to deal with fractions.

Sunnyside Decorators	$60 \div 5 = 12$ jobs
G.B. Gibson and Sons Ltd	$60 \div 4 = 15$ jobs
Deluxe Interiors	$60 \div 6 = 10$ jobs

The total number of jobs all three decorators could complete in 60 days is:

$12 + 15 + 10 = 37$

One job should be completed in $60 \div 37 = 1.62$ days.
With all three companies working together on the job they will get the decorating done in under two days.

Example 7

Use prime factor trees to work out the lowest common multiple of:

1. 9 and 12

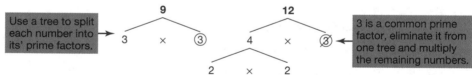

> Use a tree to split each number into its' prime factors.

> 3 is a common prime factor, eliminate it from one tree and multiply the remaining numbers.

Lowest common multiple is $3 \times 3 \times 2 \times 2 = $ **36**

2. 18 and 24

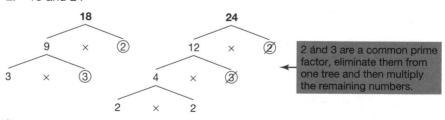

> 2 and 3 are a common prime factor, eliminate them from one tree and then multiply the remaining numbers.

Lowest common multiple is $3 \times 3 \times 2 \times 2 \times 2 = $ **72**

3.   6, 15 and 14

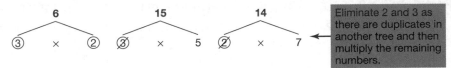

6	15	14

③   ×   ②   ③   ×   5   ②   ×   7

Eliminate 2 and 3 as there are duplicates in another tree and then multiply the remaining numbers.

Why are prime numbers important?

Prime numbers are the building blocks of all other numbers. Every positive integer is the product of a unique set of prime numbers, e.g.

$30 = 2 \times 3 \times 5$

 Lowest common multiple is $3 \times 2 \times 5 \times 7 =$ **210**

Work it out

1.   Make a prime number using the digits 2, 7 and 5.

2.   5 and 7 are prime numbers separated by one. Find four more pairs of prime numbers like this.

3.   Write down five consecutive numbers between 2 and 30, none of which are prime numbers.

4.   What are all the factors of:
   a.   18   b.   32
   c.   40   d.   72?

5.   a.   What is the smallest number with exactly four factors?
      b.   What is the smallest number with exactly six factors?
      c.   Write down two numbers with exactly five factors.

6.   Use a prime factor tree to write the following numbers as products of their primes:
   a.   24   b.   42
   c.   50   d.   66.

7.   Use a prime factor tree to work out the highest common factor of the following numbers:
   a.   54 and 48   b.   72 and 36
   c.   108 and 45   d.   105 and 120.

8.   a.   Write down the first four multiples of 9.
      b.   What is the eighth multiple of 3?

9.   Which is the smaller:
      a.   the fourth multiple of 8 or the fifth multiple of 7?
      b.   the seventh multiple of 11 or the sixth of 12?

10. Here are the multiples of two numbers with some of the values missing. Work out the missing values:
      a.   15, ☐, 25, ☐, ☐, 40
      b. ☐, 42, 49, ☐, ☐, 70.

Mathematicians love patterns in numbers, but no one, despite extensive research over the last 2 000 years, can fathom out an overall pattern for predicting primes.

Prime numbers become sparser as numbers get bigger and this is aptly demonstrated in this advertisement on the web by an organisation devoted to the discovery of new primes.

$100 000
Is yours if you come up with a prime number that has 10 million digits or more.

Hints and tips

Even numbers are numbers that can be divided by 2, odd ones can't.

11. a. Find the smallest multiple of 7 with no even digits (not including 7).
  b. Find the smallest multiple of 9 with no even digits (not including 9).

12. Use prime factor trees to work out the lowest common multiple of the following numbers:
  a. 4 and 6
  b. 3 and 7
  c. 8 and 12
  d. 9 and 18
  e. 15 and 20
  f. 45 and 10
  g. 8, 9 and 12
  g. 6, 15 and 16.

13. List all the numbers less than 30 that are not multiples of 2 or 3 and not primes.

14. A carpenter has been hired to build two sets of 'pigeon holes' for a large company. One will contain 180 slots, the second 144. It has been specified that both sets should contain the same number of slots in each row and the rows be as long as possible.
  a. What is the largest number of slots he can build in one row?
  b. How many rows will each pigeon hole contain?

15. Two people want to leave Derby by train at the same time. One is travelling to Leeds, the other to Birmingham. The trains to Leeds start at 6:00 A.M. and run every three hours. The trains to Birmingham start at 5:00 A.M. and run every five hours.

Use lowest common multiples to work out the time they can leave together.

Hints and tips

Converting hours to minutes:

0.7 hours in minutes is
$0.7 \times 60 = 42$ minutes

16. At the start of the summer season a sports centre wants to fill up its outside pool. They have three pumps that can fill up the pool in:
3 hours – pump A
4 hours – pump B
2 hours – pump C.

If all three pumps are working at the same time how long, in minutes, will it take for the pool to be full up?

17. It takes Fiona four hours to give the house its annual spring clean. Dave takes five hours to do the job and their son Dwaine eight hours. If they all worked together how long (in theory) should the cleaning take? Give your answer in hours and minutes.

18. Copy the table and use the figures on the right to complete the table. One number has already been entered.

	Number greater than 10	Factor of 60	Multiple of 3	Prime number
Factor of 36				
Multiple of 5				
Odd number				
Even number		10		

10 is both even and a factor of 60.

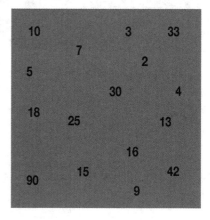

Investigation 1

It was mentioned on the news the other day that a new prime number has been discovered – three times bigger than the previous.

What is wrong with this statement?

Game for two people

On the word go you both show numbers using fingers on both your hands. These two numbers are multiplied together. If the answer is odd the first person in the pair wins a point, if even the second person wins a point. The first to ten points is the winner of the game.

- Play the game.
- Is this a fair game? Investigate.

Suppose you buy a t-shirt on the web. After typing in your credit card number it is scrambled (padlocked) into the product of two extremely large prime numbers. This is then unscrambled (unlocked) by the company you are buying the t-shirt from as they know the value of the two prime numbers.

Investigation 2 – prime numbers and web security

It is very simple to multiply two prime numbers to obtain their product, for example $13 \times 17 = 221$ but to work out the two prime factors of a big number can be a lot more challenging.

This is like a padlock, easy to lock but much harder to unlock without a key and the key in this case is the prime factors. This difficulty increases rapidly with the size of the numbers involved. This feature is used to good effect in web security.

Task 1
Work out the two prime factors of the numbers:
a. 713
b. 2 397.

Computers use not two digit primes but numbers with thousands of digits. It would literally require hundreds of years of computing time to unlock their prime factors. In this way your credit card number is kept secret from hackers.

Task 2 – for those sceptical that finding prime factors is really so difficult
An American IT security company is offering \$100 000 to anybody who can find the two prime factors of this number:

135066410865995223349603216278805969938881475605667027524485143851526510604859533833940287150571909441798207282164471551373680419703964191743046496589274256239341020864383202110372958725762358509643110564073501508187510676594629205563685529475213500852879416377328533906109750544334999811150056977236890927563.

1.3 Fractions

Key term

Fraction
A number used to express how something is divided, e.g.

 means 3 parts out of a total of 7 equal parts or 3 divided by 7.

Fractions have been around for well over 3 000 years, way before decimals. Once the Chinese, Egyptians and Babylonians had mastered adding, subtracting and multiplying whole numbers, they moved on to tackling division. Not too difficult a step you might suppose, after all it's simply the opposite of multiplication. True, but in so doing they discovered a completely new type of number – *divisions that don't go* – fractions.

Fractions have lasted the tests of time and are still widely used today, none more so than in the retail industry.

Group task

An elephant grew so fast it doubled in weight each week.

By the end of the tenth week it weighed 60 kilograms.

How long did it take the elephant to weigh half that?

Fair shares

A cake is to be shared between eight people.

Each person receives $\frac{1}{8}$.

Three people are on a diet so don't take their share.

$\frac{3}{8}$ of the cake is left on the plate.

A particularly greedy person eats one of these pieces.

Leaving $\frac{2}{8}$ or $\frac{1}{4}$.

With no sense of shame this person takes another piece.

This means $\frac{7}{8}$ of the cake has been eaten, leaving $\frac{1}{8}$ for the dog.

Example

Write down the fraction of each shape that is shaded:

a.

b.

The shape can be split into the equivalent of 4 equal parts.

2 out of the 5 equal parts are shaded.

Fraction is: $\frac{2}{5}$

4 out of the 16 equal parts are shaded.

Fraction is: $\frac{4}{16}$

This is the equivalent to 1 out of 4 equal parts shaded.

Equivalent fraction is: $\frac{1}{4}$

Equivalent fractions

Key terms

Equivalent (fractions)
Fractions equal in size.

Numerator
The top number in a fraction.

Denominator
The bottom number in a fraction.

Fraction bar
The line that separates the numerator and denominator.

These three fractions are **equivalent**:

 $\frac{1}{2}$

$\frac{2}{4}$

$\frac{4}{8}$

All three shapes are shaded the same amount.

This can be written as:

$$\overset{\times 2}{\frac{1}{2} = \frac{2}{4}}\underset{\times 2}{} \quad \textbf{or} \quad \overset{\times 4}{\frac{1}{2} = \frac{4}{8}}\underset{\times 4}{}$$

To keep the fractions equivalent the numerator and denominator are multiplied by the same value.

Example 1

Without drawing shapes complete the following:

a.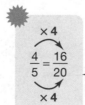
$$\frac{4}{5} = \frac{?}{20}$$

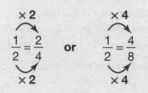
$$\overset{\times 4}{\frac{4}{5} = \frac{16}{20}}\underset{\times 4}{}$$

The denominator is multiplied by 4 so the numerator is also multiplied by 4.

▶

b.

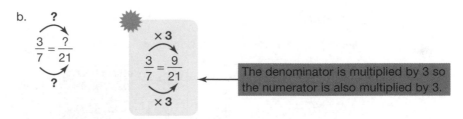

The denominator is multiplied by 3 so the numerator is also multiplied by 3.

Example 2

Write the following fractions in their **simplest form**:

a. $\dfrac{15}{25}$

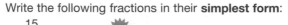

To keep the fractions equivalent the numerator and denominator are divided by the same value.

b. $\dfrac{24}{36}$

$$÷12 \quad \frac{24}{36} = \frac{2}{3} \quad ÷12$$

Example 3

After the excesses of Christmas, 120 people joined a gym. After just four months only 80 people were still attending and two months later 90 had completely given up. At the end of the year just 20 of the original 120 people were still working out at the gym.

Write as a fraction the number of new people still attending the gym after:

a. four months

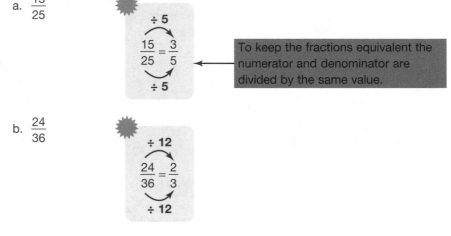

80 out of the 120 people are still attending the gym.

$$÷40 \quad \frac{80}{120} = \frac{2}{3} \quad ÷40$$

b. six months

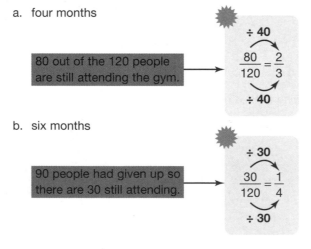

90 people had given up so there are 30 still attending.

$$÷30 \quad \frac{30}{120} = \frac{1}{4} \quad ÷30$$

c. one year

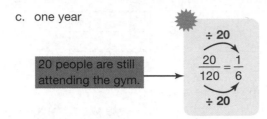

20 people are still attending the gym.

$$\frac{20}{120} = \frac{1}{6}$$

$\div 20$

$\div 20$

Work it out

1. Write down the fraction of each shape that is shaded:

a.   b.   c.   d.

e.   f.   g.   h.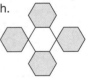

2. Match the fraction to the shape:

a. 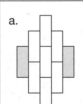   b. 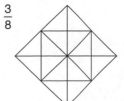   c.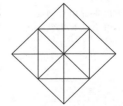

$$\frac{4}{5}$$

$$\frac{5}{6}$$

$$\frac{1}{2}$$

d.   e.

$$\frac{2}{9}$$

$$\frac{3}{8}$$

3. Copy the shapes and shade in the fractions:

Hints and tips

It may be easier to do the work on squared or graph paper.

a. $\dfrac{3}{16}$ b. $\dfrac{3}{8}$ c. $\dfrac{3}{4}$

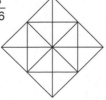

▶

d. $\frac{7}{12}$ e. $\frac{5}{6}$ f. 1

4. Which shape is the odd one out?

a.   b.   c.   d.

5. Why is this statement incorrect?

$\frac{1}{3}$ of the shape is shaded

6. Answer each of the questions using information in the adjacent text:

At the office party a Christmas log is divided fairly between all twelve members of staff.

a. What fraction of the log is each slice?

Four people don't attend.

b. What fraction of the log is extra?

Two people there have already eaten some christmas cake so don't want any.

c. What fraction of the log is eaten?

Three people claim they have not eaten any breakfast so eat another slice.

d. What fraction of the log is left?

7. Without drawing shapes complete the following:

a. $\frac{3}{4} = \frac{15}{?}$

b. $\frac{6}{10} = \frac{?}{30}$

c. $\frac{?}{5} = \frac{12}{30}$

d. $\frac{20}{45} = \frac{4}{?}$

e. $\frac{?}{4} = \frac{12}{?}$ $\times 4$

f. $\frac{20}{25} = \frac{?}{5}$

g. $\div 3$ $\frac{?}{36} = \frac{8}{?} = \frac{2}{?}$

h. $\frac{12}{42} = \frac{6}{?} = \frac{2}{?}$

i. $\frac{18}{36} = \frac{?}{4} = \frac{1}{?}$

8. Match the equivalent fractions, stating the fraction in each group which is in its simplest form. One has been done for you.

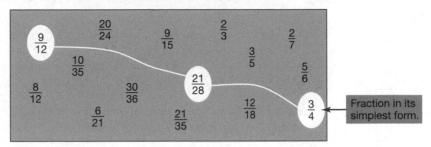

9. Write down two fractions equivalent to:

a. $\dfrac{1}{3}$

b. $\dfrac{2}{5}$

c. $\dfrac{3}{7}$

10. Write the following fractions in their simplest form:

a. $\dfrac{5}{10}$

b. $\dfrac{6}{9}$

c. $\dfrac{12}{20}$

d. $\dfrac{15}{20}$

e. $\dfrac{16}{24}$

f. $\dfrac{21}{28}$

g. $\dfrac{20}{30}$

h. $\dfrac{36}{48}$

i. $\dfrac{32}{40}$

11. What fraction of the shape is:
a. grey?
b. red?
c. white?

Write your answers as fractions in their simplest form.

12. The diagram below shows the bookings for the twelve tables in a small restaurant one Saturday night:

	Tables											
	1	2	3	4	5	6	7	8	9	10	11	12
7 P.M.	✓	✓				✓		✓				
8 P.M.	✓	✓	✓	✓	✓	✓	✓	✓	✓	✓	✓	✓
9 P.M.	✓			✓	✓	✓	✓	✓	✓	✓	✓	
10 P.M.	✓	✓	✓	✓			✓		✓		✓	✓
11 P.M.	✓	✓		✓	✓			✓	✓			

a. What fraction of the tables are booked at each time?
b. What fraction of the total possible bookings are booked for the whole evening?

Write your answers as fractions in their simplest form.

13. The clocks show when Maggie checked the time whilst sitting her finals' degree examinations.

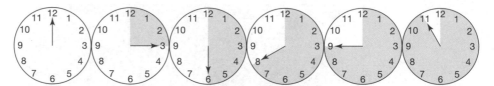

Her exam lasted an hour. Work out the six fractions, in their simplest form, of exam time left when Maggie looked at the clock.

14. Convert the figures in these sentences into fractions in their simplest form:
    a. Out of 180 people interviewed 162 said they would give up work tomorrow if they won the lottery jackpot.
    b. Out of 150 people interviewed 95 thought they looked younger than they were.
    c. Out of 200 people interviewed 124 said they regularly sneak food into the cinema.
    d. Out of 300 people interviewed 175 said they regularly bought lottery tickets.

15. This timeline shows when the evictions occur on a reality TV program. Answer each of the questions using the information in the adjacent text:

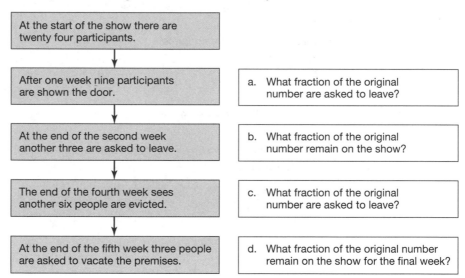

Write all fractions in their simplest form.

Hints and tips

Reduce the fractions to their simplest form and then convert them to fractions with the same denominator – then you can compare their size.

16. In a survey of 48 football supporters 36 of them said that they thought cricket supporters were a bunch of boring toffs who just used cricket as an excuse to get away from their wives. In another survey of 50 cricket supporters 40 of them said they thought football fans were a mob of chip munching hooligans who didn't have two brain cells between them.

Who had the greater love – football fans for cricket supporters or cricket fans for football supporters?

Writing fractions as words

17. As a general rule the numerator is written simply as a normal number and the denominator converts to a number position with an 's' on the end, e.g.

$\frac{2}{5}$ is written as two fifth**s**

or

$\frac{3}{7}$ is written as three seventh**s**.

Convert the fractions in the article into words:

The smoking habit

Approximately $\frac{1}{5}$ of the population smoke with a $\frac{1}{4}$ of these people smoking more than twenty a day. $\frac{2}{3}$ of the people interviewed said they wanted to quit smoking but $\frac{1}{2}$ admitted that they would find it extremely difficult to go a full day without a cigarette. $\frac{9}{10}$ stated they had already tried to quit the habit but failed. Overall $\frac{1}{6}$ said they had their first cigarette within five minutes of waking up.

Group investigation

1. Show how it is possible to make a half by combining in a fraction the digits 2, 3, 4 and 6.

2. What number must be added to the numerator and denominator of:
   a. $\frac{1}{2}$ to make $\frac{3}{4}$?
   b. $\frac{1}{3}$ to make $\frac{4}{5}$?
   c. $\frac{1}{5}$ to make $\frac{5}{6}$?

Hints and tips

Use equivalent fractions.

Adding and subtracting fractions

At the start of the day a café has three chocolate cakes, each split into eight portions. In the morning five pieces are sold; this is what is left:

▶

Key terms
Top heavy fraction A fraction where the numerator is bigger than the denominator, e.g. $\dfrac{5}{3}$ or $\dfrac{7}{2}$
Mixed number A number consisting of a whole number and a fractional part, e.g. $1\dfrac{1}{4}$ or $3\dfrac{2}{5}$

There are 19 pieces of cake left. This can be written as the **top heavy fraction** $\dfrac{19}{8}$ or the **mixed number** $2\dfrac{3}{8}$.

> Fraction to **mixed number**
> 8 into 19 goes **2** remainder **3**

$$\frac{19}{8} = 2\frac{3}{8}$$

> Mixed number to **fraction**
> **2** × 8 + **3** = 19

Example 1

Without drawing any shapes convert the following mixed numbers to top heavy fractions:

a. $3\dfrac{5}{7}$ $3 \times 7 + 5 = 26 \longrightarrow \dfrac{26}{7}$

b. $5\dfrac{3}{4}$ $5 \times 4 + 3 = 23 \longrightarrow \dfrac{23}{4}$

Example 2

Without drawing any shapes convert the following top heavy fractions to a mixed number:

a. $\dfrac{8}{5}$ 5 into 8 goes **1** remainder **3** $\longrightarrow 1\dfrac{3}{5}$

b. $\dfrac{17}{6}$ 6 into 17 goes **2** remainder **5** $\longrightarrow 2\dfrac{5}{6}$

Mapping out
Converting to top heavy fractions:
Multiply the whole number by the denominator.
↓
Add the numerator.
↓
This is the new numerator. The denominator remains the same.

Work it out

1. Convert the following mixed numbers to top heavy fractions:

   a. $1\dfrac{4}{5}$ b. $1\dfrac{3}{8}$ c. $2\dfrac{3}{7}$

   d. $3\dfrac{1}{2}$ e. $2\dfrac{5}{11}$ f. $4\dfrac{6}{7}$

2. Convert the following top heavy fractions to mixed numbers:

   a. $\dfrac{12}{7}$ b. $\dfrac{22}{9}$ c. $\dfrac{9}{5}$

   d. $\dfrac{18}{6}$ e. $\dfrac{23}{12}$ f. $\dfrac{35}{8}$

More cakes

The café has two cakes left at the end of the day, one with 5 pieces remaining, the other with three pieces.

Total number of pieces left is $5 + 3 = 8$ (one whole cake) or as fractions:

$$\frac{5}{8} + \frac{3}{8} = \frac{8}{8} = 1$$

The numerators are added together but the denominator remains the same.

At the end of another day, this was what was left:

There are three pieces left but of two different sizes:

$$\frac{2}{3} + \frac{1}{4} = \frac{3}{7}$$

You can't simply add the numerators and denominators together.

The only way the total amount of cake can be worked out is by splitting each cake into equal pieces (twelfths):

As fractions the cakes are divided:

In total there are eleven of these smaller pieces left $\frac{11}{12}$.

$$\overset{\times\,4}{\frac{2}{3} = \frac{8}{12}}, \quad \overset{\times\,3}{\frac{1}{4} = \frac{3}{12}}$$
$$\underset{\times\,4}{\phantom{\frac{2}{3}}} \quad \underset{\times\,3}{\phantom{\frac{1}{4}}}$$

Change the fractions so they have the same denominator, in this case 12 as both 3 and 4 go into 12.

$$\frac{2}{3} + \frac{1}{4} = \frac{8}{12} + \frac{3}{12} = \frac{11}{12}$$

12 is the lowest common multiple of 3 and 4.

Example

Work out:

a. $\dfrac{5}{11} + \dfrac{3}{11}$

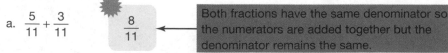

$\dfrac{8}{11}$

Both fractions have the same denominator so the numerators are added together but the denominator remains the same.

b. $\dfrac{4}{5} + \dfrac{2}{3}$

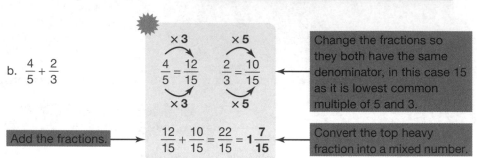

$$\overset{\times 3}{\overgroup{\dfrac{4}{5} = \dfrac{12}{15}}}\underset{\times 3}{} \qquad \overset{\times 5}{\overgroup{\dfrac{2}{3} = \dfrac{10}{15}}}\underset{\times 5}{}$$

Change the fractions so they both have the same denominator, in this case 15 as it is lowest common multiple of 5 and 3.

Add the fractions.

$$\dfrac{12}{15} + \dfrac{10}{15} = \dfrac{22}{15} = 1\dfrac{7}{15}$$

Convert the top heavy fraction into a mixed number.

c. $2\dfrac{2}{3} - 1\dfrac{5}{7}$

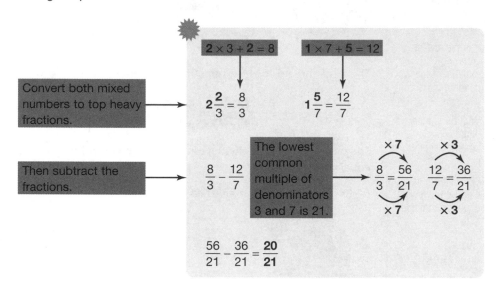

$2 \times 3 + 2 = 8$ $\qquad$ $1 \times 7 + 5 = 12$

Convert both mixed numbers to top heavy fractions.

$2\dfrac{2}{3} = \dfrac{8}{3} \qquad 1\dfrac{5}{7} = \dfrac{12}{7}$

Then subtract the fractions.

$\dfrac{8}{3} - \dfrac{12}{7}$

The lowest common multiple of denominators 3 and 7 is 21.

$$\overset{\times 7}{\overgroup{\dfrac{8}{3} = \dfrac{56}{21}}}\underset{\times 7}{} \qquad \overset{\times 3}{\overgroup{\dfrac{12}{7} = \dfrac{36}{21}}}\underset{\times 3}{}$$

$$\dfrac{56}{21} - \dfrac{36}{21} = \dfrac{20}{21}$$

Mapping out

Adding:

Add any whole numbers together.

↓

Change the fractions to equivalent ones with the same denominator.

↓

Add the numerators together but keep the denominator the same.

↓

If possible simplify the fraction.

↓

Convert a top heavy fraction to a mixed number.

↓

Add any whole numbers to the fraction/mixed number.

Entonox is used as a pain relief during labour in childbirth.

Work it out

1. Work out the following additions:

   a. $\dfrac{2}{7} + \dfrac{3}{7}$

   b. $\dfrac{4}{9} + \dfrac{1}{9}$

   c. $\dfrac{1}{10} + \dfrac{3}{10}$

   d. $\dfrac{4}{5} + \dfrac{1}{5}$

   e. $\dfrac{1}{3} + \dfrac{1}{6}$

   f. $\dfrac{1}{4} + \dfrac{1}{8}$

   g. $\dfrac{3}{5} + \dfrac{3}{10}$

   h. $\dfrac{2}{3} + \dfrac{1}{5}$

   i. $\dfrac{2}{5} + \dfrac{3}{4}$

   j. $\dfrac{5}{6} + \dfrac{5}{9}$

2. Work out the following subtractions:

   a. $\dfrac{8}{11} - \dfrac{4}{11}$

   b. $\dfrac{15}{17} - \dfrac{10}{17}$

   c. $\dfrac{1}{2} - \dfrac{1}{4}$

   d. $\dfrac{8}{9} - \dfrac{5}{18}$

   e. $\dfrac{3}{4} - \dfrac{5}{7}$

   f. $\dfrac{2}{3} - \dfrac{2}{11}$

   g. $\dfrac{9}{10} - \dfrac{2}{3}$

   h. $\dfrac{3}{4} - \dfrac{2}{5}$

3. Work out the following sums:

   a. $1\dfrac{3}{5} + \dfrac{7}{10}$

   b. $\dfrac{1}{4} + 2\dfrac{1}{2}$

   c. $1\dfrac{2}{3} + 2\dfrac{5}{6}$

   d. $2\dfrac{1}{7} - \dfrac{4}{21}$

   e. $3\dfrac{4}{5} - 1\dfrac{1}{3}$

   f. $2\dfrac{3}{8} - 1\dfrac{1}{12}$

   g. $2\dfrac{1}{2} + 1\dfrac{7}{8} + \dfrac{3}{4}$

   h. $3\dfrac{5}{6} + 1\dfrac{2}{3} - 1\dfrac{5}{12}$

4. a. At a local election Labour won $\dfrac{3}{5}$ of the votes cast and the Conservatives $\dfrac{1}{4}$.

   The rest went to the Liberal Democrats.
   What fraction of the votes did the Liberal Democrats gain?

   b. At the start of an evening shift, a midwife had a full cylinder of entonox (gas and air). One mother used three eighths of the tank, a second used one third. How much was left in the cylinder?

5. Work out the fraction of the square that is shaded.

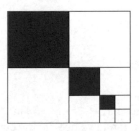

Mapping out

Subtracting:

Convert any mixed numbers to top heavy fractions.

↓

Change the fractions to equivalent ones with the same denominator.

↓

Subtract the numerators but keep the denominator the same.

↓

If possible simplify the fraction.

↓

Convert a top heavy fraction to a mixed number.

Lengths of musical notes

𝅝 A whole note (four beats)

𝅗𝅥 $\frac{1}{2}$ a note

♩ $\frac{1}{4}$ of a note

♪ $\frac{1}{8}$ of a note

𝅘𝅥𝅯 $\frac{1}{16}$ of a note

𝅘𝅥𝅭 $\frac{3}{8}$ of a note

𝅘𝅥𝅮. $\frac{3}{16}$ of a note

Musicians often write their music in groups of complete notes.

6. Dwaine is trying to lose eight pounds. He is finding he seesaws between one day losing $\frac{1}{2}$ pound and the next gaining $\frac{1}{3}$ of a pound.

   How many days will it take him to achieve his target weight?

7. Use the fractions $\frac{1}{10}$, $\frac{3}{10}$, $\frac{7}{10}$, $\frac{9}{10}$, $\frac{2}{5}$ and 1 to fill in the circles so each side of the triangle will sum to 2. Use each fraction only once.

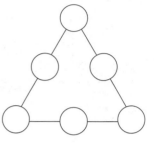

8. Use the fractions $\frac{1}{2}$, $\frac{1}{4}$, $\frac{1}{12}$, $\frac{1}{3}$, $\frac{5}{12}$, $\frac{1}{6}$ to fill in the circles so each side of the triangle will sum to 1. Use each fraction only once.

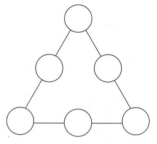

9. Fractions are used when making music.
   a. What two different symbols add together to represent
      i. $\frac{3}{4}$ of a note?
      ii. $\frac{1}{2}$ a note?
   b. Below are two incomplete bars of music. Work out what symbol needs to be added to make a complete note:

   c. What two different symbols can be added to $\frac{3}{4}$ to make a whole note?
   d. Make a complete note by using (there can be repeats):
      i. Six symbols
      ii. Nine symbols
   e. How many beats does
      i. 𝅗𝅥 represent?
      ii. 𝅘𝅥𝅮. represent?

10. How old am I?
    I started work when I was 16. I've spent $\frac{1}{10}$ of my working life as a waitress, $\frac{1}{5}$ in an office and $\frac{1}{3}$ working as a care assistant. I've been in my current job as a community care officer for 11 years.

Investigation 1

1. When subtracting mixed number fractions we first convert them to top heavy ones but do not do this when adding mixed fractions. Why is this?
   It may help to use examples.

2. a. Show how the number 3 can be produced from three 2s.
   b. Show how the number 1 000 can be produced from five 9s.

Investigation 2 – Egyptian fractions

The Egyptian civilisation left precious little mathematical evidence, largely because most of the manuscripts were written on fragile papyrus leaves that have long ago vanished to dust. However, we do know they had an interesting way of representing fractions. They used just unit fractions such as $\frac{1}{2}$, $\frac{1}{4}$ and $\frac{1}{3}$ but not $\frac{3}{4}$ or $\frac{3}{7}$ or $\frac{4}{5}$.

All fractions can be the sum of unit fractions.

For instance:

$$\frac{3}{5} = \frac{6}{10} = \frac{5}{10} + \frac{1}{10} = \frac{1}{2} + \frac{1}{10}$$

1. Write 1 as the sum of three different unit fractions.

2. Write the following fractions as the sum of just two different unit fractions:

   $$\frac{2}{3}, \frac{2}{5}, \frac{2}{7}$$

   Can you see a pattern developing?

   Use this pattern to write down the sum of $\frac{2}{9}$ and $\frac{2}{11}$.

Practical use of Egyptian fractions

Seven pizzas are to be divided equally between ten people – each person will receive $\frac{7}{10}$ of a pizza – a task difficult to carry out fairly, especially if watched by ten hungry people.

Each person could be given half a pizza; this uses up five pizzas. Of the remaining two pizzas each person receives $\frac{2}{10}$ $\left(\frac{1}{5}\right)$ – much easier to cut.

3. There are nine pies to be split between 14 people. Use Egyptian fractions to work out how the pies should be cut.

Hints and tips

Look at how the denominator of the largest fraction in each sum changes.

Multiplying and dividing fractions

One fifth of all buns in a bakery contain chocolate. One quarter of these are chocolate éclairs. What fraction of all the buns are chocolate éclairs?

▶

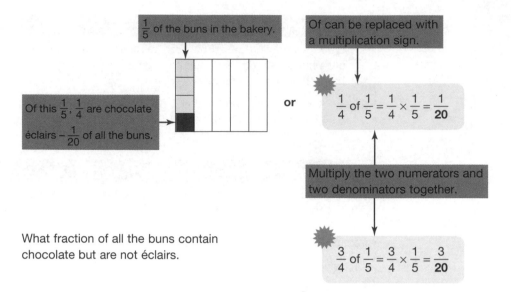

What fraction of all the buns contain chocolate but are not éclairs.

Example 1

Of the 184 people interviewed $\frac{7}{8}$ said they are unhappy about the bank charges levied on accounts exceeding the overdraft limit.

How many people are unhappy about the charges?

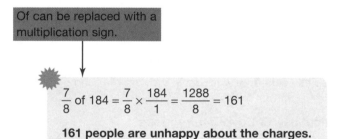

All whole numbers can be converted to top heavy fractions with a denominator of 1.

Of can be replaced with a multiplication sign.

$$\frac{7}{8} \text{ of } 184 = \frac{7}{8} \times \frac{184}{1} = \frac{1288}{8} = 161$$

161 people are unhappy about the charges.

Example 2

Work out:

a. $\frac{3}{4} \times \frac{8}{11}$

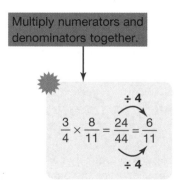

Multiply numerators and denominators together.

$$\frac{3}{4} \times \frac{8}{11} = \frac{24}{44} = \frac{6}{11}$$

b. $2\frac{1}{3} \times \frac{9}{14}$

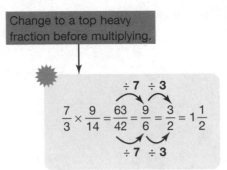

Change to a top heavy fraction before multiplying.

$$\frac{7}{3} \times \frac{9}{14} = \frac{63}{42} \underset{÷7 \quad ÷3}{\overset{÷7 \quad ÷3}{=}} \frac{9}{6} = \frac{3}{2} = 1\frac{1}{2}$$

Example 3

Work out:

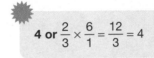

4 or $\frac{2}{3} \times \frac{6}{1} = \frac{12}{3} = 4$

a. $\frac{2}{3} ÷ \frac{1}{6}$

The question is asking 'How many sixths there are in two thirds?'

To get the answer the second fraction is flipped and the division becomes a multiplication.

b. $\frac{3}{4} ÷ \frac{1}{2}$

How many halves are there in three quarters.

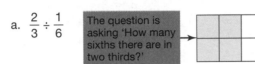

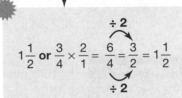

$1\frac{1}{2}$ **or** $\frac{3}{4} \times \frac{2}{1} = \frac{6}{4} \underset{÷2}{\overset{÷2}{=}} \frac{3}{2} = 1\frac{1}{2}$

c. $1\frac{4}{5} ÷ 2\frac{1}{4}$

Change to top heavy fractions before multiplying.

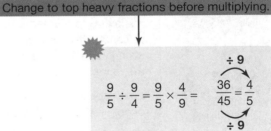

$$\frac{9}{5} ÷ \frac{9}{4} = \frac{9}{5} \times \frac{4}{9} = \underset{÷9}{\overset{÷9}{\frac{36}{45}}} = \frac{4}{5}$$

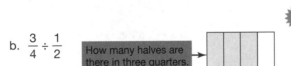

Dividin' fractions, easy as pie:

Flip the second and multiply!

Multiplyin' fractions – no big deal:

Top times top over bottom times bottom!

Work it out

1. Work out:

   a. $\frac{2}{3} \times \frac{5}{7}$
   b. $\frac{1}{4} \times \frac{1}{6}$
   c. $\frac{2}{5} \times \frac{5}{7}$
   d. $\frac{3}{8} \times \frac{2}{9}$
   e. $\frac{4}{21} \times \frac{7}{8}$

   f. $\frac{5}{12} \times \frac{4}{15}$
   g. $\frac{5}{9} \times \frac{3}{20}$
   h. $\frac{11}{14} \times \frac{21}{22}$
   i. $\frac{15}{16} \times \frac{12}{21}$

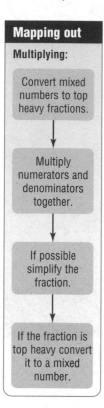

Mapping out

Multiplying:

Convert mixed numbers to top heavy fractions.

↓

Multiply numerators and denominators together.

↓

If possible simplify the fraction.

↓

If the fraction is top heavy convert it to a mixed number.

2. Work out:

   a. $1\frac{1}{4} \times \frac{7}{10}$

   b. $\frac{5}{21} \times 2\frac{1}{3}$

   c. $1\frac{3}{5} \times \frac{1}{12}$

   d. $1\frac{1}{8} \times 1\frac{2}{3}$

   e. $2\frac{1}{5} \times 1\frac{1}{3}$

   f. $1\frac{3}{4} \times 2\frac{2}{5}$

   g. $2\frac{2}{7} \times 2\frac{5}{8}$

   h. $3\frac{1}{5} \times 2\frac{1}{2}$

   i. $4\frac{1}{6} \times 2\frac{1}{10}$

3. Work out:

   a. $\frac{1}{3} \div \frac{4}{7}$

   b. $\frac{1}{5} \div \frac{1}{7}$

   c. $\frac{5}{6} \div \frac{5}{8}$

   d. $\frac{3}{7} \div \frac{6}{7}$

   e. $\frac{4}{5} \div \frac{8}{15}$

   f. $\frac{7}{11} \div \frac{21}{22}$

   g. $\frac{17}{18} \div \frac{1}{6}$

   h. $\frac{15}{16} \div \frac{21}{32}$

   i. $\frac{23}{24} \div \frac{3}{16}$

4. Work out:

   a. $1\frac{1}{5} \div \frac{2}{3}$

   b. $\frac{3}{14} \div 1\frac{2}{7}$

   c. $1\frac{2}{3} \div \frac{5}{6}$

   d. $1\frac{3}{8} \div 1\frac{1}{4}$

   e. $2\frac{2}{7} \div 1\frac{3}{5}$

   f. $2\frac{3}{11} \div 3\frac{1}{3}$

   g. $3\frac{3}{4} \div 1\frac{3}{5}$

   h. $4\frac{2}{7} \div 1\frac{5}{7}$

   i. $3\frac{8}{9} \div 5\frac{1}{4}$

5. Below is an extract from an article on the web:

Mapping out

Dividing:

Convert mixed numbers to top heavy fractions.

↓

Change the ÷ to × and turn the second fraction upside down.

↓

Work out as a multiplication.

Hints and tips

Highlight the relevant details.

DVD piracy – the big picture

Latest figures show that the total loss to the audio visual industry through copyright theft is £810 million. Half of this can be attributed to lost DVD sales, one third to lost box office takings and the remainder is lost to the rental sector.

An independent survey of 1 200 people revealed that one quarter had watched a pirate DVD in the last 12 months.

Two fifths named car boot sales as the place they would most likely buy pirate DVDs.

One tenth thought it was acceptable to download a film illegally.

---

   a. What money is lost in:
      i. DVD sales?
      ii. box office takings?
      iii. the rental sector?
   b. How many people have watched a pirate DVD in the last 12 months?
   c. How many people named car boot sales as the most likely place to buy pirate DVDs?
   d. How many people thought it was acceptable to download a film illegally?

6. Here are some supermarket offers:

a. What is the cost of four cartons of juice?

b. The original packet of crisps weighed 24 g. How much does the one on offer weigh?

c. What was the original cost of the chocolate bar?

Land use

7. $\frac{9}{10}$ of Sweden's land is rural. $\frac{5}{9}$ of this consists of forests. In the UK $\frac{4}{5}$ of land is rural with $\frac{3}{20}$ of this being made up of forest.

a. What fraction of land is forest in:
  i. Sweden
  ii. UK?

b. How many hectares of land is forest in:
  i. Sweden
  ii. UK?

> Rural land includes all agricultural, natural grassland, forests and lakes etc.
>
> **Total land**
>
> Sweden:
>   45 000 000 hectares
>
> UK:
>   24 000 000 hectares

8. Here is an extract from a report on the role of TV in our lives:

> In a survey about the nation's viewing habits, one third said they regularly watch the TV via the Internet. Of these three quarters admitted to spending at least three hours a night in front of a screen.
>
> One quarter stated they regularly watched satellite TV. Two fifths of these people rarely watched terrestrial TV.

a. What fraction of the people interviewed said they watched TV via the Internet and spent at least three hours a night in front of a screen?

b. What fraction of the people interviewed said they regularly watched both satellite and terrestrial TV?

9. Which of the following problems can involve the multiplication: $\frac{3}{4} \times \frac{1}{3}$

a. Out of all the students on an Access course, $\frac{3}{4}$ go on to study a degree. Of these, $\frac{1}{3}$ study on a joint honours degree course. What fraction of Access students study a joint honours degree course?

▶

b. $\frac{1}{3}$ of all Access students are over 35, $\frac{3}{4}$ are female. What fraction of Access students are female and over 35?

c. Alison spends $\frac{3}{4}$ of her time at university in lectures. $\frac{1}{3}$ of these lectures are in IT classrooms. What fraction of her time at university is spent in an IT classroom?

Investigation 1

Gurinder claims that to solve $\dfrac{2}{3} \div \dfrac{3}{5}$

is the same as solving $\dfrac{10}{15} \div \dfrac{9}{15}$

which is the same as solving $10 \div 9$

a. Is Gurinder correct?

b. Would his method of changing the fractions to one's with the same denominator work for all divisions?

Investigation 2

A hot air balloon is $1\frac{1}{2}$-miles high. Each time it lets gas out of the balloon its altitude falls by a half. The balloon drops to an altitude of $\frac{3}{32}$ miles.

How many times has gas been let out of the balloon?

1.4 Working with Numbers After the Decimal Point

Did you feel the earth move? Because in the last second you've moved 18.63 miles. This figure can be shown on a number line:

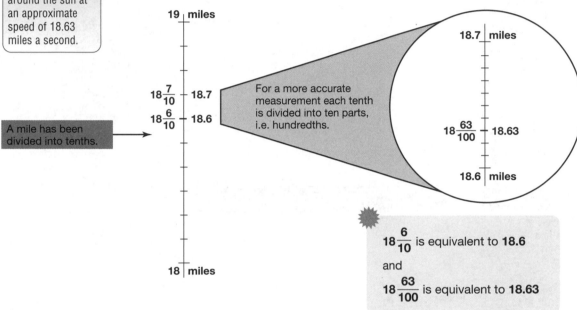

A mile has been divided into tenths.

For a more accurate measurement each tenth is divided into ten parts, i.e. hundredths.

$18\frac{6}{10}$ is equivalent to **18.6**

and

$18\frac{63}{100}$ is equivalent to **18.63**

Example 1

What is the value of 3 in the following numbers:

a. 0.739
b. 9.3527
c. 5.0136
d. 2.7503.

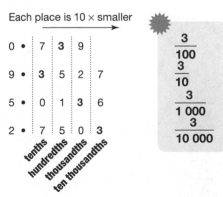

Each place is 10 × smaller

Mapping out

Converting decimals to fractions:

Numerator: the digits after the decimal point.

↓

Denominator: 1 followed by zeros equal to the number of digits after the decimal point.

↓

If required, simplify the fraction.

Example 2

Convert the following decimals to fractions in their simplest form:

a. 0.8

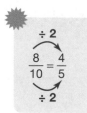

$$\frac{8}{10} = \frac{4}{5}$$
÷2 (top) ÷2 (bottom)

b. 0.45

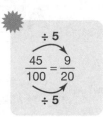

$$\frac{45}{100} = \frac{9}{20}$$
÷5 (top) ÷5 (bottom)

c. 0.060

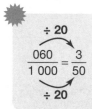

$$\frac{060}{1\,000} = \frac{3}{50}$$
÷20 (top) ÷20 (bottom)

d. 0.416

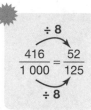

$$\frac{416}{1\,000} = \frac{52}{125}$$
÷8 (top) ÷8 (bottom)

e. 0.058

This zero can be ignored in the numerator as it is worthless.

$$\frac{058}{1\,000} = \frac{29}{500}$$
÷2 (top) ÷2 (bottom)

Mapping out

Converting fractions to decimals:

If the fraction does not already have a denominator of 10, 100, 1 000 etc. change it to do so.

↓

Number of zeros to right of decimal point:

Number of zeros in denominator minus number of digits in numerator.

↓

Add the numerator after the zeros (if there are any).

Example 3

Convert the following numbers to decimals:

a. $\frac{47}{100}$

0.47

b. $\frac{9}{1\,000}$

0.009

c. $\frac{39}{50}$

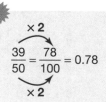

$$\frac{39}{50} = \frac{78}{100} = 0.78$$
×2 (top) ×2 (bottom)

d. $\frac{17}{250}$

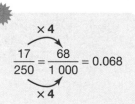

$$\frac{17}{250} = \frac{68}{1\,000} = 0.068$$
×4 (top) ×4 (bottom)

Work it out

1. Write the values marked on the scales:

a.    b.   c.

d.

2. Write down the value (as a fraction) of **7** in the following numbers:
   a. 0.7**5**   b. 0.1**3**72
   c. 0.00**7**1   d. 0.0**7**01.

3. Copy the scale onto graph paper and mark on the decimals:
   a. 1.69   b. 1.620
   c. 1.679   d. 1.603.

1.60   **1.70**

4. Convert these decimals to fractions in their simplest form:
   a. 0.9   b. 0.65
   c. 0.08   d. 0.104
   e. 0.025   f. 0.005.

5. Convert these fractions to decimals:
   a. $\dfrac{8}{10}$ b. $\dfrac{55}{100}$
   c. $\dfrac{15}{1\,000}$ d. $\dfrac{5}{1\,000}$
   e. $\dfrac{32}{50}$ f. $\dfrac{3}{4}$
   g. $\dfrac{9}{200}$ h. $\dfrac{1}{25}$

6. Which is bigger:
   a. 0.30 or 0.03?   b. 0.0099 or 0.01?
   c. 0.088 or 0.089?   d. 0.0777 or 0.707?

7. Write these numbers in order of size, starting with the smallest:
   a. 0.307, 0.073, 0.037 and 0.703
   b. 0.010, 0.101, 0.011 and 0.110
   c. 0.099, 0.909, 0.990 and 0.09.

8. Work out the width of these blocks (all measurements are in centimetres):

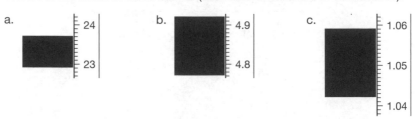

a. 24 / 23

b. 4.9 / 4.8

c. 1.06 / 1.05 / 1.04

9. In which of these numbers does leaving out the zero make no difference to the value of the number:

a. 0.14?   b. 1.042?

c. 2.304?   d. 3.60?

Multiplying and dividing by 10, 100, 1 000 etc.

A foetus is 0.011 centimetres long two weeks after conception. It increases in size 1 000 times between weeks two and 12. What is its length after 12 weeks?

$0.011 \times 1\,000 \rightarrow 0.0\,1\,1 \rightarrow$ **11 centimetres**

Moving the point three places to the right increases the value by 1 000.

Example 1

This diagram shows some sizes relative to the dimensions of a dust mite.

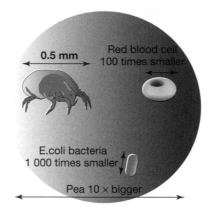

0.5 mm

Red blood cell
100 times smaller

E.coli bacteria
1 000 times smaller

Pea 10 × bigger

What is the size of the pea?

$0.5 \times 10 \rightarrow 0.5 \rightarrow$ **5 millimetres**

Moving the point one place to the right means the number becomes 10 times bigger.

What is the width of the red blood cell?

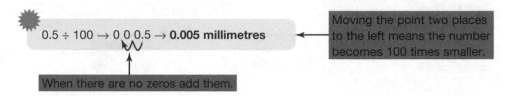

$0.5 \div 100 \rightarrow 0\ 0\ 0.5 \rightarrow$ **0.005 millimetres**

When there are no zeros add them.

Moving the point two places to the left means the number becomes 100 times smaller.

What is the width of the e.coli bacteria?

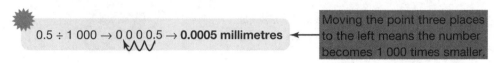

$0.5 \div 1\ 000 \rightarrow 0\ 0\ 0\ 0.5 \rightarrow$ **0.0005 millimetres**

Moving the point three places to the left means the number becomes 1 000 times smaller.

Example 2

Work out:

a. 0.24×100

$0.2\ 4 \rightarrow$ **24**

Moving the point two places to the right means the number becomes 100 times bigger.

b. $2.05 \times 10\ 000$

$2.0\ 5\ 0\ 0 \rightarrow$ **20 500**

Moving the point four places to the right means the number becomes 10 000 times bigger.

When there are no zeros add them.

Move the decimal point to the right when multiplying by:

10:    one place
100:   two places
1 000: three places.

Move the decimal point to the left when dividing by:

10:    one place
100:   two places
1 000: three places.

Hints and tips

If you run out of digits when moving the point add zeros.

Work it out

1. Work out:
    a. $0.56 \times 1\ 000$
    b. 0.4×100
    c. $0.092 \times 10\ 000$
    d. $0.015 \times 1\ 000$
    e. $1.62 \times 10\ 000$
    f. $2.07 \times 1\ 000$

2. Copy and fill in the missing figures:
    a. $0.04 \times \square = 400$
    b. $0.8 \times 10 = \square$
    c. $0.02 \times \square = 2$
    d. $\square \times 1\ 000 = 54$
    e. $\square \times 10 = 0.05$
    f. $\square \times 10\ 000 = 66$

3. Work out:
    a. $6 \div 100$
    b. $720 \div 1\ 000$
    c. $3\ 200 \div 10\ 000$
    d. $43 \div 1\ 000$

4. Copy and fill in the missing figures:
    a. $520 \div \square = 5.2$
    b. $0.8 \div 10 = \square$
    c. $7.5 \div \square = 0.075$
    d. $\square \div 1\ 000 = 73$
    e. $\square \div 10 = 0.02$
    f. $\square \div 1\ 000 = 0.31$

> **Do whole numbers have decimal points?**
>
> Yes – after the last digit; however, it's usually not written.

5. Work out the division or multiplication that is occurring within each calculator:

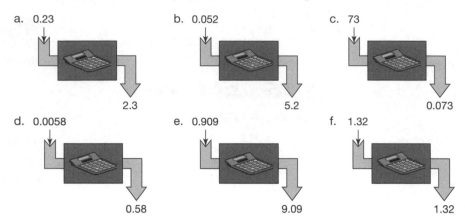

a. 0.23 → 2.3

b. 0.052 → 5.2

c. 73 → 0.073

d. 0.0058 → 0.58

e. 0.909 → 9.09

f. 1.32 → 1.32

Paired work

1. Copy and complete these 'multiplication' and 'division' tables:

a.

×	10	100	1000
0.003	0.03		
5.62			
0.04			

b.

÷	10	100	1000
15	1.5		
2.3			
278			

2. Create your own 'multiplication' and 'division' tables. Give them to your partner to complete. Check your partner's results are correct.

Investigation

Without doing the sum, which will give a bigger answer:

1. multiplying a number by 0.01 or multiplying by 0.001?
2. dividing a number by 0.1 or dividing by 0.01?
3. multiplying a number by 0.01 or dividing by 0.01?

Money matters

A recent survey showed that at Christmas each household in the UK spends on average:

£390.00   on gifts
£162.50   on food and drink
£223.40   on socialising and travel

£117.50   on new clothes
£81.60   on decorations and home improvements

How much in total does the average household spend at Christmas?

> 390 + 162.50 + 223.40 + 117.50 + 81.60 = **£975**

How many hours will an office cleaner earning £6 an hour need to work to cover the cost of Christmas?

> 975 ÷ 6 = **162.5 hours**

How many hours will a supply teacher earning £120 a day need to work to cover the cost of Christmas?

Assume supply teachers work a six hour day.

> Hourly rate of pay: 120 ÷ 6 = £20
>
> Number of hours needed to work: 975 ÷ 20 = **48.75 hours**

Work it out

Assume a footballer works a seven hour day.

1. a. Using the information above, work out the number of hours needed to be worked to cover the cost of Christmas by:
        i.   a lawyer earning £78 per hour
        ii. a Premiership footballer earning £2 275 per day.
    b. How much does the footballer earn each minute?

2. Battersea Dogs Home states that:
    *   On average it costs £9.50 to feed a medium size dog each week.
    *   All dogs need worm and flea treatment every six months – this combined can cost £40.
    *   Pet insurance is vital in this day and age – this can cost £28.60 a month.
    a. How much is the annual cost of keeping a dog?
    b. How much is the lifetime cost of keeping a dog if it lives 11 years?

3. For every two bottles of lager bought at the normal price, a third can be purchased for 50p. A shopper spends £8.22 on nine bottles of lager.

    What is the normal price of one bottle?

4. Here are three shopping baskets:

Work out the cost of a loaf of bread, a jar of jam and a jar of coffee.

5. A shop selling a fridge offers its customers two methods of payment:

> Price: £340
>
> Or
>
> £50 deposit followed by twelve monthly
> instalments of £28.50

What is the difference in cost between these two forms of payment?

6. Ahmed, Harry and George book three tickets for a music concert. The total cost is £67.50. Ahmed only has £4.10 on him; Harry contributes £27.70 and George pays the rest.
    a. How much does each ticket cost?
    b. How much does George pay?
    c. Ahmed gives back all the money he owes to Harry. How much does Harry receive?
    d. How much does Harry give George so that they have all paid the same amount?

7. Marlena has recently set up a business supplying food to childrens' parties. She estimates the cost of food will be £1.20 per child but will charge customers £3.90 per child.
    a. How much gross profit (the difference between the cost of the food to the customer and the cost of the food to Marlena) will she make per child?
    b. At a party she makes a gross profit of £56.70. How many children were at the party?

8. The Joseph Rowntree Foundation researched the cost of bringing up a child to the age of 16 and found that:

    First child costs: £70.10 per week
    Second child costs: £58.10 per week.

    How much will a family with twins pay for their children's upbringing:
    a. each year (there are 52 weeks in a year)?
    b. to the age of 16?

9. The flow chart illustrates the costs involved when purchasing an item off the web:

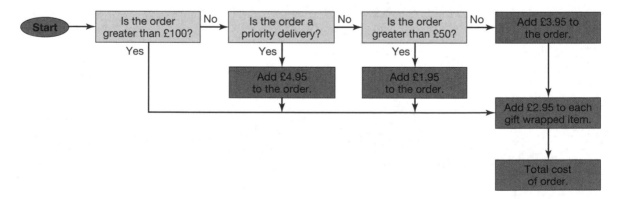

    a. A man buys a pair of trousers from the website for £24.99 and chooses the priority delivery (guaranteed next day delivery).
How much will it cost him in total?

    b. A man is charged £62.80 for one gift wrapped item that is sent by standard delivery (to be delivered within four days).
How much was the original item?

    c. A company director orders five bottles of champagne to be gift wrapped and to be sent by priority delivery. It costs him £111.20.
How much is each bottle of champagne?

10. A web designer is setting up a website selling 'white goods' (washing machines, fridges, etc.) to UK and European residents. She has been given this information:

- All European sales are charged £24.45 for each delivery.
- If a customer requires extended warranty they are charged an extra £12.50 per item.
- If a UK sale is over £500 delivery is free of charge, otherwise delivery costs £10 per item.
- If a customer requires installation, a charge of £30 is made per item.

    a. To help her design the website she wants to draw a flow chart of these costs – do it.

    b. A person living in France orders a washing machine priced at £280. He does not want the machine installed but has chosen to purchase the extended warranty. How much will it cost?

    c. A UK resident will be charged £620 for a fridge/freezer that is advertised on the web as costing £577.50. What options has he chosen?

Investigation

Dan, Greg and Liz are organising a party. Dan has already bought 30 bottles of wine and Greg 20. The total cost of all the bottles is £150 so Liz gives them £50, £30 to Dan and £20 to Greg. Dan is not happy with this arrangement.

Has it been done fairly? Investigate.

1.5a Approximations

Approximations or **roundings** are often used to make numbers easier to understand. Here are two ways of presenting the same information:

Number of broadband
users is 3,217,605

Number of broadband
users tops 3 million

Rounded to the
nearest million.

Just because we've got the detail doesn't mean we have to use it. Too much detail can sometimes distract from the actual magnitude of a number.

Group work

Estimate the following amounts, stating the accuracy of your measurement, e.g. to the nearest foot, pound etc.:

1. The height of the room you are in.
2. The amount a lottery jackpot winner receives.
3. Population of the UK.
4. Train ticket to London.
5. Average length of a pregnancy.
6. Weight of an adult brown trout.
7. Average time people spend food shopping each week.

Rounding

Example 1

Round 26 to the nearest 10.

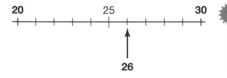

The answer is either 20 or 30.
26 is nearer 30 than 20.
Answer: 30

Example 2

Round 355 to the nearest 10.

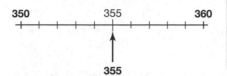

The answer is either 350 or 360.
355 is in the middle. It could be rounded either way; however, it is customary to round number in the middle up.
Answer: 360

Example 3

Round 348 to the nearest 100.

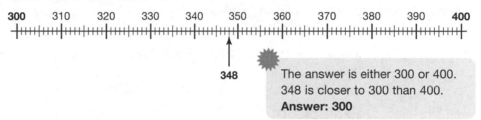

The answer is either 300 or 400.
348 is closer to 300 than 400.
Answer: 300

Example 4

Round 12 500 to the nearest 1 000.

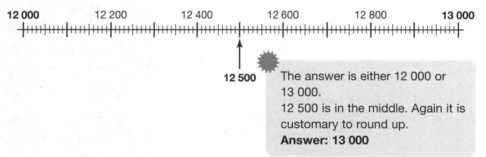

The answer is either 12 000 or 13 000.
12 500 is in the middle. Again it is customary to round up.
Answer: 13 000

(**Work it out**

1. Round the following to the specified degree of accuracy (it may help to draw a number line):
   a. 89 to the nearest 10
   b. 222 to the nearest 100
   c. 2 377 to the nearest 10
   d. 5 632 to the nearest 1 000
   e. 45 480 to the nearest 1 000.

2. Copy and complete the sentences, describing your method of rounding:
   a. To round 54 to the nearest 10 you. . . .
   b. To round 3 567 to the nearest 100 you . . .

Paired work

Tom performed this rounding on the number 2 448 to the nearest 1 000:

Round to nearest 10	2 450
Round to the nearest 100	2 500
Round to the nearest 1 000	3 000

Investigate why Tom's final answer for rounding 2 448 to the nearest 1 000 is incorrect.

Rounding without a number line

It is not always convenient to draw a number line especially when dealing with large figures.

Example 1

Round the following: **Mapping it out**

1.   21 637 to the nearest 1 000 ◀— **1.** Count the number of zeros: 3.

21│637 ◀— **2.** From the right, count in 3 digits and draw a vertical line to the left of this number.

21│**6**37 ◀— **3.** Size of number to right of vertical line: 5 and above: number to left increases by 1 Below 5: number to left remains the same.

22 000 ◀— **4.** Pad out with zeros: Replace the figures to the right of the line with 3 zeros.

2. 342 508 to the nearest 10 000 ◀— 4 zeros – from the right count 4 digits and draw a vertical line to the left of this number.

34│**2** 508 ◀— 2 is below 5 so the 4 remains the same.

340 000 ◀— Pad out with 4 zeros.

3. 8 750 382 to the nearest 100 000 ◀— 5 zeros – from the right count 5 digits and draw the vertical line to the left of this number.

8 7│**5**0 382 ◀— 5 is in the middle and so 7 is rounded up.

8 800 000 ◀— Pad out with 5 zeros.

Example 2

Organisers of a music festival estimated that the crowds numbered approximately 14 000 rounded to the nearest 1 000. What is the maximum and minimum possible audience size?

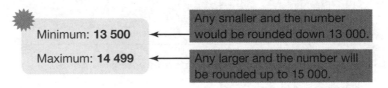

Minimum: **13 500** ← Any smaller and the number would be rounded down 13 000.

Maximum: **14 499** ← Any larger and the number will be rounded up to 15 000.

Work it out

Potential pitfall

Round 32 741 to the nearest 1 000:

32|741 → 33 ✗

3 zeros need to be added:

33 000 ✓

1. Round the following to the stated degree of accuracy:
   a. 383   nearest 10   b. 2 340   nearest 100
   c. 87 242   nearest 100   d. 43 290   nearest 1 000
   e. 239 870   nearest 10 000   f. 999   nearest 10.

2. Copy and complete the following:

	Nearest 100	Nearest 1 000	Nearest 10 000	Nearest 100 000	Nearest 1 000 000
2 450 231					
14 281 340					
2 340 000					

3. Write down the accuracy to which the following numbers have been rounded:
   a. 227   ⟶ 200
   b. 48   ⟶ 50
   c. 1 350   ⟶ 1 400
   d. 32 460   ⟶ 30 000
   e. 5 784 200   ⟶ 5 800 000
   f. 45 987   ⟶ 45 990
   g. 8 899   ⟶ 8 900.

4. Mark Harry's work. If the answer is incorrect provide the correct one:

> Distance in miles to London
> 1. Barcelona, Spain 707 miles ⟶ 700 (nearest 10)
> 2. Hong Kong, China 5 994 miles ⟶ 6 (nearest 1 000)
> 3. Cape Town, South Africa 6 009 miles ⟶ 6 000 (nearest 100)
> 4. Warsaw, Poland 1 078 miles ⟶ 1 080 (nearest 100)
> 5. Sydney, Australia 10 568 miles ⟶ 10 000 (nearest 1 000)
> 6. Delhi, India 3 065 miles ⟶ 3 070 (nearest 100)

5. Work out the smallest and largest possible original numbers when the rounded values are:
   a. 600   nearest 100
   b. 600   nearest 10
   c. 8 000   nearest 1 000
   d. 140 000   nearest 10 000.

6. Here is a web advertisement:

> **Make thousands from the comfort of your own home**
>
> Here are the facts:
>
> In one year you can make a massive $1\,000_1$ sales, each providing **you** with £30_2. You can also achieve 200_3 online consultations for a fee of £40_4 **each!**
>
> **And it takes no maths genius to work out you can earn £$40\,000_5$ a year!**

> The small print:
>
> 1: rounded to the nearest 1 000
> 2, 4: rounded to the nearest 10
> 3: rounded to the nearest 100
> 5: rounded to the nearest 10 000
>
> *These figures are based on their best sales person.*

a. Use the figures in the advertisement to work out the potential income.
b. Use the values (not including pence) in the small print to work out the:
   i. minimum potential income
   ii. maximum potential income.

Group work – errors in rounding

There are several methods of rounding, one being called **round to even**.

Method for 'round to even':

Odd digit before a 5 ⟶ round up
Even digit before a 5 ⟶ round down

For example:

Round to the nearest 10

25 ⟶ 20
135 ⟶ 140

Round to the nearest 100

750 ⟶ 800
16 650 ⟶ 16 600

The figures below show the amount of profit made in a month by ten companies:

£12 500   £8 500   £6 500   £3 500   £9 500
£5 500   £2 500   £7 500   £1 500   £4 500

1. Work out the accurate sum of all the numbers.
2. Work out the sum of the numbers when each figure is rounded to the nearest £1 000 using the normal method of rounding.
3. Work out the sum of all the numbers when each figure is rounded to the nearest £1 000 using the 'round to even' method of rounding.
4. What are the **rounding errors** for the two methods?

> **Key Terms**
>
> **Round to even**
> A method of rounding used when dealing with large numbers of figures.
>
> Customarily the number five is always rounded up despite it being the middle number. This can distort rounded figures. Rounding to even can help prevent the bias towards rounding up.
>
> **Rounding error**
> The difference between the accurate answer and the rounded answer.

1.5b Rounding to Decimal Places

A national paper prints this headline:

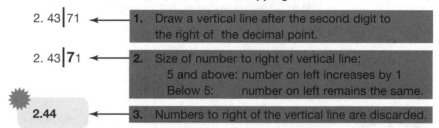

Rate of inflation now
3.1467%

When dealing with just 32 babies this ranking is possible but for data to have the credibility needed for extrapolating information to be used as standards there needs to be a far bigger sample. For example, when answering the question What is the expected birth weight of a white European baby: the data below

When dealing with just 32 babies this ranking is possible but for data to have the credibility needed for extrapolating information to be used as standards there needs to be a far bigger sample. For example, when answering the question What is the expected birth weight of a white European baby: the data below

There is too much detail for the ordinary reader. If it was a specialised financial paper the accuracy may be appropriate but here an accuracy of 1 decimal place is sufficient.

Rate of inflation now
3.1%

When dealing with just 32 babies this ranking is possible but for data to have the credibility needed for extrapolating information to be used as standards there needs to be a far bigger sample. For example, when answering the question What is the expected birth weight of a white European baby: the data below

When dealing with just 32 babies this ranking is possible but for data to have the credibility needed for extrapolating information to be used as standards there needs to be a far bigger sample. For example, when answering the question What is the expected birth weight of a white European baby: the data below

Example

Round the following:

1.   2.4371 to two decimal places (d.p.)

Mapping it out

2. 43|71 ←   **1.**   Draw a vertical line after the second digit to the right of the decimal point.

2. 43|**7**1 ←   **2.**   Size of number to right of vertical line:
     5 and above: number on left increases by 1
     Below 5:   number on left remains the same.

2.44 ←   **3.**   Numbers to right of the vertical line are discarded.

2.   0.04632 to three decimal places (d.p.)

0.046|**3**2 ←   Draw a vertical line after the third digit to the right of the decimal point.

0.046 ←   3 is less than 5 so 6 remains the same.
     Numbers to right of the vertical line are discarded.

Potential pitfall

Round 0.4032 to two decimal places:

0.40|32 → 0.4 ✗

It only shows accuracy to one decimal place. Correct answer:

0.40 ✓

Work it out

1.   Round the following to the stated degree of accuracy:
   a.   5.56   to 1 decimal place
   b.   0.254   to 1 decimal place
   c.   23.5499   to 2 decimal places
   d.   0.00345   to 3 decimal places
   e.   0.9999   to 3 decimal places
   f.   0.054   to 1 decimal place.

Hints and tips

Rounding to zero
decimal places
means rounding
to the nearest
whole number.

2. Copy and complete the following:

	To zero decimal places	To 1 decimal place	To 2 decimal places	To 3 decimal places
19.8946				
0.03039				
0.98989				

Hints and tips

If the rounded
number 0.8 was
originally a
number with
4 decimal
places then:
maximum value
of the original
number is:
  0.8499
minimum value of
the original
number is:
  0.7500

3. Write down the smallest and largest possible original measure when the values have been rounded:
a. 0.6   Original had 2 decimal places
b. 0.6   Original had 3 decimal places
c. 0.01   Original had 3 decimal places

4. The display on the calculator shows the result of 51 ÷ 7

7.285714286

What is the result correct to two decimal places?

5. Work out these calculations giving your answers correct to the specified accuracy:
a. 5.2×3.68 correct to 1 d.p.
b. 0.023×0.68 correct to 3 d.p.
c. $31.3 \div 6$ correct to 2 d.p.
d. $12.7 \div 0.83$ correct to 2 d.p.

Hints and tips

When dealing
with money,
answers need to
be rounded to 2
decimal places.

6. A group of seven work colleagues won £217.50 in one lottery prize.
a. How much will each receive?
b. Will there be any money left over?

7. In a sale everything is half price. How much is the cost of a pair of jeans that originally cost £37.75?

When the rounding rules should be ignored

8. a. A lecturer overseeing a practical biology exam can only supervise seven students at a time. There are 66 students to be examined.
        How many practicals will she conduct?
     b. Jim is buying fence panels for his garden. The length of the garden requiring fencing is 36.5 metres and each panel is 1.8 metres wide.
        How many panels should he buy?

> When rounding up to the nearest 10p all pence are shifted up
>
> £1.33 → £1.40

9. Nina is buying a round of drinks. She orders four pints of beer, two glasses of wine, one coke and two mineral waters. She is concerned that the £18 in her purse is not enough to pay for the round. Whilst the drinks are being poured she makes a quick calculation, erring on the cautious side by rounding all drinks up to the nearest 10p.

| Pint of beer .... £2.42 |
| Glass of wine .... £1.98 |
| Mineral Water .... £1.31 |
| Coke .... £1.25 |

a. What is her estimation?

b. Accurately work out the cost of the drinks.

c. Does she have enough money?

Rounding to significant figures

Key term

Significant figure: The most valuable digits in a number, e.g. the most significant digit in 256 is 2 because it is worth 200, the least significant is the 6 as it is only worth 6 units.

Rounding to **significant figures** is a means of combining rounding whole numbers and decimals.

Example

Round the following:

1. 6 432 to two significant figures

Mapping it out

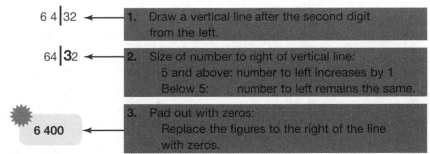

2. 8.0372 to three significant figures

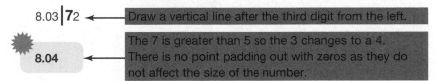

3. 0.00235 to two significant figures

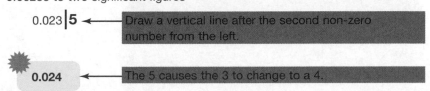

Work it out

1. Round the following to the stated degree of accuracy:

a.	274	to 1 significant figure
b.	3 425	to 3 significant figure
c.	3.542	to 2 significant figure
d.	1.0235	to 3 significant figure
e.	0.0105	to 2 significant figure
f.	1.00356	to 1 significant figure
g.	0.000067215	to 1 significant figure
h.	9.99	to 2 significant figures.

2. Copy and complete the following:

	To 1 significant figure	To 2 significant figures	To 3 significant figures
21 876			
409 622			
32.456			
1.0028			
0.004567			

3. Who am I?

I am a four figure whole number that when rounded to 1, 2 or 3 significant figures gives the same five figure number?

4. Estimate both readings correct to one and two significant figures:

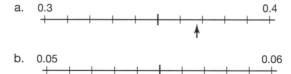

a.   0.3   0.4

b.   0.05   0.06

5. Each question on the left matches a rounded answer on the right.

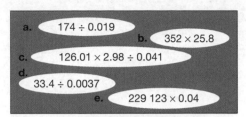

a. $174 \div 0.019$

b. 352×25.8

c. $126.01 \times 2.98 \div 0.041$

d.

$33.4 \div 0.0037$

e. $229\ 123 \times 0.04$

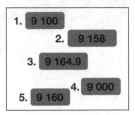

1. 9 100
2. 9 158
3. 9 164.9
4. 9 000
5. 9 160

Use your calculator to match the pairs and in each case state, in significant figures, the rounding that has occurred.

6. Here are some headline quotes from a newspaper:

24 000 homes were damaged by the floods.

Government promises £450 million to improve flood defences.

It took the fire services three hours to rescue a pensioner from the floods.

a. What is the smallest and largest possible number of damaged homes if the figure reported is rounded to two significant figures?

b. What is the smallest and largest possible amount of money the government has promised to improve flood defences if the figure reported is rounded to two significant figures?

c. What is the shortest and longest time it took the fire services to rescue the pensioner if the time reported is rounded to one significant figure?

Group work

The figures below are to be placed in various articles in a Sunday supplement. The editor wants to perform rounding to make them palatable to his readers. Suggest the rounding and the value of the rounded number:

1. The average Britain owes £3 175 in unsecured loans such as credit cards.

2. The number of students studying at college or university is 2 880 145.

3. The average number of litres drunk by a camel in one 'sitting' is 509.23 litres.

4. People spend 69 hours 23 minutes on the phone each year.

5. On average adults drink 34.72 bottles of wine each year.

6. The number of football fans attending a match was a record 43 810.

1.6 Estimation

Estimates are an everyday occurrence:

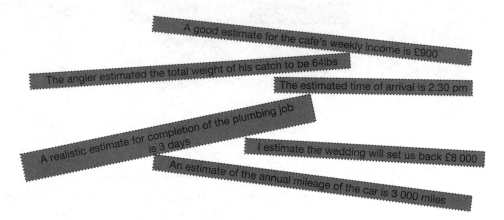

Key term

Estimations
An approximate calculation of a sum.

Reliable **estimations** are usually based on some maths that can normally be worked out without the need to reach for a calculator.

Example 1

Carol, a flight attendant, was asked to help clean a plane due to staff shortages. She found a total of £18.91 in short change that had been accidentally left by passengers.

Work out approximately how much money could be made from all the planes landing at the airport in one year.

323 902 passenger planes landed at the airport last year. A cleaner cleans 1 872 planes a year.

Round £18.91 to one significant figure: £20

Round 323 902 to one significant figure: 300 000

Estimate of the total money found on all planes: 20 × 300 000 = **£6 000 000**

Should Carol, earning £21 000 a year as a flight attendant, switch jobs?

Round 1 872 to one significant figure: 2 000

Approximate money to be made by one cleaner: 2 000 × 20 = **£40 000**

Carol should definitely think seriously about changing career!

Example 2

The accuracy of estimations

Work out estimates for the sale price of a flat screen TV that normally costs £489.99 by rounding to both one and two significant figures.

Half price sale

Rounding £489.99 to 1 significant figure:

estimate $= \frac{1}{2}$ of £500 = **£250**

Rounding £489.99 to 2 significant figures:

estimate $= \frac{1}{2}$ of £490 = **£245**

This will provide a more accurate result but the sum is a bit more difficult.

Example 3

Estimations can be useful when checking calculator work as it is easy to press the wrong button on a calculator.

The display on the calculator shows the result of the sum:

$12.12 \times 215.2 \div 3.83$

Without using a calculator check if it is correct.

9989.4979

Rounding each number to 1 significant figure:

$10 \times 200 \div 4 = \mathbf{500}$

The display is incorrect – the ⊠ button was pressed instead of the ⊡ button.

Work it out

Unless the question specifies otherwise round the numbers to one significant figure.

1. Estimate the answers to these calculations:

    a. $\frac{1}{2}$ of £79

    b. $\frac{1}{4}$ of 102 kg

    c. $\frac{1}{3}$ of £897

    d. $\frac{1}{5}$ of 189 km

2. Use estimation to check Haroon's work:

    > 1. a. $482 + 308 = 3\,528$
    >   b. $1\,056 - 126 = 88$
    >   c. $48 + 9 + 32 = 92$
    >   d. $31 + 39 - 58 = 150$
    >   e. $102 + 99 + 199 = 500$
    >   f. $799 + 42 - 27 = 814$
    >
    > 2. a. $441 \times 9 = 3\,969$
    >   b. $1\,056 \div 12 = 48$
    >   c. $863 \times 21 = 18\,123$
    >   d. $513 \div 19 = 27$
    >   e. $58 \times 51 = 41\,202$

List the answers you think are incorrect.

3. Each question on the left matches an estimated answer on the right. Connect the pairs.

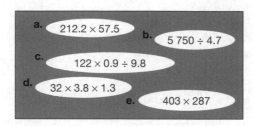

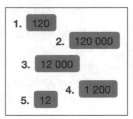

4. Use estimation to establish if:
    a. 23 × 24 = 552 or 52 or 5 250
    b. 183 ÷ 61 = 32 or 3 or 321
    c. 32 × 27 × 28 = 24 192 or 2 419 or 249.

5. Estimate by rounding the amounts to the nearest pound the savings to be made on:
    a. a blouse marked £20.90
    b. a shirt marked £32.55
    c. a pair of shoes marked £39.45.

Third off everthing!

6. Dan wants to change £197 to dollars. The current exchange rate is £1 = $1.7021. Estimate the number of dollars he will receive.

There are 365 days in a year.

7. Joe wins £18.50 when he gambles on line for the first time. Excited about his success he wants to work out how much money he will make if he goes on line once a day for a whole year. Estimate this for him.

8. Over the loudspeaker system at a rugby match the fans are told that the spectators numbered 18 732. Bob bought a standard ticket for £28.20. He wants to work out how much money the club has made from just the seats.
    Estimate this for him.

1 pound (lb) = 16 ounces (oz).

9. Alex catches five fish weighing: 2 lb 3 oz, 5 lb 9 oz, 4 lb 6 oz, 6 lb 12 oz and 3 lb and 8 oz.
    By rounding each weight to the nearest pound estimate the total weight of his catch.

About cars

10. Anil wants to work out his approximate annual car mileage for insurance purposes. Here are the exact figures:

Time = distance ÷ speed.
Anil's car goes 8.2 miles for every litre of petrol consumed. Petrol costs 97.5p per litre.

Drive to work each day for 47 weeks	52 miles round trip
Five holidays/breaks	Each averaging 410 miles
46 shopping/family visits	15 miles round trip

And here is Anil's estimate:

```
    50 × 50 = 250
    5 × 400 = 2 000
    40 × 20 = 800
Total miles: 3 050 miles
```

> Average annual CO2 emission from a car:
>   4.98 tonnes
> Total UK annual CO2 emissions from all cars:
>   19.2 million tonnes

a. Is Anil's estimate correct? If not, what should it be?

b. Anil is about to drive 214 miles, mainly on the motorway, at a speed of 70 mph. Estimate:
   i. how long the journey will take
   ii. how many litres of petrol will be consumed
   iii. the cost of the journey.

c. The current population of China is 1 321 851 888. Most Chinese get around by bike; however, this is fast being replaced by the car.
   If just one tenth of them possessed a car, estimate:
   i. the number of cars in China
   ii. the emissions from these cars (write your answer in millions of tonnes)
   iii. the difference in CO2 emissions between the UK and emissions from these cars.

> There are 52 weeks in a year.

11. The average teenager has four tantrums a week each lasting 32.6 minutes. The average toddler has twenty three tantrums a week each lasting 5.4 minutes. Estimate the total number of minutes:

a. a teenager spends having tantrums each year.

b. a toddler spends having tantrums each year.

c. Convert your answers to a. and b. to hours. Give your answers to the nearest hour.

Our daily habits

12. The average person in the UK lives to the age of 78.

a. On average, a person spends 7 hours 45 minutes asleep each day.
   i. Estimate how many hours in a life are spent sleeping.
   ii. Have you under or over estimated the accurate answer?
   iii. Use your answer to i. to estimate how many:
     • days, to the nearest day, are spent sleeping in a lifetime
     • years, to the nearest year, are spent sleeping in a lifetime.

b. On average a person spends 122 minutes 10 seconds watching adverts on telly each week.
   i. Estimate how many minutes in a life are spent watching adverts.
   ii. Convert your estimate to hours.
   iii. Use your answer to ii. to estimate how many days, to the nearest day, are spent watching adverts in a lifetime.

1.7 Negative Numbers

The diagram shows a cross-section of land both above and below sea level.

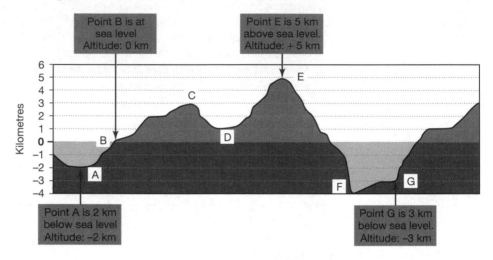

Point B is at sea level
Altitude: 0 km

Point E is 5 km above sea level.
Altitude: + 5 km

Point A is 2 km below sea level
Altitude: –2 km

Point G is 3 km below sea level.
Altitude: –3 km

Movement between points

km = kilometres

Adding numbers: move up

Subtracting numbers: move down

D to E	**E to D**
1 **+ 4** = 5	5 **− 4** = 1

+ 4

− 4

Change in altitude:

D to E: **+ 4**
A gain of 4 km in height

E to D: **− 4**
A loss of 4 km in height

D to F	**F to D**
1 **− 5** = −4	−4 **+ 5** = 1

− 5

+ 5

Change in altitude:

D to F: **− 5**
A loss of 5 km in height

F to D: **+ 5**
A gain of 5 km in height

Work it out

1. Write down the altitudes of points C, D and F.

2. Write down the change in altitude for the movements:
   a. C → B
   b. B → C
   c. C → D
   d. D → C
   e. E → C
   f. C → E.

3. What are the two possible pairs of points when there is a change of altitude of −7 km?

4. List these altitudes in ascending order:
10 km	−5 km	−6 km	8 km	0 km
−8 km	−2 km	1 km	−4 km	−7 km.

Number line

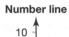

Example 1

Use the number line to work out the sums:

a. $3 + 5 = 8$ ← From 3 count up 5.

b. $2 - 5 = -3$ ← From 2 count down 5.

c. $-4 - 3 = -7$ ← From −4 count down 3.

d. $-10 + 3 = -7$ ← From −10 count up 3.

e. $6 - 8 + 5 = 3$ ← From 6 count down 8, then up 5.

f. $-10 + 7 - 3 = -6$ ← From −10 count up 7 then down 3.

Number line

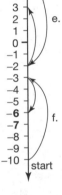

Example 2 – why two minuses make a plus

Using arithmetic to work out a change in altitude

How do we work out the change in altitude?

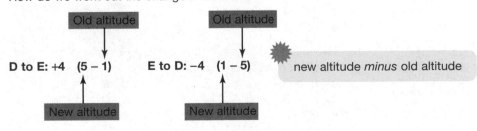

Old altitude

Old altitude

D to E: +4 (5 − 1)   **E to D: −4 (1 − 5)**   new altitude *minus* old altitude

New altitude   New altitude

▶

Using this formula:

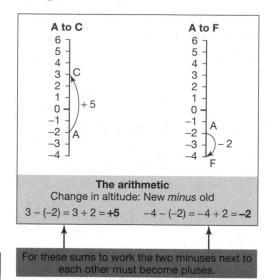

The arithmetic

Change in altitude: New *minus* old

$3 - (-2) = 3 + 2 = \textbf{+5}$ $-4 - (-2) = -4 + 2 = \textbf{-2}$

For these sums to work the two minuses next to each other must become pluses.

Mapping out

Sums with negative numbers:

Mark the first figure on the number line.

If the next symbol is a:
+ → move up
– → move down
The amount moved depends on the figure that follows the sign.

Hints and tips

Subtracting a larger number from smaller: the answer is always negative.

Subtracting a smaller number from larger: the answer is always positive.

Work it out

It may be useful to draw a number line for these questions.

1. Write down the bigger number in the following pairs:
  a. 2, –4
  b. –7, –8
  c. –5, –2
  d. –3, 3.

2. Work out:
  a. $7 - 3$
  b. $3 - 7$
  c. $10 - 11$
  d. $-4 + 3$
  e. $-2 + 2$
  f. $-5 - 1$
  g. $0 - 9$
  h. $-3 - 4.$

3. Copy and fill in the missing figures:
  a. $4 - 5 = \square$
  b. $8 - \square = -2$
  c. $-2 + 6 = \square$
  d. $\square + 3 = 0$
  e. $\square + 2 = -3$
  f. $-2 - \square = -5.$

4. Work out:
  a. $3 - 3 + 5$
  b. $-2 + 3 - 1$
  c. $-4 - 4 - 4$
  d. $3 + 1 - 7$
  e. $-2 - 3 - 1$
  f. $-5 + 1 - 2.$

5. Use arithmetic (new altitude – old altitude) to work out the change in altitude when a person moves from point:
  a. $E \rightarrow G$
  b. $B \rightarrow A$
  c. $A \rightarrow B$
  d. $D \rightarrow A$
  e. $G \rightarrow F$
  f. $A \rightarrow F.$

Key rule

When there is no figure separating two negative symbols they can be replaced by a plus.

$-- \rightarrow +$

6. Work out:

a. $2 - (-6)$

b. $-1 - (-3)$

c. $-2 - (-6)$

d. $4 - (-1)$

e. $-8 - (-8)$

f. $-5 - (-10)$.

7. Use the two number lines to write out the sums a–e and their answers.

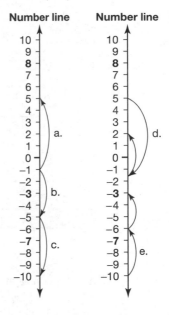

8. The table shows details about the goal scoring of four, not very successful, football teams:

Goal difference:

Number of goals scored − Number of goals conceded

	Number of goals for (scored)	Number of goals against (conceded)	Goal difference
Oker Utd	6	7	
Darley Town	6		−2
Rowsley Utd	4	8	
Tansley		9	−5

a. Copy and complete the table.

b. What team has the best goal difference?

9. Copy and complete these 'difference' tables:

a.

−	−6	3	−4
−1	5		
−5			
4			

b.

−	−2	3	−1
−1	1		
−3			
5			

c. Create your own 'difference' table and give it to your partner to complete. Check your partner's results.

10. Copy and complete these 'difference' bricks, the first one has been done for you:

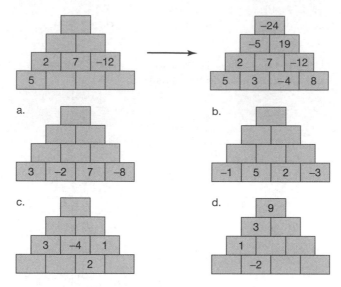

11. a. The temperature on Tuesday was −1°C, on Wednesday it increased by 2°C, on Thursday it dropped by 5°C and Friday it dropped by 3°C. Work out Friday's temperature.

b. The sum below shows the temperature for the next four days, starting with a decrease in temperature of −3°C on Saturday:

$$-3 + 5 - 2 + 1$$

Write these values as a sentence, similar to the one in task a.

c. Work out the temperature on the last day.

12. This is a statement of Karen's current bank account:

Your transactions 18th April to 18th of May

	Description	Money in	Money out	£ Balance
18 May	Balance brought forward from previous statement			**−220.00**
Mon 20 May	Payment to TESCO STORE		35.00	−255.00
Fri 24 May	Cash		100.00	
Mon 27 May	Bank Giro, *CHILD TAX CREDIT*	42		
Wed 29 May	Payment to CINEWORLD		24.00	
Wed 29 May	Payment made by cheque serial no 00173		112.00	
Thurs 30 May	Bank Giro Credit, *GELLERT LTD*	1 800		
Mon 3 June	Cash		120.00	
Thurs 6 June	Direct Debit payment to HALIFAX		670.00	
Mon 10 June	Transfer out using e-banking		690.00	
Mon 17 June	Transfer in using e-banking	52.00		

A bank account in credit:
    positive amount
overdrawn:
    negative amount

a. What is Karen's bank balance by the end of:
    i. Wednesday, 29 May?
    ii. Thursday, 6 June?
    iii. Monday, 17 June?
b. Oh Tuesday, 18 June, Karen pays into her account a cheque which takes her bank balance to £114 in credit. How much was the cheque?

Group investigation

Copy the grid.

By trying different routes through the grid, work out one that will provide you with:

a. the smallest total
b. the largest total.

Rules of movement:

You can move either horizontally or vertically but not diagonally. You can move up to six times.

This 2ⁿᵈ move gives –1

0	–1	–3	–6	END
–2	+4	+6	0	–4
+1	–3	–1	–5	–8
START	+2	+3	–1	–2

The move into the END box is not counted as a move as it involves no arithmetic.

Example 1

Going into the red

Debbie is overdrawn in three accounts:

Account A: overdrawn by £20
Account B: overdrawn by £35
Account C: overdrawn by £45.

She decides to consolidate her debt by putting all her 'monies' into Account A. What will be its new balance?

New balance =
    balance in account A + balance in account B + balance in account C
    = –20 + (–35) + (–45) = –20 – 35 – 45 = **–100**
                    Debbie's new balance is £100 overdrawn.

A plus and a minus next to each other make a minus.

Example 2

Work out:

a. 2 + (–7)

$2 - 7 = \mathbf{-5}$

b. –6 + (–6)

$-6 - 6 = \mathbf{-12}$

c. –3 + (–2) – (–4)

$-3 - 2 + 4 = -1$

Key rule

When there is no figure separating a plus and minus sign they can be replaced by a minus.

$- + \rightarrow -$

Work it out

1. Work out

a. 3 + (–4)

b. –3 + (–7)

c. –1 + (–5)

d. 3 + (–10)

e. –1 + (–3) + (–4)

f. –3 – (–3) + (–3)

g. 5 + (–4) – (–8)

h. –4 + (–6) – (–10).

2. The empty boxes are filled by adding the two preceding numbers. The first has been done for you.

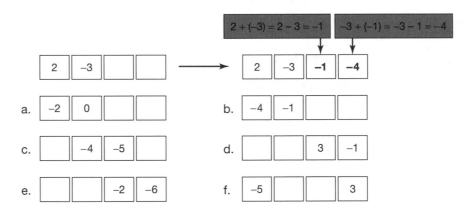

| 2 | –3 | | |

$2 + (-3) = 2 - 3 = -1$ $-3 + (-1) = -3 - 1 = -4$

| 2 | –3 | **–1** | **–4** |

a. | –2 | 0 | | |

b. | –4 | –1 | | |

c. | | –4 | –5 | |

d. | | | 3 | –1 |

e. | | | –2 | –6 |

f. | –5 | | | 3 |

3. a. Andy has overdrafts of £500, £750 and £800 in three accounts but is in credit by £1 200 in a fourth account. When he combines all four accounts into one, what will be his bank balance?

   b. He then pays a cheque into this new account. This takes his overdraft to £200. What was the value of the cheque?

Group work – magic squares

Copy the three grids and fill in the empty boxes:

−2		
	3	
	−9	8

−3	0	
	−2	
	−4	

	−3	
−9	−4	1
−1		

Multiplication and division

Multiplying a positive and negative number gives a negative number

4×3 can be written as four 3s → $3 + 3 + 3 + 3 = $ **12**

4×-3 can be written as four −3s → $-3 + -3 + -3 + -3 = $ **−12**

Multiplying two negative numbers gives a positive number

What is -4×-3?

$-(4 \times -3) = -(-12) = $ **12**   ⟵   Two minuses next to each other make a plus.

Dividing a positive and negative number gives a negative number

$4 \times 3 = 12 \quad \rightarrow \quad 12 \div 3 = 4$

In the same manner:

$4 \times -3 = -12 \quad \rightarrow \quad 12 \div -3 = $ **−4**

Dividing two negative numbers gives a positive number

What is $-12 \div -3$?

$-(12 \div -3) = -(-4) = $ **4**

Example 1

Four directors own a company. The company has a debt of −£1 000. How big is the debt for each director?

$-1\ 000 \div 4 = $ **−£250**

Example 2

Use the rules of multiplication and division to work out:

a. -5×-5 **25**

b. $24 \div -3$ **-8**

c. $-3 \times -2 \times -4$ **(-3 × -2) × -4 = 6 × -4 = -24** ◄—— Work out the sum as you see it – from left to right.

d. $-15 \div 3 \times -8$ **(-15 ÷ 3) × -8 = -5 × -8 = 40** ◄——

Key rule

Rules of multiplication and division

negative × positive
positive × negative } **negative**
negative ÷ positive
positive ÷ negative

positive × positive
negative × negative } **positive**
positive ÷ positive
negative ÷ negative

Work it out

Hints and tips

Two negatives make a positive.

Work out the figures first and then the sign of the answer.

1. Work out:
   a. -7×2 b. $20 \div -5$
   c. -7×-7 d. $-32 \div 4$
   e. $-1 \times -1 \times -1$ f. $-48 \div -12$
   g. 10×-3 h. $-5 \times -3 \times 2$
   i. $33 \div -11 \times 2$ j. $-40 \div -2 \div -5$
   k. $-2 \times -2 \times -2 \times -2$ l. $-3 \times 2 \times -4 \times 1$
   m. $100 \div -25 \times 4$ n. $-40 \div -4 \div -2$

2. Copy and complete these boxes. The empty boxes are filled by multiplying the two preceding numbers. The first one has been done for you.

| -4 | 2 | | | ——► | -4 | 2 | -8 | -16 |

a. | -1 | -3 | | | b. | | -2 | 10 | |

c. | | -7 | -7 | | d. | -3 | | | -75 |

3. Work out the missing numbers, the first has been done for you:

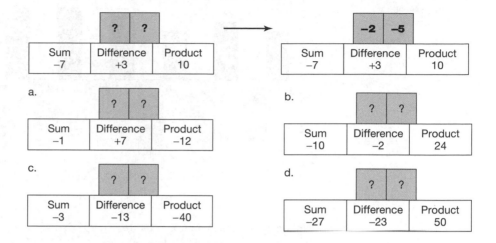

4. The temperature of a chemical compound at 8 a.m. is 4°C. It then falls steadily by 3°C each hour for the next seven hours.
   a. What is the temperature at:
      i. mid-day?
      ii. 3 pm?
   b. When is the temperature –2°C?

5. Here are the results of a tough TV quiz:

	Correct answers	Incorrect answers	Number of answers	Total points
Sam	4	8	1	?
Haroon	?	7	0	–8
George	5	?	3	0

   a. Copy and complete the table.
   b. Who is the winner?

6. Bill runs a small café. After the first six months he plots his income against expenses for each month: ▶

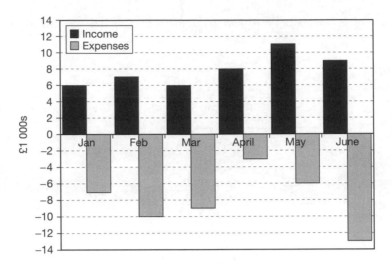

Going into the red:

when income is
less than expenses.

a. What two months is he not in the red?
b. How much money does he lose in:
   i. February?
   ii. June?
c. At the beginning of January Bill had a bank balance of –£200. What is his
   bank balance at the end of June?
d. He intends to pay off this overdraft by paying £80 into his account each
   month. How long will it take him to clear his debt?

7. A computer game about world domination can be played by two people who fight
    it out with their respective armies. Both players start with 1 000 soldiers. The rate
    of recruitment/killings for the first four minutes are:

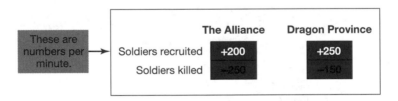

a. How many soldiers does each army possess at the end of the four minutes?
b. In the following five minutes the game changes:

   Number of soldiers recruited per minute:
   The Alliance increases by 50. Dragon Province: decreases by 100.
   Number of soldiers killed per minute:
   The Alliance: decreases by 50. Dragon Province: increases by 150.

   How many soldiers are in each army after nine minutes?

c. If the battle continues at the same rate of recruitment/killings, how long will it
   be before there is an outright winner, i.e. one army is wiped out?
d. Who is the winner?

Group work

The map shows times around the world:

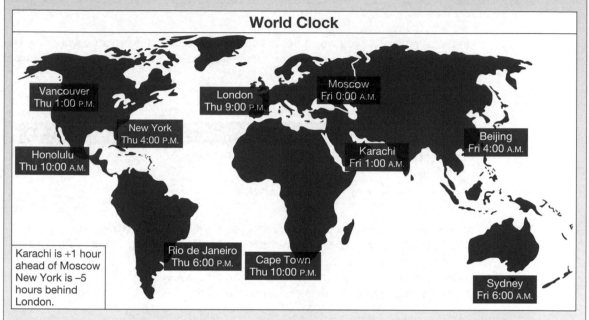

World Clock

Vancouver
Thu 1:00 P.M.

London
Thu 9:00 P.M.

Moscow
Fri 0:00 A.M.

New York
Thu 4:00 P.M.

Beijing
Fri 4:00 A.M.

Honolulu
Thu 10:00 A.M.

Karachi
Fri 1:00 A.M.

Rio de Janeiro
Thu 6:00 P.M.

Cape Town
Thu 10:00 P.M.

Sydney
Fri 6:00 A.M.

Karachi is +1 hour ahead of Moscow New York is –5 hours behind London.

The times of places throughout the world are normally calculated using Greenwich Mean Time (GMT) in London. For instance Moscow is +3 hours ahead of London.

a. Copy the time scale, adding the cities in the appropriate positions.

London
↓

–12 –10 –8 –6 –4 –2 0 2 4 6 8 10 12

← Behind   Ahead →

Use your line to answer these questions:

b. How many hours is Sydney ahead of Rio de Janeiro?
c. How many hours is Honolulu behind New York?
d. What pair of cities have a time difference of 16 hours?
e. I'm in a city that is 7 hours behind Karachi, what city am I in?
f. I'm in a city that is 10 hours ahead of Rio de Janeiro, what city am I in?
g. The table below shows some flight details. Copy and complete the table. The first one has been done for you.

For example, New York is –9 hours behind Karachi.

The time the plane arrives in New York (local time):

Wed 10:00 A.M.
+ 22 – 9
= Wed 10:00 A.M.
+ 13
= Wed 11:00 P.M.

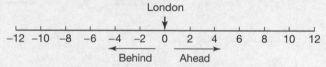

	Flight time	Departure time (local)	Arrival time (local)
Karachi to New York	22 hours	Wed 10:00 A.M.	Wed 11:00 P.M.
London to Karachi	10 hours	Wed 6:00 A.M.	?
London to Vancouver	10 hours	?	Wed 9:00 P.M.
London to Honolulu	20 hours	?	Wed 1:00 P.M.
Sydney to Moscow	24 hours	Wed 10:00 A.M.	?
Beijing to New York	?	Wed 9:00 A.M.	Wed 5:00 A.M.

1.8 Priorities in Arithmetic

In the same way as you would not put your trousers on before your pants (unless you are Superman) there is an order to arithmetic sums. You need to prioritise to avoid expressions that end like this:

)))))

Investigation

Without using a calculator perform the sum:

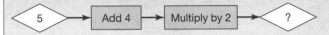

Now perform the same task on the calculator. What do you notice?
Write out three of your own flow charts similar to the one above but using different numbers and arithmetic symbols ($+$, $-$, $\times$ or $\div$).
Compare your answers with what you get on the calculator.
What do you notice? What are your conclusions?

Key priorities

In an arithmetic sum:

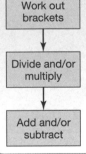

Work out brackets

Divide and/or multiply

Add and/or subtract

Example

Work out:

a. $3 + 4 \times 2 =$ $7 \times 2 = \mathbf{14}$ ✗   ← When read like English, from left to right.

Calculator answer:

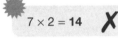
$$3 \quad + \quad 8 \quad = 11 \ \checkmark$$

← The operations have been prioritised – multiplication before addition.

b. $10 - 12 \div 3 + 5 \times 4$

$$10 - 12 \div 3 + 5 \times 4 = 10 - 4 + 20 = \mathbf{26}$$

← Multiplication and division have the same level of priority so can be worked out at the same time.

c. $5 \times (3 + 4) - 2 + 4 \times 8$

$$5 \times (3 + 4) - 2 + 4 \times 8$$
$$= 5 \times 7 - 2 + 4 \times 8$$
$$= 35 - 2 + 32 = \mathbf{65}$$

← Brackets are always the first to be worked out.

← When there is just addition and subtraction, work out the sum from left to right.

It may be helpful to highlight the operations that are top priority.

Work it out

1. Work out these sums:

    a. $2 + 3 \times 5$

    b. $12 \div 3 + 5$

    c. $4 - 2 \times 6 + 1$

    d. $21 - 3 \times 2 - 4$

    e. $14 \div 2 + 3 \times 8$

    f. $108 \div 12 - 6 + 8 \times 3$

    g. $4 + 10 \times 10 - 88 \div 11$

    h. $5 + 22 \times 2 \div 11$

    i. $3 \times 6 - 2 + 24 \div 8$

    j. $40 \div 5 - 3 \times 2 + 6$

    k. $(6 + 2) \times 3 - 3 \times 3$

    l. $10 + 3 \times (6 - 3) + 7 \times 2$

    m. $7 \times (9 - 7) + 80 \div 8 - 8$

    n. $20 - 10 \times (3 + 5) \div 4 + 8$

2. Match the sum with the correct answer:

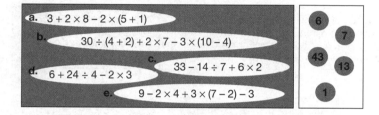

a. $3 + 2 \times 8 - 2 \times (5 + 1)$

b. $30 \div (4 + 2) + 2 \times 7 - 3 \times (10 - 4)$

c. $33 - 14 \div 7 + 6 \times 2$

d. $6 + 24 \div 4 - 2 \times 3$

e. $9 - 2 \times 4 + 3 \times (7 - 2) - 3$

6   7   43   13   1

Potential pitfall

Don't be tempted to work the sum out like a sentence from left to right unless it is made up of just multiplications and divisions or additions and subtractions.

3. Use all the digits and symbols in the box to create a sum that provides the:

    a. largest possible whole number

    b. smallest possible whole number.

    The digits cannot be combined to make a bigger number.

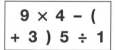

$$9 \times 4 - ($$
$$+ 3) 5 \div 1$$

Order of priority:

Brackets	**Bl**ack
Division/ Multiplication	**D**ays **M**ean
Addition/ Subtraction	**A**stounding **S**kies

4. For each box create two sums, both including all the digits and symbols in the box. The answer to the sums must equal the value below the box.

    a.
    $$6 - 3 \times 5$$
    $$(+ 2)$$
    10

    b.
    $$7 \times 2 - ($$
    $$+ 3 \times 4) 1$$
    18

    The digits cannot be combined to make a bigger number.

5. Write the following activities as sums and work out the answers:

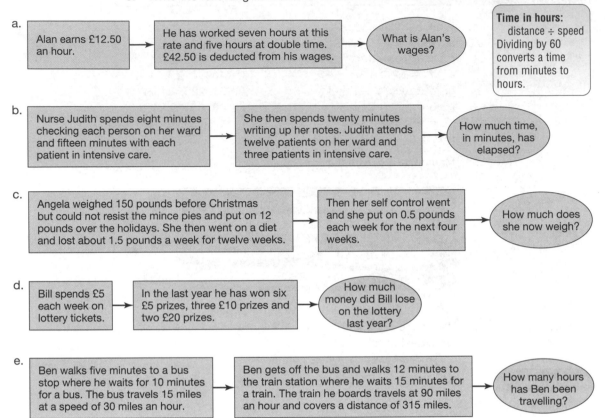

a.

| Alan earns £12.50 an hour. | → | He has worked seven hours at this rate and five hours at double time. £42.50 is deducted from his wages. | → | What is Alan's wages? |

Time in hours:
distance ÷ speed
Dividing by 60 converts a time from minutes to hours.

b.

Nurse Judith spends eight minutes checking each person on her ward and fifteen minutes with each patient in intensive care. → She then spends twenty minutes writing up her notes. Judith attends twelve patients on her ward and three patients in intensive care. → How much time, in minutes, has elapsed?

c.

Angela weighed 150 pounds before Christmas but could not resist the mince pies and put on 12 pounds over the holidays. She then went on a diet and lost about 1.5 pounds a week for twelve weeks. → Then her self control went and she put on 0.5 pounds each week for the next four weeks. → How much does she now weigh?

d.

Bill spends £5 each week on lottery tickets. → In the last year he has won six £5 prizes, three £10 prizes and two £20 prizes. → How much money did Bill lose on the lottery last year?

e.

Ben walks five minutes to a bus stop where he waits for 10 minutes for a bus. The bus travels 15 miles at a speed of 30 miles an hour. → Ben gets off the bus and walks 12 minutes to the train station where he waits 15 minutes for a train. The train he boards travels at 90 miles an hour and covers a distance of 315 miles. → How many hours has Ben been travelling?

There may be more than one number that satisfy the condition.

Investigation

Find one number, between 1 and 4, that you can combine five times with either a plus, minus, multiplication, division or brackets to obtain the given value (the first one has been done for you):

    2   → (3 + 3) ÷ 3 + 3 − 3
a. 12
b. 4
c. 7

In each case write down the sum.

Working with the fraction bar

Example 1

Work out the value of:

a. $\dfrac{2 + 10}{6 - 2}$

The fraction bar is the same as a division with brackets.

$(2 + 10) \div (6 - 2)$

$= 12 \div 4 = 3$

b. $\dfrac{28 - 4}{6 \times 2} + 3 \times 5$

$(28 - 4) \div (6 \times 2) + 3 \times 5$

$= 24 \div 12 + 3 \times 5$

$= 2 + 15 = \mathbf{17}$

Example 2

Using a calculator to work out sums

Work out the value of:

a. $3 + 2 \times (4 + 5)$

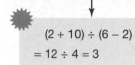

$\boxed{3}\ \boxed{+}\ \boxed{2}\ \boxed{\times}\ \boxed{(}\ \boxed{4}\ \boxed{+}\ \boxed{5}\ \boxed{)}\ \boxed{=}$ **21**

Type the whole expression into the calculator.

b. $\dfrac{20}{4 + 1}$

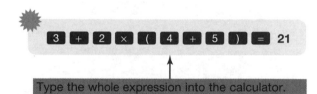

You can simply type the whole expression into the calculator:

$\boxed{20}\ \boxed{\div}\ \boxed{4}\ \boxed{+}\ \boxed{1}\ \boxed{=}$ 6 ✗ but you'll get it wrong

$5 + 1 = \mathbf{6}$

Brackets are required:

$\boxed{20}\ \boxed{\div}\ \boxed{(}\ \boxed{4}\ \boxed{+}\ \boxed{1}\ \boxed{)}\ \boxed{=}$ 4 ✓

$20 \div 5 = \mathbf{4}$

c. $\dfrac{9 + 3}{8 - 2}$

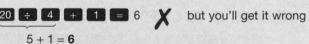

$\boxed{(}\ \boxed{9}\ \boxed{+}\ \boxed{3}\ \boxed{)}\ \boxed{\div}\ \boxed{(}\ \boxed{8}\ \boxed{-}\ \boxed{2}\ \boxed{)}\ \boxed{=}$ **2**

Type the whole expression into the calculator, adding brackets for the sums above and below the fraction bar and replacing the bar with a division sign.

Mapping out

Sums with the fraction bar:

Put brackets round the sums above and below the bar.

↓

Replace the bar with a division sign.

Work it out

1. Solve these sums:

    a. $\dfrac{4 + 12}{21 - 5}$

    b. $\dfrac{32 - 7}{9 - 4}$

    c. $\dfrac{20 - 2}{3 \times 3}$

    d. $\dfrac{8 \times 3}{11 - 5}$

    e. $\dfrac{50 - 2}{5 + 7} + 3 \times 6$

    f. $3 \times 9 - \dfrac{17 - 3}{3 + 4}$

    g. $\dfrac{2 + 5 \times 2}{10 - 3 \times 2}$

    h. $\dfrac{33 - 3 \times 4}{15 - 2 \times 4} + 5 \times 3$

2. Use a calculator to work out the following sums. Check your answers by working them out 'manually':

    a. $\dfrac{20 + 16}{10 - 4}$

    b. $\dfrac{61 - 6}{25 \div 5}$

    c. $\dfrac{4 \times 12}{22 - 6}$

    d. $\dfrac{36 - 2 \times 6}{22 + 2}$

    e. $\dfrac{11 + 3 \times 8}{17 - 2 \times 5}$

    f. $\dfrac{15 + 18 \div 2}{26 - 2 \times 7}$

    g. $\dfrac{52 - 32 \div 4}{12 + 4 - 5} + 2 \times 7$

    h. $\dfrac{22 + 5 \times 2}{20 - 3 \times 4} + 50 \div 10$

3. a. Match the calculator button presses with sums.

    b. Work out the answers to each sum.

---

a. (10 − 2) ÷ 4 + 5 × 3 =

b. 10 − (5 − 3) ÷ 2 + 4 × 6 =

c. (10 − 2) ÷ (5 − 3) + 4 =

d. 10 × (2 + 5) − 3 =

e. (10 + 2) ÷ (5 − 1) =

---

1. $\dfrac{10 - 2}{5 - 3} + 4$

2. $10 \times (2 + 5) - 3$

3. $(10 - 2) \div 4 + 5 \times 3$

4. $10 - \dfrac{5 - 3}{2} + 4 \times 6$

5. $\dfrac{10 + 2}{5 - 1}$

1.9 Percentages

Key term

Percentage
A fraction of 100, e.g. if 50% are male then 50 out of every 100 are male.
or

$\frac{50}{100} = \frac{1}{2}$ are male.

The world is teeming with **percentages**:

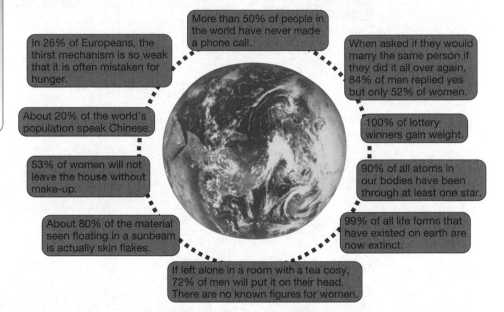

In 26% of Europeans, the thirst mechanism is so weak that it is often mistaken for hunger.

More than 50% of people in the world have never made a phone call.

When asked if they would marry the same person if they did it all over again, 84% of men replied yes but only 52% of women.

About 20% of the world's population speak Chinese.

100% of lottery winners gain weight.

53% of women will not leave the house without make-up.

90% of all atoms in our bodies have been through at least one star.

About 80% of the material seen floating in a sunbeam is actually skin flakes.

99% of all life forms that have existed on earth are now extinct.

If left alone in a room with a tea cosy, 72% of men will put it on their head. There are no known figures for women.

Group task

List four instances of how percentages are used in everyday life.

Provide an example of when 100% can be used.

Example

A survey of Access students

In one year 70% of Access students progressed on to a degree course.

This can be represented diagrammatically in a 10 by 10 square:

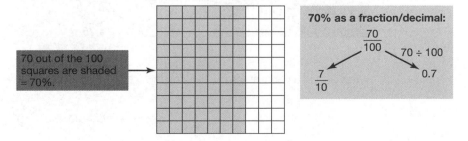

70 out of the 100 squares are shaded = 70%.

70% as a fraction/decimal:

$\frac{70}{100}$

$70 \div 100$

$\frac{7}{10}$

0.7

▶

At the end of the degree course 25% of the same Access students gained a first class honours degree, 10% obtained a third and the rest qualified with a second class degree.

This can be represented diagrammatically:

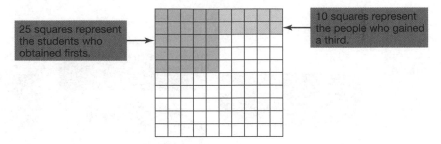

25 squares represent the students who obtained firsts.

10 squares represent the people who gained a third.

What percentage of Access students obtained a second class degree?

There are 65 out of the hundred squares not shaded – 65% of the students obtained a second class degree

or

$100 - 25 - 10 = \mathbf{65\%}$

Write these percentages as fractions and decimals in their simplest form.

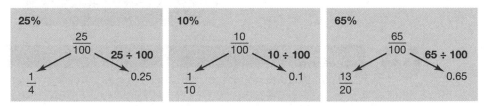

25%

$\frac{25}{100}$ $25 \div 100$

$\frac{1}{4}$ 0.25

10%

$\frac{10}{100}$ $10 \div 100$

$\frac{1}{10}$ 0.1

65%

$\frac{65}{100}$ $65 \div 100$

$\frac{13}{20}$ 0.65

37.5% of Access graduates obtained a job related to their degree within three months of qualifying and within the year $\frac{4}{5}$ were using their degree at work.

Write 37.5% as a fraction.

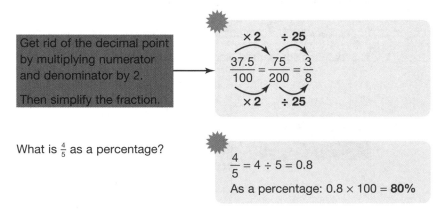

Get rid of the decimal point by multiplying numerator and denominator by 2.

Then simplify the fraction.

$\times 2$ $\div 25$

$\frac{37.5}{100} = \frac{75}{200} = \frac{3}{8}$

$\times 2$ $\div 25$

What is $\frac{4}{5}$ as a percentage?

$\frac{4}{5} = 4 \div 5 = 0.8$

As a percentage: $0.8 \times 100 = \mathbf{80\%}$

Conversions

- Numerator: percentage
- Denominator: 100
- Simplify fraction

Decimals × 100 → ÷ 100 Percentages

- Numerator ÷ denominator
- × 100

Fractions

Work it out

1. Use the shaded diagrams to work out the percentage, decimal and fraction, in their simplest form for the:
- grey squares
- red squares
- white squares

a. 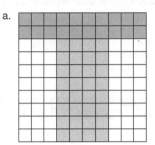   b.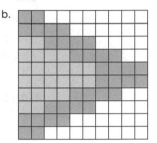

2. Connect the percentage with fraction (a. is done for you):

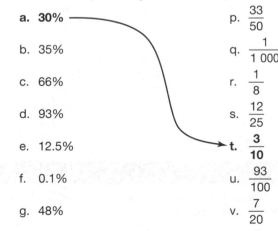

a. **30%**

b. 35%

c. 66%

d. 93%

e. 12.5%

f. 0.1%

g. 48%

p. $\dfrac{33}{50}$

q. $\dfrac{1}{1\,000}$

r. $\dfrac{1}{8}$

s. $\dfrac{12}{25}$

t. $\dfrac{3}{10}$

u. $\dfrac{93}{100}$

v. $\dfrac{7}{20}$

3. By converting these values to percentages write them in ascending order:

a. 32%, $\dfrac{1}{4}$, 0.313, $\dfrac{3}{10}$, 31%

b. $\dfrac{17}{20}$, 0.82, $\dfrac{4}{5}$, 86%, 0.84

4. In a survey 85% of people interviewed admitted they lie about their weight. Write this percentage as a decimal and fraction in its simplest form.

5. In a survey concerning marriage, 16.5% of people questioned admitted to having forgotten the date of their wedding anniversary and $\frac{3}{20}$ of all the people interviewed confessed to having proposed over the phone. Unfortunately, there is no information on the nature of the replies to these proposals.
    a. Write 16.5% as a:
        i.   decimal
        ii. fraction in its simplest form.
    b. Write $\frac{3}{20}$ as a percentage.

Investigation 1

Why bother with percentages when we've got fractions?

Investigate – consider comparing values as fractions and percentages. Use an example to support your answer.

Investigation 2

About 13% of the world's male population are illiterate and 23% of the female population. These percentages are shown diagrammatically:

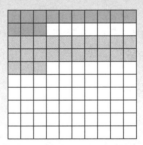

What is wrong with the diagram and how can it be fixed?

Investigation 3

40% of all sick days for a company are on either Monday or Friday. Should the company clamp down on sick days?

Converting to percentages

In a survey of 400 women with new born babies, 328 said that if they had the money they would prefer to stay at home to look after their baby.

What is the percentage of women who prefer to stay at home?

As an unsimplified fraction: $\dfrac{328}{400}$

As a percentage: $328 \div 400 \times 100 = $ **82%**

Example

Using percentages to compare statistics

This article appeared in a national paper:

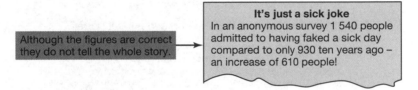

Although the figures are correct they do not tell the whole story.

It's just a sick joke
In an anonymous survey 1 540 people admitted to having faked a sick day compared to only 930 ten years ago – an increase of 610 people!

Here are all the figures behind the headline:

Number of employees who answered 'Yes' to the question: *'Have you ever phoned in sick when you weren't?'*

Ten years ago	930 out of 1 500
Today	1 540 out of 2 800

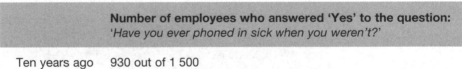

Because the number of people who participated in the survey are different the only fair way to make a comparison is by using percentages.

Ten years ago:

$930 \div 1\,500 \times 100 = $ **62%**

Today:

$1\,540 \div 2\,800 \times 100 = $ **55%**

Maybe the headline should read:

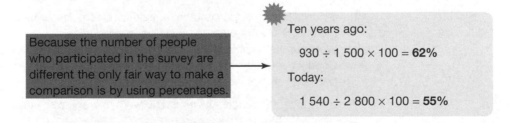

Is the UK on the road to recovery?

> ## Work it out

If required, round your answer to one decimal place.

1. Write the following as a percentage:
   a. 27 out of 54
   b. 112 out of 180
   c. 39 out of 88
   d. 12 out of 300
   e. 1.2 out of 4
   f. 10 out of 10.

> ### Key formula
>
> **Getting a percentage:**
>
> Number to be considered ÷ total possible × 100

2. Thirty four out of 50 students achieved a Maths GCSE. What percentage of students:
   a. obtained a GCSE?
   b. did not obtain a GCSE?

3. Out of a total of 640 seats in a cinema 526 are occupied. What was the percentage of seats:
   a. occupied?
   b. left empty?

4. A student obtained a mark of 24 out of 28 in Maths and 32 out of 37 in IT. Use percentages to work out which was his best result.

5. Here is the headline that appeared in a local paper:

> **Women are braver than men**
> In an anonymous survey it was discovered that more women were prepared to walk alone at night in our town.

Here are the figures behind the article:

	Number who answered 'yes' to the question: *'Are you prepared to walk alone at night in town?'*
Males	124 out of 146
Females	141 out of 985

   a. By calculating the percentage of males and females who answered 'yes' to the question work out if the headline is misleading.
   b. Work out the combined percentage of all males and females who answered yes.
   c. Conduct your own survey of students within your classroom and work out the two percentages for male and females.

6. A survey of 5 000 people, of whom 700 were over 65, was undertaken in 1970 and repeated in 2008. The results are:

	1970	2008
Total number of people with no natural teeth:	1 900	500
Number of people older than 65 with no natural teeth:	560	245

a. Copy the table but replace the figures with percentages.
b. Add another row to the table for people aged 65 or less with no natural teeth. Work out the percentages for 1970 and 2008.

7. The Food Standards Agency recommends a traffic light labelling approach to nutritional content of food. Retailers can use the system on their packaging of food.

For fat, the lights mean:

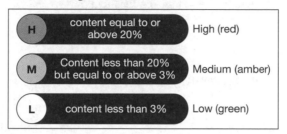

H content equal to or above 20%	High (red)
M Content less than 20% but equal to or above 3%	Medium (amber)
L content less than 3%	Low (green)

Here are the fat contents for some common foods:

Crisps	8.5 g per 25 g pack
Cheddar cheese	80 g per 240 g slab
Natural yoghurt	21 g per 500 g pot
Pizza	24.6 g per 200 g slice
Crunchy nut cornflakes	25 g per 250 g box.

Work out the traffic light level for each food.

Investigation

At MI5's Christmas party 80% of the people attending wore dark glasses and 65% wore false moustaches. All who attended wore either a pair of dark glasses or a false moustache.

What percentage wore both dark glasses and a false moustache?

Calculating percentages of an amount

Example

Working out percentages without a calculator

Calculate:

a. 87% of £350

10% is	350 ÷ 10	= £35	
80% is	8 × 35		= £280.00
1% is	35 ÷ 10	= £3.50	+
7% is	7 × 3.50		= £24.50
87% is	280 + 24.50		= **£304.50**

▶

b. 37.5% of £220

Key formula

Percentage of an amount:

Percentage
÷
100
×
amount

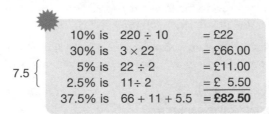

7.5 {

10% is	220 ÷ 10	= £22
30% is	3 × 22	= £66.00
5% is	22 ÷ 2	= £11.00
2.5% is	11 ÷ 2	= £ 5.50
37.5% is	66 + 11 + 5.5	= **£82.50**

Example

Working out percentages using a calculator

Calculate:

a. 43% of 480 kilograms

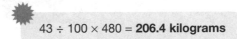
43 ÷ 100 × 480 = **206.4 kilograms**

b. 72.4% of £560

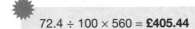
72.4 ÷ 100 × 560 = **£405.44**

Work it out

1. Without using a calculator, work out:
   a. 50% of £60
   b. 25% of 90 metres
   c. 14% of 20 kilograms
   d. 12.5% of 70 kilometres
   e. 0.1% of £2 000.

2. Use a calculator to work out:
   a. 82% of 40 kilometres
   b. 33% of £300
   c. 58.4% of 300 grams
   d. 3.1% of £240
   e. 0.07% of $6 000.

3. Armadillos sleep on average 75% of the day. How many hours do they sleep each day?

4. Which bottle contains the most alcohol, a 200 ml bottle of alcopops containing 6% alcohol or a 250 ml bottle of beer of 5% strength?

Group work

The chart shows the approximate percentage of the population dead by the end of the World War II for several countries:

Population at start of war:

China   536 million
Germany 60 million
Poland   40 million
UK   40 million
USSR   213 million

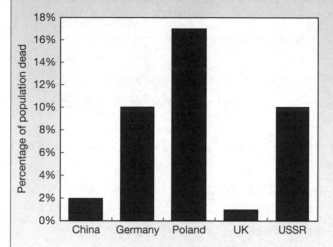

1. Although the chart does give an indication of the losses for each country it does not provide the whole picture. Why is this?
2. Work out the number of casualties for each country.

Group investigation

A doctor tested two different medicines, Zylon and Binderin, in two hospitals, for the same disease:

At Woddington Hospital:
- 100 patients were treated with the medicine Zylon and 55 were cured, a 55% success rate.
- 200 were treated with the medicine Binderin and 120 were cured, a 60% success rate.

At Torridon Hospital:
- 200 patients were treated with Zylon and 150 were cured, a 75% success rate.
- 100 were treated with Binderin and 80 were cured, a 80% success rate.

Doctor's conclusion:
- Binderin has had a better success rate and so is obviously the better medicine.

Is the doctor's conclusion correct? Investigate.

Percentage increases and decreases

Over the last year, a TV channel increased its ratings for a sit com by 8%. At the beginning of the year approximately 380 000 people sat down to watch the programme.

What are the audience figures for the end of the year?

Increase in viewers: 8 ÷ 100 × 380 000 = 30 400

Audience at end of year: 380 000 + 30 400 = **410 400**

In the same year a reality TV show saw a 24% decrease in the number of its viewers from a high of 32 000.

What are the audience figures for the end of the year?

Decrease in viewers: 24 ÷ 100 × 32 000 = 7 680

Audience at end of year: 32 000 − 7 680 = **24 320**

At the start of the year a current affairs programme commanded an audience of 112 000. By the end of the year there were 126 000 people watching.

What is the percentage increase in viewers?

Increase in viewers: 126 000 − 112 000 = 14 000

Percentage increase in viewers: 14 000 ÷ 112 000 × 100 = **12.5%**

Always divide by the original value.

Example

A university department is to purchase a new printer. The price including VAT at 17.5% is £152.75. As an educational establishment they don't pay VAT.

Work out the price the university will pay for the printer.

Price of printer + VAT   = £152.75
        100% + 17.5% is £152.75
           117.5% is £152.75
             1% is 152.75 ÷ 117.5 = £1.30
          100% is 100 × 1.30 = £130
        The university pays £130 for the printer.

Mapping out

Working out a new value:

Work out the change:
percentage
÷
100
×
original value

↓

Add or subtract this value from original amount.

Mapping out

Working out the percentage change:

Work out the difference between the two sets of figures.

↓

Change in values
÷
original value
×
100

Key formula

Calculating original value:

100
×
new value
÷
percentage

Work it out

If required, round your answers to two decimal places.

1. What is the value when:
   a. 200 metres is increased by 25%?
   b. £140 is increased by 66%?
   c. 70 kilograms is decreased by 30%?
   d. £18.20 is decreased by 15%?
   e. £112 is increased by 17.5%?
   f. 850 grams is decreased by 37.5%?

2. A typical graduate with ten years' work experience earns 77% more than the average earnings of £23 244.
   What are the average earnings of a graduate?

3. All employees of a company are to have a 6% pay rise. What will be the new salary for a person currently earning:
   a. £15 000?
   b. £58 000?

4. The average price of a standard computer has dropped by 22% in the last five years. What is the cost of a computer now that sold for £760 five years ago?

5. House prices decreased by 8% last year. What is now the cost of a home that sold for £180 000 last year?

6. Work out the percentage change between:
   a. £30 and £35
   b. 50 kilometres and 80 kilometres
   c. 120 kilograms and 90 kilograms
   d. £22.50 and £20
   e. £120 and £85
   f. 47 grams and 52 grams.

7. Over the space of a year Sam's weight has increased from 70 kilograms to 82 kilograms. What is this increase as a percentage?

8. Each year Dan, a photocopier salesman, is given the target of increasing his sales by 10% on the previous year. This shows his sales figures for four years:

2005	2006	2007	2008
£350 000	£392 000	£450 000	£486 000

   Are there any years when Dan does not meet his target?

9. The price of a pair of jeans increases by 50% then decreases by 40% in the sales. The jeans originally cost £32, what do they cost now?

10. Work out the original figure when the new value is:
    a. 200 kilograms, 125% of the original
    b. £30, 25% of the original
    c. £240, 120% of the original
    d. 20 kilometres, 40% of the original.

11. The sale price of a mobile phone is £35, 20% of its original price. What was the original value?

12. When an out of town superstore opens, the number of shoppers in the town centre is reduced to 3 600 per day, 45% of the original number.

    How many people used to visit the town before the opening of the superstore?

13. A person consumes 27 000 kilograms of food in his lifetime. This is 36 000% of his adult body weight. How much does he weigh?

Group investigation 1

Below is an extract from a web article:

Britain's poorest day

It's official – 17th January is the poorest day of the year in the UK as households reach a 'cash crisis'. For more than 15 million **(A%)** households December is the most expensive month of the year, leading to a grim spending hangover in January. Over 6 million **(B%)** households received their December pay cheque up to two weeks early, meaning they have to wait for up to 44 days for pay day instead of the more usual 31, an increase of **C%** days.

The average spending per household in December rose by £700 to £2 400, an increase of **D%**. According to research, the average monthly electricity bill rose from £67 to £82 (all those Xmas lights), an increase of **E%** and monthly spending on mobile phones rose from £40 to £48 another **F%** increase.

The addition of percentages within the article would provide the reader with better grasp of proportions.

Work out the percentages **A–F** to the nearest whole number.

Group investigation 2

1. Over a five year period the pass rate for a course increases from 80% to 90%. Does this mean there is a 10% increase in the pass rate?
   Investigate.

2. The price of a mp3 player increases by 10% then decreases by 10%.
   Is the new price the same as the original?
   Investigate.

3. This advert appeared in a local paper:

   Reduce your insurance bills
   We can reduce your home insurance by 20% and your car insurance by 20%.
   That's a reduction of 40% on your insurance bills.

   Have they got the maths right? Investigate.

You can have 50% (half) or 100% (the whole lot) of a carton of orange juice but not 150% as there is no more than the whole carton. But you can consume more than 100% of your daily vitamin C requirements as the vitamin C available to you is technically limitless.

Group work – working with more than 100%

1. Which of the following sentences make sense?
    a. I answered 146% of the questions in the assignment.
    b. I spend 120% of my leisure time surfing the net.
    c. House prices have increased by 110%.
    d.   House prices have decreased by 110%.
    e. The bus is punctual 127% of the time.
    f. 114% of the audience liked the show.
    g. There is a 132% chance it will snow today.

2. Write one sentence using percentages over 100% that make sense and one sentence that do not.

3. **Is this statement true:**

    'When the cost of something increases by 200% the price doubles.'

    Explain your answer.

The facts:

Borringham

Number of crimes each year:
    now: 800
    5 years ago: 600
Population
    now: 600 000
    5 years ago:
                 500 000

Whetherington

Number of crimes each year:
    now: 800
    5 years ago: 500
Population
    now: 303 000
    5 years ago:
                 300 000

Group work – using percentages to support an argument

Two opposing politicians are due to be interviewed for a TV programme about the crime in their towns, Borringham and Whetherington.

The interviewer's opening remark is:

   'Well, looking at the figures, both cities are equally crime-ridden – both have recorded 800 incidents for this year alone.'

Split the group in half – one to defend Borringham and the other Whetherington. Use the facts and percentages to voice your argument.
You may consider comparing the:

*   percentage increases in crime
*   percentage increase in population
*   crime rate (percentage crimes per member of the population).

Which town has the best record for crime?

Job description:

Kath is a senior midwife in a large maternity unit in the north of England. She leads a team of midwives that delivers nearly six thousand babies a year.

What Kath says:

'I chose to do midwifery because I felt it was a very positive area of nursing and even now, several years into the job, I feel emotion when holding a newborn baby.

In my job I use maths for evaluating statistics and when administering drugs – a time when you definitely can't put your decimal point in the wrong place.

CASE STUDY

Using Maths at Work: Kath – a midwife

Over the last decade we have seen an increase in the number of HIV infected pregnant women. The NHS now has a policy of screening pregnant women for the infection. I have been asked to give a talk to senior midwives in the region about the prevalence of HIV in pregnant women and their new born babies. Here are some of the notes I've already made:

- 63 500 adults are estimated to be living with HIV in the United Kingdom, of these it is estimated that 20,100 are unaware of their infection. In 2005, 7 450 new HIV cases were diagnosed – nearly a 100% increase in the number diagnosed in 2000.
- The frequency of HIV infection in women giving birth is approximately 6 in every 10 000 births.
- Interventions such as an elective caesarean, treatment with the drug Zidovudine and the avoidance of breast feeding can reduce dramatically the risk of mother-to-child HIV transmission.
- This table compares the number of babies born in the UK to HIV infected mothers in 1991 and 2006:

	Infected	Indeterminate*	Not infected
1991	153	53	184
2006	17	370	695

* Because antibodies from an HIV-positive mother may remain in her baby's bloodstream for a few months after birth, the results of early HIV antibody tests may be inconclusive.

Tasks

If required, round your answers to one decimal place.

1. What percentage of adults that are HIV infected are unaware of their infection?
2. Approximately how many people were diagnosed with the infection in 2000?
3. What percentage of women giving birth in the UK are infected by HIV?
4. How many HIV mothers gave birth in:
   a. 1991?
   b. 2006?
5. What is the percentage change in number of HIV pregnant women between 1991 and 2006?
6. What is the percentage of infected babies born to HIV-infected mothers in:
   a. 1991?
   b. 2006?
   c. The total for this period?
7. What is the percentage of babies not infected born to HIV-infected mothers in:
   a. 1991?
   b. 2006?
8. Why do you think the change in percentage of babies infected has altered so dramatically between 1991 and 2006?

Hints and tips (6 and 7)

Use the third bullet point.

CASE STUDY (*continued*)

Another of my responsibilities is to annually collate the number and type of births that have occurred at the hospital:

	Number of births	National average
Normal vaginal delivery	2 875	42%
Emergency caesarean	752	13%
Elective caesarean	393	9%
Assisted birth (e.g. forceps or ventouse)	891	19%
Induced	873	17%

Tasks

1. How many births have there been in total?
2. Work out the percentage for each type of birth. Round all your answers to the nearest whole number.
3. How does the unit compare with the national averages?

1.10 Ratios

In a TV games show the contestants can win either cash or a 'Mystery' prize that can vary from a weekend away for two to just a fountain pen. Their prize is randomly selected by rotating the wheel.

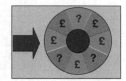

The **ratio** of the 'Mystery' prizes to cash prizes is:

   3 : 5

The producer decides to add an element of risk by increasing the number of options on the wheel and also introducing two 'exit' options – if these are selected the participant leaves the show empty handed.

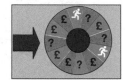

The ratio of the 'Exits' to 'Mystery' prizes to cash prizes is:

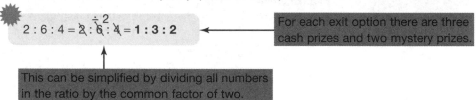

$$2 : 6 : 4 = 2 : 6 : 4 = \mathbf{1 : 3 : 2}$$

For each exit option there are three cash prizes and two mystery prizes.

This can be simplified by dividing all numbers in the ratio by the common factor of two.

Example

Write these ratios in their simplest form:

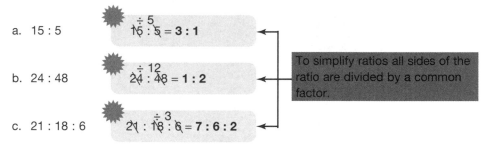

a. 15 : 5

$$15 : 5 = \mathbf{3 : 1}$$

b. 24 : 48

$$24 : 48 = \mathbf{1 : 2}$$

c. 21 : 18 : 6

$$21 : 18 : 6 = \mathbf{7 : 6 : 2}$$

To simplify ratios all sides of the ratio are divided by a common factor.

Work it out

1.   Write the ratio, in its simplest form, of cash prizes to 'Mystery' prizes.

   a. 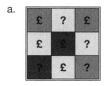   b.   c.

Hints and tips

Simplifying ratios:
Divide each figure in the ratio by a common factor. If there is no number that will go into the figures then the ratio is in its simplest form.

Ratios with decimal points:
Ratios in their simplest form should not have decimal points. To get rid of the decimal point multiply all numbers in the ratio by a number that will get rid of the decimal and then simplify.

2. Write each of these ratios in their simplest form:
   a. 2 : 4
   b. 16 : 24
   c. 60 : 84
   d. 1 000 : 3 000
   e. 0.5 to 2
   f. 4 : 6 : 8
   g. 30 : 150 : 90
   h. 64 : 32 : 80

3. Match ratios that are the same, the first has been done for you:

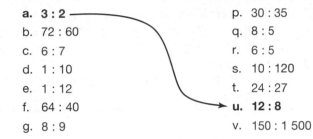

   a. 3 : 2
   b. 72 : 60
   c. 6 : 7
   d. 1 : 10
   e. 1 : 12
   f. 64 : 40
   g. 8 : 9

   p. 30 : 35
   q. 8 : 5
   r. 6 : 5
   s. 10 : 120
   t. 24 : 27
   u. 12 : 8
   v. 150 : 1 500

4. Convert these quantities to the same units and then write them as ratios in their simplest form:
   a. £2, 50p
   b. 20 minutes, 1 hour
   c. 2 minutes, 1 minute 30 seconds
   d. £2.40, 720p
   e. 460p, £5.20.

5. Complete the following ratios:
   a. 1 : 5 = 6 : ☐
   b. 4 : 3 = 12 : ☐
   c. 7 : 5 = ☐ : 25
   d. 3 : 8 = ☐ : 24
   e. 10 : 1 = 1 000 : ☐
   f. 200 : 50 = ☐ : 5

Hints and tips

When changing units always convert to the smallest e.g. change pounds into pence, minutes into seconds and so on.

6. Leah wants to share some sweets fairly between her two daughters. What is the ratio by which she will share them?

7. 86 400 football fans attended a match. 10 800 burgers are cooked in cafés around the stadium.
   a. Write as a ratio, in its simplest form, the number of burgers to fans.
   b. Complete the sentence 'There is 1 burger for every ??? fans.'
   c. The cafés cook chips in a ratio of 1 : 6 (one portion of chips to six fans). How many portions of chips are cooked?

8. On a hospital ward there are six nurses and 81 patients.
   a. Write as a ratio in its simplest form the number of nurses to the number of patients.
   b. Complete this sentence 'There is one nurse to every ??? patients.'

9. A company states that the ratio of money it spends on advertising to the company's profit should be 2 : 13.
   a. Complete this sentence 'For every pound spent on advertising the company aims to make ??? profit.'
   b. In one year the company spends £12 000 on advertising and makes a profit of £79 000. Do these figures meet the ratio?

Hints and tips

3 : 4 : 2 =
144 : 192 : ?

10. In a wood there are 144 beech trees, 192 birch trees and 84 oak trees.
   a. Write as a ratio in its simplest form the number of beech to the number of birch to the number of oak trees.
   b. A conservationist recommends that the ideal ratio is 3 : 4 : 2. How many oaks need to be planted to obtain this ratio?

About electronic entertainment

11. In a survey 82 out of a total of 697 people showed signs of Internet addiction.
    a. Write as a ratio in its simplest form the number of people who showed signs of addiction to the number who didn't.
    b. Complete the sentence '1 in every ??? people interviewed showed signs of Internet addiction.'
    c. Several more people are surveyed but none of them showed any signs of Internet addiction. The final conclusion to the survey is that one in every nine people showed signs of Internet addiction. How many more people are surveyed?
    d. Here are some statistics about the number of TVs owned by the populations of three countries:

Bermuda	2 020 TVs for every	2 000 people
Burma	68 TVs for every	10 000 people
UK	2 016 TVs for every	4 000 people

Work out the ratio of TVs to people in the form – one TV : number of people, to the nearest whole number for each country.

Sharing amounts in a given ratio

Share £360 in the ratio 5 : 3

Total parts: $5 + 3 = 8$
8 parts is £360
1 part is $360 \div 8 =$ £45
5 parts is $5 \times 45 =$ £225
3 parts is $3 \times 45 =$ £135
£360 is divided into £225 and £135

Example 1

A web designer has decided that the ideal web page consists of pictures, text and white space in the ratio 3 : 5 : 4.

A web page has an area of 900 cm².

Work out the respective areas.

Total parts: $3 + 5 + 4 = 12$
12 parts is 900 cm²
1 part is $900 \div 12 = 75$ cm²
3 parts is $3 \times 75 = 225$ cm²
5 parts is $5 \times 75 = 375$ cm²
4 parts is $4 \times 75 = 300$ cm²
The web page should be divided as:
    Pictures: **225 cm²**
    Text: **375 cm²**
    White space: 300 cm²

Example 2

The true art in making a Margarita cocktail lies in the ratio. It should be 3 : 2 : 1, tequila: cointreau: lime juice.

A person pours 72 centilitres of tequila into a jug.

Work out the quantities of cointreau and lime juice required to make a good mix. How much Margarita is made?

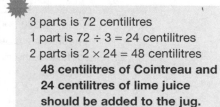

3 parts is 72 centilitres
1 part is 72 ÷ 3 = 24 centilitres
2 parts is 2 × 24 = 48 centilitres
48 centilitres of Cointreau and 24 centilitres of lime juice should be added to the jug.

There will be:
    72 + 48 + 24
    = **144 centilitres of Margarita**

Mapping out

Calculating ratios:

Total shares:
   Sum of all figures in the ratio.

↓

One part:
   Divide the amount by the total shares.

↓

Value of each 'share':
   Multiply each figure in the ratio by the value of one part.

Work it out

1. Share:
   a. £20 in the ratio 3 : 2
   b. £60 in the ratio 7 : 5
   c. 24 kilograms in the ratio 3 : 5
   d. 88 kilometres in the ratio 5 : 6
   e. £320 in the ratio 1 : 3
   f. £28 in the ratio 1 : 2 : 4
   g. 36 kilograms in the ratio 1 : 2 : 3
   h. £50 in the ratio 5 : 3 : 2.

2. A wildlife group is creating a wildflower meadow. They are using the ratio of 4 : 1 – grass seed to wildflower seed. They have mixed together 3 000 grams of seed. How much of it is:
   a. grass seeds?
   b. wildflower seeds?

3. Jack, Morgan and Sam buy lottery tickets together. Jack spends £6, Morgan £3 and Sam £9. They will share the winnings in the same ratio.
   a. Write the ratio of their winnings in its simplest form.
   b. How much will each receive if they win a total of:
      i. £36
      ii. £300
      iii. £120 480?
   c. One week they do win the lottery. Sam receives £676.50. How much money do Jack and Morgan win?

4. For a particular concert the conductor of an orchestra specifies that he wants the ratio of strings to woodwind to bass to be 6 : 2 : 1. The total number of musicians in the orchestra is 47 including two on percussion. Work out the number of musicians playing:
   a. a string instrument
   b. a woodwind instrument
   c. a bass instrument.

5. Three company directors, Simon, Jim and Fiona, are found guilty by a court of embezzlement. Simon stole £8 400 000 from the company, Jim £2 400 000 and Fiona £6 000 000. The judge decides to punish them in the same ratio as the amount they stole. Fiona is to be imprisoned for 15 months.
    For how many months will:
    a. Simon go to gaol?
    b. Jim go to gaol?

6. In a World War II battle the Allied tanks outnumbered the Axis tanks by 3 : 2 and the Allied ground troops outnumbered Axis troops by 5 : 3.
    The Allies had 480 tanks and Axis forces had 72 000 ground troops.
    a. How many tanks did the Axis forces have?
    b. How many tanks were there in total?
    c. How many ground troops did the Allies have?
    d. How many ground troops were there in total?

About a university

University managers have stated that the ideal ratio of lecturers to students is 1 : 8 and in the library the ideal ratio of computers to students visiting the library is 1 : 3.

7. a. On the Geography course there are 7 lecturers and 72 students. How many more lecturers do they need in order to achieve the ideal ratio?
    b. On a History course they have managed to attain the ideal ratio. The combined total of lecturers and students is 108.
        i.   How many lecturers work in the History department?
        ii. How many students are on the course?
    c. The library has 70 computers. At lunch time there are regularly 240 visitors. How many more computers need to be purchased in order to meet the ideal ratio?
    d. The ratio of males to females in a History lecture is 2 : 3. There are 14 males. How many females attend the lecture?
    e. The university is at the planning stage of building a new car park. The designers know that for every student that comes by bike, 17 come by car. They intend to cater for 918 students.
        i.   How many car parking spaces do they need to build?
        ii. How many bike spaces do they need to build?

8. After Christmas one out of four adults go on a diet.
    a. Write as a ratio, in its simplest form, the number of people on a diet to the number of people not on a diet.
    b. Out of 300 people how many will be dieting?

9. For every tackle a Premiership footballer makes 0.2 of them result in a foul.
    a. Write the ratio, in its simplest form, of clean tackles to dirty tackles.
    b. If in one game a footballer makes 30 tackles, how many of them will result in a foul?

10. Here is the recipe for a popular cocktail:
    a. Write the ingredients for Cosmopolitan as a ratio in its simplest form.
    b. The cocktail is made up using 33 centilitres of the orange liqueur. Work out the amounts required of the rest of the ingredients.
    c. How many centilitres of Cosmopolitan will be mixed?

Cosmopolitan	
Parts	**Ingredients**
1.5	vodka
0.75	orange liqueur
2.5	cranberry juice
0.5	lime juice
(teaspoon of sugar)	

About gambling

> When placing a bet on a horse a gambler is given the betting odds of say 3 : 4. This in effect means that for every £4 the gambler bets the bookie bets £3. If the horse wins the gambler takes all the money (3 + 4 = £7) but if it doesn't the bookie keeps the lot.

11. a. Neil has placed a bet of £12 on a horse with the odds of 2 : 3. If the horse wins, what will Neil receive from the bookie (including his initial stake)?
    b. He places a £20 bet on a horse with odds of 5 : 4. How much will he now receive from the bookie if this horse wins the race?
    c. Neil's horse wins a third race and he collects £27 from the bookies. The odds for the race were 2 : 7. How much money did Neil place on the horse?
    d. Will a gambler receive more winnings when placing a £10 bet if the odds are 5 : 2 rather than 2 : 5?
    e. The odds for a horse in one race is 100 : 1. Is the horse expected to perform well?

Group work 1

Which of these sentences make sense?

1. A ratio of 1 : 5 means 1 out of every 5.
2. The ratio 2 : 3 is the same as the fraction $\frac{2}{3}$.
3. The ratio 4 : 5 is the same as the two fractions $\frac{4}{9}$ and $\frac{5}{9}$.
4. Four out of five students pass the course. The ratio of pass to fail can be written as 4 : 5.

Group work 2

A company currently employs 120 males.
If it hires 20 more women the ratio of males to females becomes 10 : 3.
How many women does the company currently employ?

Group work 3

A decorator wants to mix blue and white paint in the ratio 1 : 4 in order to create a pale blue paint. He already has some tins of paint mixed in the ratio blue to white of:

1 : 2 – Tin A
1 : 5 – Tin B

1. How many tins of A and B will he need to use in order to obtain the correct ratio?
2. On another job he wants to mix a ratio of 1 : 3. How many tins of A and B will he need to use in order to obtain the correct ratio?

Group work 4

Scott is throwing an eighteenth birthday party for his mates. He is making a vodka punch and has already mixed 100 centilitres of vodka with 200 centilitres of lemonade.

1. What is the ratio, in its simplest form, of vodka to lemonade?
2. His mum tastes it and reckons it's too strong. She takes out 60 centilitres of the mixture and replaces it with lemonade.
    What is the ratio, in its simplest form, of vodka to lemonade now?
3. She is still not happy with the mixture and takes out a further 30 centilitres and replaces it with lemonade. What is the ratio, in its simplest form, of vodka to lemonade now?
4. Complete the sentence:

    'For one part vodka there are ??? parts lemonade.'

    Round the number to one decimal place.

1.11 The Power of Numbers

Key terms

Power of a number
A small figure placed to the upper right of a number to indicate how many times the number must be multiplied by itself.

Index form
A number to a power, e.g. 2^5

Power/index

Powers are shorthand for repeated multiplication.

Two to the power of 4 can be shortened to 2^4.

Example 1

Work out the value of these numbers that are written in **index form**:

a. 4^2

$4 \times 4 = 16$

b. 5^3

$5 \times 5 \times 5 = 125$

c. 2^5

$2 \times 2 \times 2 \times 2 \times 2 = 32$

Example 2

Simplify the following, leaving your answer in index form:

a. $3^3 \times 3^5$

$$\overbrace{3 \times 3 \times 3}^{3^3} \times \overbrace{3 \times 3 \times 3 \times 3 \times 3}^{3^5}$$ ← In long hand.

$$= 3^8$$ ← In shorthand (index form).

or

$$3^{3+5} = 3^8$$ ← Add the index numbers.

b. $8^7 \div 8^3$

$$\dfrac{\overbrace{8 \times 8 \times 8 \times 8 \times 8 \times 8 \times 8}^{8^7}}{\underbrace{8 \times 8 \times 8}_{8^3}} = 8^4$$ ← In long hand. / In shorthand (index form).

or

$$8^{7-3} = 8^4$$ ← Subtract the index numbers.

c. $5^8 \times 5^4 \div 5^5$

$$5^{8+4-5} = \mathbf{5^7}$$ ← In shorthand (index form).

d. $(6^4)^3 \div 6^2$ ← A power of a power.

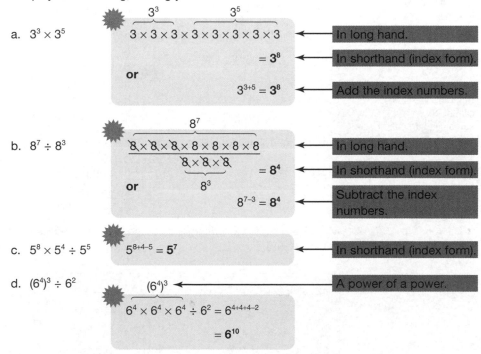

$$\overbrace{6^4 \times 6^4 \times 6^4}^{(6^4)^3} \div 6^2 = 6^{4+4+4-2}$$

$$= \mathbf{6^{10}}$$

Investigation

By using examples find a quick method of simplifying powers of powers, e.g.: $(4^5)^3$.

Work it out

Key rules

Multiplication:
Powers are added.

$$a^n \times a^m = a^{n+m}$$

Division:
Powers are subtracted.

$$a^n \div a^m = a^{n-m}$$

where a, n and m are any numbers.

Potential pitfalls

To simply multiply the two numbers together

$2^3 = 2 \times 3 = 6$ ✗

$2^3 = 2 \times 2 \times 2$

$= 8$ ✓

Different numbers cannot be combined into one index number, e.g.

$2 \times 2 \times 4 \times 4 \times 4$

$= 8^5$ ✗

$= 2^2 \times 4^3$ ✓

1. Write the following in index form:
   a. 5×5
   b. $7 \times 7 \times 7 \times 7$
   c. $3 \times 3 \times 3 \times 3 \times 3$
   d. 4

2. Without using a calculator work out:
   a. 3^2
   b. 2^4
   c. 4^4
   d. 9^2
   e. 10^5
   f. 1^{25}
   g. $(2^3)^2$
   h. $(3^2)^2$

3. Simplify the following, leaving your answer in index form:
   a. $2^4 \times 2^3$
   b. $7^5 \times 7^6$
   c. $8^7 \times 8^2$
   d. 5×5^2
   e. $3^2 \times 3^3 \times 3^4$
   f. $6^3 \times 6^5 \times 6^8$
   g. $0.2^4 \times 0.2^5 \times 0.2^4$
   h. $11 \times 11^3 \times 11^9$

4. Write the following in index form:
   a. $2 \times 2 \times 2 \times 3 \times 3$
   b. $5 \times 5 \times 5 \times 5 \times 4 \times 4 \times 4 \times 4$
   c. $8 \times 8 \times 8 \times 8 \times 9 \times 9$
   d. $7 \times 7 \times 3 \times 3 \times 3 \times 2 \times 2 \times 2 \times 2$

5. Simplify the following, leaving your answer in index form:
   a. $9^5 \div 9^2$
   b. $3^7 \div 3^3$
   c. $15^8 \div 15^7$
   d. $6^8 \div 6$
   e. $2^7 \div 2^5 \times 2^3$
   f. $10^4 \times 10^5 \div 10^3$
   g. $14 \times 14^6 \div 14^9$
   h. $21^6 \div 21 \times 21^5$
   i. $7^2 \times 7^7 \div 7^3 \times 7^6$
   j. $8^4 \div 8^2 \times 8^8 \div 8^5$

6. Simplify the following, leaving your answer in index form:
   a. $(5^4)^3$
   b. $(6^2)^5$
   c. $(7^4)^5$
   d. $(11^6)^8$
   e. $(2^5)^4 \times 2^6$
   f. $(3^4)^2 \div 3^5$
   g. $(7^3)^4 \times (7^2)^5$
   h. $(4^{10})^2 \div (4^3)^4$

7. Mark Rachel's work, writing in corrections where necessary (all answers should be in index form):

   a. $6^3 \times 6 = 18$
   b. $7^5 \times 7^2 = 7^7$
   c. $8^4 \div 8 = 8^4$
   d. $2^3 \times 4^5 = 8^{15}$
   e. $3^{10} \div 3^2 \times 3^3 = 3^{11}$
   f. $5^4 \div 5^4 = 5^1$
   g. $(4^5)^3 = 4^8$
   h. $(3^2)^7 \times 3^2 = 3^{16}$

Key actions

Squaring a number:
Multiplying a number by itself, e.g.
4 squared is 16 (4×4 or 4^2).

Cubing a number:
Multiplying a number by itself three times, e.g.
3 cubed is 27 ($3 \times 3 \times 3$ or 3^3).

8. The empty boxes are filled by multiplying the two preceding numbers. The first has been done for you, complete the rest:

2^3 | 2^4 | ☐ | ☐ ⟶ 2^3 | 2^4 | 2^7 | 2^{11}

a. 4^5 | 4^6 | ☐ | ☐   b. ☐ | ☐ | 2^7 | 2^{10}

c. ☐ | 5^7 | 5^{13} | ☐   d. 8^4 | ☐ | ☐ | 8^{12}

9. Which is bigger:
a. the cube of 3 or the square of 5
b. the square of 15 or the cube of 6?

10. 1, 4 and 9 are the first three square numbers. What are the next three square numbers?

11. Work out the missing cube numbers:
1, ☐ 27, ☐, ☐, 216

12. The square of the first number equals the cube of the second number. The numbers are different and less than ten: what are they?

Negative powers

Example

Key term

Negative powers
One divided by the power of the number.

$a^{-n} = \dfrac{1}{a^n}$

where a and n are any numbers.

Work these out, providing an answer in index form and if the power is **negative**, write the answer as a fraction:

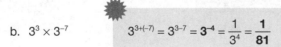
Using the subtraction rule for division.

a. $2^4 \div 2^6$

$$2^{4-6} = \mathbf{2^{-2}}$$
← In index form.

or

$$\frac{\cancel{2} \times \cancel{2} \times \cancel{2} \times \cancel{2}}{\cancel{2} \times \cancel{2} \times \cancel{2} \times \cancel{2} \times 2 \times 2} = \frac{1}{2 \times 2} = \frac{1}{2^2} = \frac{1}{4}$$
← As a fraction.

b. $3^3 \times 3^{-7}$

$$3^{3+(-7)} = 3^{3-7} = \mathbf{3^{-4}} = \frac{1}{3^4} = \frac{1}{\mathbf{81}}$$

c. $4^5 \div 4^{-2}$

$$4^{5-(-2)} = 4^{5+2} = \mathbf{4^7}$$

d. $3^6 \div 3^{-2} \div 3^4$

$$3^{6-(-2)-4} = 3^{6+2-4} = \mathbf{3^4}$$

e. $\dfrac{5^4 \times 5^5}{5^{10}}$

$$\frac{5^{4+5}}{5^{10}} = \frac{5^9}{5^{10}} = 5^{9-10} = \mathbf{5^{-1}} = \frac{1}{\mathbf{5}}$$

The power of zero

What is the value of $3^2 \div 3^2$?

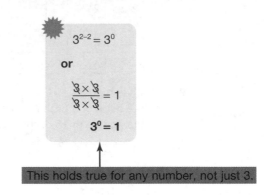

$$3^{2-2} = 3^0$$

or

$$\frac{\cancel{3} \times \cancel{3}}{\cancel{3} \times \cancel{3}} = 1$$

$$3^0 = 1$$

This holds true for any number, not just 3.

Work it out

1. Write these index form numbers as fractions:
    a. 2^{-3} b. 3^{-2}
    c. 4^{-4} d. 2^{-5}

2. Simplify the following, leaving your answer in index form:
    a. $3^7 \div 3^{10}$ b. $5^4 \div 5^9$
    c. $4^{-2} \times 4^6$ d. $2^{-3} \times 2^{-3} \times 2^{-3}$
    e. $5^{-3} \times 5^{-4}$ f. $7^2 \div 7^4$
    g. $2^{-6} \times 2^2$ h. $5^{-2} \div 5^{-4}$
    i. $6^2 \div 6^5 \div 6^4$ j. $3^{-2} \times 3^4 \div 3^{-3}$
    k. $\dfrac{5^5 \div 5^3}{5^2}$ l. $\dfrac{4^6 \times 4^5}{4^{11}}$

3. Copy and complete these arithmetic bricks. The first one has been done for you:

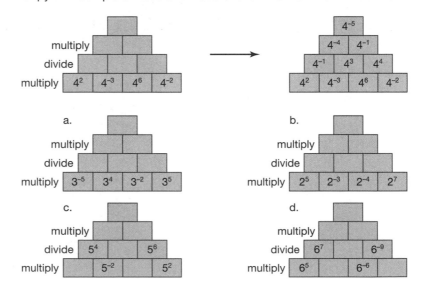

Roots of numbers

Key term

Root ($\sqrt{\ }$) of a number
A value when multiplied by itself a specified number of times results in the original number.

Square root
The second root often written as $\sqrt{\ }$ without the 2.

Cube root of a number
The third root $^3\sqrt{\ }$.

Roots are the opposite of the power of a number.

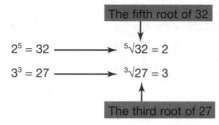

| The fifth root of 32 |

$2^5 = 32 \longrightarrow {}^5\sqrt{32} = 2$

$3^3 = 27 \longrightarrow {}^3\sqrt{27} = 3$

| The third root of 27 |

Example

Calculate:

a. $^2\sqrt{49}$

b. $^5\sqrt{243}$

c. $^4\sqrt{256}$

7 $(7 \times 7 = 49)$

3 $(3 \times 3 \times 3 \times 3 \times 3 = 243)$

4 $(4 \times 4 \times 4 \times 4 = 256)$

Hints and tips

Use examples that you know the answers to such as 2^4, 3^2, $^4\sqrt{16}$ or $^5\sqrt{243}$. Your calculator may have special buttons for square/square root values and cube/cube root values.

Investigation – using a calculator to work out powers and roots

Investigate how to use your calculator to work out:

• powers of numbers
• roots of numbers.

Write down your method in the form of a flow chart.

Work it out

If required, round your answers to two decimal places.

1. Calculate the following:
   a. $\sqrt{25}$ b. $\sqrt{36}$
   c. $^3\sqrt{729}$ d. $^4\sqrt{2\,401}$
   e. $^3\sqrt{83}$ f. $^5\sqrt{29}$
   g. $^6\sqrt{107}$ h. $^4\sqrt{59}$

2. Calculate the following:
   a. 3.2^2 b. 1.04^4
   c. 24.45^3 d. 2.27^6

3. Calculate the following:
   a. $5.3^2 \times 4.7^3$ b. $8.9^3 \times 2.1^4$
   c. $7.9^4 \div 5.2^3$ d. $25.2^3 \div 8.9^5$
   e. $0.9^5 \div 8.3^3 \times 3.1^4$ f. $18.9^6 \div 7.3^4 \div 6.7^2$
   g. $3.1^6 \times 0.5^6 \times 1.8^2$ h. $24.6^5 \div 11.8^2 \div 5.1^3$

4. Match the sums with their answers:

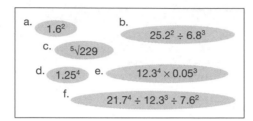

a. 1.6^2 b.
$25.2^2 \div 6.8^3$

c. $^5\sqrt{229}$

d. 1.25^4 e. $12.3^4 \times 0.05^3$

f. $21.7^4 \div 12.3^3 \div 7.6^2$

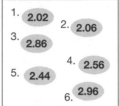

1. **2.02**   2. **2.06**
3. **2.86**
4. **2.56**
5. **2.44**
6. **2.96**

5. Which of these calculations are not possible using the normal number system?
   a. $\sqrt{-16}$ b. $^3\sqrt{-27}$
   c. $^4\sqrt{-81}$ d. $^5\sqrt{-32}$

Using powers

The invention of chess

Legend has it that King Shirham of India commissioned a mathematician called Sissa ben Dahir to come up with a new board game. The King was so thrilled with the game Sissa invented (later to be called chess) that he offered to give him anything he wanted. Sissa said:

'I would like one grain of rice for the first square of the board, two grains for the next square, four for the third and so on until all 64 squares are filled with rice.'

The king was surprised he asked for so little until he started counting out the grains of rice.

Here are the first six squares of the board filled with rice:

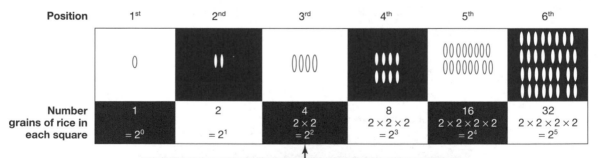

Position	1st	2nd	3rd	4th	5th	6th
Number grains of rice in each square	1 $= 2^0$	2 $= 2^1$	4 2×2 $= 2^2$	8 $2 \times 2 \times 2$ $= 2^3$	16 $2 \times 2 \times 2 \times 2$ $= 2^4$	32 $2 \times 2 \times 2 \times 2 \times 2$ $= 2^5$

There is a connection between the position of the square and the number of grains of rice when in index form:
the power is one less than the position.

There are 64 squares on a chess board.

Work out how many grains of rice there will be on the final square.

The final position is the 64th square.
The number of grains of rice on the square:

2^{63} = **9 223 372 037 000 000 000!**
(to 10 significant figures)

More rice than the King had in his entire kingdom!

Work it out

If required, round your answers to the nearest whole number.

1. The population of a village is predicted to grow at a rate of between 10% and 20% a year for the next 20 years. There are currently 1 000 people living in the village. The formulae to work out the predicted population sizes are:

    1 000 × 1.1$^{\text{no. years}}$ 10% growth
    1 000 × 1.2$^{\text{no. years}}$ 20% growth

    a. Copy and complete this table:

	Minimum growth	Maximum growth
Five years		
Ten years		

    b. What is the difference in the two predictions after:
        i.   five years?
        ii. ten years?

2. To advertise a website, Roger starts up a chain e-mail. Within the letter he asks everyone to forward the e-mail to six new people. Roger hopes people will do this but realistically he anticipates people will send about two e-mails.

    a. If everyone forwards the e-mail to six colleagues, work out the number of e-mails that have been sent at level:
        i.   two
        ii. five
        iii. ten.

    b. Repeat a. but this time use the more realistic figure of each person forwarding two e-mails.

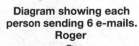

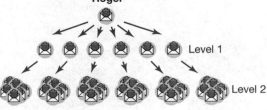

Diagram showing each person sending 6 e-mails.

Hints and tips

Use powers to work out your answers.

3. Environmentalists use this formula to predict the rate of deforestation of a particular 4 000 acres of virgin forest in South America:

    4 000 × 0.74$^{\text{no. years}}$ Number of acres left after the stated number of years.

    Work out the amount of land left after:
    a. one year
    b. five years
    c. ten years.

4. This question and answer was posted on the web:

    ### Do bigger animals live longer?

    As animals get bigger, from a tiny mouse to a huge blue whale, the pulse rate slows down and life spans stretches out longer. Mysteriously, the change in body size fits into a precise mathematical principle called fourth root scaling. For instance, an animal 16 times bigger than another will live $\sqrt[4]{16} = 2$ times longer.

    We know a mouse weighs approximately 0.05 kilograms and lives for about four years. This information can be used to calculate the lifespan of another animal:

    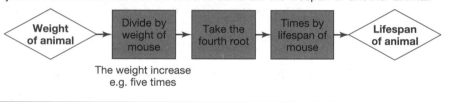

    The weight increase
    e.g. five times

    Life expectancy, in years:

    Cat: 12–15
    Horse: 20–40
    Elephant: 70–80

    a. Use the flowchart to work out the lifespan of the following animals:

	Cat	Horse	African elephant	Human
Approximate weight in kilograms	6	400	6 000	80

    b. Is the web answer correct?
    c. Would the results be different if the animals are weighed in pounds instead of kilograms?

5. A person puts £2 000 into a savings account that earns 7% interest. To work out how much money will accrue she uses the formula:

    2 000 × 1.07$^{\text{no. years}}$

    How much money will be in her savings account after:
    a. one year
    b. five years
    c. ten years?

Catching a bug

Your maths will assume Tom's body is not fighting back, i.e. killing the bug and his cold starts with just one bug.
The chess example may help.

6. Tom has caught a cold. The number of bugs in his body doubles every ten minutes. How many bugs will Tom have in his body after:
a. one hour?
b. five hours?

The bits in a computer

7. All computers store and manage information using the binary number system which consists of just two digits 0 and 1. These two figures represent the opening and closing of computer circuits.

It works in a similar way to the normal, decimal number system:

In the 10-digit decimal number system 2 562 can be split into:

Position value	1 000s (10^3)	100s (10^2)	10s (10^1)	1s (10^0)
Number	2	5	6	2

In the 2-digit binary number system 1 1 0 1 can be split into:

Position value	8 (2^3)	4 (2^2)	2 (2^1)	1 (2^0)
Number	1	1	0	1

Equivalent to 8 + 4 + 1 = **13**

a. Work out the decimal value of the binary numbers:
  i. 1001   ii. 1010
  iii. 10111   iv. 111110.
b. What is the biggest decimal value of a 4-digit binary number?
c. Work out the binary value of the decimal numbers:
  i. 7   ii. 12
  iii. 16   iv. 37.

Did you know?

The term bits comes from **b**inary dig**its**. A bit is a single binary value, either 0 or 1.
2^3 bits make a byte
2^{10} bytes make a kilobyte
2^{10} kilobytes make a megabyte
2^{10} megabytes make a gigabyte

8. Work out how many:
a. kilobytes in a megabyte
b. kilobytes in a gigabyte
c. bytes in a gigabyte.

9. Sue has 500 photos that are each approximately 1 200 kilobytes in size. She intends to store them on a 4 gigabyte memory stick.
a. How many megabytes will her photos take up?
b. How many megabytes is the storage capacity of the memory stick?
c. How much space is left on the stick?

10. Tom plans to download 2 000 songs onto his mobile phone which has 2 gigabytes of memory. Each song is approximately 5 000 kilobytes in size.
    a. How many megabytes is each song? Round your answer to two decimal places.
    b. How much space will all his songs take up
       i. in megabytes
       ii. in gigabytes?
    c. Has he enough space on his phone for all these songs?

Investigation – pyramid selling

Saira is approached by a colleague inviting her to become part of a sales group, selling body care products such as shampoos, bath oils etc. Saira will obtain a commission from sales but the main body of earnings will be generated through introducing others to the group. For every person she introduces she will receive £1 and for every person those people introduce she also receives another £1. The only catch is she needs to invest £200 initially. She is sorely tempted, especially when she does some maths. Assume that she introduces three people and each of these people introduce another three people and so on down the line. The diagram shows the amount Saira will initially receive.

1. Use index form to work out how much she could receive if there are:
   a. five levels
   b. ten levels.

2. Is it too good to be true?

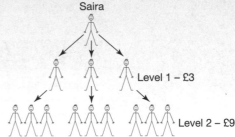

1.12 Scientific Notation

Key term

Scientific notation
A number greater than or equal to 1 but less than 10 multiplied by a power of 10.
The power can be a positive or negative whole number
e.g.
2.4×10^4

When writing either very large numbers such as the world population (6 700 000 000) or very small numbers such as the size of a chromosome (0.0000025 metres) it is easy to miscount the number of zeros. **Scientific notation** is a standard, shorthand way of writing these numbers, based on the idea that it is easier to read powers than count zeros.

Investigation

1. Key into your calculator the sum:

    8×10

    Multiply your answer by 10 and then another 10 and so on, counting the number of multiplications as you go. Stop when the way the answer displayed on the calculator changes.
    What do you think the figures on the screen represent?

2. Key into your calculator the sum:

    $8 \div 10$

    Divide your answer by 10 and then another 10 and so on, counting the number of divisions as you go. Stop when the way the answer displayed on the calculator changes.
    What do you think the values on the screen represent?

Example

1. 3.7×10^3 is in scientific form, but 0.37×10^3 is not nor is 37×10^3. Why is this?

The first number must be greater than or equal to 1 and less than 10.
3.7 is but 0.37 and 37 are not.

2. What is 3.7×10^3 in normal form?

$3.7 \times 10^3 = 3.7 \times 1\ 000 = 3\ 700$

or

$3\ 7\ 0\ 0 = 3700$

As the power is 3, move the decimal point forward 3 places, adding zeros when there are no digits.

3. What is 2.5×10^{-2} in normal form?

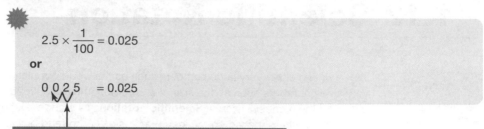

$$2.5 \times \frac{1}{100} = 0.025$$

or

$$0\,0\,2\,5 \quad = 0.025$$

As the power is –2, move the decimal point back
2 places, adding zeros when there are no digits.

4. What is 350 in scientific notation?

$$3.5 \times 100 = 3.5 \times 10^{2}$$

or

$$3\,5\,0 \quad\quad = 3.5 \times 10^{2}$$

The decimal point moves back to just after the first digit
2 places, making the power 2.

5. What is 0.0089 in scientific notation?

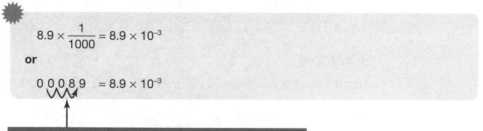

$$8.9 \times \frac{1}{1000} = 8.9 \times 10^{-3}$$

or

$$0\,0\,0\,8\,9 \quad = 8.9 \times 10^{-3}$$

The decimal point moves forward to just after the first
non-zero digit 3 places, making the power –3.

Number power

Very large numbers
such as the
distances the
planets are from
the sun are
sometimes called
astronomical
numbers.

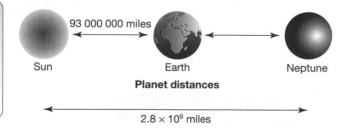

Sun — 93 000 000 miles — Earth — Neptune

Planet distances

2.8×10^{9} miles

The Earth is 93 000 000 miles from the sun. This can be written in scientific notation:

$$9\,3\,0\,0\,0\,0\,0\,0 = \mathbf{9.3 \times 10^7}$$

The decimal point moves back to just after the first digit – 7 places, making the power 7. The zeros after the 3 can be discarded as they are now worthless.

Neptune is on the outer reaches of our solar system, 2.8×10^9 miles from the sun. This can be written in normal form:

$$2\,8\,0\,0\,0\,0\,0\,0\,0\,0. = \mathbf{2\,800\,000\,000}$$

As the power is 9, move the decimal point forward 9 places adding zeros when there are no digits.

Atomic distances

Very small numbers such as the size of an atom are often called microscopic.

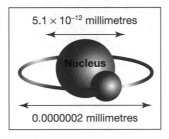

5.1×10^{-12} millimetres

Nucleus

0.0000002 millimetres

The width of an atom is about 0.0000002 millimetres. This can be written in scientific notation:

Mapping out

Converting to normal form:

Positive power: Decimal point will move to the right.
Negative power: Decimal point will move to the left.

↓

Move the decimal point on the same number of places as the power. If you run out of digits add zeros.

$$0\,.\,0\,0\,0\,0\,0\,0\,2 = \mathbf{2 \times 10^{-7}}$$

The decimal point moves forward 7 places to just after the first non-zero digit – the power is –7.

The width of a nucleus of an atom is about 5.1×10^{-12}. This can be written in normal form:

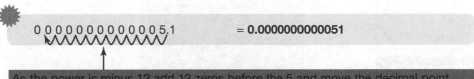

$$0\,.\,0\,0\,0\,0\,0\,0\,0\,0\,0\,0\,0\,5.1 \qquad = \mathbf{0.0000000000051}$$

As the power is minus 12 add 12 zeros before the 5 and move the decimal point back twelve places.

Work it out

1. Which of the following numbers are in scientific form?

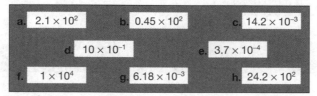

a. 2.1×10^2 b. 0.45×10^2 c. 14.2×10^{-3}

d. 10×10^{-1} e. 3.7×10^{-4}

f. 1×10^4 g. 6.18×10^{-3} h. 24.2×10^2

2. Convert the numbers from scientific notation to normal form:
a. 4.7×10^2 b. 1.38×10^4
c. 9.9×10^4 d. 2.309×10^5
e. 8.7×10^3 f. 1.5×10^1
g. 3.732×10^2 h. 8.9352×10^7
i. 8.0242×10^1 j. 6.004×10^2.

3. Convert the numbers from scientific notation to normal form:
a. 4.7×10^{-3} b. 1.38×10^{-2}
c. 6.406×10^{-2} d. 2.3×10^{-5}
e. 9.2×10^{-4} f. 1.5×10^{-4}
g. 4.65×10^{-1} h. 8.905×10^{-3}
i. 2.03×10^{-2} j. 6.0×10^{-2}.

4. Convert the numbers from normal form to scientific notation:
a. 234   b. 12 900
c. 7 500 000   d. 57.4
e. 4 500   f. 3 760 000
g. 9.9   h. 10.21
i. 1.1   j. 1 000 000 000.

5. Convert the numbers from normal form to scientific notation:
a. 0.023   b. 0.00993
c. 0.0057   d. 0.14
e. 0.092   f. 0.000304
g. 0.00001   h. 0.0000057.

6. The diagram plots out some of the features of the sea.
Convert all distances to scientific notation.

Feet

558 — Only two people have held their breath to this depth

1640 — Maximum diving depth of the blue whale

12500 — Depth of Titanic

36200 — Deepest recorded ocean depth

7. Which of these statements are correct?
   a. 4×10^6 is twice as big as 2×10^3.
   b. 9.9×10^5 is bigger than 1.2×10^6.
   c. 8×10^8 is twice as big as 4×10^8.
   d. 4.2×10^7 is ten times bigger than 4.2×10^6.
   e. 1×10^0 is a number in scientific form.
   f. 1.2×10^9 is twice as big as 6×10^8.
   g. 2.3×10^{-3} is bigger than 6.3×10^{-4}.

> Scientific notation is often called 'standard form'.

Sums using scientific notation

Example

Without using a calculator, work out the following sums, leaving your answer in scientific notation:

> Work out the two parts of the scientific notations separately and then combine to obtain the answer.

a. $(8 \times 10^3) \times (6 \times 10^2)$

$8 \times 6 = 48 = 4.8 \times 10^1$
$10^3 \times 10^2 = 10^{3+2} = 10^5$
Answer:
$\quad 4.8 \times 10^1 \times 10^5$
$\quad = 4.8 \times 10^{5+1}$
$\quad = \mathbf{4.8 \times 10^6}$

b. $(8 \times 10^5) \div (4 \times 10^7)$

$8 \div 4 = 2$
$10^5 \div 10^7 = 10^{5-7} = 10^{-2}$
Answer: $\mathbf{2 \times 10^{-2}}$

c. $(2 \times 10^2) \times (8 \times 10^{-8})$

$2 \times 8 = 16 = 1.6 \times 10^1$
$10^2 \times 10^{-8} = 10^{2+(-8)} = 10^{-6}$
Answer:
$\quad 1.6 \times 10^1 \times 10^{-6}$
$\quad = 1.6 \times 10^{1+(-6)}$
$\quad = \mathbf{1.6 \times 10^{-5}}$

Investigation

1. Without using a calculator, work out a quick method for finding the answer to:
   $3.2 \times 10^3 + 5.3 \times 10^3 + 1.1 \times 10^3$
   What is the answer in normal form?

2. Use your method to work out:
   a. $1.4 \times 10^4 + 4.1 \times 10^4 - 1.2 \times 10^4$
   b. $7.6 \times 10^5 - 3.1 \times 10^5 + 2.2 \times 10^5$
   Write both answers in normal form.

Work it out

Hints and tips

Using a calculator:

Enter the figures and symbols into your calculator exactly as they are in the sum.

1. Work out the following sums, leaving your answer in scientific notation:
   a. $(2 \times 10^3) \times (4 \times 10^2)$
   b. $(3 \times 10^4) \times (2 \times 10^3)$
   c. $(5 \times 10^4) \times (3 \times 10^3)$
   d. $(7 \times 10^6) \times (4 \times 10^2)$
   e. $(3 \times 10^{-3}) \times (3 \times 10^5)$
   f. $(5 \times 10^{-4}) \times (6 \times 10^{-3})$
   g. $(8 \times 10^5) \div (2 \times 10^3)$
   h. $(9 \times 10^7) \div (3 \times 10^2)$

2. Use a calculator to work out the following sums. For each question round your answers to two significant figures and leave it in scientific notation.
   a. $(1.1 \times 10^6) \times (4.7 \times 10^2)$
   b. $(2.9 \times 10^3) \times (1.2 \times 10^4)$
   c. $(6.9 \times 10^5) \times (4.5 \times 10^1)$
   d. $(2.8 \times 10^{-2}) \times (8.4 \times 10^6)$
   e. $(7.2 \times 10^{-3}) \times (6.1 \times 10^4)$
   f. $(2.7 \times 10^7) \div (3.9 \times 10^{-4})$
   g. $(4.4 \times 10^3) + (1.01 \times 10^2)$
   h. $(1.45 \times 10^6) - (2.36 \times 10^4)$

Million 1×10^6
Billion: 1×10^9
Trillion: 1×10^{12}
Googol: 1×10^{100}

3. Write the following in scientific notation:
   a. Half a million
   b. Two googols
   c. Eighty eight trillions
   d. Thousand millions
   e. Million billions
   f. Trillion googols.

4. Borrowing by UK individuals now totals £1.35×10^{12}.
   Work out the average debt, in normal form, of each UK citizen.

UK population:
6.1×10^7.

5. Using the diagram on page 108 work out the distance between the Neptune and earth. Write your answer in scientific notation rounded to three significant figures.

About an atom

Write your answers in scientific notation rounded to two significant figures.

Hints and tips

When dividing on the calculator by a number in scientific notation, always use brackets, e.g.

$6 \div 2 \times 10^3$
$= 3 \times 10^3$ ✗

$6 \div (2 \times 10^3)$
$= 3 \times 10^{-3}$ ✓

6. a. Using the diagram on page 109, work out how much bigger the width of an atom is compared to the width of its nucleus.
   b. An atom weighs about 2×10^{-27} kilograms (try weighing that on your bathroom scales). A penny weighs about 0.002 kilograms. Approximately many atoms are in a penny?

About insects

7. Here is an article written for a science magazine.

Insects – the most successful life form on this planet

At any one time there are estimated to be a massive 1×10^{19} insects alive on this planet! Scientists estimate that there are 3×10^7 different kinds of insects in the world, but of these only 1×10^6 species have been identified. This is despite man's destructive acts which have led to an estimated extinction of about 2.7×10^4 species a year. Conversely, the destructive act of a swarm of migrating locusts (weighing about 7.3×10^7 kilograms) can devour as much food every day as would feed 2×10^7 people for a day.

Write your answers for all these questions in scientific notation rounded to two significant figures.
a. How many insect species have not been identified?
b. If all the insects alive today were put back to back:
    i.   How long would this column of insects be?
    ii. How many times could this column circle the earth?
c. For each person on the planet, how many insects are there?
d. According to the scientists, how many insects were made extinct in the last ten years?
e. How many men are equivalent in weight to a swarm of locusts?
f. If the locusts swarmed for just one week how much food will they eat? Give your answer in terms of people's food for a day.

Circumference of earth at equator:
    4×10^7 metres
Average length of an insect:
    2×10^{-3} metres
Average weight of man:
    73 kilograms
World population:
    6.7×10^9
When figures get very big they become unimaginable and often need to be compared to everyday things.

8. The world is consuming 8.259×10^7 barrels of oil each day. The known reserves of oil total about 1.293×10^{12} barrels.
    If we continue to consume oil at today's rates, how many:
    a. days, to the nearest day, will the oil reserves last?
    b. years, to the nearest year, will the oil reserves last?
    Write your answers to both these questions in normal form.

9. The chart shows the number of Internet users worldwide:

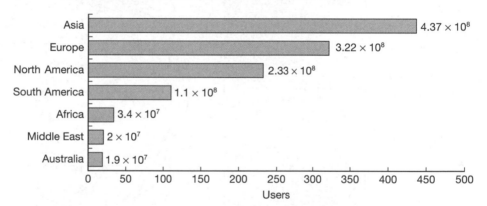

Write your answers to these questions in scientific notation, rounded to two significant figures.
a. What is the total number of Internet users worldwide?
b. What is the difference in user numbers between Asia and Australia?
c. Name the two continents that have a difference of 2.13×10^8 Internet users.

1.13 Co-ordinates

Key terms

Axis
A horizontal and a vertical line that cross at the **origin**. Numbers are placed along these lines at regular intervals.

Co-ordinates
A pair of bracketed numbers that specify the position of a point.
The first number is the horizontal distance from the origin and the second is the vertical distance from the origin.

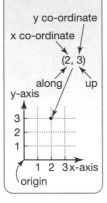

A facelift surgeon is preparing a presentation to potential customers. He decides that the best means of describing the procedure is to place a face within the framework of a grid. Here is the slide he uses:

Facelift procedure

The surgeon separates the skin from the fat and muscle. Fat can then be trimmed or suctioned from around the neck and chin to improve the contour. He then tightens the underlying muscle and membrane, pulling the skin back and removing the excess.

The diagram shows the 'anchor' points from where the tissue is tightened:

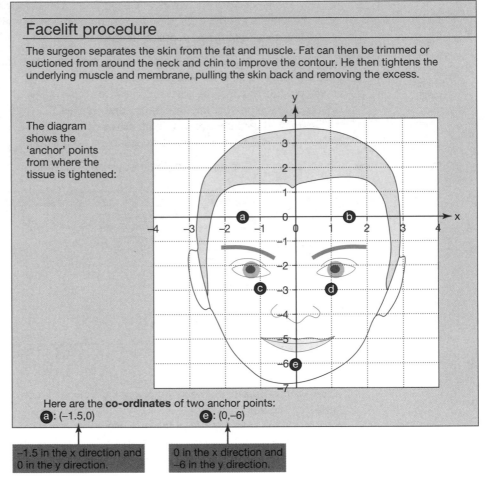

Here are the **co-ordinates** of two anchor points:

a: (−1.5,0)   **e**: (0,−6)

−1.5 in the x direction and 0 in the y direction.

0 in the x direction and −6 in the y direction.

Work it out

Remembering the order of the co-ordinates

Along the corridor then up/down the stairs.

1. What are the co-ordinates of anchor points b, c and d?

2. This second slide shows the surgeon's incisions:

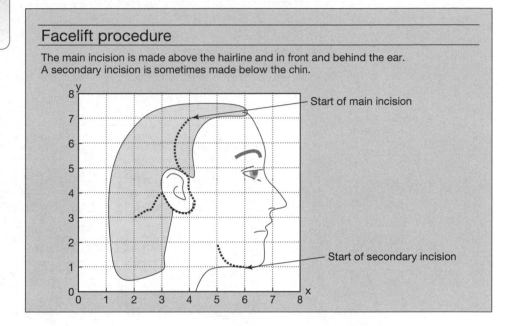

Facelift procedure

The main incision is made above the hairline and in front and behind the ear. A secondary incision is sometimes made below the chin.

What are the co-ordinates for the start and end of:
a. the main incision?
b. the secondary incision?

3. On a tour of a football stadium there is an opportunity for fans to test out their skills. Goal posts are painted on an 'electronic' wall that records the position of the ball when a player hits it. Here are several positions where a fan has hit the wall with the ball:

Points to be had:

Inside the goal: 3
On the post: 1

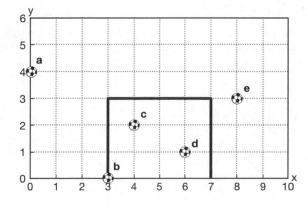

▶

   a. Write down the co-ordinates of balls a – e.

   b. How many points did the player score?

   c. Another player hit the wall at co-ordinates (2, 2), (2, 5), (7, 3), (3, 0) and (5, 5).

     i.   Copy the grid and plot the balls.

     ii. How many points did this player score?

4. a. Plot the following points, joining them up with a straight line as you go:

    (0, 5) (0.5, 3) (2, 3) (1, 1.5) (2, 0) (0.5, 0) (0, –2)

    (–0.5, 0) (–2, 0) (–1, 1.5) (–2, 3) (–0.5, 3) and (0, 5).

   b. What shape have you drawn?

5. A computer games programmer has created this electronic maze:

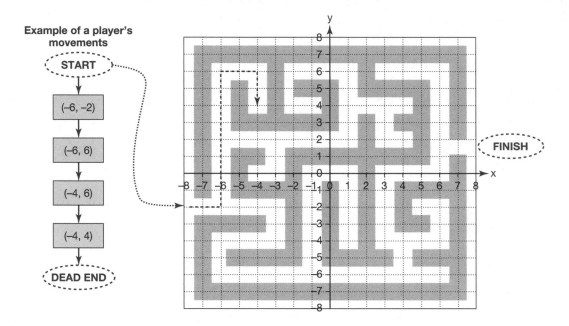

Example of a player's movements

START

(–6, –2)

(–6, 6)

(–4, 6)

(–4, 4)

DEAD END

FINISH

Record the co-ordinates each time the player changes direction.

The programmer wants to record the co-ordinates through the maze that takes a player along the shortest route from the start to the finish. Do this for him in the form of a flow chart.

6. Find the co-ordinates of the middle point of the straight lines that have start and end co-ordinates of:

   a. (1, 3) and (5, 9)

   b. (5, 0) and (17, 8)

   c. (–2, –5) and (6, 11)

   d. (–3, –1) and (–9, –7)

1.14 Interpretation and Plotting of Graphs

Graphs are a very visual way of conveying information quickly and accurately. They are used extensively by scientists, advertisers and journalists to name but a few.

A zoologist has placed a tracking device on several polar bears in Canada. The graph below shows the distance travelled by a female bear from her den in one twelve hour period.

1. How far does the bear travel from her den?

2. How far is the bear away from her den at the end of the twelve hour period?

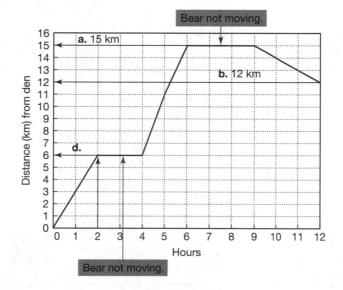

Speed = distance ÷ time.

3. How many hours is the bear not moving?

2 + 3 = **5 hours**

4. What is the bear's average speed in the first two hours?

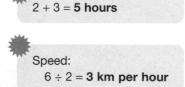

Speed:
    6 ÷ 2 = **3 km per hour**

5. What is the bear's average speed for the twelve hours?

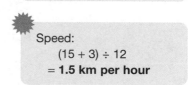

Speed:
    (15 + 3) ÷ 12
    = **1.5 km per hour**

> At birth a UK male is expected to live to 76.5 years but if they reach 65 years they can expect to live to 81.5 years.

Example

Plotting a graph

The table below provides information on the life expectancy of men living in the UK today at different ages in their life:

At birth	Age 1	Age 15	Age 45	Age 65
76.5	77	77	78.5	81.5

1. Plot these figures as a line graph.

> **Choosing the right figures for each axis:**
>
> The horizontal values affect the vertical values, e.g. the current age affects expected age of death.

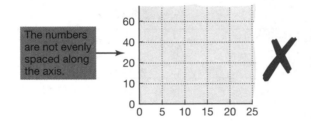

The numbers are not evenly spaced along the axis.

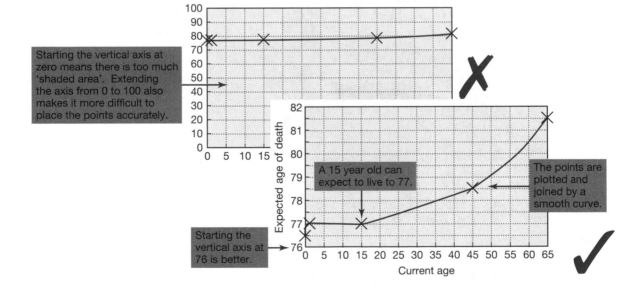

Starting the vertical axis at zero means there is too much 'shaded area'. Extending the axis from 0 to 100 also makes it more difficult to place the points accurately.

A 15 year old can expect to live to 77.

The points are plotted and joined by a smooth curve.

Starting the vertical axis at 76 is better.

2. Use your graph to estimate the life expectation of a man aged:
   a. 50
   b. 25.

3. Comment on the chart.

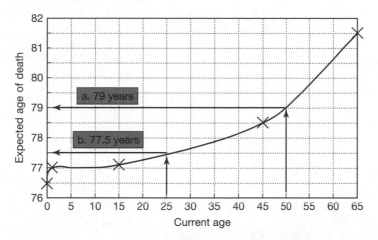

As a man gets older his life expectancy increases. This increase is most notable after the age of 45. There is a five year difference between the life expectancy at birth and 65.

Group work – what's wrong with the graph?

The graph records the temperature of the air at several heights above the ground on one day in the UK.

List three things that are incorrect about this graph:

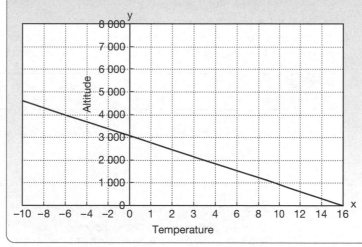

Work it out

1. With the following values, state what goes along the horizontal:
   a. number of visitors to a fun fair and the fair's income
   b. growth rate of a cow and growth hormones present in their blood

Hints and tips

Horizontal measures effect vertical measures.

c. temperature and risk of frostbite
d. speed of car and stopping distance
e. thickness of ice on a lake and weight it can withstand
f. number of bacteria in a slab of meat and temperature.

2. A zoologist has placed a tracking device on a cheetah in Kenya. The graph below shows the distance travelled by the cheetah on a hunt:

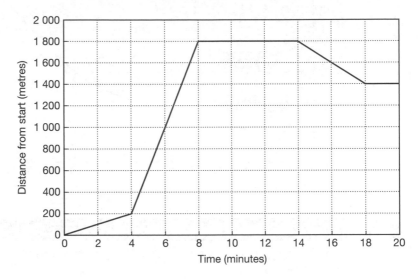

a. How far does the cheetah travel from her start position?
b. How long is the cheetah resting?
c. What is the fastest speed the cheetah reaches?
d. How far is the cheetah away from the starting point at the end of the 20 minutes?
e. Here are the distances a gazelle is from the start of the cheetah's movements:

Minutes	0	2	4	6	8	10	12	14	16	18	20
Distance (metre)	1 600	1 400	1 400	1 600	1 800	1 800	1 800	1 800	1 600	1 400	1 400

Copy the graph above and add to it the movements of the gazelle.

f. What do you think happened to the gazelle?

3. A zoologist records the movements of a group of mountain gorillas in Uganda:

> – Moved at an average speed of 2 km per hour for 1 hour
> – Moved at a speed of 0.5 km per hour for 3 hours
> – Rested for 3 hours
> – Moved at an average speed of 1.5 km per hour for 2 hours
> – Rested for 1 hour

Hints and tips

Remember to:

• Draw as large a graph as possible using an easy to read scale on both axes.
• Evenly space the numbers along each axes.
• Label both axes.
• Give your graph a title.

a. How many hours were the gorillas observed?
b. Plot these details as a line on a graph.

c. Use the graph to work out:
   i. the total distance the gorillas have travelled
   ii. their average speed while being observed
   iii. how far the gorillas travelled after 8 hours.

4. The table below provides information on the predicted life expectancy at different ages for females living in the UK:

At birth	Age 1	Age 15	Age 45	Age 65
80.9	81.3	81.4	82.2	84.4

a. Plot these figures as a line on the graph you plotted for the example on page 119.
b. Use your graph to estimate the life expectancy of a woman aged:
   i. 20
   ii. 40.
c. Comment on the difference between the life expectancy of men and women today.
d. The table below provides details of the predicted life expectancy in 1900:

	At birth	Age 1	Age 15	Age 45	Age 65
Male	44.1	53.2	60.2	67.2	75.3
Female	47.8	55.5	62.6	69.2	76.3

Plot these figures as two separate lines on a second graph.
e. Use your graph to estimate the life expectancy of a man and woman aged:
   i. 25
   ii. 50.
f. Comment on the difference between the life expectancy in 1900 and today.

> The chart does not include any special tax relief an employee may be entitled to.

5. The owner of a small company has drawn a graph to provide new employees with an idea of the approximate amount of money they will receive each month after tax and national insurance deductions. Here it is:

   a. How much can a person expect to receive each month on a salary of
       (round your answer to the nearest £100):
       i. £15 000?
       ii. £38 000?
   b. What is the salary of a person who receives each month (round your answer
       to the nearest £1 000):
       i. £1 300?
       ii. £2 600?
   c. How much are the deductions each month for a person who earns £24 000
       a year?

About student finances

This grant students
do not pay back.
The amount a
student receives is
determined by their
household income.

6. The graph below shows details of the maintenance grant available to some students.

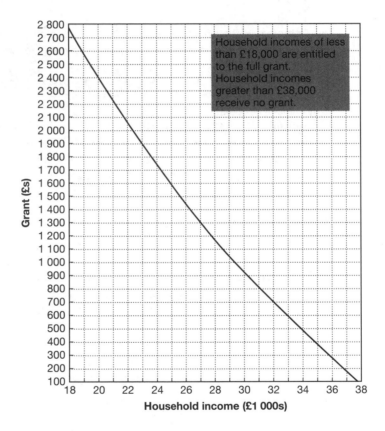

Household incomes of less than £18,000 are entitled to the full grant. Household incomes greater than £38,000 receive no grant.

   a. How much will a student receive if their total household income is:
       i. £20 000?
       ii. £34 000?
       Round your answers to the nearest £100.
   b. A student receives a maintenance grant of £1 300. What is her household
       income? Round your answer to the nearest £1 000.

c. Student loans are paid back once a graduate is earning more than £15 000. The amount a graduate repays each month depends on their income. This is illustrated in the table:

Yearly income	£15 000	£20 000	£25 000	£30 000	£35 000	£40 000	£45 000	£50 000
Monthly repayment	£0.00	£37.50	£75.00	£112.50	£150.00	£187.50	£225.00	£262.50

These questions ignore the interest accrued on the debt.

Plot a graph of this table.

d. Both Amy and Sam have accrued debts of £15 000 while studying for their degree. On graduation, Amy gets a job earning £32 000 and Sam one that pays him £26 000. Use your graph to work out the following:

i. What will be their monthly loan repayments? Round your answer to the nearest £10.

ii. How much will they each pay off in one year?

iii. If they stayed at the same salary, how long, to the nearest year, will it take Amy and Sam to repay the loan?

7. The table provides information on the monthly repayments for a specific mortgage over a 25 year period:

Mortgage	Monthly repayments	
	4% Interest rate	6% Interest rate
£50 000	£270	£330
£100 000	£530	£650
£150 000	£800	£980
£200 000	£1 070	£1 300
£250 000	£1 330	£1 630
£300 000	£1 600	£1 960

a. Plot these values as two lines on one graph.

b. Use your graph to work out the monthly repayment for a £170 000 mortgage when the interest rate is:

i. 4%

ii. 6%.

c. A person pays £600 a month, what are the two possible values of their mortgage?

d. What is the difference in monthly repayments between interest rates of 4% and 6% on a £120 000 mortgage?

Round all your answers to the nearest £50.

Goal difference:

Goals scored – goals conceded.

Investigation

Match each graph with one of the following situations:

1. Daylight hours in the UK over three years.
2. Bank balance of an office worker over several months.
3. The goal difference of a football team over several matches.
4. Number of people visiting Accident and Emergency in one week.
5. Calories burnt in a day that includes a visit to the gym.
6. New born babies weight in the first few weeks after birth.

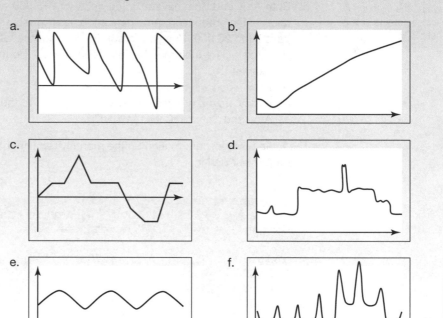

1.15 Bringing It All Together

Job description:

Pauline manages a Mental Health and Social Care Team, comprising doctors, social workers, psychologists, and other support staff. Pauline is responsible for the team's budget, ensuring the service is working efficiently and meeting the needs of the local population.

What Pauline says:

'At school I couldn't really see any use for Maths in the "grown up world" other than that which related to money, i.e. spending it (I knew then and still know now how to work out 10% off in a sale.) What an underestimation! I've now been working in social work for over seventeen years and I can honestly say that I'd have difficulty recalling a day when I didn't use maths.'

CASE STUDY

Using Maths at Work: Pauline – social worker in mental health

When putting forward a case for a new service, particularly if there are scant resources, you quickly learn that underpinning your argument with statistical data can make a big difference.

A few years ago we streamlined how the public initially made contact with us. We created a one-stop shop with a psychiatric nurse responsible for all contacts. This has made it a lot easier to monitor a person's progress through the system and ensure their needs are fully met. In fact it has been so successful we are now asking senior management for another nurse plus a social worker. To help my bid for these extra resources I have come up with the following figures.

Number of referrals 2003   : 80
Number of referrals 2008   : 300

After the initial referral people often decline to take things further (usually because of the stigma attached to mental illness) – more staff could help address this issue. Here are some figures for the last three months:

	Number of progressed	Number not progressed
January	72	20
February	64	12
March	68	16

The nurse e-mailed me these percentages for the reason for non-progression for the same period:

	Referred to another service	Person declined our service	Other reason, e.g. moved out of area
January	15%	60%	25%
February	25%	50%	25%
March	37.5%	43.75%	18.75%

Tasks

If required, round your answers to one decimal place.

1. Work out the percentage increase in referrals between 2003 and 2008.
2. Work out the percentage number of people that didn't progress in each of the three months.

▶

CASE STUDY (*continued*)

3. Pauline wants to work out the overall percentages for why people didn't progress in the first three months.
   a. Copy the second table but replace the percentages with number of people (you will need to also use the figures from the first table.)
   b. Work out the overall percentage of people in the three months who were:
      i. referred to another service
      ii. declined the service
      iii. had other reasons not to proceed.

I am also working on a more general report about mental illess. I intend to use national figures from the Layard report. So far I've got these statistics:

Size of UK adult population: 4.85×10^7
Size of local adult population: 6.38×10^4
UK Gross domestic product (GDP): £$1.25 \times \times 10^{12}$

Facts from the Layard report:

1. $\frac{1}{20}$ of adults say they are not very happy. Of these:
   - $\frac{1}{4}$ were poor (in the lowest tenth);
   - $\frac{2}{5}$ were mentally ill.

2. At any one time one in six adults are suffering from mental illness. Of those ill:
   - the ratio of people who receive treatment to people who receive no treatment is 6 : 19;
   - Only $\frac{1}{10}$ see a psychiatrist/psychologist;
   - $\frac{3}{20}$ receive medication only.

3. The annual costs of mental illness to the UK:

   Time off work or not working (including cost of carer)   £1.7×10^{10}
   GP time   £9×10^8
   Mental health trusts   £$4.9 \times \times 10^9$
   Drugs   £8×10^8
   Social services   £$1.4 \times \times 10^9$

Tasks

> Assume the numbers for the local area are in the same proportion as the nationwide figures.

1. a. What fraction of the adult population are:
      i. poor and not happy?
      ii. mentally ill and not happy?
   b. Convert your answers in **a** to percentages, rounded to the nearest whole number.
   c. Is poverty or a mental illness more likely to make you unhappy?

CASE STUDY (*continued*)

    d. Copy and complete this table of actual numbers, in normal form, of the population:

	Number of people		
	Not happy	Not happy and poor	Not happy and mentally ill
UK Local population			

    Give your answers in normal form, rounded to two significant figures.

    e. Why do the numbers in the last two columns not total the 'Not happy' column?

2. At any one time, how many people are suffering from mental illness in:
    a. the UK
    b. the local area?
    Round your answers to three significant figures.

3. Of those that are mentally ill, work out the percentage of people in the UK who:
    a. receive no treatment
    b. receive treatment
    c. see a psychiatrist/psychologist
    d. receive medication only

> Use the rounded values in question 2.

4. How many mentally ill people:
    a. receive medication only, in the local area
    b. see a psychiatrist/psychologist?

5. a. What is the total annual cost of mental illness?
       Write your answer in millions of pounds
    b. Copy and complete this table:

	Percentage of total costs
Time off work or not working (including cost of carer)	
GP time	
Mental health trusts	
Drugs	
Social services	

    c. What is this total cost as a percentage of GDP?

Assignment questions

1. The table below provides information on how the marketable wealth of this nation is shared between its population:

Percentage most wealthy people	0%	1%	5%	10%	25%	50%
Percentage wealth of the nation	0%	21%	40%	53%	72%	93%

    25% of the wealthiest people own 72% of the nation's wealth.

    a. Plot these values on a graph.
    b. Use the chart to work out:
        i. the percentage of the population who own 80% of its wealth
        ii. the percentage of the nation's wealth owned by the 15% most wealthy people
        iii. the percentage of the nation's wealth owned by the 50% least wealthy people.

2. On Matt's first day in work his boss gives him two choices for his salary. He could either start on £18 000 and get a 5% raise at the end of each year or start on £20 000 and get the same pay rise of £500 at the end of each year.
    a. For both choices, calculate how much Matt will be earning at the start of the:
        i. second year
        ii. fifth year.
    b. Which is the better choice? Explain your answer.

3. Estimate the answers to these calculations by rounding both numbers in each question to one significant figure:
    a. 52% of 71 miles
    b. 9.8% of £59
    c. 19.2% of 48.5 kilograms
    d. 24.4% of £118.20

4. Harry earns £28 910 a year. This year there is to be a 8.6% pay rise.
    Estimate by rounding the two amounts to one significant figure his pay increase.

5. A capacity crowd of 90 000 is watching the FA Cup Final at Wembley Stadium. 20% of the football supporters visit the toilets at half-time.
    a. How many people go to the toilets?
    b. There are 2 620 toilets. Approximately how many people use each toilet? Round your answer to the nearest whole number.

6. 10% of a country's population can't read. Write as a ratio, in its simplest form, the number of people who can read to the number of people who can't.

7. A student chef is making a quiche. The pastry recipe he is using gives the ingredients for one eight inch quiche dish. He only has twelve inch pastry cases.
    a. Work out the amount of each ingredient he should use in order to make 1 quiche.
    b. On another occasion he uses three teaspoons of salt when mixing the pastry. How many quiche dishes is he making?

Pastry ingredients:

8 ounces	Flour
2 ounces	Lard
2 ounces	Butter
$\frac{1}{2}$ teaspoon	Salt
3 tablespoons	Water

8. The Ryan family are planning a week's holiday on a Greek island.
The family consists of two adults and three children.
They intend to hire a car for three days while on holiday.
They have obtained costings from several different sources. These are listed below:

Travel Agents	
'All Inclusive' *{all meals and sundries are paid for}*	£587.50 per adult. There is a 65% reduction off the adult price for the first child and half price for all other children. Car hire is included.
Full Board *{all meals are paid for}*	£427.20 per adult. Each child costs 45% of the adult price. Car hire is a nominal £12 per day.
Bed and Breakfast *{breakfast is paid for}*	£312.60 per adult. The first child costs one quarter of the adult price. The other children cost two thirds of the adult price. Car hire costs £44 per day.

Internet	
{no meals or sundries are paid for}	Plane tickets cost £110 per person. Plus 5% airport tax per ticket. Self catering apartment costs £240 for the week. Car-hire costs £44 per day.

For meals that are not provided they anticipate paying:
£10 for breakfast
£18 for lunch
£28 for an evening meal
(Costs are for the whole family.)

They reckon on paying £15 a day for sundries such as drinks/ice, creams. However, this does not apply to the 'All inclusive' as these are included in the price.

a. Work out the total cost of all four options, rounding your answers to two decimal places.
b. Which is economically the best option?

9. The table below provides information on the CO_2 emissions of four countries:

	Tonnes today	Tonnes in 1990	Tonnes per square kilometre (today)	Tonnes per person (today)
Pakistan	1.3×10^8	71 000 000	160	0.8
Trinidad and Tobago	3.3×10^7	17 000 000	6 300	24
United Kingdom	5.6×10^8	590 000 000	2 300	9
United States	6.0×10^9	5 000 000 000	620	20

Average tonnes per person for the whole world: 0.0042

a. Copy the table but this time do not include the last column but:
  i. Rank the countries in order of total emissions today, the highest first.
  ii. Write the emissions today and in 1990 as millions of tonnes (e.g. 51 million).

▶

Distribution of UK emissions today:

Electricity, gas and water: 46%
Manufacturing industries: 31%
Transport and communications:
    23%

iii. Add a column for the percentage change in emissions between 1990 and today. Write the percentages to the nearest whole number.
iv. Write the tonnes per square kilometre in scientific notation.
v. Replace the final column with a column for population and work out the population size of each country.

b. In which country is C02 pollution most likely to affect your health? Explain your answer.

c. Work out today's CO2 emissions in the UK for:
   i. electricity, gas and water
   ii. manufacturing industries
   iii. transport and communication.
   Give your answer in normal form, rounded to two significant figures.

10. The chart below shows how a hatchback in good condition depreciated with mileage:

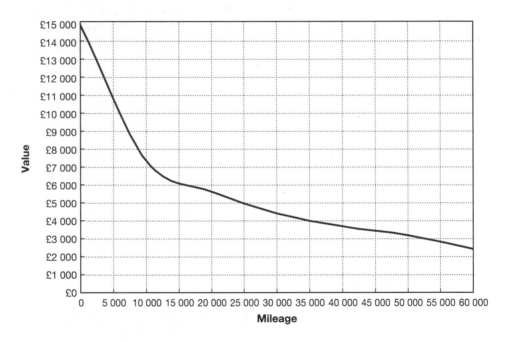

a. What is the value of the car when it has been driven:
   i. 15 000 miles?
   ii. 35 000 miles?
b. A hatchback is being sold for £5 000, what is its probable mileage? Round your answer to the nearest 5 000 miles.
c. By how much does a new hatchback depreciate after it has been driven 10 000 miles? Give your answer in:
   i. pounds, to the nearest £1 000
   ii. as a percentage of the cost of a new car.
d. The value of a new car has depreciated to 20% of its original price. What is its approximate mileage? Round your answer to the nearest 5 000 miles.

11. Complete the cross number:

1	2		3	■	4		5	6
7		■	8	9		■	10	
■		11		■		12		
■	13	·		■	14			■
15		■		16		■		17
18	19		20		21		22	
23				■	24			

Across
1. 2.346×10^3
4. $1.2 \times 10^5 \times 1.44 \times 10^{-2}$
7. Multiple of 6 and 11
8. Increase 320 by 45%
10. One quarter of 168
13. 440 is split in the ratio 8 : 3.
    The larger share
14. 10% of 3 620
18. Double a prime number
20. First three even digits
22. Factor of 132
23. $2 \times 10^5 \times 10^2 \div 10^4$
24. $1.2 \times 10^3 + 2.3 \times 10^3 + 1.4 \times 10^3$

Down
1. $26.3 \div 0.1$
2. A multiple of both 3 and 12
3. $2^2 \times 4^2$
4. Split 35 in the ratio 2 : 3. The smaller share
5. $8 \times 4 + 4 - 6 \times 2$
6. $0.008237 \times 100\,000$, rounded to the nearest whole number
9. Multiple of 3, 4, 5, 6, and 10
11. $2^2 \times 3^4 \times 12^0$
12. Two thirds of 999
15. 200% of 426
16. $(3 + 6) \times 4 - 2 \times 8 + 2 \times 7$
17. 18% of 4 500
19. 8×10^1
20. Four times a prime number
21. Cube of 4
22. One fifth of fifty

Government's daily sensible drinking benchmarks

Men: between three and four units.
Women: between two and three units.

Government's daily heavy drinking benchmarks

Men: over eight units.
Women: over six units.
A pint of lager is just over two units.
A glass of wine is about two units.

12. Here are the results of a survey of 2 948 men and 3 102 women:

	Male	Female
Number exceeding benchmark for sensible drinking on at least one day in the previous week	1 061	651
Number meeting or exceeding the benchmark for heavy drinking on at least one day in the previous week	560	269

As a result of the survey the following report was written:

Are we a nation of drunks?

An extensive survey of 5 450 men and women revealed that 56% of men and 21% of women exceeded the government benchmark for sensible drinking in the week previous to the survey.

More worryingly, nearly one fiftieth of all males can be considered as heavy drinkers compared to only one tenth of women.

▶

   a. Use estimations to check that the figures in the report are correct. If any are incorrect, work out the correct figure, rounding your answers to the nearest whole number.

   b. Work out the total combined percentage of men and women:

     i. exceeding the benchmark for sensible drinking

     ii. exceeding the benchmark for heavy drinking.

Investigation

The diagrams show the amount of disc space available on Rita's and Phil's computers. Phil claims that Rita has 20% less free space than he has. Rita claims that Phil has 25% more free space than she has. Who is right? Both have the same size hard drive. Investigate.

Rita's hard disk   Phil's hard disk

☐ Free space
■ Used space

Group work 1

This article appeared in a local paper:

Cleanliness goes down the plughole at Better Bathrooms.

After preliminary testing it has been discovered that the land around the company Better Bathrooms is heavily contaminated with lead. The council claims there is a strong possibility that this lead will be leaking into the nearby river but are still awaiting test results.

Better Bathrooms, a company that manufactures bathroom furniture, could face a fine of up to £260 000. In a statement, Rebecca Burns, a co-director said 'This is nonsense, we will fight it all the way to the courts, the waste from our factory is clean sand containing no lead. We have been on this site for only ten years, I can't believe the council has not thought of the possibility that the previous owners, a construction waste disposal company, are somewhat to blame!'

However, the council has done its homework:

- Better Bathrooms produce 10 000 kg of enamel every working day. All this enamel is used to cover baths and sinks. The factory operates a five day week and closes for twelve days each year.
- Better Bathrooms reject about 10% of all baths and sinks produced. These pieces are shot blasted to remove the enamel. The blasted off enamel is a fine powdery material that is dumped on site. The pieces are re-enamelled.
- This 'sand' contains 4% lead oxide of which 93% is lead.

▶

Group work (*continued*)

a. Work out the number of days the factory is open a year.
b. Work out the amount of enamel shot-blasted into 'sand' each day.
c. Work out the amount dumped each year of:
  i. 'sand'
  ii. lead oxide
  iii. lead.
d. Do you think Better Bathrooms are guilty?

Group work 2

Alter Ego is an interactive on-line game where players can create virtual characters (known as avatars) and use them to explore what's around them and interact with each other. It represents an idealised version of real life with shopping centres, concert halls, cinemas and museums. Initially, it was the sole domain of computer geeks but over the last few years its membership has grown phenomenally and is now attracting not only individuals but big businesses wanting to develop a presence within Alter Ego.

Land can be bought as fractions of a region.

The cost of this land is:

$\frac{1}{16}$ Region	4 096 square metres	£12
$\frac{1}{8}$ Region	8 192 square metres	£20
$\frac{1}{4}$ Region	16 384 square metres	£35
$\frac{1}{2}$ Region	32 768 square metres	£60
Entire Region	65 536 square metres	£100

Alter Ego pounds (AE£) is the 'local' currency and is used by players to watch a movie, visit an art exhibition, buy property etc.

What Gareth says:

'In real life I work in a bank, but increasingly I'm finding my Alter Ego life is more real to me. I joined two years ago, not to make money but as a fun alternative to the TV.

I soon realised it had great money making potential and now I spend at least four hours a day building up my company. As yet I don't feel secure enough to give up my day job, but the rate at which people are joining makes it a real possibility in the future.'

A virtual life:

Gareth, like other members of the on-line community, has used his avatar, Luther, to build up a business. Luther has created a small property empire, buying virtual land within Alter Ego and then developing it into luxury real estate to sell on.

Group work (*continued*)

Over the last week Luther has bought land and developed it into:

Developed into:

$\frac{1}{2}$ Region   One luxury mansion to be sold for AE£286

Entire Region   Forty luxury apartments each to be sold for AE£44

$\frac{1}{16}$ Region   A nightclub to be sold for AE£180

$\frac{1}{8}$ Region   Four luxury properties each to be sold for AE£78

> **Monthly membership fee for all players: £4.95.**

1. How much has Gareth spent on membership fees over the last two years?
2. Gareth sleeps for 8 hours a day. What fraction of Gareth's waking day does he spend within the Alter Ego community?
3. How much has Gareth spent on land in the last week?
4. What area of land does Gareth own? Give your answer as a mixed fraction of regions.
5. Estimate, by rounding the area of each region to the nearest 1 000 square metres, how much land Gareth owns.
6. If Gareth sells all his properties, how much money, in Alter Ego pounds, will he make?
7. This table shows the rate at which you can sell Alter Ego pounds for real UK pounds:

Alter Ego pounds AE£	0	500	1 000	1 500	2 000	2 500	3 000	3 500
UK pounds £	0	100	200	300	400	500	600	700

> **Profit:**
>
> Amount made on properties **minus** price paid for land

a. Plot the figures in the table as a line on a graph.
b. Use your graph to work out how many UK pounds Gareth will have if he sells all the Alter Ego pounds he makes on his properties. Round your answer to the nearest £100.
c. What will be Gareth's profit (not including membership fees)?

Introduction

Key terms

Statistics
The collecting, organising and analysing of data.

Data
Individual measurement, facts or figures e.g. salaries, ages of students etc.

Representing **data** mathematically is useful as it makes it possible to make comparisons and draw conclusions.

The importance of statistics

Two people were arguing about the reintroduction of the death penalty for the recent murder of a policewoman. Both expressed forceful, but opposing, views on this emotive subject. Although they discussed the issue for over an hour neither was having any impact on the other's opinions. Then the person against the death penalty altered the nature of the argument from one based on a personal viewpoint to one containing scientific analysis by introducing **statistics**. He claimed that in the USA there was a 44% increase in murder rates in death-penalty states compared to non-death penalty states, indicating that the death penalty was not an effective deterrent.

In this case statistics provided convincing evidence to strengthen an argument. It can also be used to help make decisions or validate a piece of scientific research.

TASK

Statistics can also be misleading. In what way could the above statistic be misleading?

An historical view

There are many incidents of statistics being used in history. Florence Nightingale used the persuasive influences of statistics to support her campaign for hospital reform.

In the nineteenth century William Farr provided the impetus for the great sanitary reform movement by providing statistics on childhood mortality rates of the rich compared to the poor.

In the mid twentieth century, Sir Austin Bradford Hill used statistics alone to indisputably prove that smoking greatly increases the risk of contracting lung cancer.

2.1 Statistics Today: Why Is Statistics so Prominent These Days?

The increase in the use of statistics is largely due to the advent of the computer. Software can now crunch large numbers of figures into meaningful statistics in seconds.

The chart shows the increase in yearly spending on statistical research into the student population at a university.

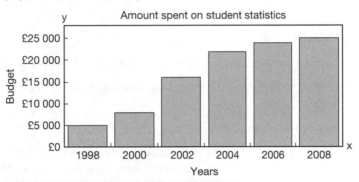

Amount spent on student statistics

Increase in spending between 1998 and 2008:
£25 000 − £5 000 = **£20 000**

In this case, a lot of the laborious slog of collecting and recording the data will be gathered at the beginning and end of a student's life, on enrolment and on receiving a qualification.

The money could be used to investigate:

- ages of students on enrolment;
- the ratio of males to females on courses;
- number of students enrolled on a course compared to the number who successfully complete the course;
- why students chose to study at the university;
- future enrolment numbers.

Discussion

By providing examples, explore how statistics could be used within the following institutions:

- hospital
- police station
- Premiership football team
- supermarket.

Group task

Statistics are used to justify everything from government policy to the health of the nation, from natural sciences to social sciences.

In groups, select one national newspaper and count how many times statistics are used on the front page.

Collate the figures of all groups.

The use and misuse of statistics

> 'There are three kinds of lies: lies, damned lies and statistics.'
> – Disraeli

It is important that we have an understanding of statistics, not only because our society is littered with them – did you know that the average person is assailed with at least six statistics a day?* But because statistics are such a powerful tool, often playing a significant role in decision making, sometimes people are tempted to misuse them.

This section will help you determine if someone is trying to pull a fast one – like the one above (*).

> Because most people have a limited understanding of statistics it is easy for those with an agenda to cherry-pick statistical measures in order to support their viewpoint.

Example

Within an advertisement, a tyre manufacturer promotes their tyres stating:

> 'Statistics have proven you are less likely to have an accident with these types of tyres.'

Quite a powerful argument.

However, on deeper investigation, to date, the tyres were only fitted to brand new cars. All the data used in the survey came from new cars which are less likely to have accidents (not necessarily because of the tyres!)

> **Group task**
>
> Use the web to investigate how statistics were used in the Sally Clarke court case on cot deaths, stating why the figures used by the prosecution were misleading
>
> **or**
>
> Investigate another legal court battle where statistics were misused to convince a jury.

The importance of gathering sound data

Not only can statistics be misused but the process of getting the data can result in biased figures. To check the validity of a survey you need to think about:

> **Key terms**
>
> **Questionnaire**
> A set of written questions used to gather data on individuals.

1. **Who is asking the questions and will they be looking for a particular outcome from the survey?**

2. **What are the questions being asked in the questionnaire?**
   Are the questions in some way biased, for example, a question on people's opinion on banning smoking in pubs could be:
   'In your opinion, should people have the freedom of choice to smoke whilst relaxing in a pub?'

or

'In your opinion, should people tolerate passive smoking whilst relaxing in a pub?'
Each of these questions will provide a distinctly different set of results.

3. Is the sample data representative?

If you are doing a survey on the eating habits of the British people you shouldn't base your study just on the people in London.

4. How many are in the survey?

For a survey to be credible there must be a reasonable number of people answering the questionnaire to prevent it being an unrepresentative sample. How large is 'large enough' depends on the variability of the data. For example, if age is an issue then the sample must be large enough to represent the variety of ages within the **population**.

5. How are the questions being asked (sampling method)?

Face-to-face, over the phone, online, postal questionnaire, a focus group etc. For example, being stopped by a person in a shopping centre armed with a clipboard and a series of questions is a face to face interview whereas a pop-up questionnaire on the web is an online survey.

Some of these methods may obtain more reliable responses than others.

6. Are there any technical errors?

A school may be promoting their good results in comparison to other local schools. But this may be because the school is selective and so the academic level is generally higher. A better comparison might be to look at the general improvement of the pupils in each school.

> **Key terms**
>
> **Sample data**
> A representative proportion of the population under investigation.
>
> **Population**
> All the people under investigation.
>
> **Sampling method**
> How the data is collected.

Example of a biased survey

A large supermarket chain is seeking planning permission for a shop on the outskirts of a small market town in the Midlands. To support its application for planning the supermarket chain submitted the results of a survey it had recently carried out. The results appeared overwhelmingly supportive:

> **What the local population think about a new supermarket**
>
> 82% of the people questioned thought they would use the new supermarket.
>
> 66% thought the supermarket would provide more jobs.
>
> 79% thought the supermarket would be better for the environment.

The survey was undertaken outside a nearby jobcentre.

The sample size was extremely small. Here are the questions asked to obtain the results:

> **Questionnaire on the proposed new supermarket**
>
> 1. Do you think you would shop at the supermarket in its first year?
>
> 2. Do you, like the majority of people, think the building of a new supermarket will provide new jobs?
>
> 3. The nearest competitor is over 10 miles away. Do you think it is better for the environment for local people to shop at their local supermarket?

The local council's unbiased survey

To obtain a true picture of local people's opinion on the proposed supermarket plans the council could simply send out a postal questionnaire to all houses in the region. The problem here is the response rate is likely to be very poor and replies may be dominated by those with strong views and so won't provide a representative sample.

Despite the expense, the council opted for face to face interviewing as it tends to achieve a high response rate and fewer questions go unanswered.

A good cross-section can be assured by using a large sample size and quotas that reflect the population of the region. For instance, interviewers may be asked to select fifty men and fifty women over the age of 60, seventy men and seventy women between the ages of 45 and 60 etc.

All interviewers used are trained to be unbiased in the manner in which they ask questions.

> **Questionnaire on the proposed new supermarket**
>
> 1. Do you think the region will benefit from a new supermarket?
>
> 2. Do you think the building of a new supermarket will increase long term employment in the area?
>
> 3. Do you think it will bring any advantages to the environment, e.g. shoppers using their car less?

Paired work

1. Improve these questions by making them unbiased or clearer:
    a. If there was an election tomorrow, who would you vote Labour or Conservative?
    b. Have you eaten at a restaurant recently?
    c. Most people think education is failing our children. Do you agree with this?
    d. Are you against a ban on children in pubs?
    e. Do you use Orange or Virgin network for your mobile phone?

2. Which of these surveys would result in biased data? Provide reasons for your answers.
    a. A survey was undertaken outside a pet shop asking whether it is cruel to keep animals as pets.
    b. Students were asked what they thought of their course at a graduation ceremony.
    c. A list of the ages of pregnant women from a hospital database.
    d. A survey of the number of people visiting an art show on a Monday morning to discover the average weekly attendance at the show.
    e. The ages of people fined for speeding offences. The data being obtained from the DVLA.

Group task 1

The government has recently introduced a policy allowing the police to demand on-the-spot fines for people who drop litter. It wants statistics to prove that the policy is effective.

- Create a biased survey, taking into account the factors previously mentioned.
- Write down a question that could be used in the survey, stating how they will be asked and who will be asked.
- How would you improve your survey to make it unbiased?

Group task 2

For the scenarios below state:

- the sampling method, providing reasons for your choice
- who you would survey in order to obtain an unbiased survey.

1. The government has commissioned a survey on the ages of students on ACCESS courses.
2. The Administration at the University wishes to carry out a survey on the parking requirements of students attending the university.
3. The company Iceberg is in the business of producing and selling frozen meat products. It is concerned that eating of meat is in decline and would like to carry out a survey to establish that eating meat is a healthy (or otherwise) option.
4. Cancer Research has commissioned a survey to ascertain whether there has been an increase in breast cancer over the last 10 years.
5. A survey to discover the modes of transport students use to get to college.
6. The Royal Society for the Protection of Birds wants to determine if sparrows are on the decline in UK gardens.

Questions used in questionnaires

Key terms

'Closed' question
Respondents can answer the question in a limited number of ways, often from a list.

A survey was undertaken to discover people's opinion on the most significant event in the last century. A **'closed' question** was asked, in that people had to select an option from a list. The results were:

Most significant in invention:

Atomic power	17%
Penicillin	35%
Computer	24%
Television	13%
Don't know	11%

But an important issue was missed from the list of options – 'The web'. When the survey was repeated with this extra entry the results were very different:

Most significant in invention:

Atomic power	7%
Penicillin	19%
Computer	11%
Television	6%
The Web	54%
Don't know	3%

Closed questions can miss out important issues, but you can easily do Maths on them (as has been performed above).

Open questions mean there is no pre-defined list of options so a wide range of answers will be obtained, but this can make analysis harder.

Work it out – comparing open and closed questions

1. A mobile phone company intends to improve the features of their phone while retaining those that are important to their users. They asked a number of people the question:

> **Mobile Phone Questionnaire**
>
> What do you most like about your mobile phone?

    a. How would *you* answer the question?
    b.   i. Provide an alternative closed question.
        ii. In this case, is one question better than the other and why?

2. The holiday company Holidays4You asked customers to complete a questionnaire on the last day of their holiday. Here are some of the questions:

> **HOLIDAYS4YOU QUESTIONNAIRE**
>
> 1. What did you enjoy most about your holiday?
> 2. What did you enjoy least about the holiday?
> 3. What is your opinion on the cost of the holiday?
> 4. What did you think of your accommodation?
> 5. How did you hear about the holiday?
> 6. Would you use Holidays4You again?

    a. What is the purpose of the survey?
    b. Why would the data from this survey be difficult to analyse?
    c. Rewrite your own questionnaire so that the data can more readily be analysed.

2.2 Charting Data

Once the data has been collected it can be transformed into useful information in the form of a chart. How data is transformed depends on how it is classified.

Key terms

Discrete data
Data that can be categorised so that there are distinct intervals between any two values. The data is often obtained by counting and is usually whole numbers.

Continuous data
Data that can be any value, including decimals or fractions, often obtained by measuring.

Discrete data

Usually data is **discrete** if it can be counted, for example, the number of:

- puppies in a litter
- people who watch EastEnders
- TVs owned by each household
- shoe size (here there can be halves, but because all the values between the halves and whole numbers are meaningless the data is discrete).

Continuous data

Continuous data is often obtained by measuring. All values between whole numbers have meaning, for example the:

- speed of cars on a motorway
- level of carbon monoxide pollution in towns and cities
- weights of newborn babies
- length of feet.

Task

State whether the following data is discrete or continuous:

a. type of mobile phone people own
b. weight of individuals
c. age of undergraduates
d. type of holiday people go on
e. mode of transport students use to get to university
f. newspaper people read
g. height of trees in a wood
h. dress size.

Example 1

A group of ACCESS students were asked what subject they intended to study as an undergraduate. These were the results:

Computing	Business Studies	Combined Studies	Computing	Media Studies
Education	Nursing	None	Education	Nursing
Media Studies	Education	Combined Studies	Health Studies	Health Studies
Education	Education	Health Studies	Combined Studies	Health Studies
Education	Nursing	Business Studies	None	Combined Studies
Business Studies	Computing	Nursing	Business Studies	None
Health Studies	Computing	Health Studies	Nursing	Health Studies
Combined Studies	Health Studies	Nursing	Nursing	Business Studies

1. How many students are in the survey?

> **40** – simply count the number of answers

2. Is the data discrete or continuous?

> **Discrete** – the data can be split into distinct categories e.g. Computing etc.

Key term

Frequency table
This is a table that summarises the data. It records the number of people within a particular category or group.

3. Create a **frequency table** for the data:

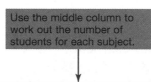

> Use the middle column to work out the number of students for each subject.

Key symbol

I Represents one person.
IIII Represents five people.

Subject	Tally	Number of Students
Computing	IIII	4
Business Studies	IIII	5
Combined Studies	IIII	5
Education	IIII I	6
Health Studies	IIII III	8
Nursing	IIII II	7
Media Studies	II	2
None	III	3
Total		**40**

> The largest value in the final column is 8 on a chart so the scale on the vertical axis could extend to the rounded value of 10.

Note: The subjects can be placed in any order.

4. Draw a **bar chart**.

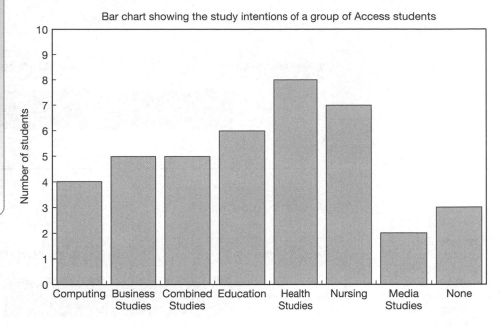

Bar chart showing the study intentions of a group of Access students

Example 2

A number of keen football fans were asked how many live matches they attended last season. The results are shown in the table:

2	12	20	32	45	52	54	8
23	22	19	8	6	42	12	22
2	23	20	10	18	44	14	19
1	28	28	12	21	42	18	15
12	24	32	37	27	35	22	8

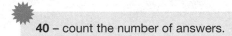

This fan attended 27 matches.

1. How many fans are in the survey?

   40 – count the number of answers.

2. Is the data discrete or continuous?

   Discrete – the figures are obtained by counting. The values between the whole numbers are meaningless, for example fans can't attend $4\frac{1}{2}$ matches.

▶

3. Create a frequency table for the data:

We could simply create a table like the one below:

Number of matches	Tally	Number of fans
1		
2		
6		
etc.		
Total		**40**

The problem here is there is too much information and the resulting chart would be very confusing.

Key term

Grouping data
Preferably there ought to be 4–8 groups in each frequency table. The groups should always be of the same size.

The data can be **grouped** in 5s:

Number of matches	Tally	Number of fans
1–5		
6–10		
11–15		
etc . . .		
Total		**40**

The problem here is that because the groups are small there is still too much information and the ensuing chart would be confusing.

The data can be grouped in 20s:

Number of matches	Tally	Number of fans
0–20		
21–40		
41–60		
Total		**40**

The problem here is that information can be lost when the groups are too large.

Ideally the data is grouped in 10s:

Number of matches	Tally	Number of fans
0–10	‖‖ ‖‖ ‖	8
11–20	‖‖ ‖‖ ‖	12
21–30	‖‖ ‖‖	10
31–40	‖‖	4
41–50	‖‖	4
51–60	‖	2
Total		**40**

4. Draw a **histogram**.

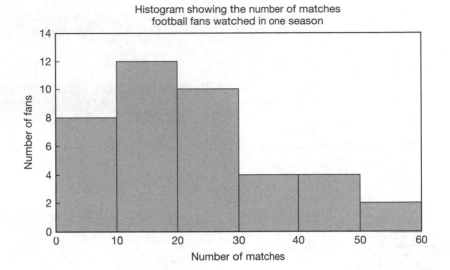

Histogram showing the number of matches
football fans watched in one season

Example 3

A survey was undertaken to work out why children under 5 didn't know common nursery rhymes. The parents of 3 and 4 year olds were asked how long their child watched TV every day (including Playstation etc.). The results of the survey are shown below:

2	0.5	2	3.25	4	4.5	7	2.25	3.5	1.5
3.25	2	2.5	4.75	3.25	8.5	8.75	6.5	5	6.75
6	7.25	8.25	2.75	3	5.5	8	8.5	9	4.75
3	2.75	6	4.5	4	6	7	7.5	2.75	9.25
3.5	3.75	4.5	5	2.75	3.75	5	2	1.75	1

a. How many children are in the survey?

50

b. Is the data discrete or continuous?

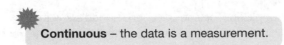

Continuous – the data is a measurement.

▶

c. Create a frequency table for the data.

The data can be grouped:

Time in hours	Tally	Number of toddlers
1–2		
3–4		
5–6		
7–8		
9–10		
Total		

7–8 means all the toddlers who spend between 7 and 8 hours watching TV. The problem here is where do you put 8.25 etc.?

Much better is:

To understand the symbols read from the centre out:
4 < Time ≤ 6
Time is greater than 4 hours, but less than or equal to 6 hours.

Time in hours	Tally	Number of toddlers
0 < time ≤ 2	ⵏⵏⵏ ⵏⵏⵏ	8
2 < time ≤ 4	ⵏⵏⵏ ⵏⵏⵏ ⵏⵏⵏ ⵏⵏ	17
4 < time ≤ 6	ⵏⵏⵏ ⵏⵏⵏ ⵏⵏ	12
6 < time ≤ 8	ⵏⵏⵏ ⵏⵏ	7
8 < time ≤ 10	ⵏⵏⵏ ⵏ	6
Total		**50**

Key symbols

> greater than
  e.g. 6 > 4
≥ greater than or
  equal to
< less than
  e.g. 5 < 9
≤ less than or
  equal to

d. Chart the data:

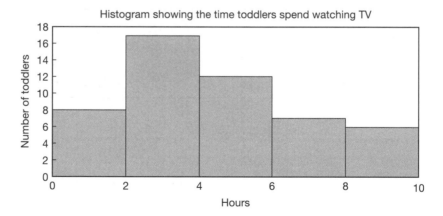

Histogram showing the time toddlers spend watching TV

e. Is there anything wrong with this survey?

It is too simplistic. The number of hours toddlers watch TV may have nothing to do with how many nursery rhymes they know. Further research is required.

Mapping it out

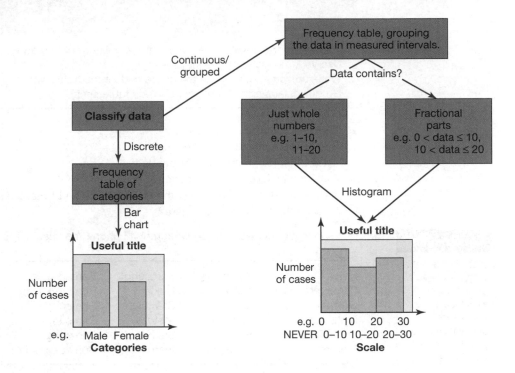

Work it out

1. State which of the following are correct:
   a. $6 > 8$
   b. $8 < 9$
   c. $5 \leq 4$
   d. $7 \leq 7$
   e. $4 < 4$
   f. $8 \geq 11$

2. Choose one of the following figures {2, 8, 10, 0} to complete the inequalities:
   a. $6 > \square$
   b. $\square \leq 9$
   c. $\square \geq 2$
   d. $7 > \square$
   e. $4 > \square$
   f. $\square \leq 0$

3. Use either the symbols > or < or the numbers 3, 120 or 52 to complete the blank squares:
   a. $2 \quad \square \quad 6 > \square < 10 \quad \square \quad 20$
   b. $110 < \square > \square > 40 \quad \square \quad 100$
   c. $2 < \square < 8 > \square > 1$

4. A number of people were asked the closed question:

   'If, in the middle of the night, you awoke to the sound of strange noises coming from downstairs, what would you do?'   ▶

The results are shown in the table:

Options	Number of people
Hide under the duvet in the hope that the noise would go away.	17
Use your mobile to phone the police.	22
Wake up somebody else in the house and let them deal with it.	19
Go downstairs armed with your bedside table lamp.	6

a. How many people took part in the survey?

b. Is the data discrete or continuous?

c. Draw an appropriate chart for the data.

d. Can you think of a missing option?

e. Ask fellow students to answer the question and chart these results.

f. How do the two charts compare?

5. In a survey people were asked what mobile phone they used. The results were:

Nokia	Samsung	Samsung	Samsung	Motorola
Samsung	Nokia	Nokia	Sony Eriksson	Sony Eriksson
Siemens	Siemens	Siemens	Samsung	Motorola
Motorola	Motorola	Motorola	Samsung	Motorola
Sony Eriksson	Siemens	Siemens	Samsung	Motorola
Motorola	Siemens	Siemens	Sony Eriksson	Motorola

Hints and tips

When creating the frequency table, strike through each type of phone with a different coloured pen. Then count the numbers.

a. How many people took part in the survey?

b. Is the data discrete or continuous?

c. Create a frequency table of the data.

d. Draw an appropriate chart for the data.

6. A number of people were asked to select from a list who they thought had 'made Britain great'. The results were:

Churchill	Nelson	Wellington
Richard the Lion Heart	Churchill	Sir Walter Raleigh
Churchill	Nelson	Queen Victoria
Queen Victoria	Sir Walter Raleigh	Churchill
Queen Victoria	Churchill	Nelson
Churchill	Richard the Lion Heart	Nelson
Churchill	Wellington	Churchill
Churchill	Churchill	Nelson
Wellington	Churchill	Sir Walter Raleigh
Nelson	Nelson	Sir Walter Raleigh

a. How many people took part in the survey?

b. Is the data discrete or continuous?

c. Draw an appropriate chart for the data.

7. The table below shows the number of people who voted in four elections:

General Election	23 million
Strictly Come Dancing	22 million
Celebrity Big Brother	25 million
Eurovision Song Contest	12 million

   a. Draw an appropriate chart for the data.
   b. Comment on the chart.

8. Over the period of a week midwives recorded the length of labour for several women. Here are the results in hours:

2.5	12.5	7	8.5	14.5	7.5	22.5	29	18.5	3.5
8	10.5	9.5	14.5	27	2	22	19.5	15	6
19.5	7	8	20.5	4.5	2	12.5	19	1	20

   a. The data will need to be grouped. Select the best grouping, stating why you rejected the other groups:

   i.

   ```
   0–10
   11–20
   21–30
   etc. . . .
   ```

   ii.

   ```
   0–5
   5–10
   10–15
   etc. . . .
   ```

   iii.

   ```
   0 < time ≤ 20
   20 < time ≤ 30
   30 < time ≤ 40
   ```

   iv.

   ```
   0 < time < 10
   10 < time < 20
   20 < time < 30
   ```

   v.

   ```
   0 < time ≤ 5
   5 < time ≤ 10
   10 < time ≤ 15
   etc. . . .
   ```

   vi.

   ```
   0 < time ≤ 10
   10 < time ≤ 20
   20 < time ≤ 30
   ```

   b. Create a grouped frequency table.
   c. Draw an appropriate chart for the data.
   d. Comment on the chart.

9. A group of people were asked to name as many TV celebrities as they could within one minute. The numbers were recorded:

2	6	14	12	25	8	42	23
9	28	11	8	18	3	1	28
8	31	3	16	23	30	9	5
21	12	36	8	44	19	39	14

a. How many people took part in the survey?
b. Is the data discrete or continuous?
c. Create a grouped frequency table.
d. Draw an appropriate chart for the data.
e. What can you conclude from the chart?

10. A survey was carried out to discover how much students on an academic course spent on course text books in one term. The results are shown in the table:

£50	£25	£36	£14	£18	£32	£44	£27	£15	£14
£12	£22	£67	£51	£63	£29	£52	£39	£19	£31
£19	£35	£37	£56	£31	£30	£47	£25	0	£45
£10	£19	£58	£29	£32	£19	£52	£36	£8	£12
£29	£33	£43	£31	£36	£23	£45	0	0	£28

a. How many people are in the survey?
b. Is the data discrete or continuous?
c. Create a grouped frequency table.
d. Draw an appropriate chart for the data.

11. A Web Design company investigated how many hours their employees actually worked on a computer during a week in January 2009. These are the results, in hours:

21.5	4	22	22	12.5	32	31	28.25	13	18.75
12.25	13.5	20	10	22.25	28	30	8.5	32	34.25
28	23	30	8	12	18.5	19	23.25	4	4
30	16	18.25	33	28	29	19	20	27	31.5
22	15.25	14.75	27.25	33	29.75	25	7	11	26
26	28.75	6	24	19.5	28	31	24.25	18.5	25.5

a. How many employees took part in the survey?
b. Create a grouped frequency table.
c. Display the data as a histogram.
d. Comment on the chart.

Investigation

The histogram below shows the number of days spent away from home in one year by a group of people:

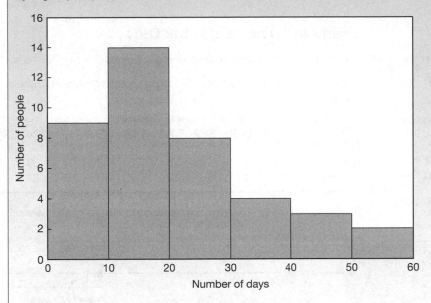

a. Work out the number of people in the survey.
b. Create the grouped frequency table for the chart.

Project

Create a mini-questionnaire to find out how many hours people on your course work, in paid employment each week, and what type of work they are employed in (you will need to provide a list of options).

Use an open question to determine how they are balancing their course work and other commitments.

a. Ask 15 people to complete your questionnaire.
b. Produce two frequency tables to summarise the data.
c. Draw two charts displaying the data.
d. Comment on all your results.

2.3 Frequency Polygons

Example 1 The rise of the DVD

Key term

Frequency polygons
Line charts, often used when comparing two or more sets of discrete or continuous data. The chart describes the 'shape' of the data.

A shop renting and selling films keeps a record of its performance.

The table shows the sales of DVDs compared to rentals (in thousands) since 1998 (year ending):

	1998	1999	2000	2001	2002	2003	2004	2005	2006	2007	2008
DVD sales	1	3	4	5	11	17	24	38	55	96	108
DVD rentals	12	19	30	52	70	75	69	67	61	58	50

a. On the same graph draw a **frequency polygon** of the two sets of data.

The biggest value in the table is 108 thousand, so the axis extends to the rounded figure of 110 thousand.

Key is essential

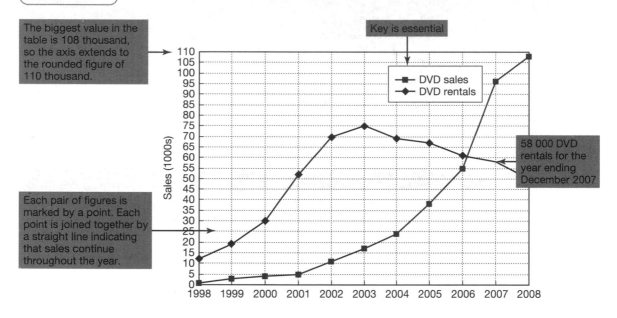

58 000 DVD rentals for the year ending December 2007

Each pair of figures is marked by a point. Each point is joined together by a straight line indicating that sales continue throughout the year.

b. When did DVD sales rise most quickly?

During the year of 2007 – the line is at its steepest.

c. In which year did the DVD sales become greater than the DVD rentals?

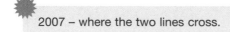

2007 – where the two lines cross.

d. Below are the figures for the rental of videos from the shop. Add the data to the chart:

	1998	1999	2000	2001	2002	2003	2004	2005	2006	2007	2008
Videos rentals	89	88	76	75	64	55	45	22	18	8	6

Summing it up:

Total sales/rentals of all films:
1998: (1 + 12 + 89)
= 102
thousand
2008: (108 + 50 + 6)
= 164
thousand
We're watching a lot more films these days!

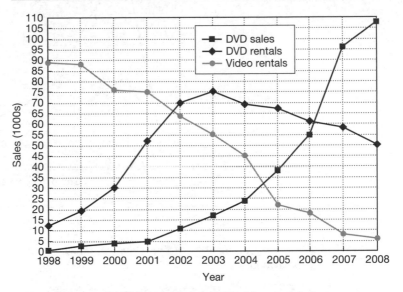

e. In what year did DVD rentals overtake video rentals?

2002 – where the two lines cross.

Example 2 Who is more law abiding?

Statistics of the recorded crime for one year as a percentage of the population has been separated by both age and gender in the table:

	Males	Females
0 < age ≤ 10	0%	0%
10 < age ≤ 20	5.5%	1.9%
20 < age ≤ 30*	4%	1.2%
30 < age ≤ 40	1.8%	0.8%
40 < age ≤ 50	1%	0.3%
50 < age ≤ 60	0.5%	0.1%
60 < age ≤ 70	0.3%	0%
over 70	0.1%	0%

* Between the ages of twenty and thirty 4% of the male population commit crimes compared to 1.2% of females.

▶

Charting this data

A chart plots a thousand figures.

The chart illustrates the data in a manner figures just can't match.

A point is plotted at the midpoint of each group: 5.5% of males between 10 and 20 years is plotted at 15 along and 5.5 up.

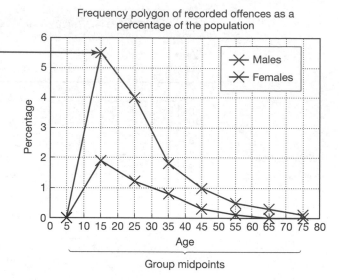

Frequency polygon of recorded offences as a percentage of the population

---

Work it out

1. The average life expectancy of the entire population of the world is compared to that of Botswana:

	1975	1980	1985	1990	1995	2000	2005	2010	2015	2020	2025
World	59	61	62	63	64	65	66	67	69	70	72
Botswana	54	58	61	60	48	38	35	39	45	50	53

   a. Plot the two sets of data as frequency polygons on the same chart
   b. What reasons can you give for the shape of Botswana's polygon?

2. Here is an extract from a newspaper article:

   Frequency polygons can be used effectively with just one set of data.

   a. There are too many figures here which may not keep the attention of the reader. Replace the figures with a frequency polygon.
   b. Between what two consecutive years did the distance increase the most?
   c. What are your conclusions about the rat population of London?

   Is London becoming another Hamelin?
   Do Londoners require the services of the Pied Piper? Here are the statistics to help you make up your mind.

   Average distance a person is from a rat at any one time!

2000	14 m
2001	12 m
2002	11 m
2003	10 m
2004	10 m
2005	15 m
2006	18 m
2007	19 m
2008	21 m

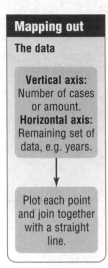

Mapping out

The data

Vertical axis:
Number of cases
or amount.
Horizontal axis:
Remaining set of
data, e.g. years.

Plot each point
and join together
with a straight
line.

3. A newly graduated fashion designer starts her own business in January 2000. At the end of each year she recorded her income, the money coming into the business from the sale of her clothes and her expenses, the money going out of the business to pay for wages, advertising, fuel bills etc. Here is the table of these figures:

Year ending	2001	2002	2003	2004	2005	2006	2007	2008
Income	18 000	22 000	25 000	26 000	29 000	30 000	30 000	33 000
Expenses	27 000	24 000	26 000	24 000	25 000	22 000	18 000	21 000

   a. Draw two frequency polygons of the data on the same chart.
   b. In what year did the business break even (income is the same as expenditure)?
   c. In what year did income rise the most rapidly?
   d. Profit = Income − Expenses.
     In what two years were the profits exactly the same?
   e. Work out the profits for each year and add this data to the chart as a third frequency polygon.

The changing face of students

4.   a. At a university the age of students at the start of their first year was recorded in 1967/68 and compared with 40 years later. Here are the results:

	1966/1967 (%)	2007/2008 (%)
10 < Age ≤ 20	89	54
20 < Age ≤ 30	8	24
30 < Age ≤ 40	2	12
40 < Age ≤ 50	1	7
50 < Age ≤ 60	0	2
60 < Age ≤ 70	0	1

     i. Create one chart for both frequency polygons.
    ii. What are your conclusions?

▶

Where will zero hours be plotted?

If the groups are

0 < Time ≤ 5,

5 < Time ≤ 10,

then the group is

–5 < Time ≤ 0

If there are 30 people with a time of zero hours then 30 will be plotted at the midpoint –2.5

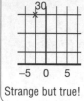

Strange but true!

Mapping out

Grouped data:

Vertical axis:
Number of cases or amount.
Horizontal axis:
Start at the first value of the first group and extend to the final value in of the final group.

↓

Plot each point in the middle of the group
e.g. If there are 2 people in the group 30 < Age ≤ 40 then mark a point at 35 along and 2 up.

↓

Use a ruler to join each point.

b. Another survey investigated how many hours students work in paid employment whilst studying as undergraduates:

Hours in paid work each week	1967/1968	2007/2008
None	30	8
0 < Time ≤ 5	7	6
5 < Time ≤ 10	2	7
10 < Time ≤ 15	1	9
15 < Time ≤ 20	0	5
25 < Time ≤ 30	0	2
30 < Time ≤ 35	0	3

i.   Draw one chart for both frequency polygons.

ii. What are your conclusions?

About technology

5. a. Two groups of people, all using the same spam protection software, were asked how many spam e-mails they receive each week.

First Group: People who use the web for e-shopping.

64	45	27	56	78	52	63	44	32	64
68	58	69	38	44	56	79	20	28	68
67	42	52	77	68	70	88	58	98	67
49	78	98	89	88	68	88	94	87	49

Second Group: People who rarely use the web for e-shopping.

4	1	10	8	25	12	15	18	5	4
4	21	11	8	9	11	14	16	22	4
3	4	4	1	1	6	6	7	8	3
12	5	6	1	31	10	6	11	9	12

i.   Create a grouped frequency table for both groups.

ii.   Plot both frequency polygons on the same chart

iii. What conclusion can you draw?

Hints and tips

Use the same grouping for both sets of data.

Potential pitfalls

When choosing the grouping avoid groups such as:
11–20, 21–30
as the midpoints will be 15.5, 25.5.
Much better:
$10 < \text{Data} \leq 20$,
$20 < \text{Data} \leq 30$
where the midpoints are 15, 25 etc.

b. A group of 14 year olds were asked: 'How many of the following Web words do you comprehend?'

Blog	Cyberspace	Burning	E-mail	USB port
Cookie	Posting	Chatroom	Encryption	JPEG
Uploading	Dithering	Bot	Wi Fi	Burning
Ripping	Virus	Byte	Shareware	Hacker
Wiki	Forum	Firewall	Browser	HTML

The results out of 25 were:

5	16	10	25	12	22	12	22	20	25
9	14	4	13	18	7	6	23	19	23
14	25	20	5	22	23	18	15	19	9

i.   Create a grouped frequency table for the data.

ii. Draw a frequency polygon.

iii. Ask 30 fellow students to answer the same question. Add this to your table and draw another frequency polygon on your chart.
     If you are unable to ask as many as 30 students, how can you compare the two sets of data on the same chart?

Investigation 1

A small survey was undertaken to compare 'eating out' habits in the UK and USA. Here are the charted results:

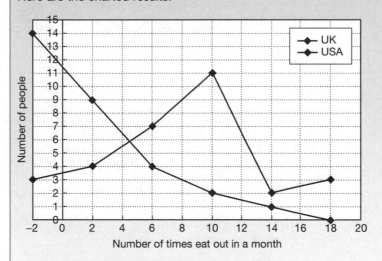

1. Use the chart to work out how many people took part in the survey in each country.

2. To obtain this chart the data was grouped.

    a. Create the original frequency table that was used to construct the chart.

    b. Why are there values at –2?

    c. Comment on the chart.

Investigation 2

The chart below shows the amount of vigorous exercise undertaken by two groups of people in one week:

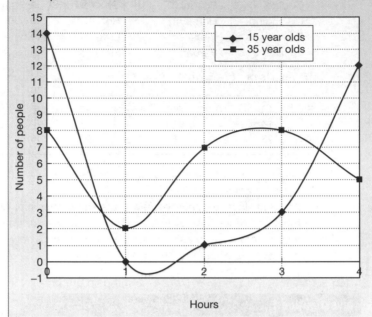

Here is the frequency table used to create the chart:

Amount of vigorous exercise each week	15 year olds	35 year olds
None	14	8
0 < hours ≤ 1	0	2
1 < hours ≤ 2	1	7
2 < hours ≤ 3	3	8
3 < hours ≤ 4	12	5

1. What's wrong with the chart?
2. Draw a correct frequency polygon for the two sets of data.
3. Comment on your chart.

2.4 Pictograms

Pictograms can be effectively used to display data without looking too mathematical.

Example

In order to raise the public awareness on how far products have flown to get onto our shop shelves, a government intends to make compulsory the displaying of the number of airmiles every food product has flown. They will use an aeroplane to symbolise 1 000 miles:

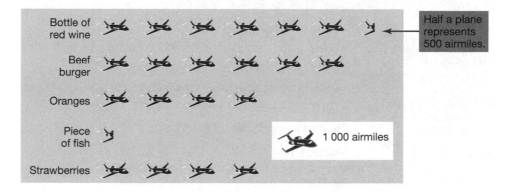

a. How many airmiles did the strawberries travel?

> There are 4 plane symbols, therefore the number of airmiles = **4 000**

b. How many airmiles did the red wine travel?

> There are $6\frac{1}{2}$ plane symbols, therefore the number of airmiles = **6 500**

c. If your shopping basket contained a piece of fish, a box of strawberries and a packet of beef burgers, what would the total airmiles be?

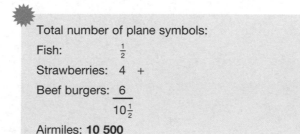

> Total number of plane symbols:
> Fish: $\frac{1}{2}$
> Strawberries: 4 +
> Beef burgers: 6
> ─────
> $10\frac{1}{2}$
> Airmiles: **10 500**

Work it out

1. The pictogram shows the approximate carbon dioxide emissions each year:

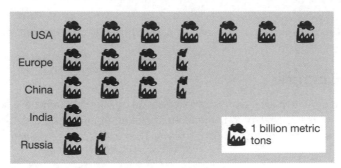

   a. What are the carbon dioxide emissions of Europe?
   b. How much more carbon dioxide does the USA emit compared to Russia?
   c. What are the total emissions for all five countries?

2. A national newspaper rates films from 0 to 5, 5 being a 'must see' film and 0 'don't go even if it's free with a bottle of wine'.

   The ratings are shown for the films:

Casino Royale	5
Click	3
The Reef	1
The Queen	5

   Using your own symbol, draw a pictogram of the ratings.

3. At the end of a package holiday to Spain holiday makers were asked to complete a 'customer satisfaction' form giving ratings out of 10 (10 being 'excellent', 0 being 'never again'). Their average scores are listed below:

Location	9
Food	6
Room	4
Facilities	7

   Display this information as a pictogram.

2.5 Drawing Angles

Metric angle

After the French revolution the leaders wanted to break away from the traditions of the past. One of their proposals was that a right angle should be 100 degrees. This system of measuring was briefly introduced and the military used it for decades. Today it is still occasionally employed by surveyors.

Why 360°? Why not a nice round number like 100? Blame the Babylonians. Their ancient astronomers noted that it took about 360 days for the sun to complete a year's circuit. Consequently they divided a circular path into 360 degrees, a degree being the space or distance travelled by the sun each day.

360° was originally applied to the Zodiac where one sign represents a month.

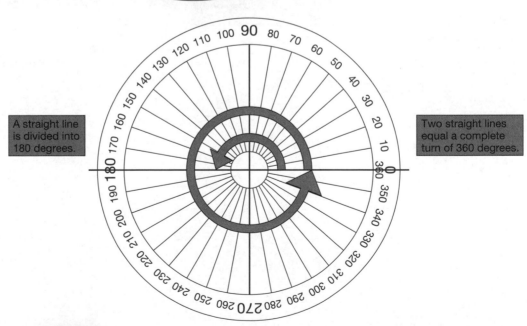

A straight line is divided into 180 degrees.

Two straight lines equal a complete turn of 360 degrees.

How large is one degree? ——————————————— = 1°

Measuring angles using a protractor

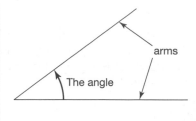

arms

The angle

Place the protractor over one arm of the angle:

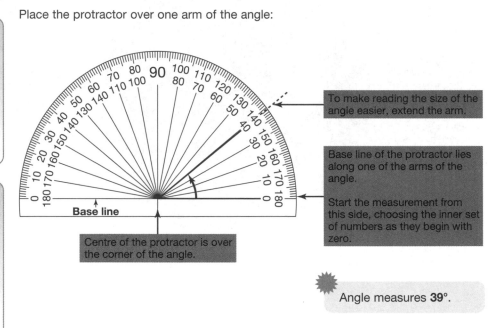

Base line

To make reading the size of the angle easier, extend the arm.

Base line of the protractor lies along one of the arms of the angle.

Start the measurement from this side, choosing the inner set of numbers as they begin with zero.

Centre of the protractor is over the corner of the angle.

Angle measures **39°**.

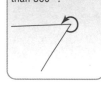

Paired work – drawing and measuring angles

Task 1

- Without your partner seeing, draw two acute and two obtuse angles.
- Give them to your partner for measuring.
- Check the answers.

Task 2

Draw the following angles and ask your partner to check them:

a. 32°

b. 104°

c. 167°

d. 88°

Task 3

Measure and name the following angles:

a.

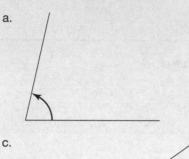

b.

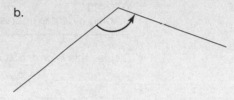

c.

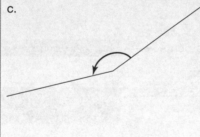

d.

e.

f.

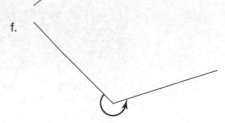

2.6 Pie Charts

Key term

Pie chart
A circular chart that displays data as slices of pie. The bigger the proportion of data the bigger the slice of pie.

Pie charts are useful when showing how the sample data is divided into its parts or slices of pie.

Example

ACCESS students were asked what they were intending to do next year. Here are the results:

Continuing with the ACCESS to HE programme	32
Don't know	5
Working	20
Starting a degree course	63

Display this information as a pie chart:

Mapping it out

Total in survey:

$32 + 5 + 20 + 63 =$ **120 students** ← 1. Total numbers in survey.

Each person is represented:

$360° ÷ 120 =$ **3°** ← 2. Calculate the angle per person:

$360° ÷$ **total in survey (ans. 1)**

	Number of students	Angle Number of students × Angle per person
Continuing with the ACCESS to HE programme	32	$32 × 3 =$ **96°**
Don't know	5	$5 × 3 =$ **15°**
Working	20	$20 × 3 =$ **60°**
Starting a degree course	63	$63 × 3 =$ **189°**
Total	**120**	**360°**

3. Calculate the angle for each category:

no. people in each category × angle per person (ans. 2)

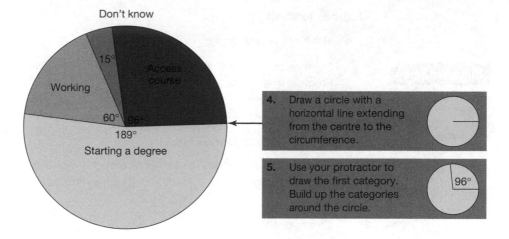

| 4. | Draw a circle with a horizontal line extending from the centre to the circumference. |
| 5. | Use your protractor to draw the first category. Build up the categories around the circle. |

> **Florence Nightingale, the 'Lady with the Lamp'**
>
> Best known for her compassionate and tireless nursing of soldiers during the Crimean War. However, she also developed the early form of the pie chart, known as the Nightingale Rose diagram. She used it to illustrate the incidence of preventable deaths in military hospitals.

Work it out

1. A student records how many hours they spend studying at college in a week. These are the results:

Attending classes	15
In the library	4.5
Study at home	9
In the bar/café	1.5

Display this information as a pie chart.

2. Is it true all we do is eat, sleep, work and watch TV?

The activities were measured of a 'typical' person. Here are the results in hours:

Sleep	8
Eating and drinking	1.4
Watching TV	2.6
Working	7
Housework	1.4
Travel	1.2
Social life	1.2
Miscellaneous	1.2

a. Draw a pie chart of the values.
b. What are your conclusions?
c. Now create a chart using your own hours and activities.
d. Is there a difference?

All about football

3. a. The types of goal scored in Premiership football matches are recorded:

From inside the penalty area	60%
From outside the penalty area	25%
From a free kick	5%
From the penalty spot	10%

Show the results as a pie chart.

b. A survey was undertaken to see what proportion of TV viewing was apportioned to what type of football. Here are the results:

Premiership	54%
Championship	12%
Lower leagues	6%
European	28%

Display the results as a pie chart.

Hints and tips

When working out angles, percentages can be treated like any other value.

4. A carbon footprint is the amount of carbon dioxide emitted through everyday activities such as cooking, having a bath, driving to work etc. in one year. Here are the results of a UK resident who is fairly careful about energy consumption:

The average 'carbon footprint' in the USA is more than double this but there are many many countries where the carbon footprint is less than a tenth of this.

	Carbon dioxide emissions (kg)
Electricity	1 080
Gas	860
Public transport	280
Holiday flights	480
Car	1 160
Food and drink	440
Clothes, shoes, personal effects	320
Household (buildings, furnishings, appliances)	720
Recreation/leisure goods and services	1 000
Share of public health services (health, education, defence)	860

a. Draw a pie chart of these values.

b. Combine some of the related categories and create a second pie with a reduced number of slices.

c. Which pie effectively summarises the data and why?

Interpreting pie charts

Example 1

When the number in the survey is known

The pie chart shows the number of students studying in the departments of a university. There are a total of 14 400 students attending the university.

Work out how many students there are in each department.

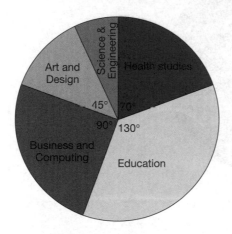

Angle for Science and Engineering:

Total known angles = 45 + 70 + 130 + 90 = 335°
Angle = 360 − 335 = **25°**

1. Calculate any missing angles.

Each 1° represents:

14 400 ÷ 360 = **40 students**

2. Work out the value of 1°:
Total in survey ÷ 360

	Number of Students Angle × Value of 1°
Health studies	70 × **40** = **2 800**
Education	130 × **40** = **5 200**
Business and Computing	90 × **40** = **3 600**
Art and Design	45 × **40** = **1 800**
Science and Engineering	25 × **40** = **1 000**

3. Number of students in each category:
Angle × Value of 1°
(ans. 2)

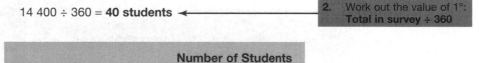

Example 2

When the number in one slice is known

A second pie chart shows the allocation of budgets between the departments. Education has a total budget of £6 750 000. Work out the budgets for the other departments.

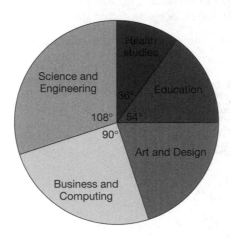

Angle for Art and Design:

Total known angles = 54 + 36 + 108 + 90 = 288°

Angle = 360 − 288 = **72°**

> 1. Calculate the missing angle.

Budget for 1°:

6 750 000 ÷ 54 = **£125 000**

> 2. Work out the value of 1°:
>   **Total for slice** ÷ **Angle of slice**

	Budget Angle × Value of 1°
Health studies	36 x **125 000** = **£4 500 000**
Art and Design	72 × **125 000** = **£9 000 000**
Business and Computing	90 × **125 000** = **£11 250 000**
Science and Engineering	108 × **125 000** = **£13 500 000**

> 3. Work out the value for each slice:
>   **Angle of slice** × **Value of 1°** (ans. 2)

Why doesn't the share of students match the share of the budget between the departments?

The distribution of the budget is not in proportion to the number of students.

Work it out

1. Moral dilemmas
    a. Ninety people were asked the question:
        'You find David Beckham's wallet lying in the street with £1 000 in it. Do you return it to him?'
        The results are shown as a pie chart.

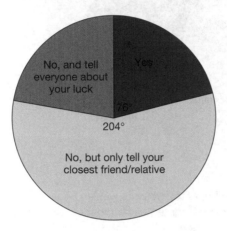

Work out the exact figures for each answer.

    b. On your promise never to tell, a friend confides to you that he has committed a serious crime. Discovering that an innocent person has been accused of the crime, you entreat your friend to confess to the police. He refuses and reminds you of your promise. What do you do? 32 people replied they would go directly to the police.
        Use the pie chart to work out how many were in the survey.

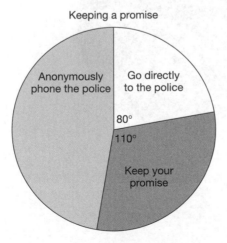

    c. Ask the same two questions to at least ten of your fellow students. Draw two pies of the results.

2. A number of people were asked to select one device that they could not live with-out from a list. Forty two selected the computer. The results are shown in the pie.
   a. Work out the numbers for each device.
   b. Carry out a similar survey within your class and plot the results as a pie.

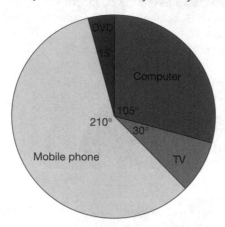

3. The pie chart shows the average weekly household spending in 1968.
   a. Work out the percentage amount spent on each category. Give your answers to 1 decimal place.
   b. Draw a table showing the amount, in percent, you spend. Display the data as a pie chart.

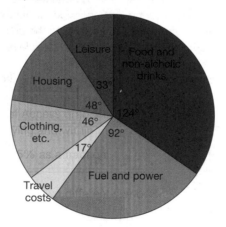

CASE STUDY

Using Maths at Work: Rachel – primary school teacher

'We've recently received the SATS results for this year. My job is to display the data as a chart that will go in the next parents' newsletter. We used to copy the local newspaper and use pie charts; however, this year I'm going to do something different as I've found pies can distort reality when dealing with small numbers.

For instance, comparing results for 2007 for our school against a local, larger school it can be seen that the results are pretty similar.'

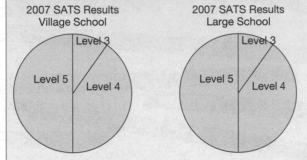

Here is the data for 2007:

	Number of children	
	Village school	**Large school**
Level 3	1	40
Level 4	4	168
Level 5	5	212

Tasks

In 2008 both schools had the same number of students sitting SATS as in 2007, both had two more achieving level 3 and 2 less achieving level 5.

a. Draw pie charts for both schools.
b. Comment on the two charts.
c. What would be a more appropriate chart for Rachel to use?

2.7 Averages

In today's world averages are everywhere:

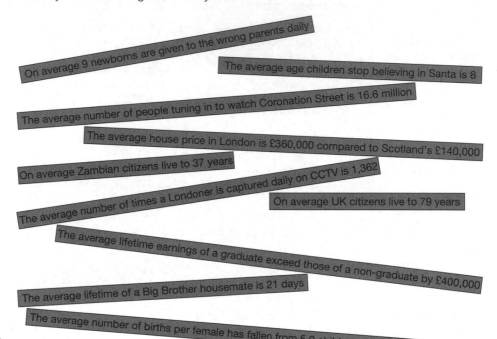

On average 9 newborns are given to the wrong parents daily

The average age children stop believing in Santa is 8

The average number of people tuning in to watch Coronation Street is 16.6 million

The average house price in London is £360,000 compared to Scotland's £140,000

On average Zambian citizens live to 37 years

The average number of times a Londoner is captured daily on CCTV is 1,362

On average UK citizens live to 79 years

The average lifetime earnings of a graduate exceed those of a non-graduate by £400,000

The average lifetime of a Big Brother housemate is 21 days

The average number of births per female has fallen from 5.9 children in the 1970s to 3.9 today

The average comfort zone between people is 80 cm in the UK, 1.4 m in Japan but only 50 cm in Spain

Key terms

Average
A number or measure that typifies a set of values. The measure could be mean, median or mode.

Mean
Total of all values divided by the number of values.

Median
The middle value once the numbers have been put in order of size.

Mode
The number that occurs most often.

Example 1

Work out the **mean**, **median** and **mode** of the following data sets:

a. 8, 3, 8, 11, 5

Mean	$8 + 3 + 8 + 11 + 5 = 35$ $35 \div 5 = 7$	Total all values. Divide by number of values.
Median	3, 5, **8**, 8, 11	Place the values in order of size, select the middle one.
Mode	8	Most common value.

b. 10, 15, 8, 10, 8, 6

Mean	10 + 15 + 8 + 10 + 8 + 6 = 57	
	57 ÷ 6 = **9.5**	
Median	6, 8, **8**, **10**, 10, 15	Because there is an even number of values
	(8 + 10) = 18	there are two 'middle' values. The median
	18 ÷ 2 = **9**	is half way between 8 and 10.
Modes	**8** and **10**	There are two most frequent values.

Example 2

Work out the **range** of the values:

3, 2, 5, 0, 6, 3

6 – 0 = 6   smallest number subtracted from the biggest.

Work it out

Work out the mean, median, mode and range for the following sets of numbers:

1. 7   3   3   4   5
2. 10   11   9   8   7   14   11
3. 17   29   17   18   17   10
4. 15   3   6   5   8   1   4
5. 4   6   8   10   2   6   0   4
6. 12.8   10.7   9.9   12.5   9.3   8.2   13.6
7. 4.1   2.4   6.5   8.2   3.5   1.2   0.4   5.7
8. 12 003   11 989   12 032   11 899   12 032
9. 0.02   0.04   0.002   0.03   0.3   0.025   0.003   0.04
10. 2.04   2.53   20.05   25.3   2.53   0.35

Example 3

The average number of claims made to a small insurance firm was 46 per day. For three days after severe gales the claims rose to 152 per day.

What is the average number of claims made for a period of ten days, seven days before and three days after the storm?

Number of claims made in the seven days before the storm:	46 × 7	= 322
Number of claims made in the three days after the storm:	152 × 3	= 456
Total number of claims for the six days:	322 + 456	= 778
Average number of claims:	778 ÷ 10	= **77.8**

Group tasks

1. The average goals scored by Wayne Rooney is 0.6 goals per match over a period of five matches. In the next match he scores a hat trick. What is his new average?

2. The average number of cars bought by five lottery millionaires is four. Three new winners both buy six cars each. What is the new average?

3. The average spending of ten households in the run up to Christmas was £1 220. Two people didn't provide statistics for January, but the average spending for the remaining eight was £870. What is the average monthly spending for both months? Give your answer to the nearest pound.

Mapping out

Finding the average from two sets of data:

Find the total for each data set.

↓

Add together both totals.

↓

Divide new total by the total number of values in both sets.

Investigation

Two sales assistants, Bob and Azim working in a large electrical shop wanted to compare their sales. During the first day Bob made three sales totalling £240, so his average was £80 per item. Azim sold six items for a total of £420 so his average was £70, £10 less per item than Bob's.

On the second day Bob went all out and sold 8 items for a total of £400 averaging £50 per item whereas Azim sold only three items for a total of £120, averaging £40 per item. Again £10 less than Bob's.

Is Bob the better salesman? Investigate.

On our roads

An ardent campaign was being driven by the residents of a village. They were tired of the noise pollution caused by the steady stream of traffic through their village and wanted the vehicles to be diverted.

An officer from the Highways Agency drove out to the village and sure enough there was a constant hum of traffic along the main street.

He set up machines to count the number of cars on the roads between 6 A.M. in the morning and 8 P.M. at night. Here are the results together with results from a nearby urban area:

	6 A.M.	7 A.M.	8 A.M.	9 A.M.	10 A.M.	11 A.M.	Noon	1 P.M.	2 P.M.	3 P.M.	4 P.M.	5 P.M.	6 P.M.	7 P.M.	8 P.M.
Village	70	82	91	72	75	78	73	74	71	78	78	85	90	74	71
Urban area	52	221	223	38	35	32	32	38	37	39	35	231	218	35	41

He worked out the mean, median and mode for the two areas.

Village setting

Mean	1 162 ÷ 15 = **77.5*** cars per hour
Median	70 71 71 72 73 74 74 **75** 78 78 78 82 85 90 91
Mode	**78 cars per hour**
Range	91 − 70 = **21 cars**

* Sum of all values ÷ number of values.

Urban area

Mean	1 307 ÷ 15 = **87.1** cars per hour
Median	32 32 35 35 35 37 38 **38** 39 41 52 218 221 223 231
Mode	**35 cars per hour**
Range	231 − 32 = **199 cars**

As a result of these figures he wrote to the campaign leader:

Dear Campaign leader,

We have investigated thoroughly your concerns about noise pollution. We set up a machine to record the number of cars on the high street each hour and analysed this data.

These results were compared with a typical urban street. The average (mean) number of cars per hour was about ten cars less in your village than the urban street,

We do sympathise fully with your situation but feel it would be unfair to act on your case when there are many others in worse situations.

Yours sincerely,
Traffic officer

Not one to be bamboozled by statistics the campaign leader replied:

Dear Traffic Officer,
Thank you for your letter.

We also have looked at your data and find that the median number (i.e. the midpoint of all the figures) of cars per hour is 75 compared to 38 in an urban area – a huge difference. This is by far a better measure of the data as the mean is distorted in the urban area by just a few hours of heavy traffic.

In our village we have to endure a constant stream of cars. This is supported in your data with the range of values being only 21 cars per hour in our village compared to 199 along the urban street.

Another measure that highlights our plight is the mode – a massive 78 cars per hour in our village compared to only 35 in an urban setting.

With these new measures I hope you are able to look again at the plight of the residents.

Regards,
Campaign Leader

Both have cherry-picked the measures to support their viewpoint.

Just because your head is in the oven and your feet in ice doesn't mean you've achieved a happy median.

Group tasks – why we need more than the mean

1. Create your two sets of figures (five in each set) that have:
   a. A mean of 10, but the ranges are very different.
   b. A medium of 10, but the means are very different.

2. The table below shows the number of cars sold in eight showrooms in the East Midlands and eight in the South East in one week.

East Midlands	13	12	11	12	11	12	11	14
South East	12	24	1	36	1	12	2	8

   a. Work out the mean, median, mode and range for each region.
   b. Put yourself in the shoes of the executive director of all sixteen showrooms and comment on these results.

3. The figures below represent the hourly rate of pay of a group of office workers and their manager.

   £8, £6, £7, £6, £5, £8, £7, £8, £5, £55

   a. Work out their mean, median, mode and range.
   b. The owner of the company is writing an article in the local paper. He wants to give the impression he's a good payer. Which measure would he use?
   c. A friend of one of the office workers is thinking of joining the company. What measure(s) would the office worker use to give her friend a realistic idea of the rate of pay?

4. There are ten people socialising in a pub. Their combined mean income is £25 000, their median is also £25 000. One man, who earns slightly more than the 'average' leaves the pub and Richard Branson walks in.
   a. Will either the mean or median remain the same?
   b. Which measure, mean or median, best typifies their income now?

5. What is wrong with this statement?

   'We're not going to rest until all students leaving school are achieving above average results.'

Investigation

Below is a list of goals scored by a premiership side in league games:

0	1	1	0	2	1	1	1	0	0
1	2	3	1	2	2	3	3	0	0

a. How many matches were played?
b. Work out the mean, median, mode and range for the figures.
c. Create a frequency table for the figures.
d. Investigate how to use the table to confirm your measures.

Example

Extracting measures from tables

The table below shows the number of goals scored by a team playing in a local league:

Number of goals	Number of matches
0	1
1	3
2	4
3	6
4	2
5	3
6	1

Three matches when just one goal is scored.

a. Calculate the mean.

The mean number of goals scored per match is:

total goals ÷ number of matches

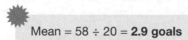

Number of goals	Number of matches	Total goals Number of goals × Number of matches
0	1	$0 \times 1 = 0$
1	3	$1 \times 3 = 3$
2	4	$2 \times 4 = 8$
3	6	$3 \times 6 = 18$
4	2	$4 \times 2 = 8$
5	3	$5 \times 3 = 15$
6	1	$6 \times 1 = 6$
Total	**20**	**58**

Add up all the matches to obtain the total number of matches played.

Two goals are scored in four matches giving a total of 8 goals.

Adding all the answers in the new column gives the total goals of all 20 matches.

Mean = 58 ÷ 20 = **2.9 goals**

b. What is the mode?

3 goals – the most popular number of goals scored in a match – it occurs in six matches.

c. Work out the range

6 – 0 = 6 goals – the range of goals scored.

d. Find the median

The median is the middle value of all the values.

- Write out the goals scored in the 20 matches as a long, ordered list:

  0 1 1 1 2 2 2 2 3 3 3 3 3 3 4 4 5 5 5 6

- Select the middle value – in this case there are two as there is an even number of matches (20):

  0 1 1 1 2 2 2 2 3 **3 3** 3 3 3 4 4 5 5 5 6

Median number of goals scored: $(3 + 3) ÷ 2 = $ **3**

Work it out

If required, round your answers to two decimal places.

1. A group of students applied to do a degree at several universities. Here are the results of their applications:

Number of offers	Number of students
0	0
1	1
2	2
3	5
4	7
5	12

a. How many students took part in the survey?

b. Work out the mean, median, mode and range for the data.

c. Comment on the results.

2. A survey was undertaken by a popular magazine to work out exactly how frequently actors appeared on our TVs as doctors. Here are the results:

Number of doctors	Number of days
0	7
1	0
2	5
3	3
4	8
5	15
6	12

a. Over how many days did the survey take place?

b. Work out the mean, median, mode and range for the data.

c. Comment on the results.

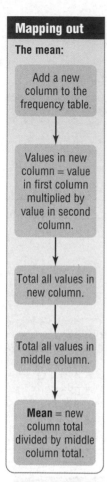

Mapping out

The mean:

Add a new column to the frequency table.

↓

Values in new column = value in first column multiplied by value in second column.

↓

Total all values in new column.

↓

Total all values in middle column.

↓

Mean = new column total divided by middle column total.

Potential pitfall

To simply divide the total for the 2nd column by the total for the 1st column. Entering the word **Total** at the bottom of the first column is not only informative but also prevents the unnecessary adding up of the column.

3. The table below shows the number of call outs each week for the mountain rescue in the Lake District:

Number of callouts	Number of weeks
1	0
2	1
3	2
4	4
5	10
6	15
7	11
8	9

a. Over how many weeks did the survey run?
b. Work out the mean, median, mode and range for the data.
c. Comment on the results.

4. The table below shows the winnings for a Saturday night lotto draw:

Winnings	Number of people
£2 482 376	3
£110 617	13
£1 331	675
£54	36 419
£10	697 490

a. How many people won something?
b. Work out the mean, median, mode and range for the data.
c. Here are the results for a Thunderball draw on the same night. By working out the averages and range compare the two sets of winnings.

Winnings	Number of people
£250 000	1
£5 000	18
£250	133
£100	2 373
£20	4 163
£10	98 400
£5	108 212

d. Would any other data be useful when comparing the two draws?

Example

Calculating averages when there is no raw data

A survey of the mortgages of first time buyers revealed the results shown below:

Mortgage (£)	Number of people
0 < mortgage ≤ 50 000	18
50 000 < mortgage ≤ 100 000	67*
100 000 < mortgage ≤ 150 000	85
150 000 < mortgage ≤ 200 000	30

*67 people take out a mortgage of more than £50 000 and less than or equal to £100 000.

a. Work out the mean mortgage per first time buyer.

   With no exact figures, only a good estimate can be calculated:

total mortgages ÷ number of first-time buyers

> As there are no exact figures, the **midvalue** of each group is used in the final column.

Mortgage (£)	Number of people	Total mortgage Mid value × Number of people
0 < mortgage ≤ 50 000	18	**25 000** × 18 = 450 000
50 000 < mortgage ≤ 100 000	67	**75 000** × 67 = 5 025 000*
100 000 < mortgage ≤ 150 000	85	**125 000** × 85 = 10 625 000
150 000 < mortgage ≤ 200 000	30	**175 000** × 30 = 5 125 000
Total	**200**	**£21 350 000**

Total number of people in survey.

Total mortgages of all first time buyers: sum all figures.

*A best guess means there are 67 people who have a mortgage of **£75 000**, half way between £50 000 and £100 000
or:
  (£50 000 + £100 000) ÷ 2 = **£75 000**

Estimated mean = £21 350 000 ÷ 200 = **£106 750**

b. What is the modal group.

The group **£100 000 < Mortgage ≤ £150 000** is the modal group as most first-time buyers have mortgage amounts lying within this group.

c. Comment on the statistics.

> There is great variation between the mortgages with a small number of first-time buyers taking out a loan of less than £50 000 whereas some are saddled with a debt of up to £200 000. However, many have a mortgage between £100 000 and £150 000 which is reflected in the mean of £106 750.

(**Work it out**)

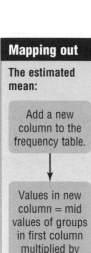

Mapping out

The estimated mean:

Add a new column to the frequency table.

↓

Values in new column = mid values of groups in first column multiplied by value in second column.

↓

Total all values in new column.

↓

Total all values in middle column.

↓

Estimated mean = new column total divided by middle column total.

If required, round your answers to two decimal places.

1. A survey was carried out on student debt. Newly graduated students were asked what their total current debt was. The results are shown below:

Debt	Number of students
£0 ≤ debt ≤ £4 000	28
£4 000 < debt ≤ £8 000	54
£8 000 < debt ≤ £12 000	68
£12 000 < debt ≤ £16 000	60
£16 000 < debt ≤ £20 000	36
£20 000 < debt ≤ £24 000	26
£24 000 < debt ≤ £28 000	20
£28 000 < debt ≤ £32 000	8

a. How many students were in the survey?
b. Work out the approximate mean.
c. What is the modal group?

2. A survey of women was carried out to find out how old they were when they first became pregnant. These are the results:

Age	Number of women
10 < age ≤ 15	8
15 < age ≤ 20	44
20 < age ≤ 25	68
25 < age ≤ 30	92
30 < age ≤ 35	70
35 < age ≤ 40	34
40 < age ≤ 45	24

a. How many women were in the survey?
b. Work out the approximate mean.
c. What is the modal group?
d. Calculate an exact mean for the students who are mothers in your class and compare it to your answer for b.

3. A group of families with young children were asked how many times they went out socialising in the last two months. This was then compared to a similar group of eighteen to twenty year olds with no children. Here are the results:

Number of times people go out a month	Families with young children	Eighteen to twenty year olds
0 < times ≤ 5	40	7
5 < times ≤ 10	6	8
10 < times ≤ 15	3	14
15 < times ≤ 20	1	10
20 < times ≤ 25	0	9
25 < times ≤ 30	0	2

a. Work out the approximate mean for both groups.
b. What is the modal group for each group?
c. Comment on the results. Do you think they reflect the social habits of each group?

4. A group of professionals were asked how long it took them to get to work. Here are the results in the form of a histogram:
a. How many people participated in the survey?

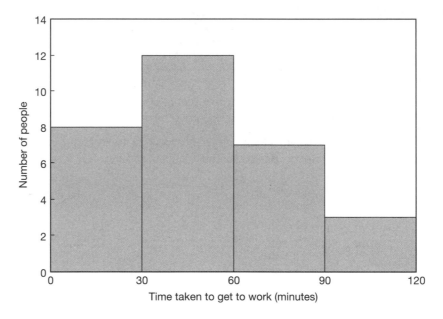

b. What is the modal group?
c. Create a grouped frequency table for the data.
d. Work out an estimated mean.

2.8 Cumulative Frequency Charts

These charts are useful when asking questions such as:

What do the top 10% of people earn?

What is the normal weight for a new born baby?

What are the acceptable limits for air pollution?

How is a course graded?

How many people live below the poverty line?

What is the expected price of a three bedroom semi?

What is middle income?

These questions can all be answered by ranking the data. This could be done simply by writing the data in one long ordered list, for example weights of new born babies:

3.5 3.6 4 4.4 4.7 5 5.3 5.3   5.6 6 6.2 6.3 6.5 6.6 6.7 7 7 7.2 7.3 7.7 7.7 8 8.1 8.2   8.4 8.6 8.8 9 9.5 10 10 10.8

One quarter of all babies are 5.3 lbs or less.

Median = 7 lbs

The middle 50% ranges from 5.6 lbs to 8.2 lbs

One quarter of all babies are 8.4 lbs or more.

When dealing with just 32 babies this ranking is possible but for data to have the credibility needed for extrapolating information to be used as standards there needs to be a far bigger sample. For example, when answering the question 'What is the expected birth weight of a white European baby?', the data below could help:

Birth weight (lbs)	Number of babies
3 < weight ≤ 4	600
4 < weight ≤ 5	2 100
5 < weight ≤ 6	4 800
6 < weight ≤ 7	8 500
7 < weight ≤ 8	9 100*
8 < weight ≤ 9	8 800
9 < weight ≤ 10	4 300
10 < weight ≤ 11	1 800

* There are 9 100 babies with a birth weight greater than 7 lb but less than or equal to 8 lbs.

Key term

Cumulative frequency
A running total calculated from accumulating the values in a frequency table. These new values are plotted freehand as a line chart.

The previous cumulative total is added to the number of babies in the current grouping.

To create a **cumulative frequency** chart add one column and one row:

Birth weight (lbs)	Number of babies		Cumulative frequency
3 < weight ≤ 4	600		600
4 < weight ≤ 5	2 100	There are 7 500 babies with a birth weight of 6 lbs or less.	2 100 + 600 = 2 700
5 < weight ≤ 6	4 800		4 800 + 2 700 = 7 500
6 < weight ≤ 7	8 600		8 600 + 7 500 = 16 100
7 < weight ≤ 8	9 400		9 400 + 16 100 = 25 500
8 < weight ≤ 9	8 800		8 800 + 25 500 = 34 300
9 < weight ≤ 10	3 900		3 900 + 34 300 = 38 200
10 < weight ≤ 11	1 800		1 800 + 38 200 = **40 000**
Total	40 000		

Total in survey equals the final value in the third column.

There are 38 200 babies with a birth weight of 10 lbs or less.

Plotting the cumulative frequency chart:

Cumulative frequency is always up the vertical axis, starting at 0.

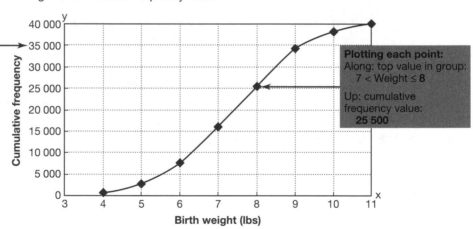

Plotting each point:
Along: top value in group:
7 < Weight ≤ **8**

Up: cumulative frequency value:
25 500

Key terms

Lower quartile
Cuts off the first quarter of the data.

Upper quartile
Cuts off the top quarter of the data.

Interquartile range:
Lower quartile subtracted from the upper quartile. It provides a measure of the spread or consistency of the middle 50% of the data.

Dividing the 40 000 babies on the vertical axis:

One quarter: 10 000
Half: 20 000
Three quarters:
             30 000

Useful information can be extracted from this chart:

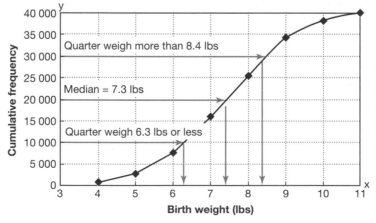

Upper quartile = 8.4 lbs
Lower quartile = 6.3 lbs
Interquartile range: 8.4 − 6.3 = 2.1 lbs

This means that the middle 50% of the data is spread over a range of 2.1 lbs.

Example

A business man has a prospective buyer for his company. In order to paint a full picture of the business over the last $2\frac{1}{2}$ years he decides to construct a cumulative frequency chart of his profits after wages, fuel bills etc.

Here is the frequency table:

Profits (£)	Number of months
0 < profits ≤ 500	12
500 < profits ≤ 1 000	8
1 000 < profits ≤ 1 500	7*
1 500 < profits ≤ 2 000	2
2 000 < profits ≤ 2 500	1

* During 7 months the profits were larger than £1 000 but less than or equal to £1 500.

Add the extra row and column to calculate the cumulative frequency:

Profits (£)	Number of months	Cumulative frequency
0 < profits ≤ 500	12	12
500 < profits ≤ 1 000	8	8 + 12 = 20
1 000 < profits ≤ 1 500	7	7 + 20 = 27*
1 500 < profits ≤ 2 000	2	2 + 27 = 29
2 000 < profits ≤ 2 500	1	1 + 29 = **30**
Total	**30**	

* For 27 months the profits were £1 500 or less.

Plotting the data:

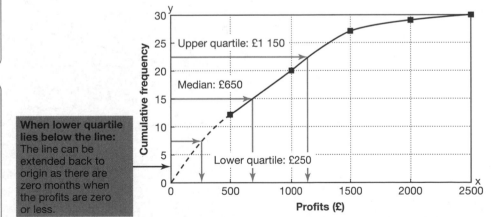

Dividing the 30 months of the vertical axis:

Half: 15
One quarter: 7.5
Three
   quarters: 22.5

During a quarter of the $2\frac{1}{2}$ years his profits were £250 or less and for a quarter of the time his profits were more than £1 150.

Interquartile range:
   1 150 – 250 =
                £900
The middle 50% of the data varied by £900.

When lower quartile lies below the line: The line can be extended back to origin as there are zero months when the profits are zero or less.

The potential buyer was concerned that the middle 50% of the data varied by £900 and a quarter of the months only showed a profit of £250 or less. He decided to look at a second business. Here is the cumulative frequency chart for this company:

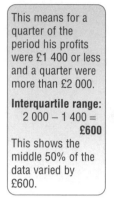

This means for a quarter of the period his profits were £1 400 or less and a quarter were more than £2 000.

Interquartile range:
2 000 – 1 400 =
£600
This shows the middle 50% of the data varied by £600.

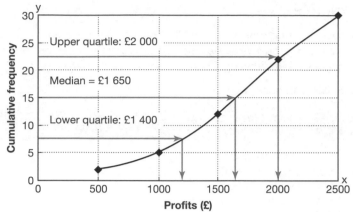

The consistency of the middle 50% of the profits is better (£600 compared to £900) and the upper and lower quartiles are showing much improved profits.

As a final check before he makes a decision, he uses the charts to work out how many months the profits are above £1 800.

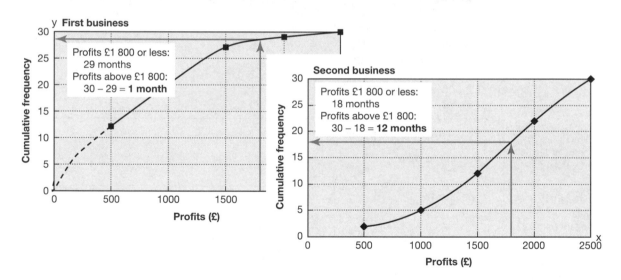

He decides to buy the second business.

Mapping out

The cumulative frequency table:

If there is no frequency table create one from the data.

↓

Work out the total in the survey and add it to the bottom of the second column of the frequency table.

↓

Create a third, cumulative frequency column.

↓

New column:

First entry: same as the first entry in the second column.
Second and subsequent entries: Add previous cumulative frequency value to current frequency value. The final value should always equal the total in survey.

> ## Work it out

1. A factory producing breakfast cereal randomly weighed the cereal boxes. The weight of the boxes should be 750 g, but inevitably there will be some variation. Here are the results (none are under 720 g).

Weight (g)	Number of boxes
720 < weight ≤ 730	8
730 < weight ≤ 740	21
740 < weight ≤ 750	27
750 < weight ≤ 760	24
760 < weight ≤ 770	14
770 < weight ≤ 780	4
780 < weight ≤ 790	2

   a. How many boxes were surveyed?
   b. Copy the table and add a cumulative frequency column.
   c. Create a cumulative frequency chart.
   d. What is the median?
   e. What are the upper and lower quartiles?
   f. Calculate the interquartile range.
   g. Boxes are rejected if their weight is either 735 g or below or above 765 g. How many boxes in this batch are rejected?

2. In the Midlands the prices of 800 houses are recorded:

House price (thousands)	Number of houses
50 < price ≤ 100	50
100 < price ≤ 150	280
150 < price ≤ 200	250
200 < price ≤ 250	150
250 < price ≤ 300	70

   a. Copy the table and add a cumulative frequency column.
   b. Draw a cumulative frequency chart.
   c. Work out the:
      i. median
      ii. lower and upper quartiles
      iii. interquartile range.
   d. How many houses are valued under £120 000?
   e. How many houses are valued over £220 000?

Mapping out

The cumulative frequency chart:

Vertical axis:
Cumulative frequency values, starting at 0.

Horizontal axis:
Start at the lowest value for all groups and extend to the highest value.

Plot each point:
Along –
maximum value for each group.
Up –
corresponding cumulative frequency value.

Use freehand to join the points.

Potential pitfall

Make sure the points are plotted at the end of the group not in the middle.

Hints and tips

The values of the quartiles and median are read from the horizontal axis.

Hints and tips

Extend the vertical scale no further than the maximum cumulative frequency value. This avoids errors when dividing the vertical into quartiles.

3. A large group of UK residents were asked their income. Here are the results:

Income (£)	Number of people (thousands)
0 < income ≤ 10 000	9
10 000 < income ≤ 20 000	25
20 000 < income ≤ 30 000	30
30 000 < income ≤ 40 000	21
40 000 < income ≤ 50 000	18
50 000 < income ≤ 60 000	7
60 000 < income ≤ 70 000	6
70 000 < income ≤ 80 000	2
80 000 < income ≤ 90 000	1
90 000 < income ≤ 100 000	1

a. How many people were surveyed?
b. Copy the table and add a cumulative frequency column.
c. Draw a cumulative frequency chart.
d. Use your chart to find the:
    i. median
    ii. upper and lower quartiles
    iii. interquartile range.
e. What do the top 10% earn and how many people are in this group?
f. If poverty is defined as having an income of less than £8 000, how many people fall into this category?

4. A survey was undertaken to discover how much time people spend on the Internet each day. These are the results (in hours):

0.5	2	2	3.5	1	0	0	1.5	2	2
3	3.5	1	4	4	3.5	2	4.5	4.5	1.5
2.5	2	2	4	5	8	3.5	7	6.5	1.5
0	0	3	3	4	3.5	2.5	2	1	4.5

a. How many people were in the survey?
b. Create a grouped frequency table of the data.
c. Add a cumulative frequency column.
d. Use the table to draw a cumulative frequency chart.
e. Use the chart to work out the:
    i. median
    ii. upper and lower quartiles
    iii. interquartile range.
f. Comment on these results.

5. A publisher is concerned about the disparity in book sales at undergraduate level. Both the Nursing Studies and English Literature courses have ten set books. A survey was conducted in which students on each course were asked how many books out of the ten they purchased. Here are the results in the form of a cumulative frequency chart:

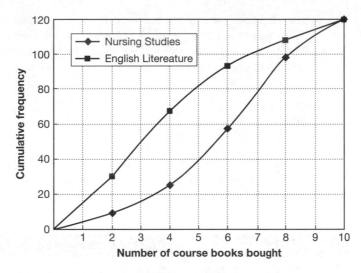

Round your answers to the nearest 10.

a. On each course, how many students were surveyed?

b. Which group of students buy more books?

c. What is the median for each course?

d. For each course, how many students buy four books or less?

e. For each course, how many students buy over eight books?

6. Here are the results for two consecutive years for an exam for a Foundation Degree exam:

Mark (%)	Number of students (2006)	Number of students (2007)
0 < mark ≤ 10	5	120
10 < mark ≤ 20	15	160
20 < mark ≤ 30	30	200
30 < mark ≤ 40	55	220
40 < mark ≤ 50	105	150
50 < mark ≤ 60	140	140
60 < mark ≤ 70	160	90
70 < mark ≤ 80	240	80
80 < mark ≤ 90	260	30
90 < mark ≤ 100	190	10

a. How many students were in each of the two surveys?

b. Copy the data and add two cumulative frequency columns.

c. Create two, separate cumulative frequency charts for these results.

d. Assessors have decided on the following grading:

0–40	Fail
41–60	Pass
61–80	Merit
80–100	Distinction.

Using this system of grading work out the number of students for each grade for each year.

e. On reflection, the assessors decide the written exams did not test the students at the correct level. Which exam was too easy?

f. The assessors decide to take this into account and change the grading system to one based on percentages:

25%	Fail
25%	Pass
25%	Merit
25%	Distinction

   i. How many students would be assigned to each grade?

   ii. List the marks required for each grade for each year.

g. Comment on the two methods of grading.

Group task – incorrect chart

Below is the frequency table showing how much time a group of retired people, all with broadband, spend on the Internet:

Time in hours	Number of people
$0 < \text{time} \leq 1$	18
$1 < \text{time} \leq 2$	9
$2 < \text{time} \leq 3$	6
$3 < \text{time} \leq 4$	4
$4 < \text{time} \leq 5$	3

Here is the cumulative frequency chart for this data:

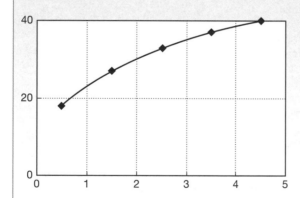

There are at least three things wrong or missing from this chart – list them.

2.9 Scatter Plots

What lies behind a headline statements is often a **scatter plot**.

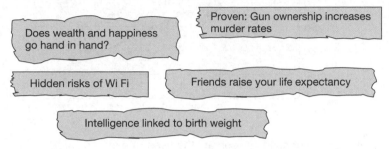

Does wealth and happiness go hand in hand?

Proven: Gun ownership increases murder rates

Hidden risks of Wi Fi

Friends raise your life expectancy

Intelligence linked to birth weight

Example 1

A study was undertaken to deduce if our heart rate changes as we get older. The table records 15 people's ages and their heart rate:

Age	15	7	3	9	4	6	11	13	2	5	10	7	1	17	16
Heart Rate	78	95	108	100	108	98	85	80	115	105	100	100	120	75	80

1. Plot these 15 sets of values on a scatter plot:

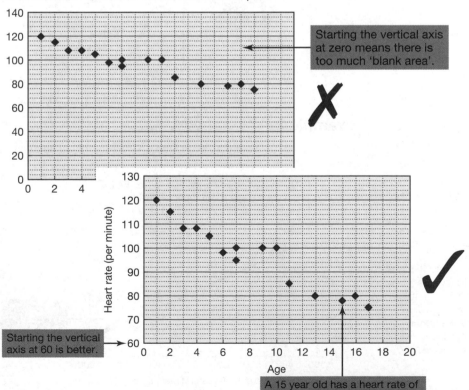

Starting the vertical axis at zero means there is too much 'blank area'.

Choosing the right data for each axis:

The horizontal data affects the vertical data, e.g. age affects heart rate.

Starting the vertical axis at 60 is better.

A 15 year old has a heart rate of 78 beats per minute. The point is marked at 15 along and 78 up.

2. Add a **line of best fit**:

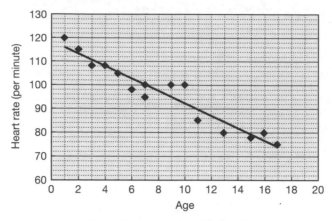

3. Use your chart to estimate the heart rate of:
   a. a 10 year old
   b. a 19 year old.

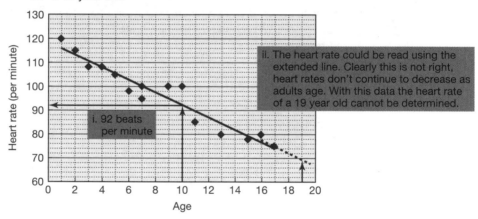

Example 2

During the 1970s scientists (with time on their hands) collected data to obtain the interesting scatter plot shown below:

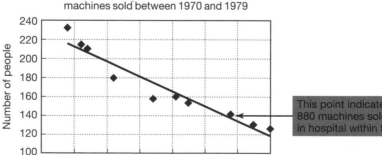

Number of people in the local psychiatric hospital against number of washing machines sold between 1970 and 1979

Types of correlation

How does one quantity affect another?

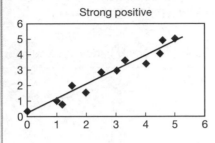

Strong positive

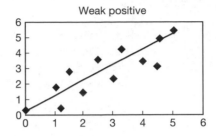

Weak positive

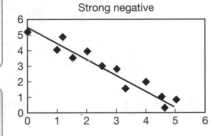

Strong negative

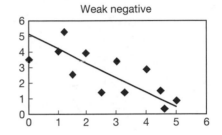

Weak negative

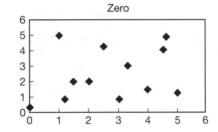

Zero

Group work – incorrect charts

A psychologist asked several couples two simple questions:

Questionnaire
Does Wealth Bring Happiness

1. What is your salary?
2. On a scale of 1–10, 10 being extremely happy, are you happy?

Here are the results:

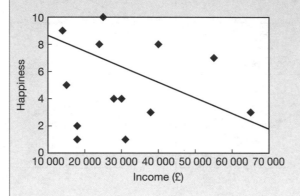

1. What is wrong with the scatter plot?

Determined to get a clear cut result, the psychologist asked a further question:

How many 'money' arguments do you and your partner have each month?

Here are the results:

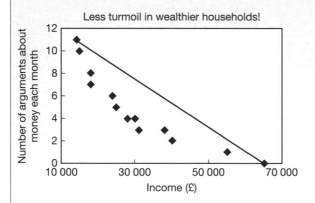

2. What is wrong with this scatter plot?
3. What is questionable about the psychologist's chart title?

Work it out

1. With the following sets of data, state what should go along the horizontal axis:
    a. age and value of a car.
    b. number of people working for a company and the profit of a company.
    c. number of cookery magazines sold and number of cookery programs on TV.
    d. number of spam e-mails and use of Internet for shopping.
    e. blood pressure and weight of a person.
    f. number of people in prison and number of crimes committed.

2. A company selling exercise bikes wants to know if their advertising campaigns have a positive influence on sales. They record their sales after each advertising campaign:

Advertising Expenditure (£)	3 900	2 200	4 900	4 600	2 700	1 300	1 100	2 700	1 500	4 500	3 500	3 200
No. bikes sold	176	117	190	188	130	110	88	154	90	176	145	132

    a. Draw a scatter plot of the data.
    b. Add a line of best fit.
    c. Describe the type of correlation.
    d. How many bikes should the company have in stock if they spent:
        i. £1 800 on advertising?
        ii. £4 400 on advertising?

3. A lecturer on an interior design course noticed the course had become increasingly popular recently. This surge in applicants was a national phenomenon. He suspected that it may be connected to the glut of makeover TV programmes. He decided to check his hunch with a bit of research. Here are the results:

Average no. TV programs each week	4	10	0	2	9	8	1	5	7	12
No. applicants each year	324	460	228	280	402	394	242	300	350	472

    a. Draw a scatter plot of the data.
    b. Add a line of best fit.
    c. Describe the type of correlation.
    d. Approximately how many applicants should the university expect if there are:
        i. 3 TV shows running per week?
        ii. 15 TV shows running per week?

4. A survey was undertaken to investigate if there is a relationship between income and the frequency of buying lottery tickets. Here are the results:

Income (£)	12 000	24 000	30 000	21 000	26 000	27 000	15 000	17 000	21 000	14 000	19 000	16 000
No. lottery tickets bought each month	8	2	0	3	1	1	5	4	3	7	4	3

a. Draw a scatter chart of the data.
b. Add a line of best fit.
c. Describe the type of correlation.
d. Approximately how many lottery tickets would a person earning
   i. £22 000 buy?
   ii. £9 000 buy?

5. A study was undertaken to discover if there is a relationship between increased use of computer games and literacy levels in 11 year olds. The 11 year olds were asked how much time they spent on the computer each day and then were given a simple literacy test in which they could score between 0 and 20. Here are the results:

Time spent playing games (hrs)	0.5	0	1	3	2	1.5	3.5	2	3	4	2.5	4.5	5
Literacy level	6.2	6.4	6	4	4.5	5.5	4.2	5	4	3.8	4.5	3.4	3.2

a. Draw a scatter plot of the data.
b. Add a line of best fit.
c. Describe the type of correlation shown.
d. What would a child's literacy level be if he played computer games for:
   i. 3.5 hours?
   ii. 6 hours?
e. Comment on your findings.
.f. What's wrong with the survey?

6. A TV channel is planning a documentary on why there is an increase in violent gun incidents within the USA.

They carried out a survey in both the USA and Canada of 20 communities (each consisting of 1 000 adults).

Those running the survey looked through local government data on gun ownership and also the average number of weekly criminal gun incidents. Here are the results:

USA households owning guns (%)	Average number of violent incidents in week	Canada households owning guns (%)	Average number of violent incidents in week
3.5	8.2	3.2	4.7
1	1.1	1.1	3
2.5	6	0	3
0.6	0.9	2.7	4.5
2	4.9	4.2	3.4
4	9.4	2.8	2.2
1.6	2.8	4.5	1.3
0	0	2.9	3.6
1.2	1.5	3.2	2.4
3	7	1.4	4
3.5	9.2	1.8	2
2.2	5.8	1.5	1.2
3	6.2	1.7	0.3
3.2	6.4	3.8	2
0.5	0.8	0.7	0
2.1	5.1	3.3	1.2
4	9.5	2.4	0.8
3.2	8	3.9	2.5
2.3	5.4	2.7	0.5
1.8	3	2.2	0.4

a. Draw two scatter plots of the data on two separate charts.
b. If possible, add a trend line to each chart.
c. Describe the correlation for each chart. Why do you think there is such a difference between the charts?
d. If the percentage of households in a community owning guns is 2% what would be the likely number of violent incidents in:
    i. USA?
    ii. Canada?
e. Are there any weaknesses in the survey?

Group discussion

A survey was undertaken to see if there exists a connection between brown rice, fish and health. Here are the results:

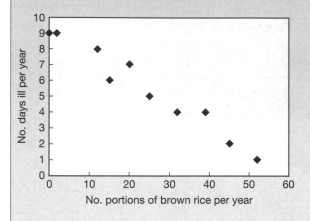

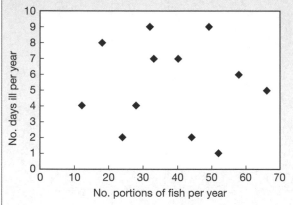

The outcome was the newspaper headline:

Forget fish, eat brown rice to stay healthy!

Fairly uncontroversial or is it? Discuss.

2.10 Probability

Probability is used widely to make predictions of an event happening. The predictions for the state of the economy, climate change, weather forecasts and gambling all rely on probabilities.

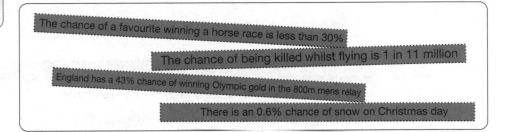

The chance of a favourite winning a horse race is less than 30%

The chance of being killed whilst flying is 1 in 11 million

England has a 43% chance of winning Olympic gold in the 800m mens relay

There is an 0.6% chance of snow on Christmas day

Expressions such as 'definitely', 'more than likely', 'possibly', 'doubtful' are widely used in the English language to describe the chances of an event happening. A scale can be used to illustrate these terms:

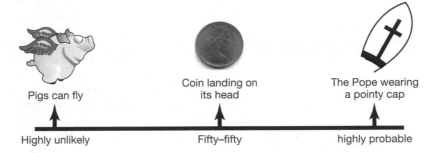

Pigs can fly | Coin landing on its head | The Pope wearing a pointy cap

Highly unlikely | Fifty–fifty | highly probable

The probability scale

Adding numbers to the scale enables predictions to be quantified.

Probabilities can range from 0 to 1:
  0 is an impossibility
  1 is a certainty.
They can be expressed as decimals, fractions or percentages.

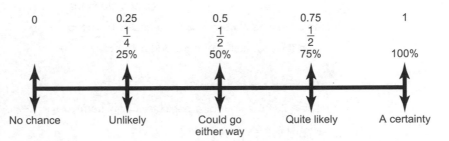

| 0 | 0.25 $\frac{1}{4}$ 25% | 0.5 $\frac{1}{2}$ 50% | 0.75 $\frac{1}{2}$ 75% | 1 100% |

No chance | Unlikely | Could go either way | Quite likely | A certainty

The roots of probability lie in gambling. A dispute over a popular dice game in 1654 led to the creation of the theory of probability.

Group task 1

1. Draw your own scale and mark the probability position of:
    a. a major Royal participating in Big Brother
    b. snow tomorrow
    c. all the answers at the back of this book are correct
    d. a new game console appearing on the market just before Christmas
    e. England winning the football World Cup.

2. Think of a certainty and an impossibility and mark them on the probability scale

3. In each of the above, state the reason for your chosen position.

Four horses compete in a race. The probability of each horse winning is not one in four, it depends on their 'form' or past performance.

Group task 2

State how the following probabilities could be calculated:

a. the probability of having dentures by the age of 65
b. the probability of a graduate earning over £200 000 at some point in their career
c. the probability of being burgled.

Probability of an event

$$\text{Probability of an event} = \frac{\text{The number of ways an event can happen}}{\text{Total number of possible outcomes}}$$

Example

Everyone's a winner – but some more so than others

At a village fete there is a stall promising prizes for everyone. The game consists of paying 50p and randomly selecting a gift from a bag. Wrapped up in the bag are:

3	£5 notes
6	£1 coins
4	Pens
7	Chocolate coins

Each time an item is chosen it is immediately replaced.

1. What is the probability of choosing a £5 note?

> Total number of items: $3 + 6 + 4 + 7 = 20$
>
> Three £5 notes out of a possible twenty items.
>
> Probability $= \dfrac{3}{20}$

2. What is the probability of choosing a coin?

> Total number coins in bag: 6 + 7 = 13
>
> Probability = $\dfrac{13}{20}$

3. Towards the end of the fair items are not replaced. All coins are still in the bag but there is only one £5 note and two pens. What is the probability of selecting a pen?

> Two pens out of a possible sixteen items.
>
> Probability = $\dfrac{2}{16} = \dfrac{1}{8}$

Work it out

1. With an ordinary dice, what is the probability of the dice landing on:
    a. a six?
    b. an even number?

2. Using a normal pack of cards what is the probability of selecting:
    a. a red card?
    b. a picture card (Jack, Queen or King)?
    c. the Ace of Hearts?

3. A game on the Internet allows participants to select one out of 16 windows. The prizes behind the window can't be revealed until the 'bet' has been placed.

£50	0	£10	£5
0	£5	0	£5
0	£10	£20	0
£5	0	0	£5

    a. What is the probability of selecting the top prize?
    b. What is the probability of going away empty handed?
    c. What is the probability of winning a prize of £10 or more?
    d. Once the prize has been won the window can't be selected again.
        A contestant wins two £5 prizes in a row, what is the probability of them winning another £5 prize?

<table>
<tr><td>

Key term

Sample space
A list of all possible outcomes of an activity. Often shown as a table.

</td></tr>
</table>

Example

A sofa is sold in three colours:

| Peach | Cream | Honey |

Cushions can also be purchased in the same colours. All possible colour combinations can be shown as a **sample space**:

Sofa	Peach	Peach	Peach	Cream	Cream	Cream	Honey	Honey	Honey
Cushions	Peach	Cream	Honey	Cream	Peach	Honey	Honey	Peach	Cream

a. What is the probability of choosing a cream sofa with honey cushions?

> 1 out of a possible 9.
>
> Probability $= \dfrac{1}{9}$

b. What is the probability of choosing the same colour for the sofa and cushions?

> 3 out of a possible 9.
>
> Probability $= \dfrac{3}{9} = \dfrac{1}{3}$

Work it out

1. In a dice game for two players the first player wins if, when two dice are thrown, the sum of the dice totals either 4, 5 or 6. The second player wins if the total is 7, 8 or 9.

   a. Draw a sample space similar to the one below. Complete all the possible outcomes when two dice are thrown:

+	**Dice 1**					
Dice 2	1	2	3	4	5	6
1	2	3				
2	3	4				
3						
4						
5						
6						

   b. Which player is more likely to win, and why?

2. In a draw for a district football league semi-finals the teams are:

    Wessington Utd   Oker Utd
    North Darley Utd   Wensley Utd

    a. Draw a sample space of all possible draw outcomes.
    b. What is the probability of Wensley Utd playing at home to Wessington Utd?
    c. If Oker Utd is drawn at home against Wensley Utd, what now is the chance of Wessington playing North Darley at home?

3. At a small private party the alcoholic drinks available are beer, lager or wine. George and Harry order drinks.
    a. Draw a sample space for all possible combinations of their order.
    b. If they randomly make their choice. What is the probability that:
        i. they both order a wine?
        ii. one orders a lager and the other a beer?

4. In a mini lottery there are five balls 1–5. Two balls are randomly selected.
    a. Draw a sample space of all possible combinations of balls.
    b. If a player chose the numbers 2 and 5 what is the chances of them winning?

Example

The probability of a 48 year old wearing glasses is 0.62. What is the probability of a 48 year old not wearing glasses?

Either they wear glasses or they don't – there is no in-between so the sum of the two probabilities must be 1. The probability of not wearing glasses: $1 - 0.62 = $ **0.38**

Probabilities from data

Example

A senior midwife has noticed an increase over the years in the number of emergency caesarean sections her maternity unit performs. Here is the data for an entire year:

Number of Caesareans	Number of weeks
0–5	2
6–10	17
11–15	19
16–20	8
21–25	4
26–30	2

There are 19 weeks when 11–15 caesareans are performed.

▶

Using the figures estimate:

a. The probability of 6–10 caesareans in a week.

> Sum of all weeks = 1 + 17 + 19 + 8 + 4 + 2 = 52
>
> Probability = $\frac{17}{52}$ (*17 possibilities out of 52*)

b. Over 20 caesareans in a week.

> Number of weeks = 4 + 2 = 6
>
> Probability = $\frac{6}{52} = \frac{3}{26}$

c. Fifteen or under caesareans in a week.

> Number of weeks = 19 + 17 + 2 = 38
>
> Probability = $\frac{38}{52} = \frac{19}{26}$

Hints and tips
The sum of all probabilities for an event is 1.

Work it out

1. The probability that it will snow on Christmas Day in Manchester is 0.1. What is the probability that it will not snow?

2. The probability of a train arriving on time is 0.6, the probability of it arriving early is 0.05. What is the probability of it arriving late?

3. A cafeteria at a university recorded the amount students spent over a period of one week:

Amount spent (£)	Number of students
0–3	240
4–6	170
7–9	64
10 and over	26

a. What is the probability a student will spend £3 or less?
b. What is the probability a student will spend between (and including) £4 and £9?

4. Ten people who used their mobile phones frequently throughout the day were asked, 'Do you have trouble sleeping at night?' These were the replies:

Yes: 7
No: 3

a. What is the probability of a mobile phone user having trouble sleeping at night?
b. What is questionable about making this extrapolation?

5. A car insurance firm keen to make sure they levied the correct amounts for each age group, recorded the activities of 8 000 of their clients. Here are the recorded claims for one year:

Ages	Number of claims	
	Male	**Female**
17–21	120	78
22–30	60	44
31–40	46	32
41–50	21	20
Over 50	14	16

a. What is the probability of a 17–21 year old male making a claim?
b. What is the probability of an over 50 year old making a claim?
c. What is the probability of a female aged 35 making a claim?

6. A factory producing MP3 players collected data on faulty machines. Out of a total of 5 000 players the faults recorded were:

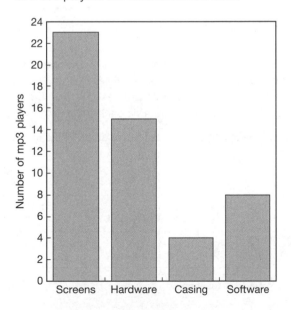

a. What is the probability of a player having a screen fault?
b. What is the probability of a player having any fault?

Discussion

1. A man is having no luck when gambling in a casino. Should he cut his losses and leave or continue in the belief that he can't have bad luck all night?

2. A person who was struck by lightning was determinedly optimistic when he stated in a local newspaper report 'Oh well, looking on the bright side at least it is extremely unlikely I'll be struck again.' Is he right?

3. **Anti-spam software**
    Spams are filtered partly by looking at the words within an e-mail subject title. Certain key words indicate the probability of the message being a spam. Here are a few:

	Probability of message being a spam
Sexy	0.99
Winner	0.95
Urgent	0.8
Member	0.88
Claim	0.90
Free	0.96

Make up a subject title using some of these words, send an e-mail to yourself using this title and see if it is labelled a spam.

A true story

A man was arrested just before getting on a plane. When asked why he was carrying a gun in his hand luggage he replied 'I was very worried about another passenger carrying a gun, so to reduce the chances of that happening I carried one. The chance of two people on a plane both with guns must be a lot less than just one.'

Probability tree diagrams

When employees go on work related trips they use one of the four company cars and one of the two company mobile phones. Phil is due to see a client and goes to pick up the keys for a car and a phone. Both phones look fine, but one is not working. One of the cars has satellite navigation, but Phil can't tell this from the keys alone.

Here is the sample space of the possible choices Phil can make:

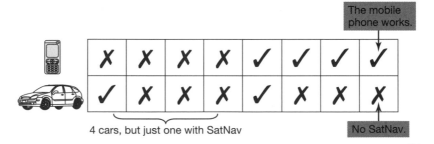

The mobile phone works.

4 cars, but just one with SatNav

No SatNav.

What is the probability Phil will select a phone that works and a car that has satellite navigation?

$\dfrac{1}{8}$

Key term

Tree diagram
A diagram showing the probabilities of all possible outcomes.

A **tree diagram** is an alternative way of showing the possible probabilities.

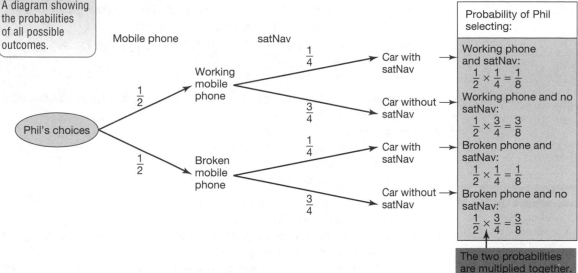

The fractions describe the probabilities.

Work it out

1. Here is a version of a roulette wheel. Two balls spin, one lands on a number and the other on a colour.
   a. In one spin a gambler places his money on a red five. This means he wins the bet if one ball lands on the red and the other lands on a five. Copy and complete this tree diagram:

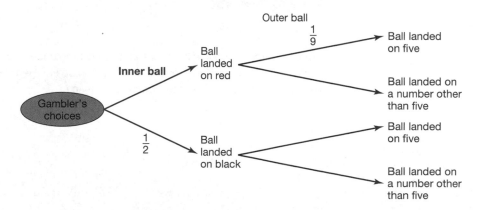

   b. i. What is the probability the gambler will win?
      ii. What is the probability the inner ball will land on a black and the outer ball will land on a number other than five?

> The type of accommodation has no influence on its position.

2. A couple want to take a holiday abroad but as cash is tight they decide to select a package deal where the accommodation will be allocated on arrival. The tour operator told them their chances of getting a hotel rather than a self-catering apartment is $\frac{1}{4}$ and the chance of them getting accommodation with a beach frontage is $\frac{1}{2}$.

   a. Show this information as a tree diagram.
   b. What is the couple's chance of being allocated:
      i. a hotel with sea frontage?
      ii. an apartment with no sea frontage?

> Assume the footballer's chance of scoring does not influence his chance of receiving a yellow card (and vice versa).

3. A professional footballer's chance of scoring in a match is 0.1 and his chance of receiving a yellow card is 0.2.

   a. Draw a tree diagram of these two probabilities.
   b. What is the probability the footballer will:
      i. score a goal and not receive a yellow card?
      ii. not score a goal but receive a yellow card?

Hints and tips

> Throwing a dice: it either lands on a six or it doesn't. Selecting a card: it is either a heart or it isn't.

4. If you were a betting person, which should you place your money on:
   i. a dice landing on a six twice in a row?
   ii. selecting a heart from a normal pack of cards twice in a row (the card is returned after the first selection)?

   To answer this question draw two tree diagrams and state the probabilities of both events.

5. Alma, the winner in a TV quiz show, can select two prizes by choosing two numbers between one and nine:

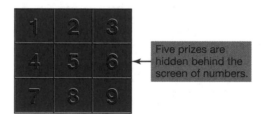

Five prizes are hidden behind the screen of numbers.

Alma can either choose a number that has nothing under it or one that has a week's holiday in the sun. If she chooses a holiday twice she gets two weeks at the same resort. She cannot select the same square twice.

This tree diagram shows some of the probabilities of Alma's selections:

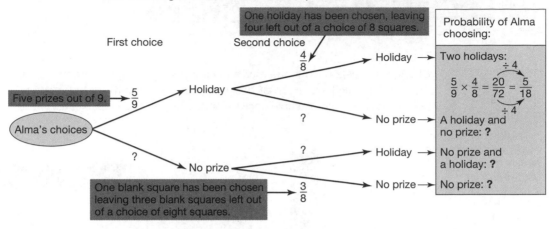

a. Copy the diagram and replace the question marks with probabilities.
b. What is the probability of Alma selecting one week's holiday?

Hints and tips

Split the diagram into the first and second draw. When one ticket has been drawn there are only 99 left.

6. At a fete Bikram buys two raffle tickets. When the raffle is drawn one hundred tickets have been sold. There are to be two prizes.
a. Draw a tree diagram for the possibility of Bikram winning both prizes.
b. What is the probability of Bikram winning:
  i. both prizes?
  ii. one prize?
  iii. nothing?

Investigation

A doctor stated that the chance of a person catching flu this winter is $\frac{1}{200}$. If someone was randomly picked out of the population the chances of them being over 65 is $\frac{4}{25}$.

This tree diagram shows the possibilities:

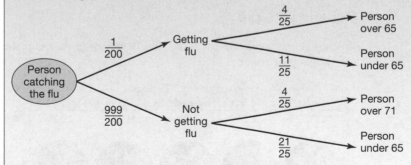

Therefore the probability of a person over 65 getting the flu is

$$\frac{1}{200} \times \frac{4}{25} = \frac{4}{5000} = \frac{1}{1250}$$

What's wrong with this conclusion?

2.11 Misleading Charts

Earlier in the chapter we discovered that the manner data is collected can create bias. Here we look out how the presentation of the statistics can also lead to a distorted picture.

Charts are widely used in the media because they can make a more powerful impact than straight numbers. But just because you see a graph doesn't mean you have to believe it. Here is an example concerning the results of a local election:

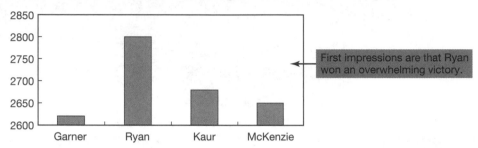

First impressions are that Ryan won an overwhelming victory.

Using exactly the same data but changing the scale tells a completely different story:

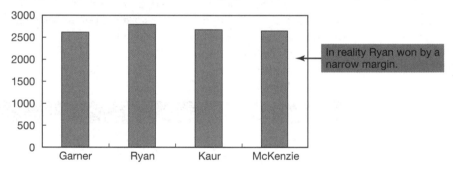

In reality Ryan won by a narrow margin.

Example

Squaring the pie

An extract from a newspaper shows the TV ratings (presumably for the whole of the UK) over a five year period:

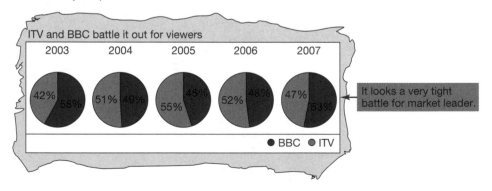

It looks a very tight battle for market leader.

The percentages all total 100, giving the impression that just the two channels command the market. A more honest approach would be to include other channels and visually, a frequency polygon is a better tool for the job.

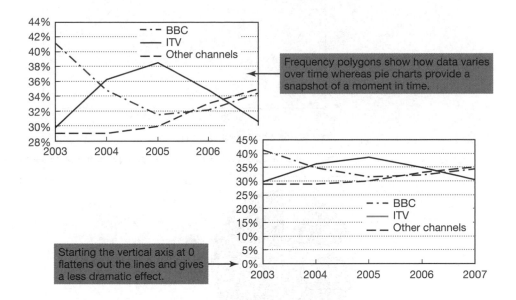

Frequency polygons show how data varies over time whereas pie charts provide a snapshot of a moment in time.

Starting the vertical axis at 0 flattens out the lines and gives a less dramatic effect.

Work it out

Governments with an agenda

1. a. In 2007 a government printed a promotional leaflet. This chart was included:

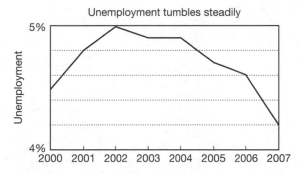

Unemployment tumbles steadily

   i. How is this chart misleading?

   ii. Extract the data from this chart and draw another that paints a truer picture.

b. Another chart was published in February 2007:

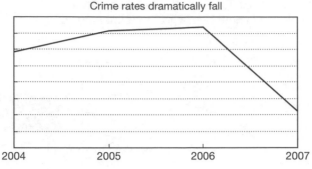

Crime rates dramatically fall

How is this chart misleading?

2. To encourage people to play in a lottery-type game the organisers published this chart.

Most winners get up to £100!

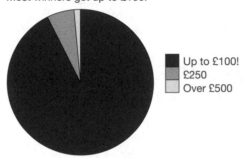

Up to £100!
£250
Over £500

Why is the chart misleading and how can it be improved?

Are statistics making us neurotic?

3. The charts below were published on the web:

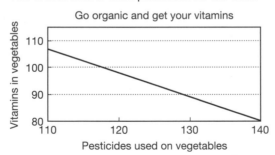

What further information is required for the charts to be credible?

4. In a leaflet to investors Cloudhoppers Airways included this chart:

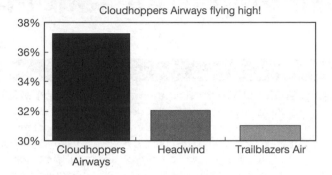

Cloudhoppers Airways flying high!

What is wrong with this chart?

 i. What needs to be added?

 ii. What would be a better chart to use?

5. One hundred people were asked to select one or more light bulb memories from a list. Here are the results:

> Light bulb memories are memories where you can remember exactly what you were doing when the original event occurred but can't remember anything about the day before or after.

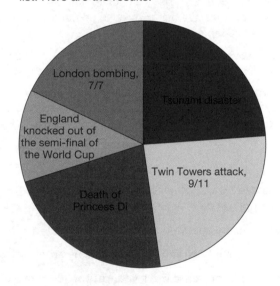

The frequency table for the data is:

Tsunami disaster	95
Twin Towers 9/11	96
Death of Princess Di	89
England knocked out of the semi-finals of World Cup	49
London bombing, 7/7	71

a. Why don't the figures add up to 100?

b. What is misleading about using a pie chart?

c. Use the table to draw a more appropriate chart.

2.12 Bringing It All Together

It is important to let the students know the purpose of the survey – especially as in this case, they will directly benefit from it.

CASE STUDY

Using Maths at Work: Emma – market research officer

At the moment I'm in the middle of developing a questionnaire that will look at the university's catering provisions. We contract out the catering to a private firm who carry out their own market research but we also like to do our own surveys. We're hoping the questionnaire will be completed by a large number of students. From experience we've worked out that you can only expect people to spend up to five minutes completing the questionnaire, so we'll avoid asking too many open questions as they take a bit longer to complete.

In the past, to save costs, we've put the survey on our Intranet or simply left the forms in the cafeteria for people to complete. However, we've found on both counts the response is poor and the questionnaires are often incomplete. So for this survey we'll bite the bullet and employ people to carry out the market research. We'll undertake the work over a week making sure we see students throughout the day and evening to achieve a representative sample.

Once we have analysed the results from the survey we'll organise a **focus group** that will concentrate on any issues that have been highlighted in the original research.

Here's a section of the questionnaire:

Catering facilities

Dear Student

We highly value your opinions on the catering facilities at the university and we would appreciate it if you could spend a few minutes answering these questions. It will help us provide a better service that more fully meets your needs.

All questionnaires are anonymous.

What's more, on completion you can enter your name in a **prize draw for an IPOD!**

To complete the form please mark your responses with a ✓ in the appropriate box. Scale: ① means very good/important and ⑤ means very bad/unimportant

Have you completed this form before? ☐

1. How often do you use the canteen:

    Every day   ☐
    2–4 times a week   ☐
    Once a week   ☐
    Once a fortnight   ☐
    Less than once a fortnight ☐

▶

We've found question b very useful. For instance, if a student is happy with a baked potato and cheese everyday and that is a regular menu item they may think there isn't much variety but don't really care as long as they get their choice.

CASE STUDY (*continued*)

2. a. What do you think of the amount of variety of food provided?

   1 ☐ 2 ☐ 3 ☐ 4 ☐ 5

   b. Is this important to you?

   1 ☐ 2 ☐ 3 ☐ 4 ☐ 5

3. a. What do you think about the waiting time to be served?

   1 ☐ 2 ☐ 3 ☐ 4 ☐ 5

   b. Is this important to you?

   1 ☐ 2 ☐ 3 ☐ 4 ☐ 5

It's really important to concentrate on questions that will be useful. For instance there's no point asking about students' opinion on décor if there is no money in the bank to improve it.

Group task

1. Write down two more questions Emma could add to the questionnaire. Here are the results of two of the questions:

Results of Catering Facilities Survey

1. How often do you use the canteen:

Every day	46
2–4 times a week	88
Once a week	178
Once a fortnight	14
Less than once a fortnight	4

2. a. What do you think of the amount of variety of food provided?

   1 2 **2** 66 **3** 92 **4** 164 **5** 6

   b. Is this important to you?

   1 0 **2** 24 **3** 36 **4** 206 **5** 64

'The managers who make the decisions do not necessarily have a high competence in Maths so I make sure the information is clear and easy to understand. The bottom line is if managers are fearful of it they won't use it.'

2. How many students took part in Emma's survey?

3. Create a report for the catering manager. Within it include any useful:
    a. charts
    b. measures of dispersion.

4. Think of two open questions Emma could use with her focus group.

▶

'It would be a meaningless venture to compare our data with say Cambridge University as we are not in their league and are not their competitors. We've developed a group of "Benchmark" universities that have a similar profile to us, i.e. attract the same type of student, are of similar size and provide broadly similar courses.'

CASE STUDY (*continued*)

Data from the web

Emma states, 'as well as designing the survey, I have been asked by senior management to have a look at how the university (Dalton) is performing. As I can access this data easily from the Internet there is no need for a costly survey.'

Here are some of the results:'

Nursing Degree – 2008

University	Number of students	Change from 2007	Ranking	Change in ranking from 2007	Overseas students	Change from 2007
Paisley	203	+7	56	+2	23	+12
Dalton	158	–40	48	–3	0	–22
Wadhurst	188	+10	53	+2	28	+6
Cottenham	207	–14	58	–5	18	–11

Note: the change is comparing the figures to the previous year; a negative value means 2008 figures are down on 2007 figures.

Note: Ranking denotes the overall quality of the course when compared to other universities (could include factors such as popularity, student retention, student results etc.)

Group task

1. What is the overall change in the total number of students studying Nursing in 2008 compared to 2007?
2. If there are a total of 105 universities in the UK which one of the four is the median? Which was the median last year?
3. Emma wants to compare the mean number of students for all four universities for 2007 and 2008 and compare these values with Dalton for both years. Calculate these values and display them as both a table and chart.
4. The Director of Student Admissions is particularly concerned with the numbers of overseas students.
    a. Why do you think that is?
    b. Work out the mean number of overseas students on the Nursing degree in 2007 and 2008 at all four universities.
    c. How does Dalton compare with these figures?

Assignment questions

If required, round your answers to one decimal place.

1. You are a graduate planning to set up a small business providing a service of burning old video footage onto DVDs. Before purchasing a high quality machine (about £500) you will need to carry out some market research. The purpose of the investigation is to discover:

- if the service would be used
- how many videos people would want to burn
- how much people would be willing to pay for the service
- the best way to advertise the service.

a. Create your own mini questionnaire to answer these questions.
b. Ask at least fifteen people to complete your questionnaire.
c. Fully analyse your results using both charts and measures of dispersion.
d. Is the business plan sound, assuming the cost of a DVD and case is 25p?

2. Below is a record of the average number of hours of daylight throughout the year in three cities:

	London, UK (51°)	Kiruna, Sweden (70°)	Nairobi, Kenya (0°)
January	8.6	2.8	12.1
February	10.4	8.0	12.1
March	12.2	12.2	12.1
April	14.3	16.8	12.1
May	15.9	24.0	12.1
June	16.6	24.0	12.1
July	15.9	24.0	12.1
August	14.3	17.3	12.1
September	12.6	13.6	12.1
October	10.3	8.0	12.1
November	8.6	2.7	12.1
December	7.8	0.0	12.1

a. Is the data discrete or continuous?
b. Which place gets the most daylight in a year?
c. Work out the mean and range for the three cities.
d. Create one chart with three frequency polygons.
e. Comment on the statistics.

3. A survey of the salaries achieved by University students in their first year of employment immediately after graduation revealed the results shown below:

Salary	Number of graduates
£10,000 < salary ≤ £15,000	48
£15,000 < salary ≤ £20,000	66
£20,000 < salary ≤ £25,000	52
£25,000 < salary ≤ £30,000	34

a. Copy the table and add a third column to calculate an estimated mean.
b. What is the modal group?
c. Display the data as a histogram.

4. A TV company researching for a programme concerning the impact of security cameras on our daily lives asked a group of people living in a rural area how many times they thought they were caught on camera each day.

▶

Here are the results:

0	1	2	0	2	4	5	6	8	2
4	3	0	2	3	3	2	1	0	1
0	2	3	4	3	5	8	9	2	7

Then the company tracked the same people for a day, recording how many times they were actually caught on camera.

Here are the results:

7	14	12	15	18	28	26	14	24	6
24	23	10	19	14	13	2	8	12	21
7	9	18	28	22	25	27	30	17	26

What a difference!

a. Show these two results on a chart of your choice.
b. Calculate appropriate measures of dispersion that will provide maximum impact for the viewers.

5. A company providing broadband is concerned that customers, once registered, are waiting too long before they are able to go online. The manager's target is that:
   • nobody waits longer than 10 working days
   • 25% of customers wait just 2 days or less
   • 50% of customers wait just 4 days or less
   • 75% of customers wait 8 days or less.

For a week they recorded how long customers had to wait:

3	5	6	10	11	12	8	7	8	7
5	8	7	6	8	4	3	6	2	4
1	3	1	2	4	5	10	7	8	2
2	5	8	9	5	4	3	3	5	2
9	11	10	8	8	9	4	3	6	5

a. Calculate the mean and range.
b. Work out how many customers are not within the manager's target of 10 days.
c. Group the data and create a frequency table.
d. Draw a histogram.
e. Add a cumulative frequency column to your table.
f. Draw a cumulative frequency chart.
g. Use this chart to work out:
   i. The median. Has the manager's target been met for 50% of customers?
   ii. What are the upper and lower quartiles? Do these meet the manager's targets?

Is work killing us?

6. Increasingly, people in the UK are working longer in order to make up shortfalls in their pensions. The government recently put forward plans to increase the retirement age for all public sector workers from 60 to 65. Concurrent with this, a team of statisticians were asked to analyse government data on retirement ages and mortality. Within the survey they only used data from people who were healthy when they retired. They compared these records with a similar number of public sector workers in Georgia (used to be part of the USSR).

    The results are shown below:

UK		Georgia	
Retirement age	Age at death	Retirement age	Age at death
60	75	61	75
55	80	60	88
47	86	56	86
65	74	65	66
70	72	70	72
64	72	64	66
59	81	67	81
54	87	54	91
50	91	72	74
61	70	78	94
60	72	67	88
67	71	67	70
63	76	84	86
55	78	55	63
58	81	80	81
68	69	68	88
48	90	68	95
50	87	56	87
52	88	62	94
62	74	65	75

    For both sets of data (on two separate sets of graph paper):
    a. Plot a scatter graph. Make sure you use an appropriate scale – remember the axes do not have to start at 0.
    b. Add the line of best fit (trend line), if possible.
    c. Describe the correlation for both charts.
    d. Use your UK line of best fit to work out the likely age of:
        i.   death of a person if they retire at the age of 52
        ii. retirement if a person dies at the age of 75.

    ▶

e. Copy and complete the tables below:

	Retirement UK	Georgia
Mean		
Range		

	Mortality (age of death) UK	Georgia
Mean		
Range		

f. Why haven't you been asked to work out the mode?

g. Analyse all your results and write a conclusion. Does the survey answer the original question 'Is work killing us?'

h. What are the strengths and weaknesses of the survey?

3 Shape, Space and Measurement

In this section you will learn:

✓ how to identify shapes and define their characteristics
✓ how to calculate angles and use bearings
✓ how to work with similar shapes and scale drawings
✓ how to solve problems using measures
✓ how to calculate areas and volumes
✓ how to calculate angles and sides of right angle triangles
✓ how to transform 2-D shapes

In this chapter you will need:

✓ a pencil
✓ ruler
✓ compass
✓ protractor
✓ calculator
✓ tracing paper
✓ graph paper

Introduction

The importance of geometry

A group of people were selected to spend one year as castaways on a desert island. Their activities were televised for a TV series.

They were given an initial set of supplies of building and storage material as well as chickens (for eggs), cows (for milk), pigs (for meat) and vegetable seeds. For the first eight months they were also supplied with food on a monthly basis. After that their food supply was drastically reduced and they were then expected to fend for themselves.

They were also provided with several **geometry** textbooks, an addition that would be both a source of vital information but also many entertaining conflicts.

Through the year geometry was used repeatedly to calculate areas for cultivation, fuel consumption, navigational bearings when out fishing and so on.

Later on in this chapter you will see how the castaways got on with this area of Maths.

Key term

Geometry
The study of measurements and properties of shapes.

Their first task

Initially, the group was housed in one large army tent but with the onset of winter looming their priority was to renovate some old outbuildings.

Supplies were limited so it was important to draw accurate scaled plans and use geometry to calculate slopes of roofs and their lengths etc. Only then would they know exactly how much material was required for each project.

Discussion

By providing examples, explore how geometry could be used within:

- architecture
- furniture making
- computer gaming.

3.1 Polygons

Shapes are found in nature, in man-made structures and in art. They form the building blocks of any construction which in itself creates a larger shape. Symmetrical shapes play an important role in ornamental art and mosques throughout the world are decorated with extremely elaborate geometrical patterns of simple shapes.

 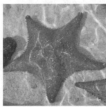    

Common shapes

| Triangle | Quadrilateral | Pentagon | Hexagon | Heptagon | Octagon |

Work it out

Which of these **polygons** are regular?

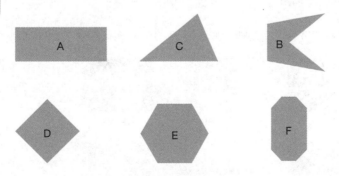

Symmetry of shapes to be found in nature, art and architecture

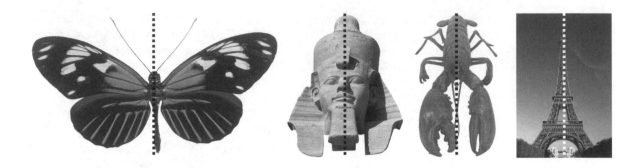

All these figures have vertical **lines of symmetry**.

Group work

List at least five shapes from nature together with five man-made objects that have one or more lines of symmetry.

Key term:

Line of symmetry
A line that divides a shape into two mirror images.
A simple test to see if a shape has a line of symmetry is to fold the shape along the line and see if the two halves match.

Task

The Guyana flag has a horizontal line of symmetry:

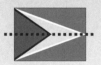

State if any of the flags below have a horizontal and/or vertical lines of symmetry:

a. UK

b. Pakistan

c. Kenya

d. Jamaica

e. Poland

f. Vietnam

Symmetry around us

Nature has a strong inclination towards symmetry, from flowers, butterflies, and leaves to the human face and seashells. These symmetrical patterns have influenced architects and artists throughout the ages and cultures and have literally shaped the world we live in today.

Group investigation

A regular pentagon has five lines of symmetry:

By sketching the following shapes work out how many lines of symmetry there are in:

a. a regular triangle?
b. a regular quadrilateral?
c. a regular hexagon?

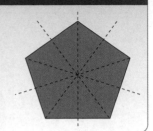

Rotational symmetry

Key Terms

Rotational symmetry
A shape has rotational symmetry if it looks the same when rotated by a number of degrees around a centre point.

Order of rotational symmetry
The number of times a shape can be matched when rotated a full circle.

Order of 1
There are no matches when the shape rotates through a full circle.

Example

Finding the order of rotation using tracing paper

Work out the **order of rotational symmetry** of a square.

1. Draw a square with all sides of length 4 cm.
2. Mark an **x** in the left top corner.
3. Place tracing paper over the square and trace it and the cross.
4. Put the point of your pencil firmly in the centre of the square. Rotate the tracing paper clockwise.
5. Count the number of times the tracing paper square exactly covers the original – this is the order of rotational symmetry.

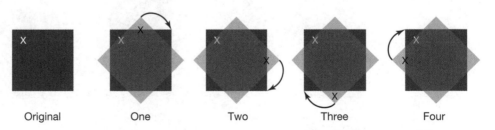

Original   One   Two   Three   Four

Order of rotational symmetry: 4

Order of rotational symmetry in road signs

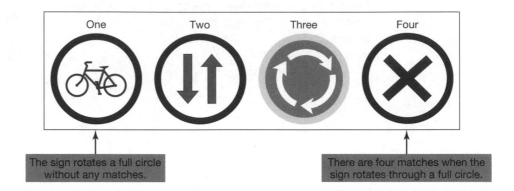

One   Two   Three   Four

The sign rotates a full circle without any matches.

There are four matches when the sign rotates through a full circle.

Work it out

1. State the order of rotation for the logos or symbols:

a.   b.   c.

d.    e.    f.

2. Design your own logo that contains either three or more rotations.

Investigation

By sketching the shapes, work out the order of rotation for:

a. a rectangle
b. a triangle with sides of different lengths
c. a regular pentagon
d. a circle.

Parallel lines in shapes

Work it out

A rectangle has two pairs of parallel sides.

1. How many parallel pairs are there in a regular:
    a. octagon?
    b. triangle?
    c. hexagon?

2. a. Match up the following shapes to make complete rectangles:

    b. What do the sloping lines in your pairs have in common?

Investigation

Which of these sets of lines are parallel?

a.   b.   c.   d.   e.

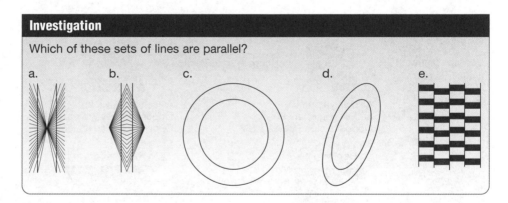

Special triangles

One or two dashes indicate the sides are equal.
One or two curves indicate the angles are equal.

Equilateral	**Isosceles**	**Scalene**	**Right angle**

All sides are equal and all angles are the same.

Two sides and two angles are equal.

All angles and sides can have different values.

A triangle with a 90° angle (indicated by the box).

Why right not left angle?

Right does not refer to position nor that the angle is correct. It probably originates from the Latin 'rectus' meaning upright wall.

Work it out

1. What triangle am I?
    a. I have no lines of symmetry and my order of rotational symmetry is one. I have one obtuse angle.
    b. I have two equal angles and one right angle.

2. Which of the following statements are true?
    a. A right angle triangle always has one line of symmetry.
    b. A triangle can have two right angles.
    c. An equilateral triangle has just one line of symmetry.

3. A wire is 15 cm long. The wire is shaped exactly into the following triangles. Provide the possible dimensions of:
    a. a scalene triangle
    b. an isosceles triangle
    c. an equilateral triangle.

Special quadrilaterals

Key term

Opposite angles of a quadrilateral

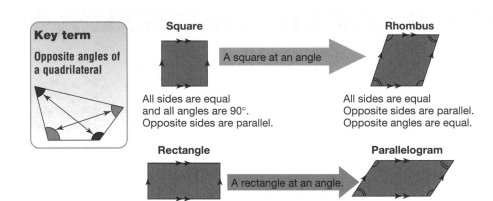

Square

All sides are equal and all angles are 90°. Opposite sides are parallel.

A square at an angle

Rhombus

All sides are equal Opposite sides are parallel. Opposite angles are equal.

Trapezium

One pair of opposite sides are parallel.

Rectangle

Opposite sides are equal and parallel. All angles are 90°.

A rectangle at an angle.

Parallelogram

Opposite sides are equal and parallel. Opposite angles are equal.

Kite

One pair of opposite angles are equal. Neighbouring sides are equal.

The diagonals of quadrilaterals

Key term

Diagonals of a quadrilateral
A straight line that connects opposite corners.

Investigative task

Accurately draw a parallelogram with sides of length 5 cm and 3 cm and one of its angles is 48°.

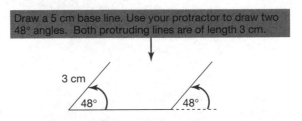

Draw a 5 cm base line. Use your protractor to draw two 48° angles. Both protruding lines are of length 3 cm.

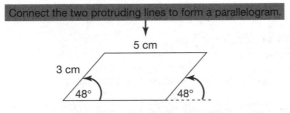

Connect the two protruding lines to form a parallelogram.

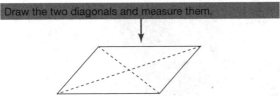

Draw the two diagonals and measure them.

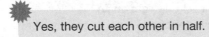

1. Are the diagonals of equal length?

    No.

2. Do the diagonals bisect each other?

   Yes, they cut each other in half.

3. Do they cut each other at right angles?

   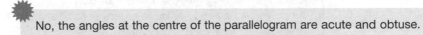 No, the angles at the centre of the parallelogram are acute and obtuse.

Work it out

1. By accurately drawing the diagonals below name the quadrilateral:

   a.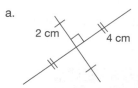

   b.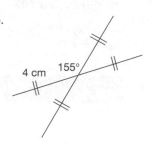

2. Describe a rhombus in terms of its:
   - lines of symmetry
   - order of rotational symmetry
   - parallel lines
   - equality of sides or angles
   - diagonals.

3. By the process of elimination identify the shape:

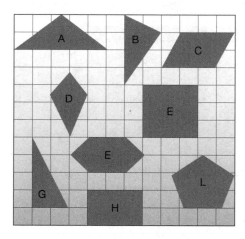

   ✓ It has less than five sides.
   ✓ The shape has at least one right angle.
   ✓ The shape had an order of rotational symmetry of two.

   Name the shape.

4. Which of the following statements are correct?
   a. All polygons have one or more orders of rotational symmetry.
   b. The order of rotation always equals the number of lines of symmetry.
   c. If the diagonals of a quadrilateral bisect each other at right angles the shape has to be a square.
   d. A trapezium could have one line of symmetry.

5. With no wastage, a wire 120 cm long is made into one of the following shapes:
   a. A square. How long is the length of each side?
   b. An equilateral triangle. What are the lengths of the sides?
   c. A regular hexagon. What is the length of each side?
   d. A kite with one side 40 cm long. How long are the other sides?
   e. A rectangle where the length is twice as long as the width. What are the dimensions of the rectangle?

Group work

How many different types of shapes can you find in the room you're in right now? Name each shape.

Investigation

Connect all corners of a regular pentagon with each other. How many isosceles triangles are there in the diagram?

3.2 Angles

We take a measure of things all the time, a pound of bacon, the speed of our car or a pint of beer, and in the same manner, angles measure a turn using degrees.

Angles are used in the daily lives of many types of professionals including engineers, architects, computer graphics developers, anyone involved in land surveys or the construction business and by artists.

Example

Work out the angles marked with letters:

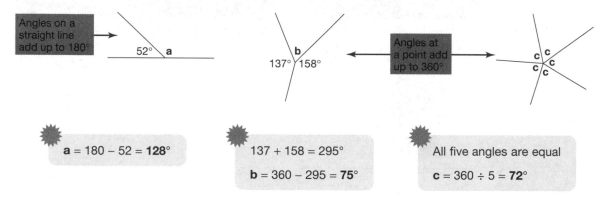

Angles on a straight line add up to 180°

52° a

b
137° 158°

Angles at a point add up to 360°

c c
c c
c c

a = 180 − 52 = **128°**

137 + 158 = 295°

b = 360 − 295 = **75°**

All five angles are equal

c = 360 ÷ 5 = **72°**

Group investigation

When two lines cross will their opposite angle always be equal?

Investigate using the diagram showing a 38° angle and its opposite.

State the reason for your conclusion.

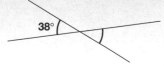

38°

Work it out

Calculate the angles marked by a letter, stating the reasons for your answers:

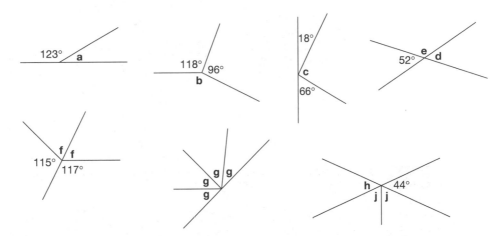

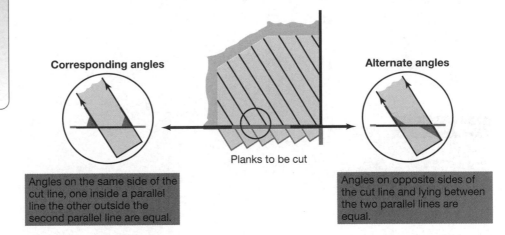

Looking at angles around parallel lines

Cut line: A line that crosses parallel lines.

Garden decking forms a series of parallel lines:

Corresponding angles

Alternate angles

Planks to be cut

Angles on the same side of the cut line, one inside a parallel line the other outside the second parallel line are equal.

Angles on opposite sides of the cut line and lying between the two parallel lines are equal.

Work it out

1. Copy the diagrams and mark all the angles that are the equal to angles **a** and **b**.

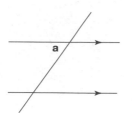

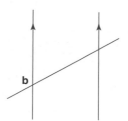

Mapping out

Angles round a line that cuts two parallel lines:

Mark the angles that are equal to the known angle.

↓

Either you've marked the angle you want or your required angle: 180 − known angle.

2. Calculate the angles marked with letters, providing reasons for your answers:

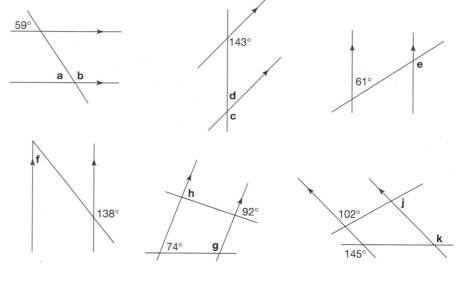

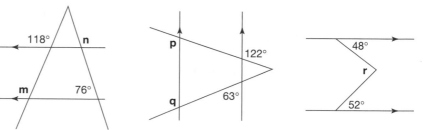

Hints and tips

When a line cuts a pair of parallel sides all acute angles are equal and so are all obtuse angles.

Two lines that cut a pair of parallel sides have nothing in common unless they are also parallel.

3. Opposite angles in a trapezium are 52° and 123°. Calculate the remaining angles.

Looking at triangles

Key term

Triangle
A three sided shape whose angles add up to 180°.

Baseline

Base angles

Why do angles in a **triangle** add up to 180°?

Draw a triangle of any size.

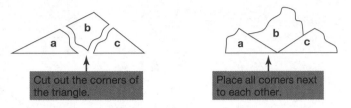

Cut out the corners of the triangle.

Place all corners next to each other.

The corners should form a line indicating that the angles in a triangle add up to 180°.

Example

Work out the angles marked with letters:

1.

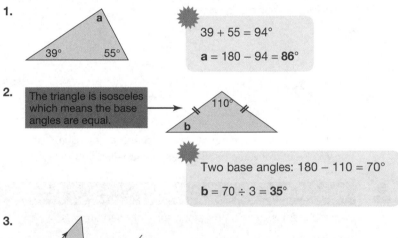

39 + 55 = 94°

a = 180 − 94 = **86°**

2.

The triangle is isosceles which means the base angles are equal.

Two base angles: 180 − 110 = 70°

b = 70 ÷ 3 = **35°**

3.

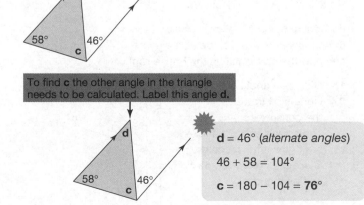

To find **c** the other angle in the triangle needs to be calculated. Label this angle **d**.

d = 46° (*alternate angles*)

46 + 58 = 104°

c = 180 − 104 = **76°**

> ## Work it out

1. Calculate the angle marked with a letter in the following triangles:

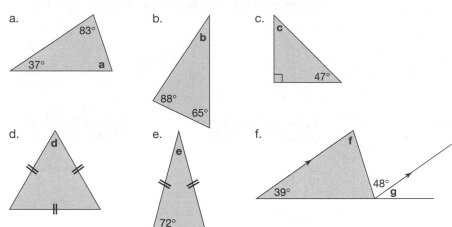

a.   83°   37°   a

b.   b   88°   65°

c.   c   47°

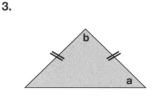

d.   d

e.   e   72°

f.   f   39°   48°   g

2. In an isosceles triangle one angle is 50°. What are the other two? There are two possible answers, give both.

3.

b   a

c   d

Angles **c** and **e** are equal. Angles **d** and **a** are equal.
Work out the value of all the angles labelled with a letter.

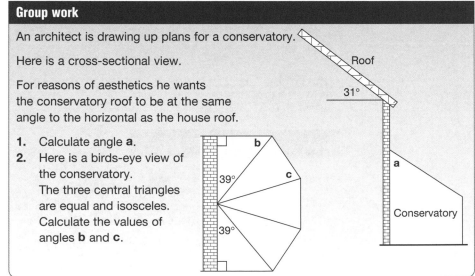

Group work

An architect is drawing up plans for a conservatory.

Here is a cross-sectional view.

For reasons of aesthetics he wants the conservatory roof to be at the same angle to the horizontal as the house roof.

1. Calculate angle **a**.
2. Here is a birds-eye view of the conservatory.
    The three central triangles are equal and isosceles.
    Calculate the values of angles **b** and **c**.

Roof   31°

b
c
39°
39°

a

Conservatory

Investigation 1 – the castaways

One of the outhouses has a mezzanine floor but no means of access. The castaways intend to fix a ladder to a supporting vertical pillar.

Work out the size of angles **a** and **b** so they can draw two **sawlines** on the wood.

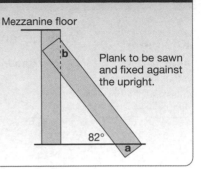

Mezzanine floor

Plank to be sawn and fixed against the upright.

82°

Sawline: this is the guide line used when sawing a piece of timber. When drawing it, it can be useful to know the size of angle **a**.

Investigation 2 – a bit of history

Over 2 000 years ago Erastosthenes, a famous philosopher and mathematician, set out to calculate the circumference of the earth.

Armed with the knowledge that the earth was a sphere, he observed that on the day of the summer solstice the sun struck the bottom of a well in the town of Syene (now known as Aswan) in Egypt. This meant the sun was directly overhead. At the same time it made an angle of approximately 83° to the horizontal in the town of Alexandria some 500 miles away.

Elevation of the sun: this is the angle the sun makes to the horizontal. When the sun is directly overhead the elevation is 90°.

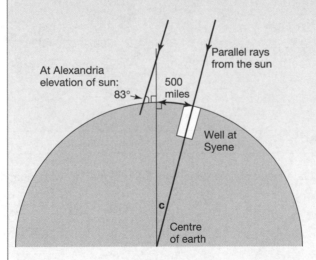

At Alexandria elevation of sun: 83°

500 miles

Parallel rays from the sun

Well at Syene

c

Centre of earth

1. What is the size of angle **c**?
2. Using the fact that there are 360° at the centre of the earth, work out the circumference of the earth according to Erastosthenes' measurements.

Looking at quadrilaterals

Key term

Quadrilateral
A four sided shape whose angles add up to 360°.

Why do angles in a quadrilateral add up to 360°?

Draw a **quadrilateral** of any size.

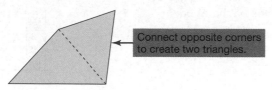

Connect opposite corners to create two triangles.

Sum of the angles in two triangles: $2 \times 180° = 360°$.

Example

Work out the angles marked with a letter in the following quadrilaterals:

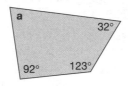

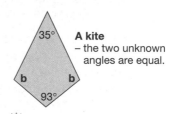

A kite
– the two unknown angles are equal.

$92 + 123 + 32 = 247°$

$a = 360 - 247 = \mathbf{113°}$

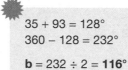

$35 + 93 = 128°$

$360 - 128 = 232°$

$b = 232 \div 2 = \mathbf{116°}$

Work it out

1. Calculate the angle marked with a letter in the following quadrilaterals:

a.

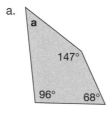

b.

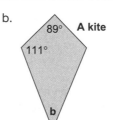

A kite

c.

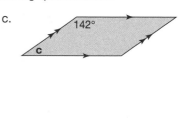

2. Two angles in a kite are 140° and 50°. What are the other two? There are three possible answers, give all of them.

Example

Angles of a regular pentagon

Sum of angles in three triangles:

   $3 \times 180 = \textbf{540}°$

Size of each angle of the pentagon:

   $540 \div 5 = \textbf{108}°$

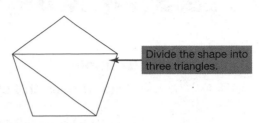

Divide the shape into three triangles.

Investigation

1. By sketching the shape, work out the size of each angle for a regular:
   a. hexagon
   b. octagon.

2. a. Copy and complete the table below that connects the number of sides of a polygon with the number of triangles it can be divided into.

Number of sides	3	4	5	6	7	8
Number of triangles						

   b. What is the connection between the two rows?
   c. Add a third row to the table labelled 'Size of each angle in a regular polygon.' Complete this row.
   d. Without drawing a regular icosagon (a 20 sided shape). Work out the:
      i. number of triangles it can be divided into
      ii. the size of each its angles.

3. Geometric patterns have been a feature of ceramic tiles throughout the ages and cultures. Medieval Islamic architecture is literally cloaked with wondrously intricate geometric designs and today geometric designs adorn both the inside and outside of many buildings.

   Here is a tile:

   Here are its properties:

   - A regular pentagon lies within a square.
   - Each point of the star makes an angle of 36°.
   - The white triangles are equal and isosceles.
   - There is one vertical line of symmetry.

   Calculate all of the angles within the shape.

3.3 Drawing Shapes

Example

Using a ruler and compass to accurately draw a triangle

a. Draw a triangle with two sides 4 cm long and a third of length 6 cm.

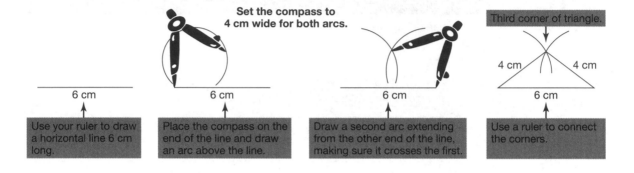

Set the compass to 4 cm wide for both arcs.

Third corner of triangle.

4 cm   4 cm

6 cm   6 cm   6 cm   6 cm

Use your ruler to draw a horizontal line 6 cm long.

Place the compass on the end of the line and draw an arc above the line.

Draw a second arc extending from the other end of the line, making sure it crosses the first.

Use a ruler to connect the corners.

b. Measure the angles in the triangle.

Two base angles: 41.5°
Third angle: **97°**
This triangle is an **isosceles** – the two base angles and two sides are equal.

(**Work it out**)

1. Construct a scalene triangle with sides of length 5 cm, 3 cm and 4 cm. Measure the angles.
2. Construct an equilateral triangle with sides of length 3.5 cm. Measure an angle.
3. Construct an isosceles triangle with a base of length of 5 cm and both base angles 32°. Measure a side.
4. Use a protractor and ruler to draw a regular pentagon with sides of length 4 cm. Measure an angle.

5.   What am I?

a.

| Draw a horizontal line 4 cm long. |

↓

| At its middle draw a vertical line, extending 2 cm above line and 3 cm below. |

↓

| Connect the ends of the two lines. |

↓

What am I?

b.

| Construct a 5 cm square. |

↓

| On both sides of the square draw a rectangle 4 cm by 5 cm, using the vertical sides of the square as one length. |

↓

| On the top and bottom of the square draw a rectangle 3 cm by 5 cm, using the horizontal sides of the square as one length. |

↓

| Connect neighbouring corners of the four rectangles. |

↓

What am I?

Investigation

- Draw four regular hexagons with sides of length 2 cm.

- From three alternate corners within each hexagon draw three lines of equal length that meet in the middle and split the hexagon into three equal parallelograms.

- Within one hexagon colour each parallelogram a different shade.

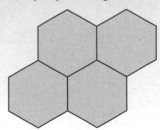

- Repeat this colouring for all four hexagons.

1.   Are these parallelograms regular?
2.   What illusion have you created?

3.4 Bearings

Imagine being lost at sea and told to turn on a **bearing** of 230°. What does that mean?

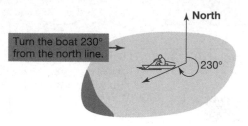

Turn the boat 230° from the north line.

Bearings are used when there are no roads to guide the way. They are a traditional measurement used to navigate our seas, airways and mountains. These days they are also used in computer graphics.

Work it out

1. In the compass diagram the pointers are separated by 45°.

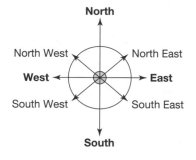

Copy and complete the table:

Direction	Bearing
North West	315°
South West	
North East	
	270°
	090°
	135°
	180°

2. State the bearing of the letters in the following diagrams:

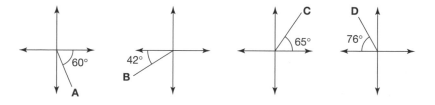

3. Three aeroplanes fly out from a local airport. One flies on a bearing of 040°, the second on a bearing of 290° and the third on a bearing of 230°.
    Plot these three directions accurately on the same diagram.

4. Sheffield is due south of Leeds. Nottingham is on a bearing of 168° from Sheffield and Manchester is on a bearing of 291° from Sheffield.
    Work out the values of the angles **a**, **b** and **c**.

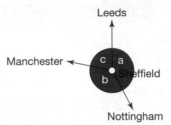

5. A family is moving to a new area. They want to make sure they are in the catchment area for a particular school which means they must be within a four mile radius of it. They also want to be within two miles of work.
    The distance between work and the school is five miles and work is on a bearing of 060° from school.
    a. Let 1 cm represent a mile and draw an accurate plan of the situation.
    b. Shade the area where both requirements are met.

The castaways

6. A couple of castaways are returning from a successful fishing expedition. The route on the map shows how to avoid protruding rocks and a sandbank.

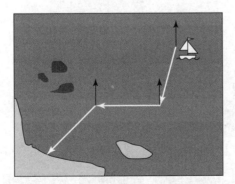

One of the castaways confidently said:

'We should first take a bearing of 164°, then 090° and finally 135°.'

The second knew that was incorrect but wasn't sure why.
a. Use the arrows to measure the three bearings and state the mistake the castaway has made.
b. What single bearing could they take?

Paired work

Check your work against your partner's.

A computer program uses bearings when drawing shapes.

1. Draw the shape created by these instructions:

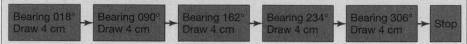

| Bearing 018°
Draw 4 cm | Bearing 090°
Draw 4 cm | Bearing 162°
Draw 4 cm | Bearing 234°
Draw 4 cm | Bearing 306°
Draw 4 cm | Stop |

- Start by drawing the line at the stated angle.
- Begin the next line at the end of the previous one.
- Continue to the end.

2. What is the shape you've drawn?

3. Create a similar set of instructions for the spiral shape opposite. The shape starts with a line of length 10 cm. Each subsequent length is 1 cm less than the previous one. Each turn is through 90° in an anti-clockwise direction.

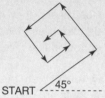

START ⟵ 45°

4. These flow diagrams can be used in computer football games.
   a. Accurately copy the outline of a football pitch:

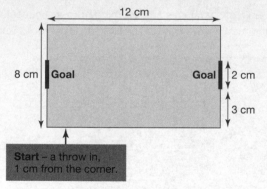

Here are the computer instructions for the movement of the ball:

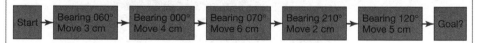

| Start | Bearing 060°
Move 3 cm | Bearing 000°
Move 4 cm | Bearing 070°
Move 6 cm | Bearing 210°
Move 2 cm | Bearing 120°
Move 5 cm | Goal? |

   b. Plot these instructions on your pitch.
   c. Is a goal scored?
   d. Draw another pitch, but this time mark in your own four movements of the ball from a throw in. Give it to your partner whose task is to establish the computer instructions to correspond to your ball movements.

3.5 Units of Measure and Compound Measures

We use measures such as length, mass, capacity and time on a regular basis, from filling the car up with petrol to checking the number of pounds gained over the Christmas break to measuring the time taken to get to work.

The metric and imperial systems

Equivalent measurements

By visualising a measurement you are more likely to remember it:

Distance

1 kilometre (km)

A bit of history

Metric system: Designed in the midst of the 1790s French Revolution. At the time there was a confusing array of measures used throughout the regions of Europe. Merchants and scientists realised that a uniform system was needed, but only in this climate of political upheaval could these radical changes be considered. Since then metrification has grown in popularity and today it is truly an international system with over 90% of the world using it.

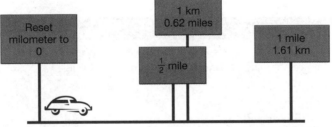

1 km is a two minute drive at 30 kmph.

1 metre (m)	1.09 yards (yd)	Distance between the end of your outstretched fingertips and your opposite shoulder.

1 centimetre (cm)	0.39 inches (″)	Width of your smallest finger.

Imperial system
Measurements that were not 'made in Britain' but largely imported by the Romans.
These units are based on a human scale of measure, e.g. an inch is approximately the width of a thumb, a yard is the length of a stride and a mile represents the distance a Roman legion could march in 2 000 paces.

Weight

1 kilogram (kg)	2.21 pounds (lb)	Four packets of butter.

1 gram (g)	0.035 ounces (oz)	A penny weighs 2 g.

Capacity

1 litre (l)	1.76 pints (pt) or 0.22 gallons (gal)	Just under 2 pints.

1 millilitre (ml)		1 teaspoon measures 5 ml.

Temperature
Celsius (°C)

30°C — Thirty is hot
20°C — Twenty is nice
10°C — Ten is cool
0°C — Zero is ice

Group work

1. To get a feel for the actual sizes within the metric system, write down an equivalent physical measurement of a real object for:
    a. one metre
    b. one centimetre
    c. one kilogram
    d. one gram
    e. one litre.

2. Estimate, using the metric system, the following measurements:
    a. height of the room you're in
    b. weight of a five year old boy
    c. height of twenty one pound coins
    d. weight of a can of baked beans
    e. height and weight of twenty ten pound notes
    f. capacity of a bottle of wine
    g. speed of a car on the motorway
    h. length of a memory stick
    i. speed of an intercity train
    j. the temperature in the UK on a summer's day
    k. size of a car's petrol tank.

Even now after over 30 years of 'metrification' there is still opposition to the system.

Here is an extract from an online forum concerning the pros and cons of the two systems:

> The metric system does away with complicated fractions – hurray!

> That's great but how can a carpenter divide a one metre length of wood into three equal parts if there is no measurement for a third of a metre?

> Choose a length of wood that will divide by three – 120 cm.

> How many people don't know how many yards in a mile but know there are 1 000 m in a km?

> Equally if a man in the street was asked his height or weight the most probable answer would be in imperial units.

> That is true because we have a pick and mix system of measures, school children learn in metric but on leaving school have to adapt to imperial units which they have not been formally taught. This gives rise to a situation where many forget the metric system but only have an imperfect grasp of imperial measures.

> But can we give up the pub pint or the British mile? Can we replace the ten yard rule in football for the 9.14 m rule?

> The bottom line is would you rather add:

   1 yd 2 ft $3\frac{1}{4}''$ + 2 yds 1 ft $11\frac{3}{8}''$

   or

   $1.607 + 2.423$?

Mixing of measures

In a DIY store customers can buy 10 m of 2 inch piping. Petrol is sold in litres but measured in miles per gallon. Surveyors measure land in acres but maps are metric. Misunderstandings, mistakes and disputes can occur when parties use different units of measurement. A spectacular example of this is the 1999 failure of the Mars space probe when it smashed directly into the red planet at a cost of $125 million to NASA. Why? Because one group of scientists worked with imperial units and another did their calculations in metric and somebody got a conversion wrong!

Group discussion

The above dialogue is by no means the whole story. What do you think of the two systems?

1. Provide at least six occurrences where imperial units are used today.
2. List the advantages and disadvantages of the two systems of measure.
3. Should we abandon completely imperial units or continue using a mixed system?

Mapping out

Converting measures:

1. Find the equivalent imperial value of one metric unit.
   e.g. 1 km = 0.62 miles.

   ↓

2. Metric value of one imperial unit:
   1 ÷ value in (**1.**)
   e.g. 1 ÷ 0.62

Paired work

Copy and complete the conversion table below, rounding your answers to two decimal places.

		Imperial	Metric
Distance		1 mile	(km)
		1 yard	(m)
		1 inch	(cm)
Weight		1 pound (lb)	(kg)
		1 ounce (oz)	1 ÷ 0.035 = 28.57 g
Capacity		1 pint (pt)	(litre)
		1 gallon	(litre)

Example 1

After metrification a village sweet shop was converting its products from ounces to grams. How much, to the nearest whole number, is 4 oz of sherbert lemons?

1 oz: 28.57 g (from table)

4 × 28.57 = **114 g**

Example 2

Which is the best value for money:

1 litre of juice costing £1.12

or

2 pints of juice costing £1.20

As we know how many pints in a litre convert the litres to pints and find out the cost of 2 pints.

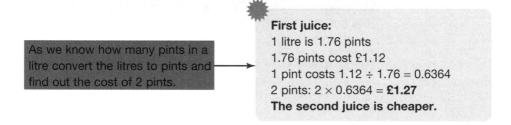

First juice:
1 litre is 1.76 pints
1.76 pints cost £1.12
1 pint costs 1.12 ÷ 1.76 = 0.6364
2 pints: 2 × 0.6364 = **£1.27**
The second juice is cheaper.

Example 3

One person walks six miles in $2\frac{1}{2}$ hours, another walks 12 km in 3 hours. Who walks the faster?

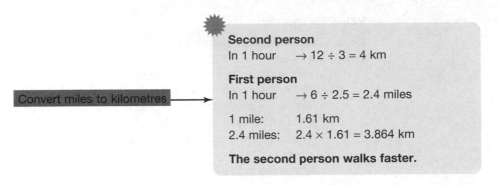

Convert miles to kilometres

Second person
In 1 hour $\rightarrow 12 \div 3 = 4$ km

First person
In 1 hour $\rightarrow 6 \div 2.5 = 2.4$ miles

1 mile: 1.61 km
2.4 miles: $2.4 \times 1.61 = 3.864$ km

The second person walks faster.

Work it out

Round your answers to one decimal place.

1 yard = 3 feet
1 foot = 12 inches
1 stone
      = 14 pounds

1. a. What is the metric weight of 2 lbs of sausages?
    b. A person is 5 foot 10 inches tall. What is that in metres and centimetres?
    c. A person weighs 10 stone 8 pounds. How much is that in kilograms?

2. Here are two similar problems for you to work out, one using imperial units, the other metric:
    a. Divide 1 yard 2 foot 6 inches into three equal parts.
    b. Divide 1.68 m into three equal parts.
    c. Which is the easier calculation?

All about cars

3. The car industry is awash with measures to help customers make an informed decision about a vehicle. Here are details for a family hatchback car:

    Acceleration: 0 to 60 mph in ten seconds
    Fuel economy: 27 miles per gallon (urban)
    Engine Size: 2 litres
    Fuel capacity: 14 gallons

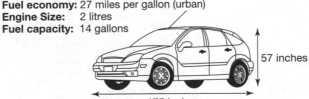

    57 inches

    175 inches

    For sale on the continent, convert these specifications to metric.

4. Does the metric or imperial system make you feel better if you are overweight by 40 lbs. Why?

5. Deonne wants to buy 9 oz of a special cream cheese but they only come in 100 g packets. How many should she buy?

6. The car braking distance on ice is approximately twice the distance under normal conditions. When driving at 30 mph in normal conditions the breaking distance is 75 feet.
    What would these two values be in metric for icy conditions?

Value for money

7. **a.** Two garages sell petrol. The first sells a litre for 90p, the second sells a gallon for £4.20.

Which is the better value for money?

b. A pint of beer costs £2.30, a 0.5 litre bottle costs £2.03.

Which is the better value for money?

c. Two lots of cheese are for sale:

Cheddar: 500 g costs £2.50

Cheshire: 14 oz costs £2.10

Which is the better value for money?

Some centuries-old measures

8. **a.** **A moment**: a medieval unit of time equal to 1.5 minutes. A person says 'Just wait a moment' but keeps you waiting 9 minutes.

How many moments have you waited?

b. **Scruple**: a traditional unit of weight equal to 1.296 grams used by apothecaries (chemists).

Lot: a unit of weight equal to about 15 grams.

One person states 'I have a lot of medicine.' To which another replies 'That may be so but I've got more scruples – fourteen to be precise.'

Who has the most medicine?

Conversions within the metric system

Key measures

Lengths:
1 km = 1 000 m
1 m   = 100 cm
1 cm = 10 mm

Weights:
1 tonne = 1 000 kg
1 kg   = 1 000 g

Capacities:
1 litre = 100 cl
1 cl   = 10 ml

Times:
1 day = 24 hours
1 hour =
      60 minutes
1 minute =
      60 seconds

Example 1

Convert the following to centimetres

a. 5 m

1 m	$\Rightarrow$	100 cm
5 m	$\Rightarrow$	$5 \times 100 = $ **500 cm**

b. 6.02 m

6.02 m	$\Rightarrow$	$6.02 \times 100 = $ **602 cm**

c. 1.45 km

1.45 km	$\Rightarrow$	$1.45 \times 1\,000 = 1\,450$ m
1 450 m	$\Rightarrow$	$1450 \times 100 = $ **145 000 cm**

Example 2

Convert the following to kg:

a. 1 250 g

1 000 g	$\Rightarrow$	1 kg
1 250 g	$\Rightarrow$	$1\,250 \div 1\,000 = $ **1.250 kg**

b. 0.02 tonnes

1 tonne	$\Rightarrow$	1 000 kg
0.02 tonnes	$\Rightarrow$	$0.02 \times 1\,000 = $ **20 kg**

c. 5.6 g

5.6 g	$\Rightarrow$	$5.6 \div 1\,000 = $ **0.0056 kg**

Work it out

1. a. Copy and complete the length conversion rules:

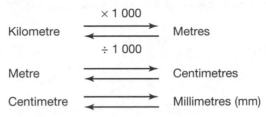

$\times 1\,000$

Kilometre ⟶ Metres
$\div 1\,000$

Metre ⟶ Centimetres

Centimetre ⟶ Millimetres (mm)

   b. Do the same for weight, capacity and time.

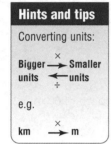
2. Convert the following lengths to metres:
   a. 12 km
   b. 0.4 km
   c. 200 cm
   d. 0.54 km
   e. 24 cm
   f. 0.07 km

3. Convert the following weights into kilograms:
   a. 16 000 g
   b. 570 g
   c. 2 tonnes
   d. 25 g
   e. 0.5 tonnes
   f. 0.0024 tonnes

4. Convert the following capacities to litres:
   a. 330 ml
   b. 25 cl
   c. 6 340 ml
   d. 2.4 cl
   e. 12 ml
   f. 0.0067 cl

5. Convert:
   a. 1 minute 30 seconds into seconds.
   b. 2 hours 20 minutes 36 seconds into seconds.
   c. 5 hours 15 minutes into hours.
   d. 10 minutes 50 seconds into minutes. Give your answer to 2 decimal places.

6. It is important to get a 'feel' for a measurement. For example, the distance 2 400 m is better written as 2.4 km.
   Convert these measurements to more manageable units:
   a. The download time for a file is 240 seconds.
   b. The thickness of a toe nail is 0.000 000 5 km.
   c. Weight of a person is 66 500 g.

7. a. Juice comes in 25 cl bottles or 500 ml cartons.
      Give two ways in which 5 litres can be purchased.
   b. Sun dried tomatoes come in 150 g, 200 g and 400 g packets. Give two ways in which 0.75 kg can be purchased.

8. A famous Premiership footballer earns £126 000 a week. Presuming he works a seven hour day for five days a week, how much does he earn:
   a. per hour?
   b. per minute?

Compound measures

Key measure

The speed triangle:

$Speed = \dfrac{Distance}{Time}$

Distance = Speed × time

$Time = \dfrac{Distance}{Speed}$

When two or more measures are used within a calculation.

Example

All about speed

1. You have been driving for 2 hours and covered 120 miles. What is your average speed?

    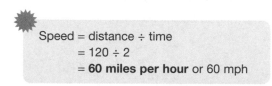

    Speed = distance ÷ time
    = 120 ÷ 2
    = **60 miles per hour** or 60 mph

2. How long does a 75 mile motorway journey take at an average speed of 60 mph?

    Time = distance ÷ speed
    = 75 ÷ 60
    = **1.25 hours** or 1 hour 15 minutes

    Convert 0.25 to minutes
    0.25 × 60 (60 minutes in 1 hr)

3. Each day Umaad drives a total of 30 km to work and back. Here are the times he spends driving in one week:

Monday	35 minutes
Tuesday	45 minutes
Wednesday	35 minutes
Thursday	40 minutes
Friday	55 minutes

    What is the average speed in mph (to the nearest whole number) for the whole week?

Key abbreviations

mph:
miles per hour

kmph:
kilometres per hour

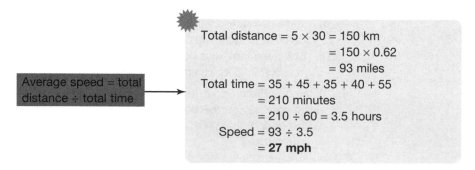

Average speed = total distance ÷ total time

Total distance = 5 × 30 = 150 km
= 150 × 0.62
= 93 miles
Total time = 35 + 45 + 35 + 40 + 55
= 210 minutes
= 210 ÷ 60 = 3.5 hours
Speed = 93 ÷ 3.5
= **27 mph**

Work it out

If required, round your answers to one decimal place.

1. Copy and compete the table:

Speed (mph)	Distance	Time (in hours and minutes)
	80 miles	2 hours
	100 miles	1 hour 30 minutes
	10 miles	15 minutes
36 mph		3 hours
60 mph	140 miles	
50 mph		2 hours 30 minutes
60 mph	100 miles	

About car travel

> **Potential pitfall**
>
> 12 minutes is not
> 0.12 hours but
> 12 ÷ 60
> = 0.2 hours

2. a. The diagram shows a car journey, the speed restrictions en route and readings from the milometer and the car clock.

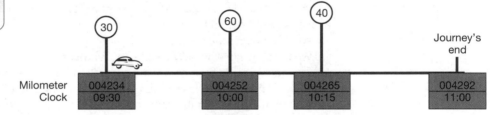

Milometer	004234	004252	004265	004292
Clock	09:30	10:00	10:15	11:00

   i.   Does the car ever break the speed limits?
   ii. What is the average speed for the whole journey?

   b. A motorbike is ridden the entire length of a stationary motorway traffic jam in 3 minutes. The speed is approximately 6 kmph. How many cars are in the jam if each car occupies about 6 m?

   c. Two cars start a journey from the same place at the same time, but one drives at an average speed of 30 mph whereas the other goes at 40 mph.
   If the journey is 60 miles how soon after the first does the second car arrive at the destination?

   d. The capacity of the petrol tank of a car is 64 litres. If the fuel consumption on the motorway is 7.2 litres per 100 km, how far could the car travel with a full tank of petrol?

3. There is an off the ball incident during a match between Liverpool and Chelsea. The Liverpool captain is 52 metres away from the referee and runs towards him at a speed of 6.5 metres per second. At the same time the Chelsea captain, who is 51 metres away, runs at a speed of 6 metres per second.
   a. Who will get to the referee first?
   b. How long will it be before the second player reaches the referee?

4.   a.   In $4\frac{1}{4}$ hours the temperature dropped by 8°C. How much did it drop per hour?

b.   George types a 626 word document in 9 minutes 50 seconds. What is his typing speed in words per minute?

c.   When an oil tanker came aground oil spilled out of its ruptured side at a rate of 250 000 litres an hour. The spillage went on for 5 days. How much oil was spilled?

5.   Here is a extract from a popular magazine about dieting:

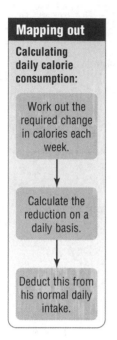

Mapping out

Calculating daily calorie consumption:

Work out the required change in calories each week.

↓

Calculate the reduction on a daily basis.

↓

Deduct this from his normal daily intake.

> **Lose those pounds**
>
> There are 3 500 calories in each pound of body fat, so if your aim is to lose one pound a week you need to either burn an extra 3 500 calories or simply not eat them. Equally if you consumed an extra 3 500 calories you would put on a pound.
>
> The average daily calorie intake of a moderately active person between the ages of 19 and 30 is:
>
> Male: 2 400   Female: 2 000

a.   A moderately active 28 year old man weighing 220 lbs wants to lose 10 lbs over a 20 week period by dieting.
   i.   What will be his weight loss per week?
   ii.   What will be his new daily calorie consumption?

b.   A twenty six year old man on a polar expedition consumes 6 000 calories a day but still manages to lose 14 lbs over a four week period!
   How much weight would the same man gain in the same period if he led a moderately active life?

6.   When Ashley is on the running track at the gym the display readings are:

Time mins	Distance km	Speed kph	Calories
12:00		13.00	90

At the time the distance display wasn't working.
a.   How far has he already run?
b.   What was the rate of calories burnt per minute?

His partner Laura is on another running track working at a different level. Her readings are:

Time mins	Distance km	Speed kph	Calories
16:00	2.80	10.50	165

c. Who was working harder (i.e. burning the most calories per minute)?
d. They both intend to run for 30 minutes. Assuming they maintain a constant speed:
    i.   how far will each have run in that time?
    ii. how many calories will they each have burned?

About drink driving

7. The government advises that men should consume no more than 4 units of alcohol and women 3 units before driving.
    The liver eliminates alcohol from the body at the rate of 1 unit an hour.
    How long will it take a man who drinks 6 pints of beer (5% strength) between 9 P.M. and 11:30 P.M. before:
    a. he has no alcohol in his body?
    b. he is legally permitted to drive?

3.6 Similar Shapes

Example 1

Key terms

Similar shapes
Two shapes are similar if their corresponding sides are in the same proportion, e.g. all sides of the second shape are double that of the first.

Scale factor
Length on second shape ÷ Corresponding length on first shape.
A scale factor of 3 means all sides are tripled in length.

The food industry often uses **similar shapes** when resizing a product. Here the two shapes are similar:

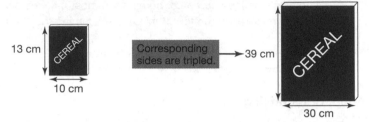

When designing a larger bottle of ketchup the manufacturer intends to keep the shapes similar. What will be the height of the new products?

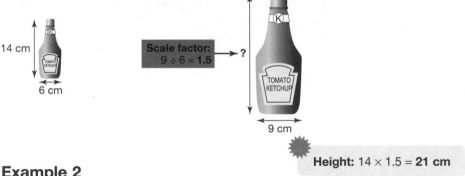

Height: $14 \times 1.5 = \textbf{21 cm}$

Example 2

By calculating the **scale factor**, work out the dimensions labelled with a letter for the following pairs of similar shapes:

1.

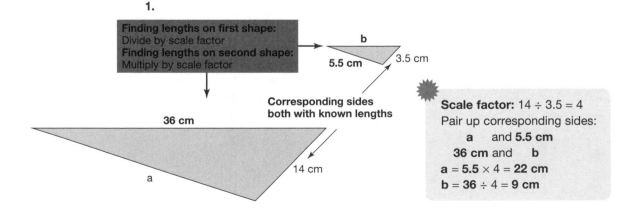

Scale factor: $14 \div 3.5 = 4$
Pair up corresponding sides:
    a   and **5.5 cm**
  36 cm and   **b**
$a = 5.5 \times 4 = \textbf{22 cm}$
$b = 36 \div 4 = \textbf{9 cm}$

2.

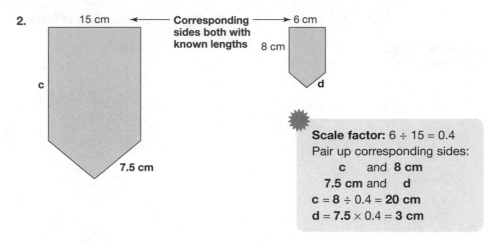

Scale factor: $6 \div 15 = 0.4$
Pair up corresponding sides:
    c   and **8 cm**
    7.5 cm and   **d**
$c = 8 \div 0.4 = \textbf{20 cm}$
$d = 7.5 \times 0.4 = \textbf{3 cm}$

Work it out

1. By measuring the dimensions of the shapes, work out which pairs are similar. If they are, state the scale factor.

a.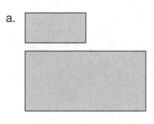

b.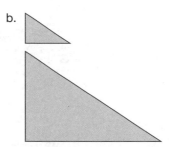

c.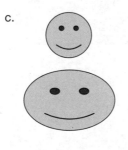

d.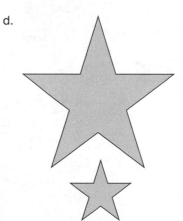

e.

2. State the scale factor and the missing dimensions of these similar shapes:

a.

b.

c.

d.

e.

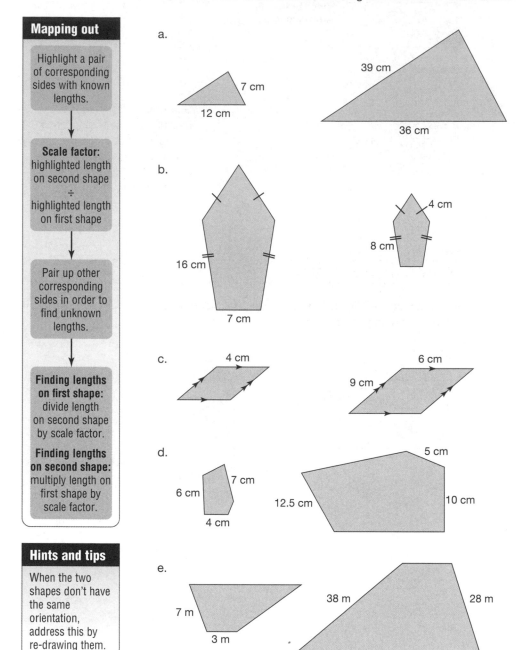

Investigation – triangles within triangles

Without measuring the lengths of the sides, state why the smaller triangle is similar to the larger one?

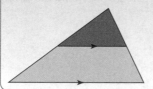

Group work

State if the following are true or false:

1. Squares are always similar.
2. Rectangles are always similar.
3. If all corresponding angles in a pair of shapes are equal then the shapes are similar.
4. Equilateral triangles are not always similar.
5. Circles are always similar.
6. If two right angle triangles have a second pair of matching angles then the triangles are similar.

Solar eclipse

Considered to be one of the most awe inspiring spectacles of nature. The halo of light is caused by the sun's super heated plasma, two million degrees centigrade in temperature.

Investigation – why do we have solar eclipses?

A solar eclipse occurs when the moon blocks out the sun. Here is a diagram of one:

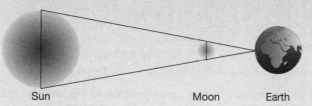

Sun   Moon   Earth

1. Draw a diagram, similar to the one on the left, of the view from Earth of the sun and moon during an eclipse but:
   a. the moon is smaller
   b. the moon is closer to the earth.
2. Here are some key dimensions that provide us with an eclipse:

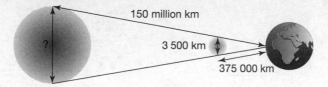

150 million km

? 3 500 km

375 000 km

Calculate the diameter of the sun.

Work it out

1. Karen wants to buy a computer monitor on the web. She currently uses a 14 inch monitor (the diagonal length of the screen) but would like to upgrade to a 21 inch one.

Existing monitor

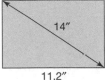

14″

11.2″

Any monitor up to 18 inch wide will be fine for her desk.
The width of her current monitor is 11.2 inches.
Use similar shapes to work out if the width of the 21 inch monitor will fit on her desk.

2. A student on a fashion design course has designed a pair of trousers for the 'smaller man' with a waist of 30 inches and an inside leg measurement of 27 inches. He now wants to use the same design but in a larger size. He decides to use similar shapes to obtain the new measurements. The waist of the new trousers is 40″.

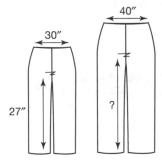

a. What will be the inside leg measurement?
b. What is wrong with the student's method?

3. An Environmental Studies student on a field trip wants to measure the height of the tallest tree in the area. Together with a fellow student he measures the length of his own shadow and at the same time the length of the shadow cast by the tree. The student is 1.95 m tall.
Here are the measurements of the two similar triangles:

1.95 m

2.5 m
shadow

32 m shadow

What is the height of the tree?

3.7 Scale Drawings and Models

Scaling down

Key terms

Scale
A comparison between a length on the 'scaled' figure and the corresponding length on the original figure, e.g. 1 cm represents 1 m.

Scale drawings and models
A two or three dimensional figure that is either reduced or enlarged in proportion to the original.

Scale does matter. The dimensions on the ground correspond to scaled down lengths on the map:

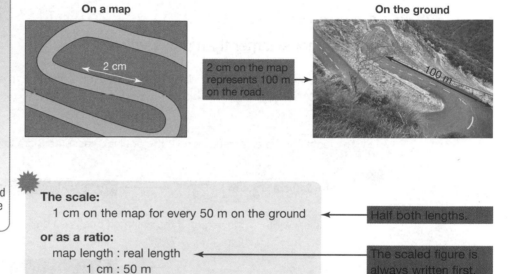

On a map

2 cm

2 cm on the map represents 100 m on the road.

On the ground

100 m

The scale:
  1 cm on the map for every 50 m on the ground ◄ Half both lengths.

or as a ratio:
  map length : real length ◄
  1 cm : 50 m
  1 cm : 5 000 cm ◄
  1 : 5 000

The scaled figure is always written first. Convert metres to centimetres.

Scaling up

The dimensions in the diagram in the book represent an enlargement of corresponding lengths on the leaf:

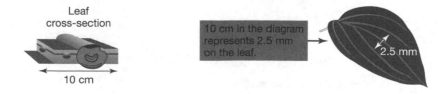

Leaf
cross-section

10 cm

10 cm in the diagram represents 2.5 mm on the leaf.

2.5 mm

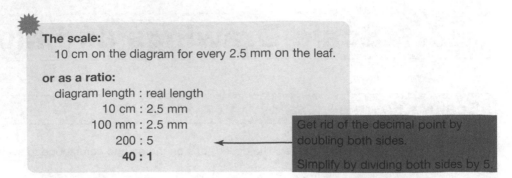

The scale:
10 cm on the diagram for every 2.5 mm on the leaf.

or as a ratio:
diagram length : real length
10 cm : 2.5 mm
100 mm : 2.5 mm
200 : 5
40 : 1

Get rid of the decimal point by doubling both sides.

Simplify by dividing both sides by 5.

30 : 1 means:
30 cm on the model represents 1 cm on the original mobile phone.

Example 1

Scaled model larger than real version

A model of a mobile phone is produced for a TV advertisement. It is enlarged from the original in the ratio 30 : 1.

Calculate:

a. The length of the enlarged phone if the original measures 8 cm long.

$8 \times 30 = 240$ cm = **2.4 m**

Multiply as the model is bigger.

b. The original width of the screen if the enlarged one is 90 cm wide.

$90 \div 30 =$ **3 cm**

Divide as the original is smaller.

Example 2

Working out a suitable scale

A scale model of a new football stadium is planned. On the ground the stadium is to be approximately 500 m long, 400 m wide and stand 50 m high.

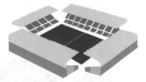

The model can be no bigger than 65 cm in any direction.

Work out a suitable scale.

Take the biggest measurement, 500 m, and try out a scale that will provide a model under 65 cm long:

> 50 cm on a model represents 500 m
> 1 cm ⟶ 500 ÷ 50 = 10 m
> Scale: 1 cm : 10 m = **1 : 100**

What are the dimensions of the model?

> Width of model: 400 ÷ 10 = **40 cm**
> Length of model: **50 cm**
> Height of model: 50 ÷ 10 = **5 cm**
>
> **Or using the scale:**
> Width: 400 ÷ 1 000 = 0.4 m = **40 cm**
> Height: 50 ÷ 100 = 0.05 m = **5 cm**

Mapping out

Scales as ratios:

Write the two measurements as a ratio:
   map/model :
   real life

↓

Convert both measurements to the same units, usually the smaller unit.

↓

Simplify the ratio.

Hints and tips

Comparing scales:

A larger scale means a larger scaled diagram. A scale of 1 : 100 will produce a larger scaled diagram than a scale of 1 : 200.

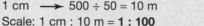

Work it out

1. Convert the following scales to ratios:

	On the map/model	In real life
a.	1 cm	5 m
b.	2 cm	6 km
c.	1 cm	0.01 mm
d.	5 inches	1 000 yards
e.	8 cm	0.8 m

2. In words the scale 1 : 1 000 can be written as:

1 cm on the model is 1 000 cm in reality.

or better

1 cm on the model is 10 m in reality.

Write these ratios in words, starting with 1 cm to:

a. 1 : 300

b. 1 : 10

c. 1 : 5 000

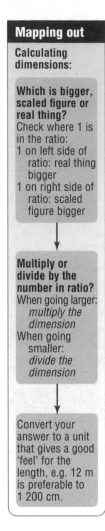

Mapping out

Calculating dimensions:

Which is bigger, scaled figure or real thing?
Check where 1 is in the ratio:
1 on left side of ratio: real thing bigger
1 on right side of ratio: scaled figure bigger

↓

Multiply or divide by the number in ratio?
When going larger: *multiply the dimension*
When going smaller: *divide the dimension*

↓

Convert your answer to a unit that gives a good 'feel' for the length, e.g. 12 m is preferable to 1 200 cm.

3. Provide the original dimensions for the following scaled measurements. Use a suitable unit of measure for your answer:

	Scaled dimension	Scale
a.	2 cm	1 : 50
b.	5 cm	1 : 2 000
c.	10 cm	20 : 1
d.	0.5 cm	1 : 300
e.	12 cm	100 : 1

4. Provide the scaled measurements for the following original lengths. Use a suitable unit of measure for your answer:

	Original dimension	Scale
a.	120 m	1 : 400
b.	2 mm	50 : 1
c.	1.5 km	1 : 10 000
d.	0.001 mm	40 000 : 1
e.	64 km	1 : 200 000

5. Which of these statements are true?
   a. A scale of 1 : 100 means the scaled figure is one hundred times smaller than the real one.
   b. A scale of 1 : 5 will produce a smaller scaled figure than a scale of 1 : 50.
   c. A scale of 3 : 1 means the model is bigger than the real thing.

6. Use a scale of your choice to display these altitudes:

Commercial aircraft flight	12 km
Highest flying bird	13 km
Height of Everest	9 km
Start of ozone layer	20 km
End of ozone layer	40 km
Normal flight of a helicopter	6 km
Height of clouds	4 km
Highest unmanned balloon	50 km
End of earth's atmosphere	100 km

Using maps

7. **a.** A map is drawn to a scale of 1 : 50 000. Calculate:
   i. the length of a reservoir that appears as 4 cm on the map
   ii. the length on the map of a nature reserve which is 12 km long in real life.

b. Serene wants to drive from Derby to Bristol. She gets her directions from a route-finder package on the web. She prints off a map of the overall route and because she doesn't know the route around Birmingham very well she zooms in on that area and prints off a second map:

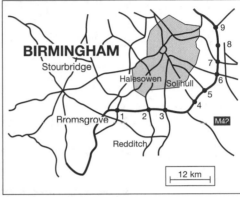

   i. By measuring with a ruler, write the scale of the two maps as simplified ratios.
   ii. Using the first map, copy and complete the route planner for the journey (write your answers to the nearest whole number):

Route planner

	Distance	Time (minutes)	Predicted speed
Derby (flag) – Lichfield			80 kmph
Lichfield – Bromsgrove			64 kmph
Bromsgrove – Bristol (flag)			96 kmph

   iii. On another journey there is a traffic jam between Exit 9 and Exit 2 on the M42 motorway. The traffic is crawling along at an average speed of 20 kmph. Use the second map to work out how long it will take her to cover this section. Give your answer to the nearest minute.

Hints and tips

Write the scale in words.

8. Here is an interior designer's plan of a kitchen. The scale is 1 : 400.
   a. What is wrong with the scale?
   b. The real length of the table is 2 m. Use this information to work on the correct scale.
   c. What is the
      i. real width of the table
      ii. real width of the work surfaces.
      iii. The inferior length and width of the kitchen.

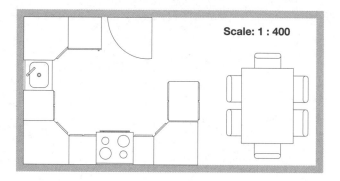

Scale: 1 : 400

Investigation

At the beginning of the growing season, a farmer uses two fertiliser sprays placed in opposite corners of his field.

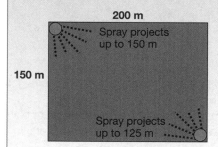

200 m

Spray projects up to 150 m

150 m

Spray projects up to 125 m

In the broccoli picking season he noticed that there was an area where the broccoli did very well and two areas where growth was poor.

Use a scale diagram to explain this phenomenon.

3.8a Area, Perimeter and Volume

The importance of these measures

Two architects are bidding for the job of designing an office block. Here are their opposing ideas:

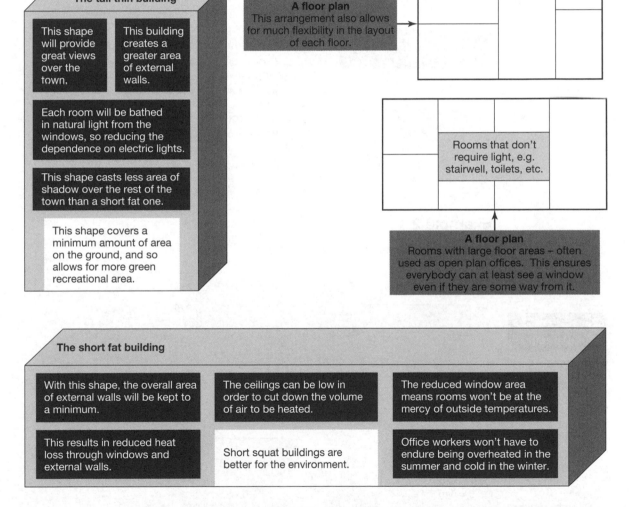

The tall thin building

This shape will provide great views over the town.

This building creates a greater area of external walls.

Each room will be bathed in natural light from the windows, so reducing the dependence on electric lights.

This shape casts less area of shadow over the rest of the town than a short fat one.

This shape covers a minimum amount of area on the ground, and so allows for more green recreational area.

A floor plan
This arrangement also allows for much flexibility in the layout of each floor.

Rooms that don't require light, e.g. stairwell, toilets, etc.

A floor plan
Rooms with large floor areas – often used as open plan offices. This ensures everybody can at least see a window even if they are some way from it.

The short fat building

With this shape, the overall area of external walls will be kept to a minimum.

The ceilings can be low in order to cut down the volume of air to be heated.

The reduced window area means rooms won't be at the mercy of outside temperatures.

This results in reduced heat loss through windows and external walls.

Short squat buildings are better for the environment.

Office workers won't have to endure being overheated in the summer and cold in the winter.

Both architects employ different measures to produce convincing arguments to support their designs.

Area of rectangles

Example 1

Find the **area** and **perimeter** of this rectangle:

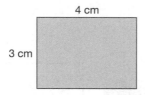

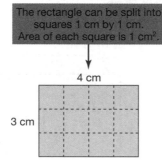

The rectangle can be split into squares 1 cm by 1 cm. Area of each square is 1 cm².

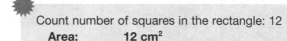

Count number of squares in the rectangle: 12
   Area: **12 cm²**
or simply
   Area: $4 \times 3 = $ **12 cm²**

Adding together all the boundary lengths:
   Perimeter: $4 + 3 + 4 + 3 = $ **14 cm**
or
   Perimeter: $2 \times 4 + 2 \times 3 = $ **14 cm**

Example 2

Calculate the perimeter and area of this shape:

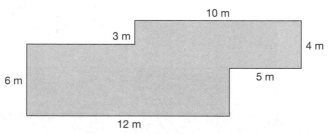

Calculate the missing lengths:

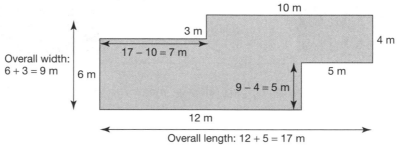

Split the rectangle into three smaller rectangles labelled **A**, **B** and **C**.
Calculate the areas of these rectangles.

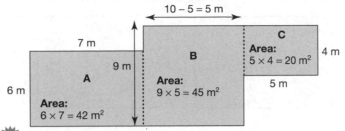

Total area of shape:
Add up the three areas:
42 + 45 + 20 = **107 m²**

Perimeter:
Add up all the lengths:
7 + 3 + 10 + 4 + 5 + 5 + 12 + 6 = **52 m**

Work it out

Hints and tips

It can help to draw the shape, even a simple rectangle.

1. Calculate the area and perimeter of the following rectangles:
   a. Length: 8 cm
      Width: 10 cm
   b. Length: 6 m
      Width: 8 m
   c. Length: 13 cm
      Width: 12 cm
   d. Length 2.6 m
      Width: 3.5 m

2. a. The area of a rectangle is 12 cm² and its width is 4 cm, what is its length?
   b. The perimeter of a rectangle is 30 m and its length is 12 m, what is its width?

3. A couple planning the table arrangements for their wedding banquet came up with three layouts:

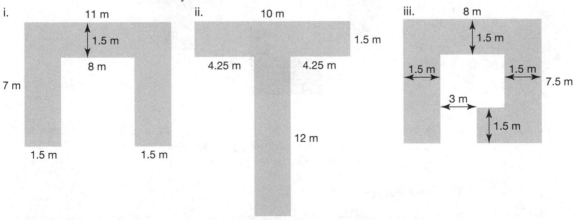

   a. Work out the area and perimeter of all three.
   b. What do you notice?
   c. Which layout would take the most number of guests?

4. An art gallery wants to maximise the amount of wall space available for paintings. Currently the gallery consists of a simple rectangle. Here are possible layouts:

Assume all walls are wafer thin.

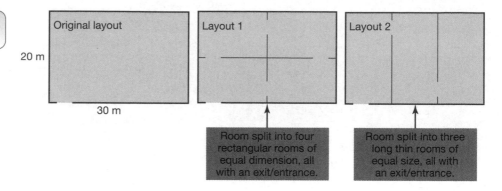

Room split into four rectangular rooms of equal dimension, all with an exit/entrance.

Room split into three long thin rooms of equal size, all with an exit/entrance.

Each entrance/exit is 1.5 m wide.

Paintings are hung along one picture rail on all of the walls. There is no rail where there is an entrance.

a. Work out the length of picture rail available for each of the three layouts.

b. Which layout should the gallery select?

Group work

1. Using the following shapes see if you can come up with a quick method of finding the perimeter.

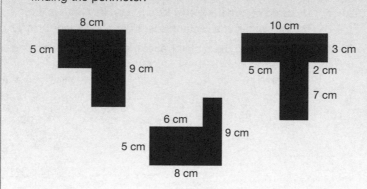

2. Do perimeter and area change in the same proportion, e.g. if the area of a rectangle is doubled, is the perimeter also doubled?

Investigate, stating the reasons for your conclusion.

The castaways

3. They have been given 24 m of fencing that is to be used around a rectangular livestock holding area. The fencing comes in 1 m sections that cannot be split. What rectangular dimensions will provide them with the maximum area?

Example 1

Does 1 m² = 100 cm²?

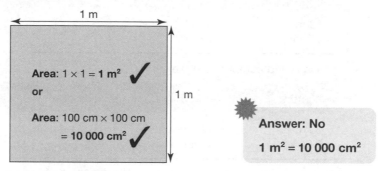

1 m

Area: $1 \times 1 = \mathbf{1\ m^2}$ ✓

or

Area: 100 cm × 100 cm
= **10 000 cm²** ✓

1 m

Answer: No

1 m² = 10 000 cm²

Example 2

Work out:

a. The area in cm²

2.5 m

1.4 m

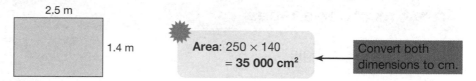

Area: 250 × 140
= **35 000 cm²**

Convert both dimensions to cm.

b. The area in m²

9 cm

15 cm

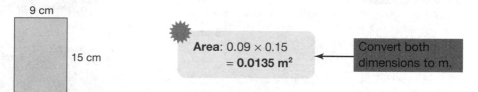

Area: 0.09 × 0.15
= **0.0135 m²**

Convert both dimensions to m.

c. The area in m²

1.2 km

0.8 km

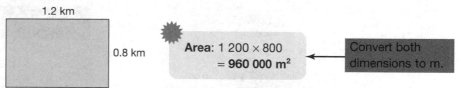

Area: 1 200 × 800
= **960 000 m²**

Convert both dimensions to m.

Work it out

1. Copy and complete the table (the first has been done for you):

Conversion	Method
m² to cm²	Multiply by 10 000
cm² to m²	
km² to m²	
m² to km²	

2. a. Copy and complete the table:

Length	Width	Area in cm²	Area in m²
12 m	15 m		
27 cm	28 cm		

b. Copy and complete the table:

Length	Width	Area in m²	Area in km²
3 km	12 km		
0.02 km	1.34 km		

3. On average, each person in the world has 0.0226 km² of space. In the UK people have less than this, on average 0.003975 km² of space.
Convert these two values into more meaningful units – m².

Area of other shapes

Triangle

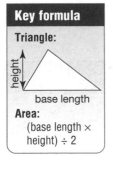

Key formula

Triangle:

height

base length

Area:
(base length ×
height) ÷ 2

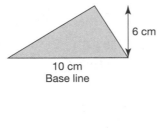

6 cm

10 cm
Base line

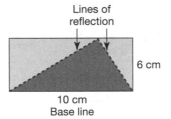

Lines of
reflection

6 cm

10 cm
Base line

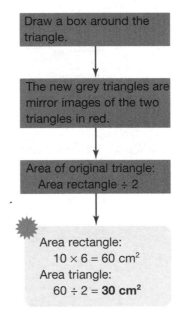

Draw a box around the triangle.

↓

The new grey triangles are mirror images of the two triangles in red.

↓

Area of original triangle:
Area rectangle ÷ 2

↓

Area rectangle:
10 × 6 = 60 cm²
Area triangle:
60 ÷ 2 = **30 cm²**

Parallelogram

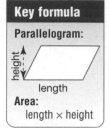
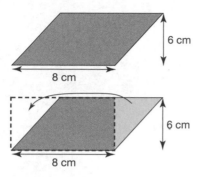

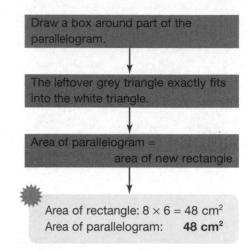

Draw a box around part of the parallelogram.

The leftover grey triangle exactly fits into the white triangle.

Area of parallelogram =
                area of new rectangle

Area of rectangle: 8 × 6 = 48 cm²
Area of parallelogram: **48 cm²**

Trapezium

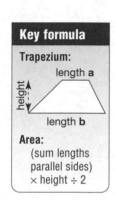

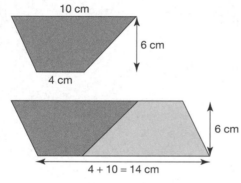

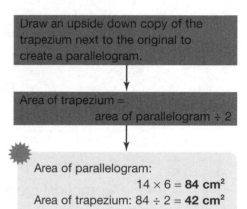

Draw an upside down copy of the trapezium next to the original to create a parallelogram.

Area of trapezium =
                area of parallelogram ÷ 2

Area of parallelogram:
                14 × 6 = **84 cm²**
Area of trapezium: 84 ÷ 2 = **42 cm²**

Work it out

Calculate the area of the following shapes:

1.

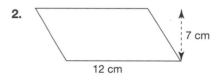

6 cm

10 cm

2.

7 cm

12 cm

3.

8 m

6 m

4.

6 cm

5 cm

14 cm

5.

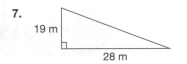

11 m

16 m

6.

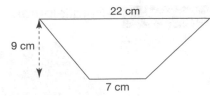

22 cm

9 cm

7 cm

7.

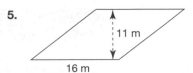

19 m

28 m

8.

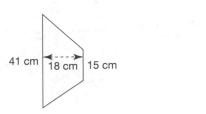

41 cm   18 cm   15 cm

9. Are any of the red shaded areas equal?

a.

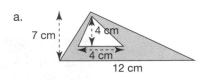

7 cm   4 cm

4 cm

12 cm

b.

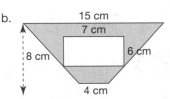

15 cm

7 cm

8 cm   6 cm

4 cm

c.

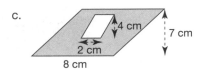

4 cm   7 cm

2 cm

8 cm

Example

A practical problem

In an area of the UK the going rate for agricultural land is approximately £8 000 per acre.

A farmer intends to sell a bit of land and would like to get a rough idea of its value before he approaches an estate agent. Here is a plan of the land:

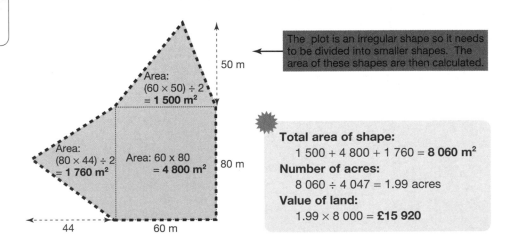

The plot is an irregular shape so it needs to be divided into smaller shapes. The area of these shapes are then calculated.

50 m

Area:
(60 × 50) ÷ 2
= **1 500 m²**

Area:
(80 × 44) ÷ 2
= **1 760 m²**

Area: 60 × 80
= **4 800 m²**   80 m

44   60 m

Total area of shape:
    1 500 + 4 800 + 1 760 = **8 060 m²**
Number of acres:
    8 060 ÷ 4 047 = 1.99 acres
Value of land:
    1.99 × 8 000 = **£15 920**

> # Work it out

The Castaways

1. a. The group of 12 will eventually receive only part of their food supply, the rest they will need to grow. They estimate that 200 m² of land per person should be cultivated in order to have enough vegetables to see them through the winter. This is the land they have available:

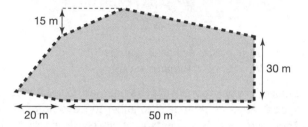

Here are the calculations of one group member:

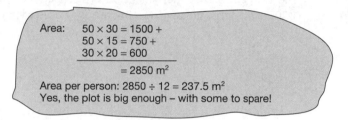

Area: 50 × 30 = 1500 +
50 × 15 = 750 +
30 × 20 = 600
_____
= 2850 m²
Area per person: 2850 ÷ 12 = 237.5 m²
Yes, the plot is big enough – with some to spare!

   i. These workings are incorrect. Why?
   ii. What is the area of the land?
   iii. Is there enough land for the 12?

b. The group plan to tile the main building. The coverage for the roofing tiles they have is approximately 26 per m². Work out:

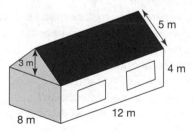

   i. the roof area
   ii. the number of tiles required.

▶

c. The outside walls are to be rendered.

The other side wall is an exact copy of the visible one.

The second end wall is not to be covered. All four windows are 2 m by 1.5 m high. Here is one member's calculation for the area to be rendered:

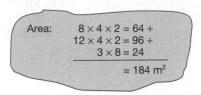

Area: $8 \times 4 \times 2 = 64 +$
$12 \times 4 \times 2 = 96 +$
$3 \times 8 = 24$
_____
$= 184 \text{ m}^2$

i. What mistakes has she made?

ii. What should the area be?

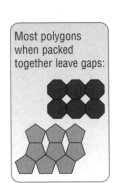

Most polygons when packed together leave gaps:

2. Bees create hexagonal cells to store their honey. These six-sided polygons are great space savers as they pack together to leave no gaps unlike most other polygons. They also have the advantage of closely resembling a circle which happens to be the shape of a bee's cross-section.

The diagram shows the dimension of a typical cell. If a 'frame' of a beehive is 1 200 cm², approximately how many honey cells will there be?

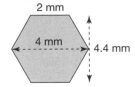

2 mm

4 mm

4.4 mm

3. a. The floors of a six storey building are rectangular, each with dimensions 40 m by 30 m.

i. What is the perimeter of each floor?

ii. What is the total floor area of all six storeys?

b. i. Find the width of a rectangular four storey building that has the same total floor area and its length is 60 m.

ii. What is the perimeter of each floor of the second building?

c. A third building consists of three equal trapeziums:

i. What is the total floor area of one floor?

ii. What is the perimeter of one floor?

iii. How many storeys would be required to match the floor area of the first building?

d. Which building would you prefer to work in and why?

Hints and tips

For part d. think about what the perimeter of the building provides in terms of light, heat loss, fresh air, views etc.

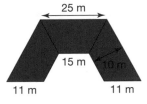

25 m

15 m 10 m

11 m   11 m

Area and circumference of a circle

The different parts to a circle:

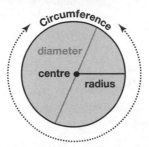

Paired work

You will need a measuring tape and four circular containers such as cans or tubes.

1. Use the tape measure to accurately record the circumference and diameter of each container. What number when multiplied by the diameter approximately gives the circumference?

2. Apply this relationship to calculate the circumference of a circle with diameter:
    a. 12 cm   b. 8 cm   c. 15 cm

3. Find the button for π (pi) on your calculator. This is the accurate value of your answer to question one.
    What is its value to:
    a. two decimal places
    b. eight decimal places

Key term

Pi or π
A number used in the calculation of the area and circumference of a circle. There are an infinite number of decimal places to the right of the decimal point. Pi to 5 decimal places is **3.14159**.

Example 1: Working out the area

About Pi (π)

Pi has been around for over 4 000 years. It is a Greek letter meaning perimeter. Throughout history mathematicians have searched for an exact value for pi and today with the advent of the computer it can be calculated to nearly 70 billion places!

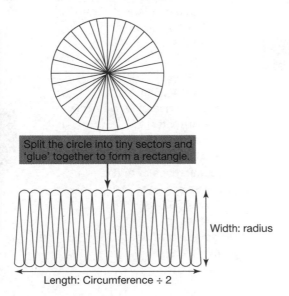

Split the circle into tiny sectors and 'glue' together to form a rectangle.

Width: radius

Length: Circumference ÷ 2

▶

Key formula

Circumference:

$\pi \times$ diameter
or
πd

Area: length $\times$ width
$\quad$ = (circumference $\div$ 2) $\times$ radius
$\quad$ = ($\pi \times$ diameter $\div$ 2) $\times$ radius
$\quad$ = $\pi \times$ **radius** $\times$ **radius**

Example 2

Calculate the area and circumference of the following shapes, rounding your answers to two decimal places:

Key formula

Area:

$\pi \times$ radius $\times$ radius

or in shorthand

πr^2

1.

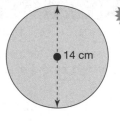

14 cm

Radius: $14 \div 2 = 7$ cm
Area: $\pi \times$ radius $\times$ radius
$\quad\quad\quad = \pi \times 7 \times 7$
$\quad\quad\quad =$ **153.94 cm²**
Circumference:
$\quad\quad\quad \pi \times$ diameter
$\quad\quad\quad = \pi \times 14$
$\quad\quad\quad =$ **43.98 cm**

Quick calculator method:

Press the buttons:

$\boxed{\Pi}$ $\boxed{\times}$ $\boxed{7}$ $\boxed{x^2}$ $\boxed{=}$

Note: to obtain π you often need to first press the shift button.

2.

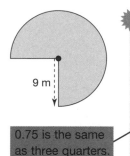

9 m

Area of whole circle:
$\quad \pi \times$ radius $\times$ radius
$\quad = \pi \times 9 \times 9$
$\quad = 254.4690049$ m²
Area three quarters of circle:
$\quad 0.75 \times 254.4690049$
$\quad =$ **190.85 m²**
Diameter:
$\quad 2 \times$ radius
$\quad = 2 \times 9 = 18$ m
Circumference of whole circle:
$\quad \pi \times$ diameter
$\quad = \pi \times 18$
$\quad = 56.54866776$ m
Circumference of three quarters of circle:
$\quad 0.75 \times 56.54866776$ m
$\quad = 42.41$ m
Perimeter of shape:
$\quad 42.41 + 9 + 9$ m
$\quad =$ **60.41 m**

Keep this number in your calculator for the next part of the calculation.

0.75 is the same as three quarters.

Keep this number in your calculator for the next part of the calculation.

Work it out

Work out the circumference (or perimeter) and area of the following shapes, rounding your answers to two decimal places:

1.

6 cm

2.

5 m

3.

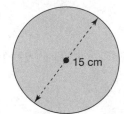

15 cm

4.

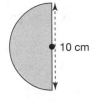

10 cm

Hints and tips

To prevent rounding errors, do the whole calculation in one go, e.g. to find the area of one quarter of a circle calculate the area of a whole circle and then immediately divide your calculator answer by 4.

5.

1.6 m

6.

7 cm

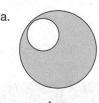

7.

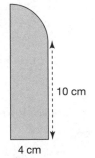

9 m

9 m

8.

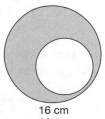

10 cm

4 cm

9. Are any of the shaded areas equal?

a.

b.

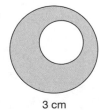

c.

	a.	b.	c.
Red circle radius:	4 cm	16 cm	3 cm
White circle radius:	9 cm	11 cm	8 cm

10. Copy and complete the table of dimensions of some of the planets within our solar system:

	Earth	Sun	Jupiter	Mars
Radius (km)	6 378	695 500		
Circumference (km)			449 216	21 344

Write your answers to the nearest km.

Example

A practical problem

An architect is designing the layout for a small theatre. The seating will ring a circular stage as shown:

Diameter of stage: 15 m

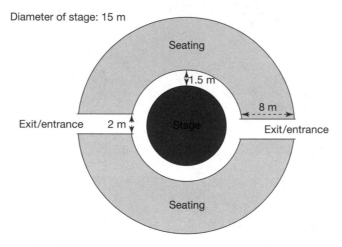

a. Actors like to know the area of stage they will be working on. What is it?

Radius: 15 ÷ 2 = 7.5 m
Area: π × radius × radius
= π × 7.5 × 7.5
= **176.71 m²**

b. The stage will be edged with vertical wooden boards.
How many of these will be required?

Vertical planks:
16 cm wide

Circumference:
  π × diameter
  = π × 15
  = **47.1238898 m**
  = 4712.38898 cm
Number of vertical planks required:
  4712.38898 ÷ 16
  = 294.5
This will mean purchasing **295** planks and cutting one of them.

Convert to cm to match the dimensions of the planks.

Circumference divided by width of plank.

To prevent their being a gap it is best to round the answer up.

The diagram shows the seating arrangement:

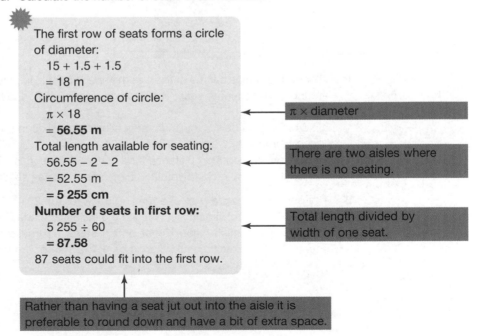

c. Work out how many rows will fit within the seating area.

A seat plus the gap between rows is 1 m.
According to the plan the seating extends to 8 m, so **8** rows should fit in the theatre.

d. Calculate the number of seats in the first row.

When calculating the number of seats in a row, use the inner circumference.

row of seats

The first row of seats forms a circle of diameter:
  15 + 1.5 + 1.5
  = 18 m
Circumference of circle:
  π × 18
  = **56.55 m**
Total length available for seating:
  56.55 − 2 − 2
  = 52.55 m
  = **5 255 cm**
Number of seats in first row:
  5 255 ÷ 60
  = **87.58**
87 seats could fit into the first row.

π × diameter

There are two aisles where there is no seating.

Total length divided by width of one seat.

Rather than having a seat jut out into the aisle it is preferable to round down and have a bit of extra space.

Work it out

Round your answers to two decimal places.

1. Using the dimensions in the example on page 282, calculate the number of seats on the final row of the auditorium.

2. A table 2.2 m in diameter has to fit eight people around seated on chairs that are 65 cm wide. Is this possible?

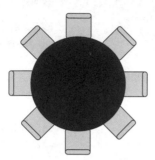

3. In drought conditions a farmer uses a spray to water his crops. He places the spray in the middle of the field where the water can project 40 m.
   How much area of the farmer's field does not get sprayed?

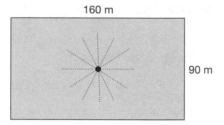

4. 'Comfort' distance can be defined as the space people in different cultures need all around them to feel at ease. The average comfort distance for a culture A person is 1.4 m.
   a. What should be the minimum area allowed for six culture A people to feel comfortable?
   b. The average comfort distance for a culture B person is 60 cm. How many culture B people could you fit in the same space as six culture A people?

5. The diagram shows a plan of a running track for the 2012 Olympics. Each lane is 1.22 m wide. Great Britain is running in the inside lane and France is in the outside. All runners will finish where Great Britain starts. To make the race fair, how far ahead of Great Britain should France be at the start of the race?

Note: Presume that each runner runs in the middle of the track.

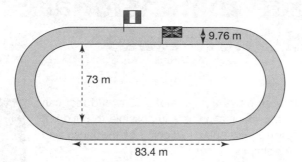

Hints and tips

It may help if you refer back to the castaways investigation earlier in this section.

Investigation – efficiently using fencing

The castaways have been given 400 m of fencing to enclose an area for their livestock. They want to enclose the largest possible area. Should they use a circle or a rectangle? Investigate.

3.8b Three-dimensional Shapes and Their Nets

Here is an example of a picture of a 3D world that can only live in the imagination. It is impossible to build but can be drawn by complex realigning of the faces and edges of the shapes.

In this section we will be looking strictly at those 3D shapes that can be both drawn and realised as solid shapes.

Faces, edges and vertices

Key terms

Face
A flat surface.

Edge
A line between two faces.

Vertex
A corner or point where edges meet.

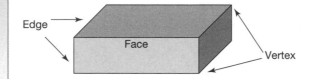

Edge

Face

Vertex

Cube
All faces are square

Cuboid
All faces are rectangular

Cylinder
Two circular ends connected by straight sides

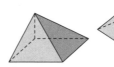

Square or triangular pyramids
The faces extend from the base to meet at a vertex

Triangular prism
Two triangular ends connected by rectangular sides

Work it out

1. When a square pyramid is sliced horizontally, the face revealed is a square.

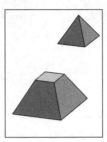

What is the shape of the face revealed when a square pyramid is sliced vertically down the middle?

A cuboid sliced at angle from end to end:

A chocolate cake sliced vertically:

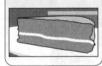

2. Copy and complete the table, stating the shape of the faces revealed:

	Sliced horizontally	Sliced vertically	Sliced at an angle from end to end
Upright cylinder			–
Cube			
Cuboid			Rectangle
Triangular prism			

3. How many edges, faces and vertices does a square pyramid possess?

What am I?

4. a. I have two edges and three faces.
   b. I have nine edges and five faces.

5. Twenty seven 1 cm cubes are put together to make one large cube.
   a. What are the dimensions of this cube?
   b. The outside cubes are all painted blue.
      Copy and complete the table, about the number of 1 cm cubes within the large cube with a specific number of painted faces.

Number of faces painted	0	1	2	3	4
Number of cubes	1*				

* There is one cube that has no painted faces.

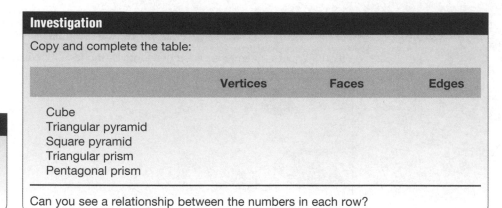

Investigation

Copy and complete the table:

	Vertices	Faces	Edges
Cube			
Triangular pyramid			
Square pyramid			
Triangular prism			
Pentagonal prism			

Can you see a relationship between the numbers in each row?

Hints and tips

Add and/or subtract all the figures in each row to come up with a pattern.

Prisms

Key term

Prism
A 3D shape that has the same cross-section along its length.

Here are some: examples of **prisms**:

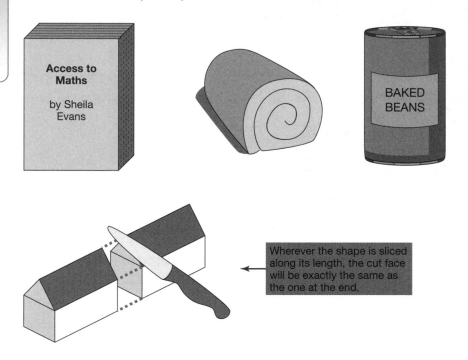

Access to Maths

by Sheila Evans

BAKED BEANS

Wherever the shape is sliced along its length, the cut face will be exactly the same as the one at the end.

Group work

Which shapes are prisms?

a. 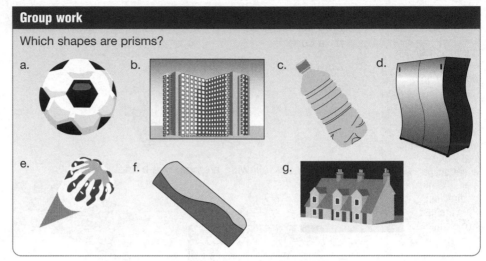   b.   c.   d.

e.   f.   g.

Nets – the link between 3D and 2D

Key term

Net
A 3D shape that has been opened up and flattened out by cutting along its edges. One shape can have several nets.

The opening up of a cube to obtain its **net**:

Nets are predominantly used in the production of containers. This could be the container for your box of teabags, can of tuna or tube of toothpaste.

(**Work it out**)

1.   What 3D shapes are these the net of:

a.   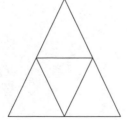   b.   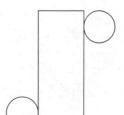   c.

2. Draw two different nets of:
   a. a square pyramid
   b. a cuboid.

3. Draw the net of this shape:

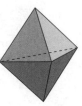

4. Which of the following are nets of a triangular prism?

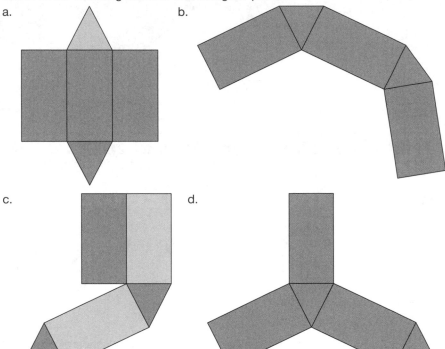

   a.   b.

   c.   d.

5. Draw the 3D front of this box of chocolates:

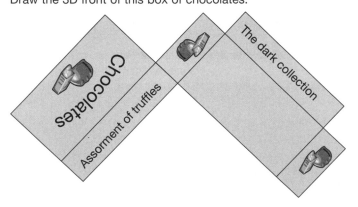

6. Three of these nets are part of the net of a cube.

a. Which are the correct ones?

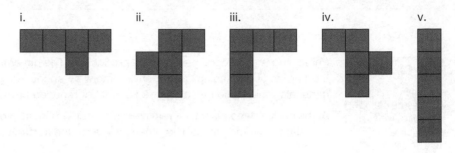

i.   ii.   iii.   iv.   v.

b. Complete the net of these.

3.8c Volume and Surface Area

Packaging is an integral part of retail production. The government is seeking to reduce the impact of packaging on the environment by encouraging producers to use fewer materials, which also has the added benefit of reduced production costs.

At the design stage manufacturers need to consider both the **volume** of their product (e.g. how much is in the can of baked beans) against the **surface area** (i.e. their packaging).

Example

Calculate the volume and surface area of the following shape:

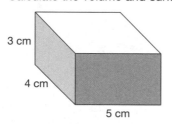

3 cm
4 cm
5 cm

The cuboid can be split into cubes of sides 1 cm. The volume of each cube is 1 cm³.

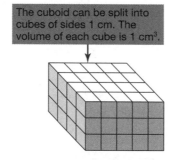

Total number of cubes: $3 \times 4 \times 5 = 60$
Volume: **60 cm³**

Net the cuboid to obtain the surface area.

Find the area of each face.

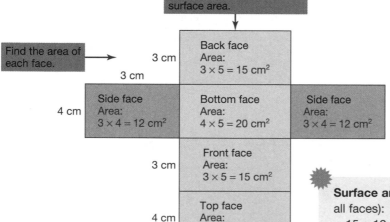

Back face
Area:
$3 \times 5 = 15$ cm²

3 cm
3 cm

Side face
Area:
$3 \times 4 = 12$ cm²

4 cm

Bottom face
Area:
$4 \times 5 = 20$ cm²

Side face
Area:
$3 \times 4 = 12$ cm²

Front face
Area:
$3 \times 5 = 15$ cm²

3 cm

Top face
Area:
$4 \times 5 = 20$ cm²

4 cm

5 cm

Surface area of cuboid (total area of all faces):
$15 + 12 + 20 + 12 + 15 + 20 =$ **94 cm²**

> ## Work it out

Calculate the volume and surface area of the following cuboids. If required, round your answer to two decimal places.

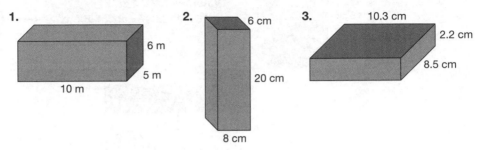

1.   6 m
          10 m   5 m

2.   6 cm
          20 cm
          8 cm

3.   10.3 cm   2.2 cm
          8.5 cm

Example

Find the volume and surface area of the following prisms. If required, round your answer to one decimal place.

> ### Key formula
>
> **Volume of a prism:**
>
> Length × area of cross-section.

1.

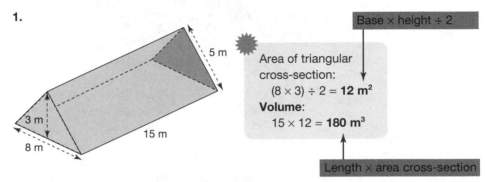

5 m

3 m

8 m

15 m

Base × height ÷ 2

Area of triangular cross-section:

$(8 \times 3) \div 2 = \textbf{12 m}^2$

Volume:

$15 \times 12 = \textbf{180 m}^3$

Length × area cross-section

Net the triangular prism to obtain the surface area.

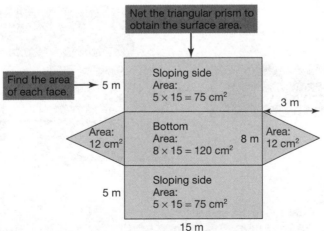

Find the area of each face.

5 m

Sloping side
Area:
$5 \times 15 = 75 \text{ cm}^2$

3 m

Area:
12 cm²

Bottom
Area:
$8 \times 15 = 120 \text{ cm}^2$

8 m

Area:
12 cm²

5 m

Sloping side
Area:
$5 \times 15 = 75 \text{ cm}^2$

15 m

Surface area (total area of all faces):

$75 + 120 + 75 + 12 + 12 = \textbf{294 m}^2$

2.

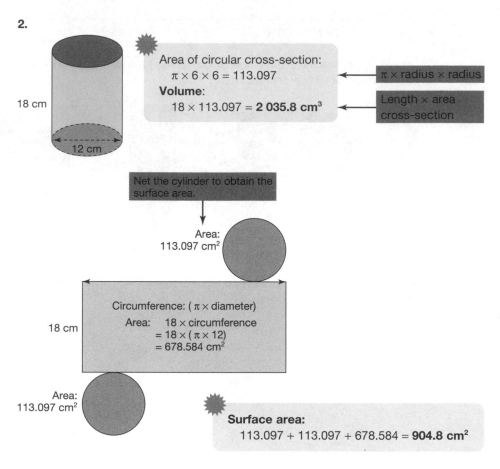

Area of circular cross-section:
$\pi \times 6 \times 6 = 113.097$
Volume:
$18 \times 113.097 = \mathbf{2\ 035.8\ cm^3}$

$\pi \times$ radius $\times$ radius

Length $\times$ area cross-section

18 cm

12 cm

Net the cylinder to obtain the surface area.

Area:
113.097 cm²

18 cm

Circumference: ($\pi \times$ diameter)
Area: $18 \times$ circumference
$= 18 \times (\pi \times 12)$
$= 678.584\ cm^2$

Area:
113.097 cm²

Surface area:
$113.097 + 113.097 + 678.584 = \mathbf{904.8\ cm^2}$

3.

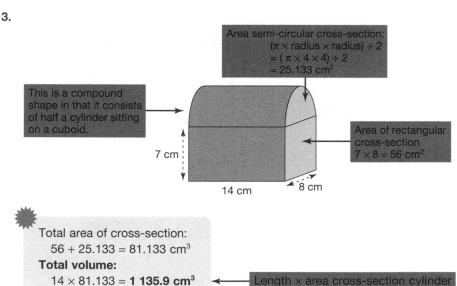

Area semi-circular cross-section:
$(\pi \times$ radius $\times$ radius$) \div 2$
$= (\pi \times 4 \times 4) \div 2$
$= 25.133\ cm^2$

This is a compound shape in that it consists of half a cylinder sitting on a cuboid.

Area of rectangular cross-section
$7 \times 8 = 56\ cm^2$

7 cm

14 cm

8 cm

Total area of cross-section:
$56 + 25.133 = 81.133\ cm^3$
Total volume:
$14 \times 81.133 = \mathbf{1\ 135.9\ cm^3}$

Length $\times$ area cross-section cylinder

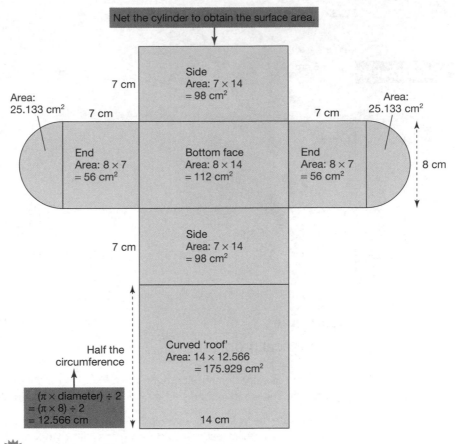

Net the cylinder to obtain the surface area.

Side
Area: 7 × 14
= 98 cm²

7 cm

Area:
25.133 cm²

7 cm

7 cm

Area:
25.133 cm²

8 cm

End
Area: 8 × 7
= 56 cm²

Bottom face
Area: 8 × 14
= 112 cm²

End
Area: 8 × 7
= 56 cm²

Side
Area: 7 × 14
= 98 cm²

7 cm

Half the
circumference

Curved 'roof'
Area: 14 × 12.566
= 175.929 cm²

(π × diameter) ÷ 2
= (π × 8) ÷ 2
= 12.566 cm

14 cm

Surface area (total area of all faces):
98 + 112 + 98 + 175.929 + 56 + 25.133 + 56 + 25.133 = **646.2 cm²**

Mapping out

Volume:

Identify the cross-section that has the same face along its length.

↓

Calculate the area of this cross-section.

↓

Multiply this area by its length.

Work it out

Work out the volume and surface area of the following prisms, if required round your answers to one decimal places:

1.

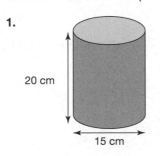

20 cm

15 cm

2.

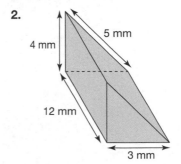

5 mm

4 mm

12 mm

3 mm

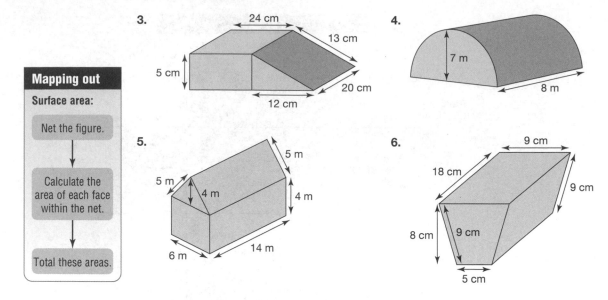

3.

24 cm

13 cm

5 cm

20 cm

12 cm

4.

7 m

8 m

5.

5 m

5 m

4 m

4 m

6 m

14 m

6.

9 cm

18 cm

9 cm

8 cm

9 cm

5 cm

Example

A practical problem

When the forestry commission cuts down logs they are initially piled up before transportation. The wood is then sold by volume to commercial outlets.

To calculate the volume of wood in each pile without having to tediously measure the radius and length of each individual log they first work out the volume of the prism formed by the pile and then estimate the wood to make up 70% of this.

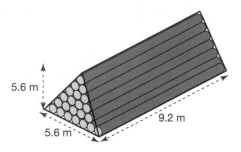

5.6 m

5.6 m

9.2 m

Is this a good estimate for a pile of twenty two logs shown in the diagram, all of radius 0.4 m?

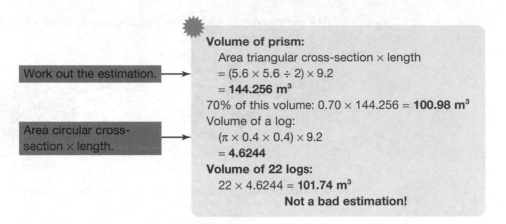

Work out the estimation.

Area circular cross-section × length.

Volume of prism:
Area triangular cross-section × length
= (5.6 × 5.6 ÷ 2) × 9.2
= **144.256 m³**
70% of this volume: 0.70 × 144.256 = **100.98 m³**
Volume of a log:
(π × 0.4 × 0.4) × 9.2
= **4.6244**
Volume of 22 logs:
22 × 4.6244 = **101.74 m³**
                    Not a bad estimation!

At the timber yard the wood is cut into planks and stacked:

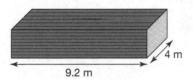

9.2 m

4 m

If the volume is 101.74, how high will the pile be?

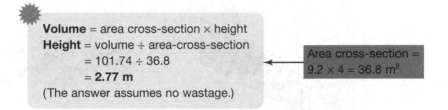

Volume = area cross-section × height
Height = volume ÷ area-cross-section
        = 101.74 ÷ 36.8
        = **2.77 m**
(The answer assumes no wastage.)

Area cross-section =
9.2 × 4 = 36.8 m²

Work it out

If required, round your answers to two decimal places.

1. The diagram shows a net of a box of chocolates:
    a. Calculate the volume.
    b. What will be the area of packaging for
        20 boxes?

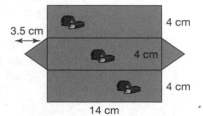

3.5 cm

4 cm

4 cm

4 cm

14 cm

2.   a. The same beer comes in two types of glasses. Which holds the more liquid?

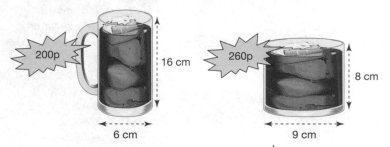

200p   16 cm

260p   8 cm

6 cm

9 cm

Height = volume ÷ area cross-section.

b. A third glass has a volume of 462 cm³. What is the height?

230p   ?

Hints and tips

Calculate the cost of 1 cm³ of beer for each glass.

7 cm

c. Which glass is the best value for money?

3. A crisp manufacturer decides to change the shape of his packaging from a triangular prism to a box while keeping the volume, length and width the same.

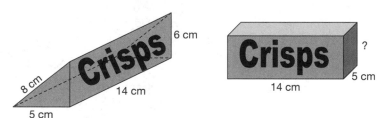

6 cm

8 cm

14 cm

5 cm

Crisps

14 cm

?

5 cm

a. What is the volume of a box crisps?
b. What is the height of the new box?
c. Which shape produces less packaging?

1 m³ = 1 000 litres.

4. In bad weather a ship overturns leaving 20 people trapped in a room. Fortunately for them, the room forms an air pocket and the 20 remain there as it is too dangerous to swim. But for how long can they survive? The dimensions of the room are 8 m by 6 m by 4 m high. One person consumes approximately 8 litres of air a minute if they are barely active.
a. How many litres of air are in the room?
b. How many hours will the 20 last in the room?
c. What assumption have you made?

The Castaways

5. a. The group have allotted four identical tanks for the storage of oil. They are expecting a delivery of 22 000 litres of oil.

Dimensions of a tank

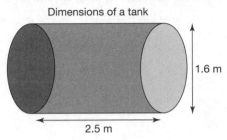

1.6 m

2.5 m

    i. What is the volume of the oil to be delivered?
    ii. Calculate the total volume of all four tanks.
    iii. Have they allotted enough tanks?

b. The Castaways possess a rectangular water storage tank. At the moment it is half full. They fill it with another 10 000 litres of water.

Dimensions of tank

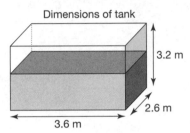

3.2 m

2.6 m

3.6 m

    i. What is the original volume of water?
    ii. What is the new volume of water?
    iii. What is the new depth of the water in the tank?
    iv. How many days will this water last if each of the 12 is rationed to an average of 15 litres a day?

6. In November 2002 the tanker The Sea Empress ran aground on rocks at the entrance to Milford Haven harbour in Pembrokeshire. In the following week approximately 19 million gallons of oil spilled into the sea.

Oil slicks are approximately 0.254 mm thick.

a. What is the volume, to the nearest whole number, of oil spilt?
b. How big an area would this cover? Give your answer to the nearest whole number in:
    i. m^2
    ii. km^2

Mapping out

Using the conversion:
Volume, in m^3:
  no. gallons ÷ 220

↓

Surface area:
  volume ÷ depth

Investigation 1

Four cuboids all have edges of length 2 cm, 6 cm and 6 cm.

Work out how they can be glued together to obtain the minimum surface area.

Vital statistics

Total surface area of earth that is covered in sea: 360 million km²

Dimensions of ice sheet:
Area: 1 700 000 km²
Depth: 1.5 km

Assumptions:

1. The surface area of the sea will remain constant. In reality it will increase as the sea will spread over land.
2. Ice occupies the same volume as water – it dosen't.

However, these assumptions do not negate the problem as it provides a good feel for the extent of the issue.

Job description:

Hugh is part of a team responsible for the protection and expansion of woodlands over a large area in the south of England. His work can include the removal of invasive species or managing woodlands in a manner that will encourage the increase of a specific plant or animal. Part of Hugh's job is also to raise public awareness of the value of woodlands and of the care they need to survive.

Investigation 2

It is now widely recognised that global warming is causing the ice sheets of Greenland and Antarctica to melt. But what exactly is happening to the sea levels?

The scenario: The whole of the Greenland ice sheet melts.
The question: By how much will the sea level rise?

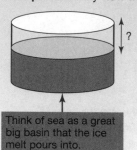

Think of sea as a great big basin that the ice melt pours into.

Volume of ice sheet:
   area × depth
   = 1 700 000 × 1.5
   = 2 550 000 km³
Rise in sea levels:
   2 550 000 ÷ 360 000 000
   = 0.007083 km
   = **7.083 m**

Sea rise:
   volume ÷ surface area of sea

Using the values given in the above example work out the sea level rise, to the nearest metre, if:

1. the Antarctic ice melts
   area: 12 000 000 km²; depth 2.45 km
2. both ice sheets melt.

CASE STUDY

Using Maths at Work – Hugh: woodland officer

A couple of months ago we granted Peter Beauson, the owner of an ancient chestnut wood, a licence to thin it. We gave him permission to fell 200 trees.

Unfortunately, we later received several angry complaints from local residents about the number of trees felled. A trainee and I followed these complaints up by visiting the site.

We counted 357 logs lying on the ground; however, 47 of these could be discounted because they were old windblown ones.

We then measured the length and mid-diameter of every tenth new log and worked out the average dimensions of all the logs:

   length: 11.4 m
   diameter: 38 cm.

CASE STUDY (*continued*)

Tasks
Round your answers to two decimal places.

1. How many unlicensed trees did the owner fell?

2. How many logs were measured?

3. Work out the average volume in m^3, of wood per log.

4. a. Use your answer to **3.** to work out the volume of wood Peter felled.
   b. How much money did he make from the wood?

'I pointed out to the trainee that the trees had been coppiced, so there could be more felled logs than felled trees. On further investigation we found there were 264 new stumps, indicating that some trees had indeed produced more than one log.'

5. On average, how many logs are there per tree?

6. Using your answer to questions 3 and 5 work out:
   a. the number of logs Peter had licence to fell
   b. the volume of unlicensed wood felled.
   c. How much did Peter make from the unlicensed wood?

7. Here is a map of the area. Each square on the grid represents an area of 625 m^2.
   a. What is the length, in metres, of each square?
   b. By counting squares, work out the approximate area of the wood:
      i. m^2
      ii. hectares.

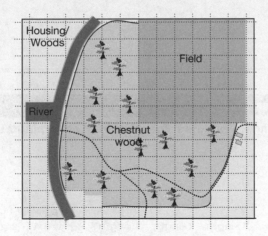

8. Before felling, the density of wood was 179 trees per hectare.
   a. How many trees were originally in the wood?
   b. What is the density of trees per hectare after the felling?
   Round both your answers to the nearest whole number.

What Hugh says:

'I have worked for the Forestry Commission all over Britain and I use maths on a daily basis to calculate the number of trees per hectare, timber volumes, percentage stocking of woods and values of grant aid to owners.'

Local value for timber: £25 per m^3.

Coppiced tree:

a tree that has been pruned in such a manner that it results in multiple trunks.

Hints and tips

The owner had a licence to fell 200 trees not 200 logs.

---

1 hectare
= 10 000 m^2.

3.9a Right-angled Triangles and Pythagoras' Theorem

The special properties of right-angled triangles allow us to answer questions such as:

How does GPS work?
What is the altitude of that helicopter?
How high is this mountain?
How much does the leaning tower of Pisa lean?
How far is it to the horizon?
How big is the planet Pluto?
How does the cursor move around a computer screen?
What is the slope of that roof?
Exactly where did the murder take place?

Key term

Hypotenuse
The longest side in a right-angled triangle. The side opposite the right angle.

Task – identifying the hypotenuse

When working with right-angle triangles it is important to be able to identify the **hypotenuse**.

Label the hypotenuse in the following triangles:

a.

b.

c.

Investigation

Discovering Pythagoras' theorem in twenty minutes

Part 1
Copy the table:

	Length a	Length b	Length c	Area square A $a \times a = a^2$	Area square B $b \times b = b^2$	Area square C $c \times c = c^2$
Triangle 1	3 cm	4 cm				
Triangle 2						
Triangle 3						
Triangle 4						

▶

Investigation (*continued*)

Use this table to record your measurements for Parts 2–4

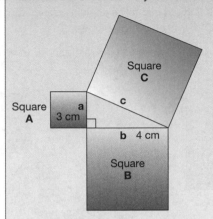

Part 2

- Accurately draw the right-angled triangle in the diagram.
- Label the sides **a**, **b** and **c** making sure **c** is the hypotenuse.
- Measure the length of **c**.
- Draw the **squares** extending from the sides as shown.
- Work out the areas of these squares.
- Record your measurements in the table.

Part 3

Repeat all of **Part 2**, but now drawing right-angled triangles with sides:

- 5 cm (**a**) and 12 cm (**b**).
- 7 cm (**a**) and 24 cm (**b**).

Part 4

Repeat **Part 2** but now use your own dimensions to draw a right-angled triangle.

Part 5

Can you find a relationship between the areas? This is Pythagoras' theorem.

Investigation

1. Does Pythagoras' Theorem work with triangles that do not contain a right angle? Investigate by constructing at least three scalene triangles with no 90° angle and calculating the area of their protruding squares.

2. Use your relationship from the previous investigation, to work out the missing areas:

   a.

   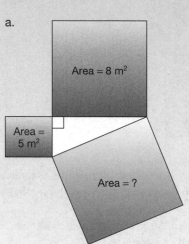

   b.

   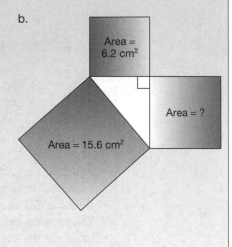

3. a. Does the relationship work, if instead of adding squares to the side of the right-angle triangle, triangles with the same base length and perpendicular height are used?

   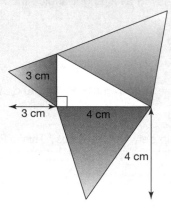

   b. Name one shape when added to the sides of a right-angle triangle that would not obey the relationship.

Example

The sides of a triangle have three associated squares:

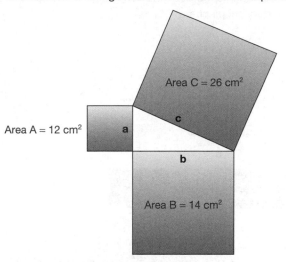

Area C = 26 cm^2

Area A = 12 cm^2

a

c

b

Area B = 14 cm^2

Does this triangle have a right angle?

Yes
Area **C** = Area **A** + Area **B**
  26   =   12   +   14

What are the lengths of each side of the triangle?
Give your answer to two decimal places.

$a \times a = 12$
  $a = \sqrt{12} =$ **3.46 cm**
$b \times b = 14$
  $b = \sqrt{14} =$ **3.74 cm**
$c \times c = 26$
  $c = \sqrt{26} =$ **5.10 cm**

Use the square root button on the calculator: ▢

Work it out

Hints and tips

The biggest area belongs to the square extending from the hypotenuse.

Are any of the following triangles right angled? If they are, calculate the lengths of their sides, rounding your answers to two decimal places.

1. Triangle with squares of area 30 m^2, 18 m^2 and 12 m^2

2. Triangle with squares of area 28 cm^2, 11 cm^2 and 17 cm^2

3. Triangle with squares of area 36 cm^2, 18 cm^2 and 20 cm^2

Example – calculating the length of the hypotenuse

Work out the missing lengths in the following right-angled triangles. Round your answers to two decimal places.

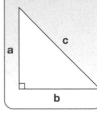

Key term

Pythagoras' theorem
The square of the hypotenuse equals the sum of the squares of the other two sides:

$$c^2 = a^2 + b^2$$

1.

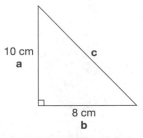

10 cm
a

c

8 cm
b

Add squares **A**, **B** and **C** to the diagram. Label the hypotenuse **c** and the remaining two sides **a** and **b**.

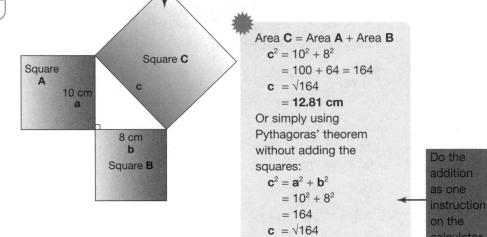

Square **C**

Square **A**
10 cm
a

c

8 cm
b
Square **B**

Area **C** = Area **A** + Area **B**

$c^2 = 10^2 + 8^2$
$\quad = 100 + 64 = 164$
$c = \sqrt{164}$
$\quad = \textbf{12.81 cm}$

Or simply using Pythagoras' theorem without adding the squares:

$c^2 = a^2 + b^2$
$\quad = 10^2 + 8^2$
$\quad = 164$
$c = \sqrt{164}$
$\quad = \textbf{12.81 cm}$

Do the addition as one instruction on the calculator.

2.

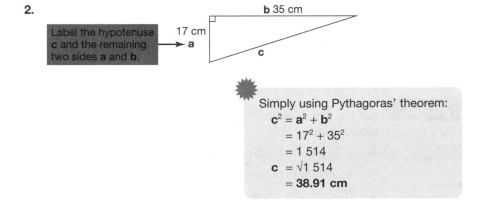

Label the hypotenuse **c** and the remaining two sides **a** and **b**.

b 35 cm

17 cm
a

c

Simply using Pythagoras' theorem:

$c^2 = a^2 + b^2$
$\quad = 17^2 + 35^2$
$\quad = 1\,514$
$c = \sqrt{1\,514}$
$\quad = \textbf{38.91 cm}$

Work it out

Use Pythagoras' theorem to find the length of the missing side in the following triangles. Round your answers to two decimal places:

1.
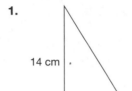
14 cm
6 cm

2.
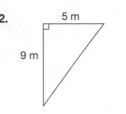
5 m
9 m

3.
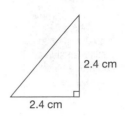
2.4 cm
2.4 cm

4.
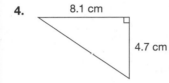
8.1 cm
4.7 cm

5.
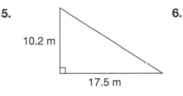
10.2 m
17.5 m

6.
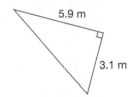
5.9 m
3.1 m

Example – when the missing side is not the hypotenuse

Work out the missing lengths in the following-right angled triangles. Round your answers to two decimal places.

Label the hypotenuse **c**, the unknown side **a** and the remaining side **b**.

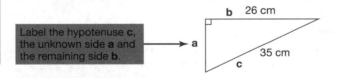
b 26 cm
a
35 cm
c

Using Pythagoras' theorem:
$$c^2 = a^2 + b^2$$
$$35^2 = a^2 + 26^2$$
$$1\,225 = a^2 + 676$$
To total 1 225:
$$a^2 = 1\,225 - 676 = 549$$
$$a = \sqrt{549}$$
$$= \mathbf{23.43\ cm}$$
Or simply:
$$a^2 = c^2 - b^2$$
$$a^2 = 35^2 - 26^2$$
$$= 549$$
$$a = \sqrt{549}$$
$$= \mathbf{23.43\ cm}$$

Do the subtraction as one instruction on the calculator.

Mapping out

Calculating the length of a side that is not the hypotenuse:

Label the hypotenuse **c**, the unknown side **a** and the remaining side **b**.

↓

Use Pythagoras' theorem: Subtract the square of **b** from the square of **c**.

↓

Length of side a: Square root the answer.

↓

Round the answer to the required degree of accuracy.

Hints and tips

The whole calculation can be done as one sum on the calculator.

Work it out

Find the length of the missing side in the following triangles. Round your answers to two decimal places:

1.
12 m
20 m

2.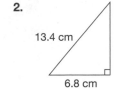
13.4 cm
6.8 cm

3.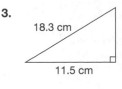
18.3 cm
11.5 cm

4.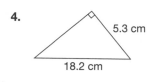
5.3 cm
18.2 cm

5.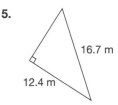
16.7 m
12.4 m

6.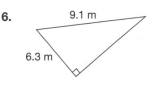
9.1 m
6.3 m

Investigation

1. Triangles where all three sides are whole numbers are known as Pythagorean triplets, for example a right-angled triangle with sides of length 3, 4 and 5 cm forms a triplet.
   Find four more triplets.
   Hint: Start with an odd number, square it, split the answer into two numbers that differ by one e.g. $3^2 = 9$, 9 can be split into 4 and 5 that differ by one. The triplet is 3, 4 and 5.

2. a. Ancient Egyptians, armed with rope with knots evenly spaced along its length and a practical version of the theorem, constructed perfect corners for their buildings and pyramids. Without using a protractor, use their idea to construct accurately a right angle. Describe how you used the system of knots.
   b. List three practical situations where right angles are used today.

3. a. Without using a calculator, draw as accurately as possible the lines of length:
   i. $\sqrt{34}$ cm
   ii. $\sqrt{18}$ cm
   iii. $\sqrt{40}$ cm
   Hint: Use the given square root as the length of the hypotenuse in a right-angled triangle. First draw two arms of the right angle, making sure the squares of the lengths of these arms total the square of the hypotenuse (i.e., 34 for part i).
   b. Create one square root for your partner to draw.

Example

Have you ever wondered, when standing on the waters' edge, just how far out to sea you can see?

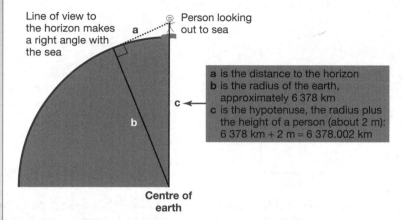

Line of view to the horizon makes a right angle with the sea

a

Person looking out to sea

b

c

Centre of earth

a is the distance to the horizon
b is the radius of the earth, approximately 6 378 km
c is the hypotenuse, the radius plus the height of a person (about 2 m): 6 378 km + 2 m = 6 378.002 km

Using Pythagoras' theorem:

$$a^2 = c^2 - b^2$$
$$a^2 = 6\ 378.002^2 - 6\ 378^2$$
$$a^2 = 25.512\ \text{km}$$
$$a = \mathbf{5.05\ km}$$

A person 2 m tall can see approximately 5 km out to sea.

Work it out

Round all your answers to two decimal places

1. a. If you were standing on top of a 1 000 m mountain next to the sea, how far out to sea could you see (assume you are 2 m tall?).

1 000 m

28 m

b. What is the maximum distance you can be away from a lighthouse that stands 28 m tall and still be able to see the light? Assume you are at the surface of the sea.

c. What must be the elevation of an observer if he can see an object 50 km away? Give your answer in metres.

Pythagoras

A Greek mathematician living in the late 6th century B.C. He organised a secret religious society called the Pythagoreans. Members owned no personal possessions and were vegetarians.

Who did discover the theorem?

Pythagoras has long been associated with the theorem. However, ancient clay tablets dated 1 000 B.C. provide evidence that the Babylonians understood the relationship of the sides of a right-angled triangle. The ancient Egyptians were also familiar with it but left precious little evidence of their maths as it was written on papyrus which decays easily. Pythagoras was probably the first person to actually prove the theorem.

Hints and tips

Draw a diagram of the situation.

About driving

2. a. Two cars start at the same point on a straight road but face opposite directions.
Each car drives 12 km, takes a right turn and drives for another 8 km.
How far apart are the two cars?

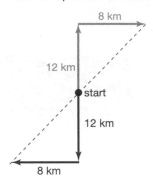

b. A driver setting out for home from work has enough petrol to go 40 miles.
He would prefer to drive along **Route A**, because although it is longer the roads are faster and he will get home quicker.
He knows **Route B** is 36 miles and the second leg of **Route A** is 22 miles.
Has he enough petrol to take **Route A**?

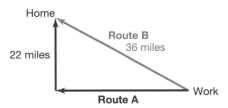

3. A shopper wants to buy on-line both a TV and a pine 'entertainment centre' for the TV. The TV measures 27″ along the diagonal and the dimensions of the area where the TV would sit is 24″ wide by 18″ high.
Will the TV fit in the space?

The castaways

4. a. The group are having a shed delivered. On arrival the shed will need to be covered with roofing felt which comes in strips 1.8 m wide.
An extra 50 cm will be required for each edge the roof meets the shed.
Using the diagram a member came up with these calculations:

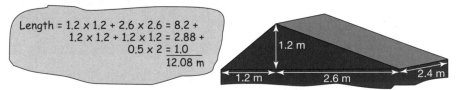

i. What errors has she made?
ii. How much felt should they order?

b. The group are planning to convert the 'attic' of the main building into one large open plan bedroom. Here are their plans for the stairs:

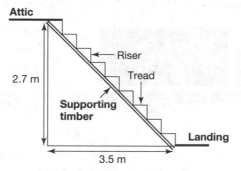

One member of the group was asked these three questions:

1. The risers are to be 18 cm. How many steps will be required?

2. How wide will be each tread?

3. What should be the length of the supporting piece of timber?

And he came up with these answers:

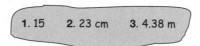

1. 15   **2.** 23 cm   **3.** 4.38 m

i. Are any of them correct?
ii. Rectify any incorrect answers.

5. A drug dealer was arrested for selling drugs to an undercover police man. In court the prosecution argued that as the crow flies he was within 1 000 feet of a school and so should be given a heavier sentence. The defence argued that crows do not sell drugs.

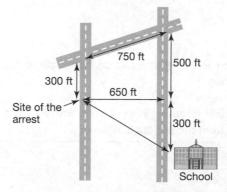

a. How far would the defence argue he was from the school?
b. How far would the prosecution argue he was from the school?

6. A business person dealing in the buying and selling of timber is about to purchase some new trucks for his company. The dimension of the 'trailer' part of the truck is shown below:

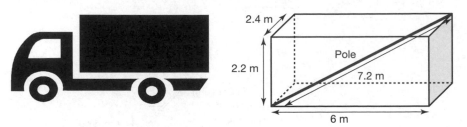

a. Occasionally he transports wooden poles that are 7.2 m long. Would one fit inside the trailer if positioned opposite corner to opposite corner? Justify your answer.
Hint: You will need to use Pythagoras twice.

b. If not, what is the minimum length for the trailer that could take this pole (keep the width and height the same)?

Spirals in nature

From hurricanes to sea shells these patterns form an optimum 'packing' arrangement.

Investigation

Investigation – Maths in Nature

a. For each triangle, write down the lengths of the hypotenuse **c–g**. Do not obtain a decimal value, but leave your answer as a square root, for example:

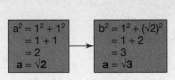

$$a^2 = 1^2 + 1^2$$
$$= 1 + 1$$
$$= 2$$
$$a = \sqrt{2}$$

$$b^2 = 1^2 + (\sqrt{2})^2$$
$$= 1 + 2$$
$$= 3$$
$$a = \sqrt{3}$$

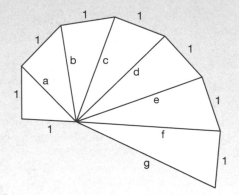

b. If this pattern continued, what would be the length of the:
  i. 10th hypotenuse?
  ii. 100th hypotenuse?
c. Construct the spiral in the diagram, starting with a right-angled triangle with the sides extending from the 90° angle of length 1″.

3.9b Right-angled Triangles and Trigonometry

Naming the sides in a right-angled triangle

Here are two identical triangles that are labelled with respect to the marked angle.

Key terms

Opposite side
The side opposite the angle under consideration.

Adjacent side
The side next to the angle under consideration.

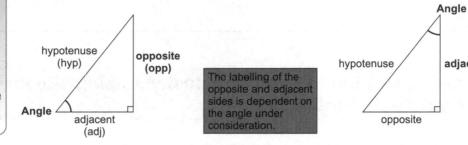

The labelling of the opposite and adjacent sides is dependent on the angle under consideration.

Work it out

Copy and name the sides of the right-angled triangles in respect to the angle marked **a**:

1.

2.

3.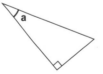

 Group task

- Each member draws four right-angle triangles like the one in the diagram. The lengths can be any size, but the angle size for each triangle should be 30°, 45°, 50° and 60°, respectively.
- Label the hypotenuse, opposite and adjacent sides.
- Copy and complete the table below, making sure you measure the sides of your triangles accurately.
- Compare your answers with other members of the group.
- Can you draw any conclusions?

▶

Group task (*continued*)

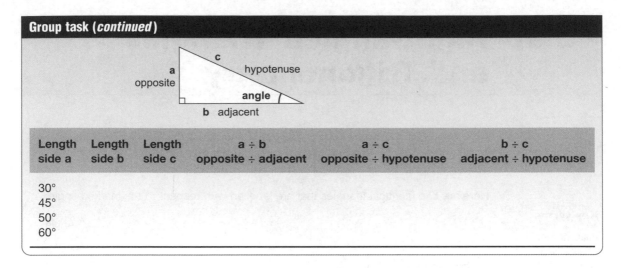

Length side a	Length side b	Length side c	a ÷ b opposite ÷ adjacent	a ÷ c opposite ÷ hypotenuse	b ÷ c adjacent ÷ hypotenuse
30°					
45°					
50°					
60°					

An explanation of your conclusions using similar right-angled triangles

The two triangles are similar as all the sides in the large triangle are four times bigger than corresponding ones in the smaller triangle.
Corresponding angles are equal.

The sides are labelled with respect to angle **a**.

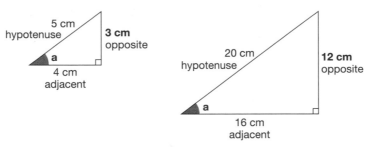

Division of the sides

Giving the division a name	Abbreviated to:	Division of sides	Small triangle	Large Triangle
Tangent of angle a	Tan **a**	$\dfrac{\text{opposite}}{\text{adjacent}}$	$\dfrac{3}{4} = 0.75$	$\dfrac{12}{16} = 0.75$
Sine of angle a	Sin **a**	$\dfrac{\text{opposite}}{\text{hypotenuse}}$	$\dfrac{3}{5} = 0.6$	$\dfrac{12}{20} = 0.6$
Cosine of angle a	Cos **a**	$\dfrac{\text{adjacent}}{\text{hypotenuse}}$	$\dfrac{4}{5} = 0.8$	$\dfrac{16}{20} = 0.8$

When triangles are similar the division of two sides is always the same.

This information can be used to find unknown sides of similar right-angle triangles without the need for measurement:

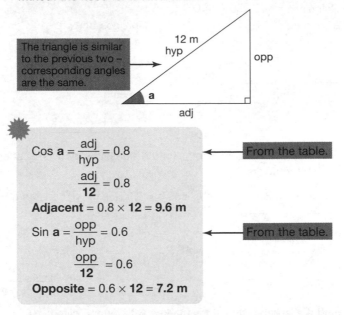

The triangle is similar to the previous two – corresponding angles are the same.

$$\text{Cos } \mathbf{a} = \frac{adj}{hyp} = 0.8$$

From the table.

$$\frac{adj}{12} = 0.8$$

Adjacent $= 0.8 \times \mathbf{12} = \mathbf{9.6 \text{ m}}$

$$\text{Sin } \mathbf{a} = \frac{opp}{hyp} = 0.6$$

From the table.

$$\frac{opp}{12} = 0.6$$

Opposite $= 0.6 \times \mathbf{12} = \mathbf{7.2 \text{ m}}$

Investigation

1. Sketch a right-angled triangle *similar* to the ones above, providing the dimensions for corresponding sides.
2. Label angle **a** to correspond to the **a** marked in the previous triangles.
3. Using your dimensions work out:
    a. tan **a**
    b. sin **a**
    c. cos **a**
4. Do they equal the answers in the example?

Example

When only one piece of information is provided there are countless possible answers.

Provide possible lengths for the adjacent and opposite sides in the triangle below when tan **b** = 0.4

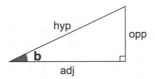

$$\text{tan } \mathbf{b} = \frac{opp}{adj} = 0.4$$

Opposite: 4 cm
Adjacent: 10 cm
$(4 \div 10 = 0.4)$
Alternatively:
Opposite: 8 cm
Adjacent: 20 cm
$(8 \div 20 = 0.4)$

Investigation

1. Calculate:
   a. tan **a**

   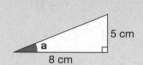

   b. cos **b**

   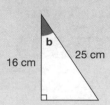

2. Find a pair of possible lengths for the sides labelled with a letter (there are many possible answers):

   a. sin **a** = 0.2

   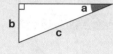

   b. cos **b** = 0.9

   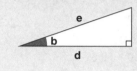

   c. tan **c** = 1.2

   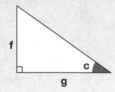

3. Find the length of the sides marked with letters, given:

   a. cos **60°** = 0.5

   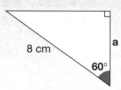

   b. tan **45°** = 1

   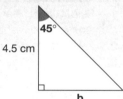

4. By drawing two pairs of similar triangles that don't contain a right-angle investigate if the division of corresponding sides are the same.

Key trigonometric functions

Tangent of a:

Abbreviated to:

Tan a =

$$\frac{\text{opposite}}{\text{adjacent}}$$

Sine of a:

Abbreviated to:

Sin a =

$$\frac{\text{opposite}}{\text{hypotenuse}}$$

Cosine of a:

Abbreviated to:

Cos a =

$$\frac{\text{adjacent}}{\text{hypotenuse}}$$

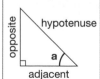

In the time before calculators

Less than 50 years ago the divison of sides for each angle were listed in tables, here is part of one:

Angle	Sin	Cos	Tan	Angle	Sin	Cos	Tan
26°	0.44	0.90	0.49	41°	0.66	0.76	0.87
27°	0.45	0.89	0.51	42°	0.67	0.74	0.90
28°	0.47	0.88	0.53	43°	0.68	0.73	0.93
29°	0.49	0.88	0.55	44°	0.70	0.72	0.97
30°	0.50	0.87	0.58	45°	0.71	0.71	1.00

Group work

Use the table at the bottom of page 316 to answer the first two questions.

1. Work out the angles marked with letters:

a.

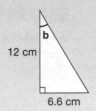

20 cm

13.6 cm

a

b.

b

12 cm

6.6 cm

c.

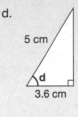

c

10 cm

5.3 cm

d.

5 cm

d

3.6 cm

2. a. Work out how to use your calculator to obtain:
    i. sin 30°
    ii. cos 27°
    iii. tan 45°
    Use the table on page 316 to check your answers.

    b. Work out how to use your calculator to obtain the angle **a**, when:
    i. cos **a** = 0.89
    ii. tan **a** = 0.93
    iii. sin **a** = 0.5
    Use the table to check your answers.

Hints and tips

Always remember to label all three sides of the triangle with respect to the marked angle.

Example

Using trigonometry to calculate the lengths of sides in a right-angled triangle

Calculate the length of the side marked by a letter.

1.

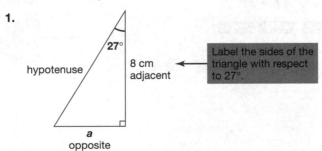

27°

hypotenuse

8 cm
adjacent

Label the sides of the triangle with respect to 27°.

a
opposite

▶

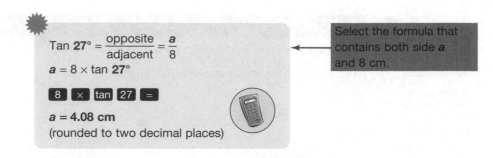

$$\text{Tan } 27° = \frac{\text{opposite}}{\text{adjacent}} = \frac{a}{8}$$

$$a = 8 \times \tan 27°$$

8 × tan 27 =

a = 4.08 cm
(rounded to two decimal places)

Select the formula that contains both side **a** and 8 cm.

2.

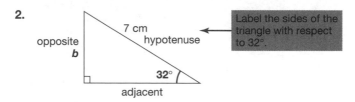

Label the sides of the triangle with respect to 32°.

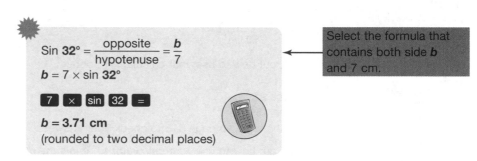

$$\text{Sin } 32° = \frac{\text{opposite}}{\text{hypotenuse}} = \frac{b}{7}$$

$$b = 7 \times \sin 32°$$

7 × sin 32 =

b = 3.71 cm
(rounded to two decimal places)

Select the formula that contains both side **b** and 7 cm.

3.

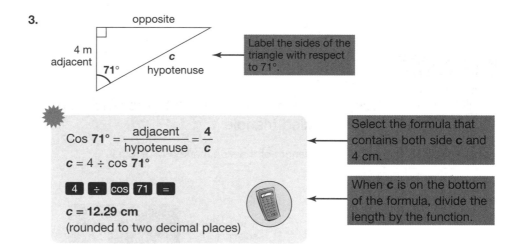

Label the sides of the triangle with respect to 71°.

$$\text{Cos } 71° = \frac{\text{adjacent}}{\text{hypotenuse}} = \frac{4}{c}$$

$$c = 4 \div \cos 71°$$

4 ÷ cos 71 =

c = 12.29 cm
(rounded to two decimal places)

Select the formula that contains both side **c** and 4 cm.

When **c** is on the bottom of the formula, divide the length by the function.

Mapping out

Finding a length:

Label the sides with respect to the angle.

↓

Select a formula that contains both the given side and the side with the letter.

↓

If in the formula the letter is on top:
Unknown length:

length × function angle =

or

If in the formula the letter is on the bottom:
Unknown length:

length ÷ function angle =

Note: function is either cos, tan or sin.

Work it out

Find the lengths of the sides marked with a letter. Round your answers to two decimal places.

1.
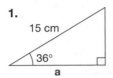
15 cm, 36°, a

2.
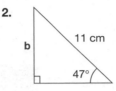
b, 11 cm, 47°

3.
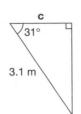
c, 31°, 3.1 m

4.
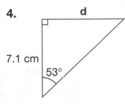
d, 7.1 cm, 53°

5.
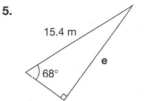
15.4 m, 68°, e

6.
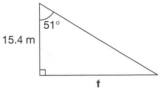
51°, 15.4 m, f

7.
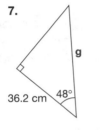
g, 36.2 cm, 48°

8.
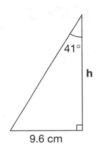
41°, h, 9.6 cm

9.
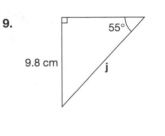
55°, 9.8 cm, j

10.
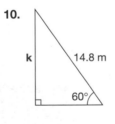
k, 14.8 m, 60°

11.
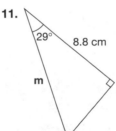
29°, 8.8 cm, m

12.
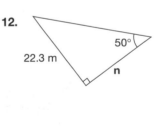
50°, 22.3 m, n

Potential pitfall

When answering the question 'Find a' – the solution is not:

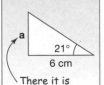
a, 21°, 6 cm
There it is

A mnemonic

To help you remember the three formulas, sin, cos and tan:

Six **O**verweight **H**effalumps   **S**in = **O**pp/**H**yp
Came **A**nd **H**eavily   **C**os = **A**dj/**H**yp
Trod **O**n **A**rthur   **T**an = **O**pp/**A**dj

Or you may remember this from your school days:
SOH CAH TOA

Example

Calculating an angle when two sides are given

Calculate the angle marked by a letter.

1.

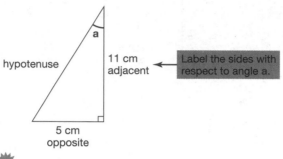

hypotenuse

11 cm
adjacent

Label the sides with
respect to angle a.

5 cm
opposite

$$\tan a = \frac{\text{opposite}}{\text{adjacent}} = \frac{5}{11}$$

shift tan 5 ÷ 11 =

a = 24.4°
(rounded to 1 decimal place)

Select the formula that contains
both the 5 (opposite) and 11
(adjacent).

Finding the angle is the inverse
of finding a side, so the shift
button on the calculator is used.

2.

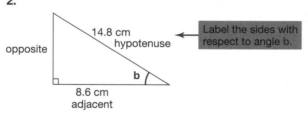

14.8 cm
hypotenuse

Label the sides with
respect to angle b.

opposite

b

8.6 cm
adjacent

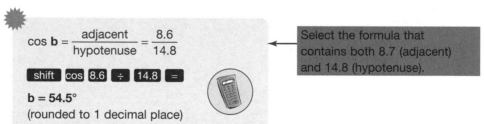

$$\cos b = \frac{\text{adjacent}}{\text{hypotenuse}} = \frac{8.6}{14.8}$$

shift cos 8.6 ÷ 14.8 =

b = 54.5°
(rounded to 1 decimal place)

Select the formula that
contains both 8.7 (adjacent)
and 14.8 (hypotenuse).

Mapping out

Finding an angle:

Label the sides with respect to the unknown angle.

↓

Select a formula that contains both the given sides.

↓

Use your calculator to find the angle remembering to press the keys:

shift function

Division of two sides

=

Work it out

Round your answers to one decimal place.

Find the angles marked with a letter.

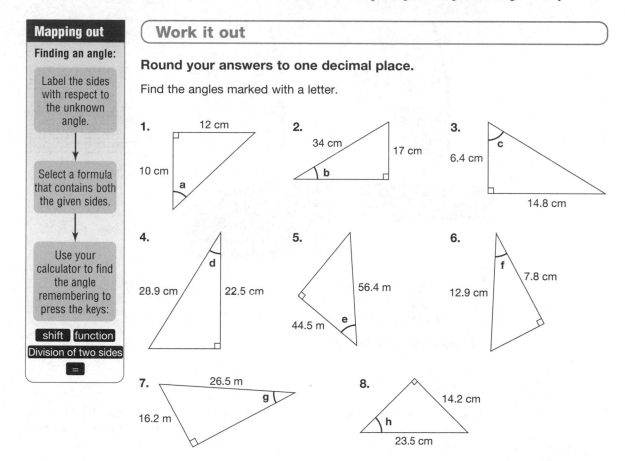

1. 12 cm, 10 cm, a

2. 34 cm, 17 cm, b

3. c, 6.4 cm, 14.8 cm

4. d, 28.9 cm, 22.5 cm

5. 56.4 m, 44.5 m, e

6. f, 7.8 cm, 12.9 cm

7. 26.5 m, g, 16.2 m

8. 14.2 cm, h, 23.5 cm

Practical uses of trigonometry

These are situations where either an angle or side can't be measured but trigonometry can be used to obtain a measurement.

Example 1

A person is laying lino in their kitchen. There is an odd angle between the wall and cupboards. What angle do they cut the lino?

▶

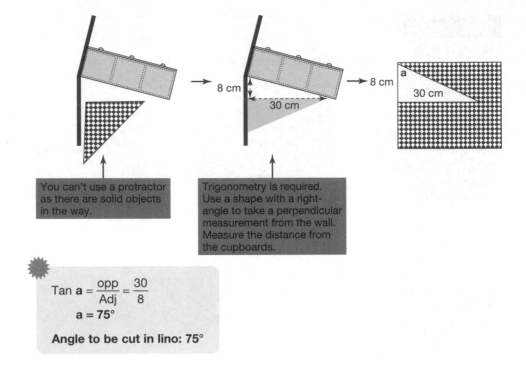

You can't use a protractor as there are solid objects in the way.

Trigonometry is required. Use a shape with a right-angle to take a perpendicular measurement from the wall. Measure the distance from the cupboards.

$$\text{Tan } \mathbf{a} = \frac{\text{opp}}{\text{Adj}} = \frac{30}{8}$$
$$\mathbf{a} = \mathbf{75°}$$

Angle to be cut in lino: 75°

Example 2

Flaring occurs when the suns rays bounce off the satellite and reflect back to earth.

On a clear summer evening it is possible to see satellites in the night sky. They look like faint stars and certain ones can suddenly brighten (known as flaring) and may even outshine every star in the sky.

When this happens we can calculate, without any use of computers, the distance the satellite is from earth.

On one occasion, a satellite flared for nine seconds and travelled the distance of a thumb when held at arms length.

This is equivalent to about 5° of sky.

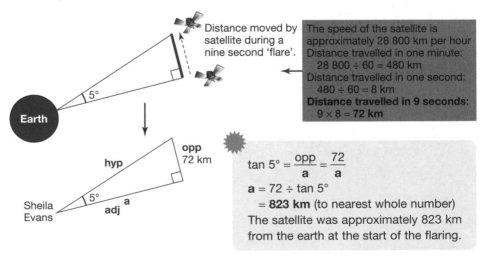

Distance moved by satellite during a nine second 'flare'.

The speed of the satellite is approximately 28 800 km per hour
Distance travelled in one minute:
28 800 ÷ 60 = 480 km
Distance travelled in one second:
480 ÷ 60 = 8 km
Distance travelled in 9 seconds:
9 × 8 = **72 km**

$$\tan 5° = \frac{\text{opp}}{\mathbf{a}} = \frac{72}{\mathbf{a}}$$
$$\mathbf{a} = 72 \div \tan 5°$$
$$= \mathbf{823 \ km} \text{ (to nearest whole number)}$$
The satellite was approximately 823 km from the earth at the start of the flaring.

Work it out

Round your answers to one decimal place.

1. Using the figures in Example 2, calculate the distance the satellite is from earth at the end of the flaring.

2. A woman drives from her house on a bearing of 036° for 48 km. She then heads east until she is exactly due north of her home. How many kilometres is she away from her starting point?

The castaways

3. The group are creating a timber frame for the roof of an outhouse. Here is the diagram they are using:

Supporting struts

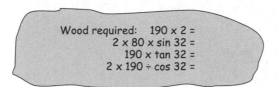

32°			32°
80 cm	110 cm	110 cm	80 cm

They have been given 10 m of timber and now want to check that this is enough. Here are the workings of one group member:

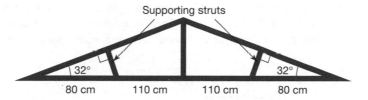

Wood required: 190 × 2 =
2 × 80 × sin 32 =
190 × tan 32 =
2 × 190 ÷ cos 32 =

They haven't completed it because they can't find the calculator, but the workings are correct.

  a. Copy the sums but now work out each calculation, to the nearest cm and state each length being calculated.

  b. Work out the total amount of wood required.

  c. Is 10 m enough?

4. At the scene of a road accident where a motorbike has careered off the road a collision investigator noted down the measurements shown in the diagram.

   For his report he also had to record the angle the bike came off the road. What is it?

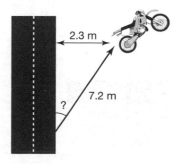

2.3 m

7.2 m

?

5. It is impossible to use a protractor when working out the angle the leaning tower of Pisa makes with the ground.

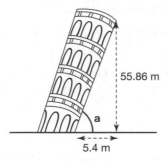

Using the measurements in the diagram work out the size of angle **a**.

6. A person laying a patio using stone slabs knew the house did not make a right angle with the fence so the first slab would have to be cut at an angle. It was imposs-ible to use a protractor to find the angle, so he decides to use trigonometry.

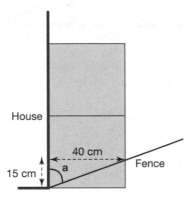

Using the measurements in the diagram calculate the angle **a**.

7. Students on an Environmental Science degree course are on a field trip. They are investigating whether the number and variety of plants growing on a hillside is affected by the slope. They have already recorded the plants and drawn this diagram:

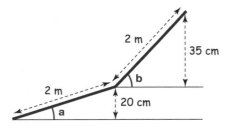

Hints and tips

Use trig to work out the horizontal distances.

a. Calculate the angle of elevations **a** and **b**.

b. What is the overall angle of elevation between the start and end of the slope?

Investigation – forensics

When a forensic investigator visits the scene of a violent crime one of their first tasks is to determine the location of the victim when hit by a weapon.

This requires careful analysis of any blood stains.

Here is a bit of theory that lies behind their work:

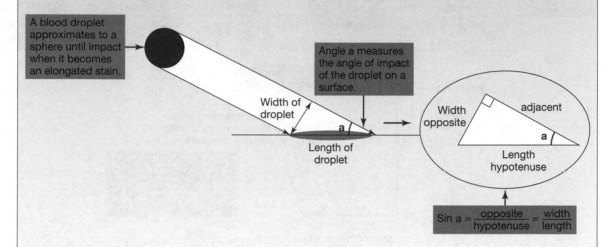

A blood droplet approximates to a sphere until impact when it becomes an elongated stain.

Angle a measures the angle of impact of the droplet on a surface.

Width of droplet

Length of droplet

Width opposite   adjacent

Length hypotenuse

$$\text{Sin } a = \frac{\text{opposite}}{\text{hypotenuse}} = \frac{\text{width}}{\text{length}}$$

Work out the angle of impact for the following blood stains:

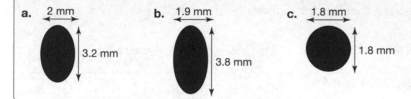

a. 2 mm

3.2 mm

b. 1.9 mm

3.8 mm

c. 1.8 mm

1.8 mm

The first step in identifying the victim's location is the recognition of a group of blood spatters that have been generated by the same violent incident:

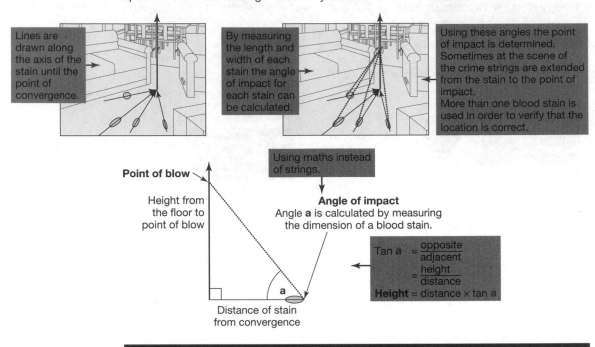

Lines are drawn along the axis of the stain until the point of convergence.

By measuring the length and width of each stain the angle of impact for each stain can be calculated.

Using these angles the point of impact is determined. Sometimes at the scene of the crime strings are extended from the stain to the point of impact.
More than one blood stain is used in order to verify that the location is correct.

Point of blow

Using maths instead of strings.

Height from the floor to point of blow

Angle of impact
Angle **a** is calculated by measuring the dimension of a blood stain.

$$\text{Tan } a = \frac{\text{opposite}}{\text{adjacent}}$$
$$= \frac{\text{height}}{\text{distance}}$$
Height $= \text{distance} \times \text{tan } a$

a

Distance of stain from convergence

Task

Here is a grid of a floor plan that contains three blood stains:

1. Copy the grid, using a scale of 1 cm for each unit along both axes.
2. Accurately mark on the stains.
3. The point of convergence is (9, 15). Measure the distance of each stain to the point of convergence (to the nearest cm).
4. Here are the dimensions of the three stains:

There is just one point of impact but three blood stains are used in order to confirm the measurements are correct.

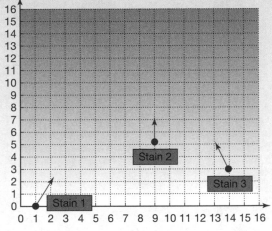

	Width	Length
Stain 1	9.946 mm	10 mm
Stain 2	9.981 mm	10 mm
Stain 3	9.968 mm	10 mm

Work out the angle of impact to one decimal place for all three stains.

5. Determine the approximate height of the impact of each stain.
6. What is the likely height of impact?

3.10 Transformations

Key term

Transformations
Changing the position, shape or size of an object.

Transformations are now a vital component of the world of computing.

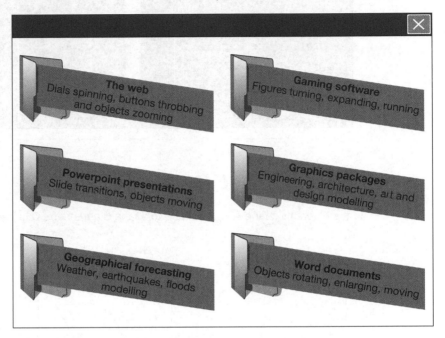

Transformation is a general term for translations, reflections, rotations and enlargements. In this section we will look at all four.

Translations

Key term

Translation
The movement of a shape along a straight line.

When a football is passed along the ground it is undergoing a **translation**:

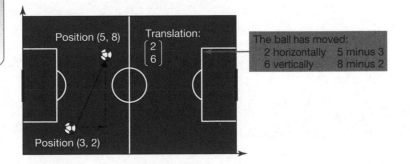

Task

State the translations for these passes:

a.

b.

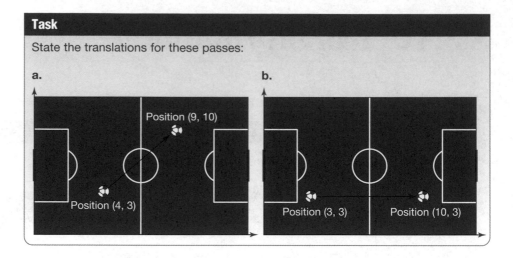

Example 1

In the diagrams shape **A** is translated to shape **B** and shape **C** is translated to shape **D**.

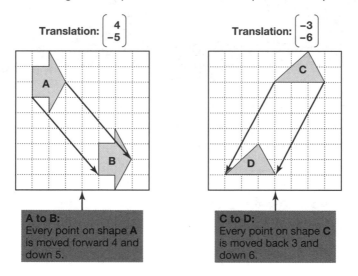

Translation: $\begin{pmatrix} 4 \\ -5 \end{pmatrix}$

Translation: $\begin{pmatrix} -3 \\ -6 \end{pmatrix}$

A to B:
Every point on shape **A** is moved forward 4 and down 5.

C to D:
Every point on shape **C** is moved back 3 and down 6.

Plotting on a grid
Transformations tend to be plotted on a grid as this allows us to accurately describe a shape's original and final position.

Example 2

Plot the quadrilateral **Z**, with vertices (0, 2), (3, 1), (4, 2) and (3, 4). Move the shape along the translations:

a. $\begin{pmatrix} -6 \\ -5 \end{pmatrix}$ to the shape **A**

b. $\begin{pmatrix} 0 \\ -6 \end{pmatrix}$ to the shape **B**

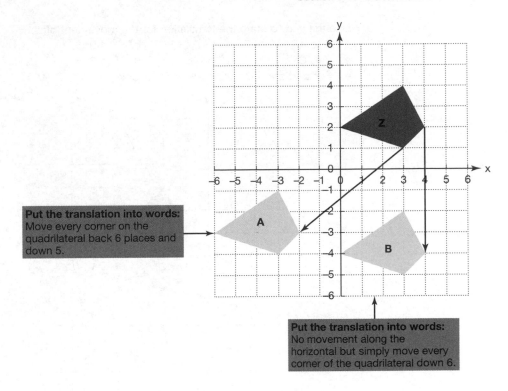

Put the translation into words:
Move every corner on the quadrilateral back 6 places and down 5.

Put the translation into words:
No movement along the horizontal but simply move every corner of the quadrilateral down 6.

Work it out

Hints and tips

In a translation:
First number: movement along the horizontal or x axis.
Second number: movement along the vertical or y axis.

1. There are four pairs of translations in the diagram. Each pair consists of the original triangle and its translation. Match the pairs and state the translation, starting with the shape that comes first in the alphabet:

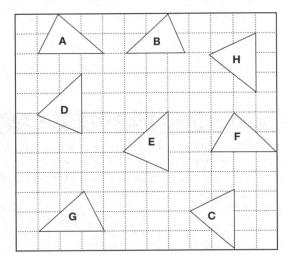

2. Use the grid to state the translation for the movement of:
    a. Z to A   b. Z to B
    c. Z to C   d. Z to D
    e. For **a–d** state the translations in reverse, i.e. A to Z etc.

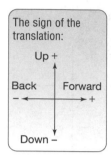

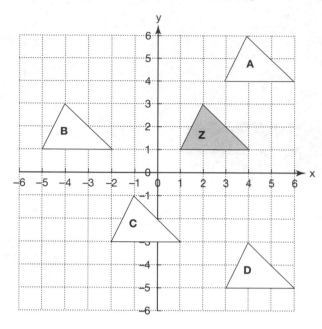

3. Draw a grid that extends from –6 to +6 on both axes. Plot the triangle with vertices at the points (2, 1), (5, 1) (3, 3). Move it along the translations:

    a. $\begin{pmatrix} 1 \\ 3 \end{pmatrix}$ b. $\begin{pmatrix} -3 \\ 0 \end{pmatrix}$ c. $\begin{pmatrix} -2 \\ -5 \end{pmatrix}$

    In all three cases state the co-ordinates of the new triangle.

4. Draw a grid that extends from –6 to +6 on both axes. Plot the trapezium with vertices at the points (–1, 4), (3, 4) (1, 2) (0, 2). Move it along the translations:

    a. $\begin{pmatrix} 3 \\ 2 \end{pmatrix}$ b. $\begin{pmatrix} 1 \\ -5 \end{pmatrix}$ c. $\begin{pmatrix} -4 \\ -3 \end{pmatrix}$

    In all three cases, state the co-ordinates of the new trapezium.

Investigation

Without plotting the shape, find a quick method of working out the co-ordinates of a newly translated shape (your answers to questions 3 and 4 may help).

Use your method to calculate the new co-ordinates of a triangle with original vertices (1, 3) (2, 5) and (6, 0) when translated along:

a. $\begin{pmatrix} 2 \\ 3 \end{pmatrix}$ b. $\begin{pmatrix} -2 \\ 4 \end{pmatrix}$

Reflections

The movement of a shape or point across a line of **reflection**.

Mirror line or line of reflection.

Investigation

Place a flat object such as a key or protractor on one half of a sheet of paper and draw its outline.

1. Fold the paper so there is an imprint on the other half.
2. Draw its outline.
3. Measure the distances from the fold line.
4. What reflection rule are the measurements obeying?

Example 1

Reflect the trapezium **A** along the mirror line.

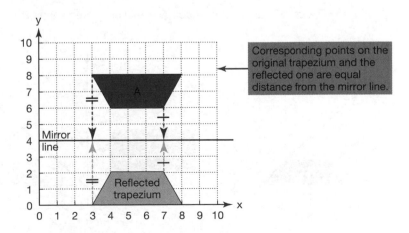

Corresponding points on the original trapezium and the reflected one are equal distance from the mirror line.

Example 2

Getting the distances right

Each of the points in shape **A** are to be reflected onto a shape an equal distance on the other side of the mirror line.

Measure the perpendicular distance to the mirror line.

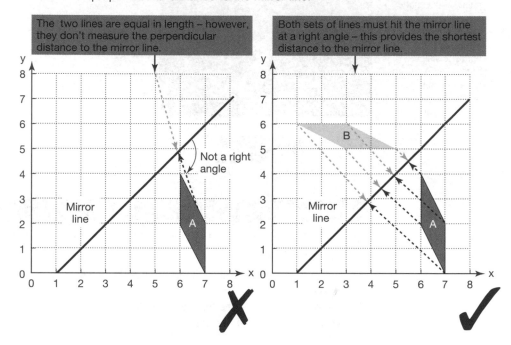

The two lines are equal in length – however, they don't measure the perpendicular distance to the mirror line.

Both sets of lines must hit the mirror line at a right angle – this provides the shortest distance to the mirror line.

Not a right angle

Mirror line

Mirror line

Example 3

Drawing the mirror line

Plot the line of reflection when shape **A** is reflected onto shape **B**.

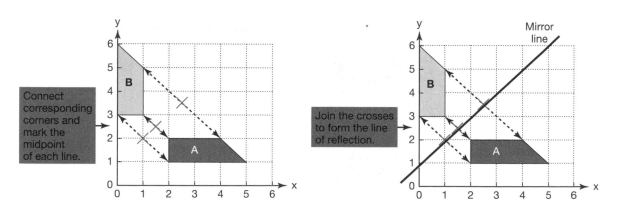

Connect corresponding corners and mark the midpoint of each line.

Join the crosses to form the line of reflection.

Mirror line

Work it out

1. State which of the following correctly measures the perpendicular distance to the mirror line.

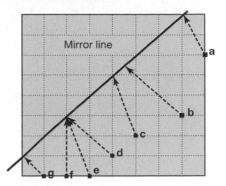

2. The coloured line is the mirror line. Copy the grid and draw in the reflected shapes.

a.

b.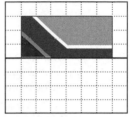

c.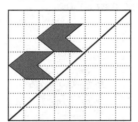

d.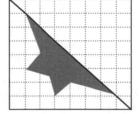

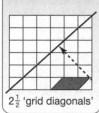
3. Copy the diagram and reflect the triangle about the three mirror lines **a**, **b** and **c**.

In each case, state the co-ordinates of the new triangle.

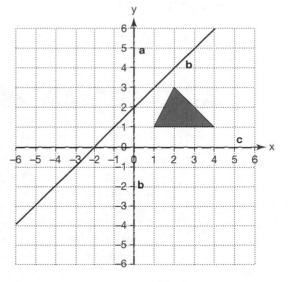

4. Copy the grid and the shapes. Draw on the mirror lines that reflect:
   a. A to B
   b. A to C
   c. A to D
   d. A to E.

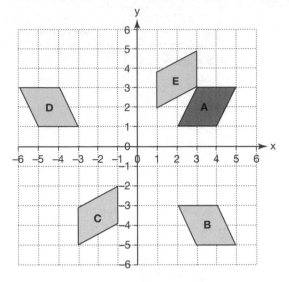

5. The grid shows the reflection of shape **D** to **E** along a mirror line.
   a. Copy the three grids, mirror lines and shapes.
   b. Reflect each shape along its mirror line.
   c. State the co-ordinates of the new shape.

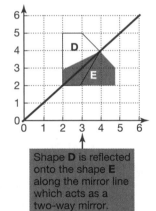

Shape **D** is reflected onto the shape **E** along the mirror line which acts as a two-way mirror.

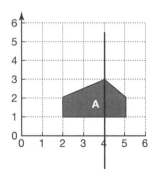

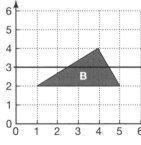

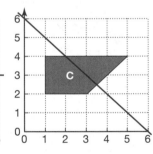

Group investigation 1

On a grid that extends between −6 and +6 on both axes, draw the mirror line joining the points (6, 6) and (−6, −6).

1. Plot any two triangles and reflect them across the mirror line.
2. Write down the original and new co-ordinates of the vertices of the triangles.
3. Investigate the relationship between corresponding co-ordinates and come up with a rule.
4. A quadrilateral has co-ordinates (2, 1), (5, 2), (6, 4) and (3, 5).
   Without plotting the shape, use your rule to state the co-ordinates of the shape when reflected along the line.

Group investigation 2

Which of these reflections are incorrect:

1.   **A** to **B** along the line **p?**
2.   **A** to **C** along the line **q?**

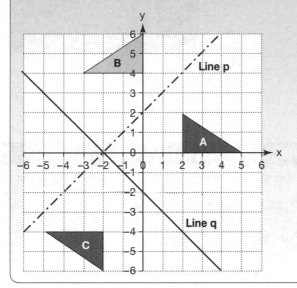

Paired work

An architect is designing a 'U' shaped building.

He has created the first section and wants to use the blue lines of reflection to create the rest.

1.   Copy the grid and the first section.
2.   Reflect the shape over the mirror line **a**.
3.   Reflect this new shape over the mirror line **b** to complete the building.

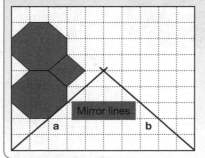

Rotation – a shape on a lead

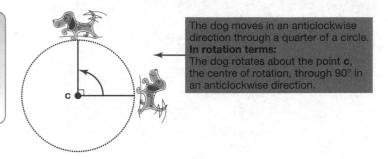

Key term

Rotation
The rotation of a shape about a fixed point in a clockwise or anticlockwise direction.

The dog moves in an anticlockwise direction through a quarter of a circle.
In rotation terms:
The dog rotates about the point **c**, the centre of rotation, through 90° in an anticlockwise direction.

Task – rotating shapes using tracing paper

1.   The shape is to be rotated 90° in a clockwise direction about the point (1, 6).

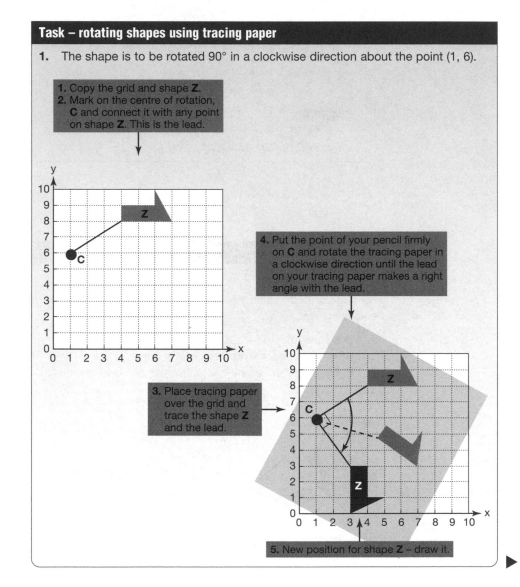

1. Copy the grid and shape **Z**.
2. Mark on the centre of rotation, **C** and connect it with any point on shape **Z**. This is the lead.

4. Put the point of your pencil firmly on **C** and rotate the tracing paper in a clockwise direction until the lead on your tracing paper makes a right angle with the lead.

3. Place tracing paper over the grid and trace the shape **Z** and the lead.

5. New position for shape **Z** – draw it.

Task (*continued*)

2. Rotate the shape through 180° about the point (1, 2):

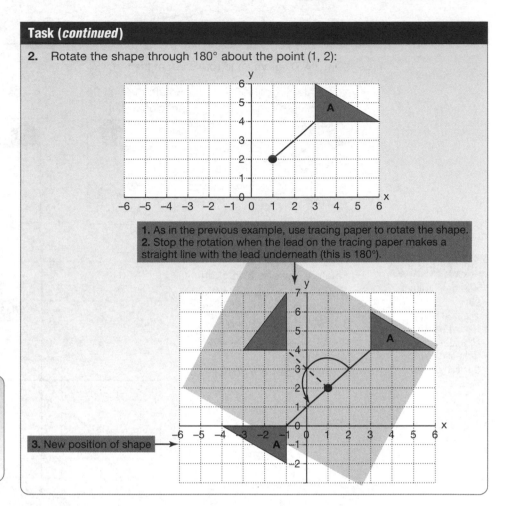

1. As in the previous example, use tracing paper to rotate the shape.
2. Stop the rotation when the lead on the tracing paper makes a straight line with the lead underneath (this is 180°).

3. New position of shape

Because the shape is rotated through 180° it can be rotated in either direction – it will still end in the same place.

Example

Finding the centre of rotation for 180° turns

Shape **Z** is rotated to shape **A**.

To find the centre of rotation join up three or more corresponding corners.

Centre of rotation **(1, 0)**.

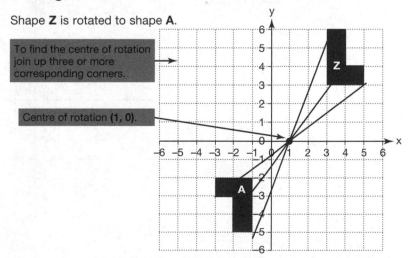

Work it out

1. Copy the diagrams and rotate about the dots:

   a. Rotate through 90° clockwise

   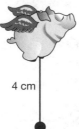

   4 cm

   b. Rotate through 90° anticlockwise

   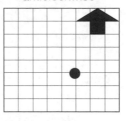

   c. Rotate through 180°

   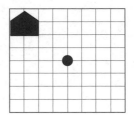

Hints and tips

Rotation through 90°:
The lead on the tracing paper should make a right angle with the lead on the grid.

---

2. Copy the diagram.
   Rotate the shape **Z** through:
   a. 90° clockwise about the point (1, 3)
   b. 180° about the origin
   c. 90° anticlockwise about the point (1, 1)
   d. 180° about the point (2, 0)

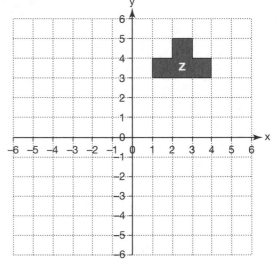

3. Write down the co-ordinates of the centre of rotation when shape **Z** rotates through 180° to:
   a. shape **A**
   b. shape **B**
   c. shape **C**

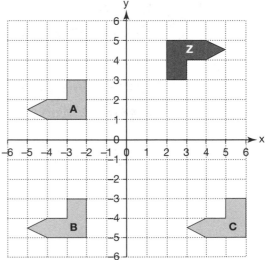

Rotations on the computer

In many computer packages such as Word and PowerPoint, shapes can be rotated.

○←**Centre of rotation**

Investigation

A garden designer has planned out part of a garden next to a house. To maintain balance in her design she wants the shapes she has already drawn rotated through 180° around a centre point. The patio in the rotated area will be replaced by a raised pond. Copy the diagram, find the centre of rotation and complete the garden.

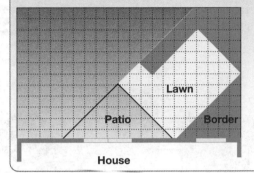

Group work – replacing one type of transformation with another

1. Draw a grid that extends from –8 to 8 on both axes.

2. Plot the triangle **A** with co-ordinates (5, 1), (8, 1) and (5, 5).

3. Move the triangle along the translation $\begin{pmatrix} -10 \\ 0 \end{pmatrix}$.
   Name your new triangle **B**.
   a. Draw two lines of reflection to move the triangle **A** to the position of triangle **B**.
   b. Is your set of mirror lines unique or are there other combinations that would perform the same movement?
   c. Is it possible to use three lines of reflection to obtain the same movement?

4. Similarly, a rotation can be replaced by two reflections. Now rotate triangle **A** through 180° about the origin. Name your new triangle **C**.
   Draw two lines of reflection to move the triangle **A** to the position of triangle **C**.

Enlargements

This transformation dilates or shrinks an object in the same way as the pupil of an eye changes size.

When enlarging photos only the scale factor is important. However, it is often useful to know the position of the new image as well as its size.

All these faces in red have been enlarged by a scale factor of two but only one is in the correct position. The **centre of enlargement** determines the position.

Example 1 – finding the centre of enlargement

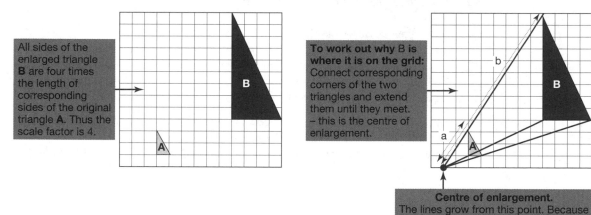

All sides of the enlarged triangle **B** are four times the length of corresponding sides of the original triangle **A**. Thus the scale factor is 4.

To work out why B is where it is on the grid: Connect corresponding corners of the two triangles and extend them until they meet. – this is the centre of enlargement.

Centre of enlargement.
The lines grow from this point. Because the scale factor is 4: $b = 4 \times \text{length } a$.

The distances between the centre and the corners of **B** are exactly four times the distances between the centre and the corresponding corners of **A**.

Example 2

Enlarge the trapezium **A** by a scale factor of 2 with centre of enlargement (1, 2).

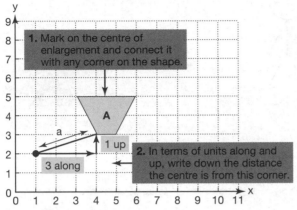

1. Mark on the centre of enlargement and connect it with any corner on the shape.

a

1 up

3 along

2. In terms of units along and up, write down the distance the centre is from this corner.

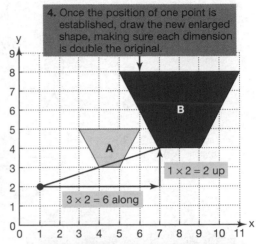

4. Once the position of one point is established, draw the new enlarged shape, making sure each dimension is double the original.

B

A

$1 \times 2 = 2$ up

$3 \times 2 = 6$ along

3. Extend the red horizontal and vertical lines to the point where each line is double the initial length (the shape is to be enlarged by 2). This is the corner of the new enlarged shape.

Mapping out

Centre of an enlargement:

Join corresponding points of the two shapes.

↓

Extend these to the point where they meet – this is the **centre of enlargement**.

Scale factor:

1. Measure the length of one side of the smaller shape (**a**).
2. Measure the length of the corresponding side of the enlarged shape (**b**).

↓

Scale factor: $b \div a$

The length **a** is not used in the enlargement as it is not usually a whole number and so inaccuracies can creep in when scaling up its length.

Work it out

1. Copy the grids and shapes.
Work out the co-ordinates of the centre of enlargement and the scale factor in the following enlargements:

a.
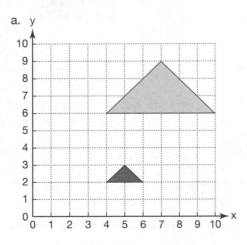

b.
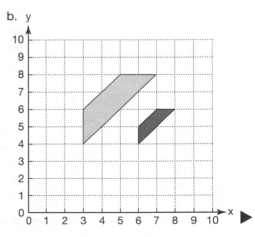

▶

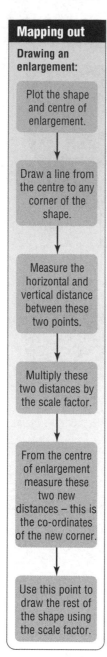

Mapping out

Drawing an enlargement:

Plot the shape and centre of enlargement.

↓

Draw a line from the centre to any corner of the shape.

↓

Measure the horizontal and vertical distance between these two points.

↓

Multiply these two distances by the scale factor.

↓

From the centre of enlargement measure these two new distances – this is the co-ordinates of the new corner.

↓

Use this point to draw the rest of the shape using the scale factor.

Enlargements look a lot bigger than they should because it is the area you initially notice not the lengths of the sides.

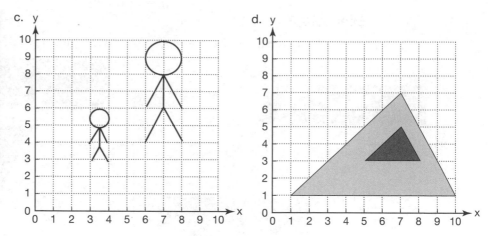

c.

d.

2. Copy the grids and using **c** as the centre of enlargement draw the new image of the shape:

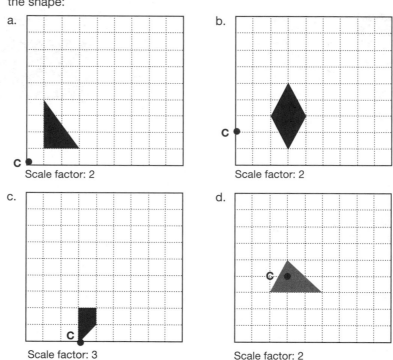

a.

Scale factor: 2

b.

Scale factor: 2

c.

Scale factor: 3

d.

Scale factor: 2

3. On grids that extend from 0 to 10 on both the x and y axes, plot:
   a. A triangle with co-ordinates (3, 2), (5, 2) and (3, 3). Enlarge it using a scale factor of 2 and centre (2, 0)
   b. A rectangle with co-ordinates (5, 4), (8, 4), (8, 6) and (5, 6). Enlarge it using a scale factor of 1.5 and centre (10, 10).
   c. A trapezium with co-ordinates (4, 3) (5, 3), (6, 5) and (3, 5). Enlarge it using scale factor 3 and centre (4, 4).

4. When blowing up a balloon where is the centre of enlargement?

Computer graphics

When a computer zooms in on a figure it is important to know not only how much the shape needs to grow but also where it is to be positioned. A screen grid is used to describe the position of objects.

Maths in IT

5. Computer windows can be enlarged or shrunk. Expanding them from the corners can keep the sides in proportion and the corners act as a centre of enlargement.

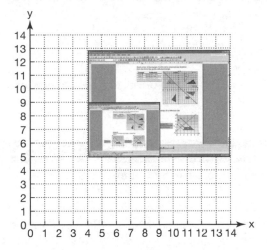

a. What is the scale factor in this enlargement?
b. What corner has the smaller window been pulled from?
c. What are the co-ordinates of the centre of enlargement?
d. If the smaller window was expanded from the bottom left corner of the window by a scale factor of 1.5, what would be the co-ordinates of the new window?

Art in motion

A whole new area of art has evolved over the last decade – computer art. At its very core is transformations. Here is a static picture of shapes that 'grow' from the centre.

These shapes are being translated and enlarged.

6. In most computer software packages, you are able to zoom in on text or pictures. For instance:

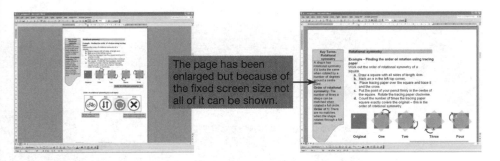

The page has been enlarged but because of the fixed screen size not all of it can be shown.

a. What is the scale factor of the enlargement?
b. Describe in words the approximate position of the centre of enlargement.

Investigation

Draw a grid that extends from 0 to 12 on both the x and y axes. Plot the triangle (1, 1), (2, 1) and (2, 4). Draw a new triangle using the origin as the centre of enlargement and a scale factor of

a. 2

b. 3

c. 1.5.

d. Can you find a quick method of working out the new co-ordinates without plotting the triangles?

Group work – combining transformations

This is when two or more different types of transformations are used to achieve a movement.

The TV weather presenters put together a sequence of wind pictures using arrows to show the wind over a specific time period. These pictures are then displayed in quick succession. The presenters receive details of wind forecasts from the 'Met' office. These are then converted into computer code.

A dataflow diagram is a useful way of mapping out how each 'parcel' of information is transferred into code:

The weather forecast

Every day on TV the weather forecasts use transformations. Wind arrows are translated to demonstrate movement, enlarged to indicate strength and rotated to show direction.

Computer instructions

1. Translate: $\begin{pmatrix} 1 \\ 1 \end{pmatrix}$
Arrow size: 2
Rotate: 90° clockwise about (1, 1)

Translation initially is from this position:

0 1

2. Translate: $\begin{pmatrix} 3 \\ 0 \end{pmatrix}$
Enlarge: –
Rotate: 45° anticlockwise about (4, 2)

Resulting arrows. These appear not on a grid but on top of a map of Britain.

3. Translate: $\begin{pmatrix} 3 \\ 1 \end{pmatrix}$
Enlarge: 1.5 centre (7, 3)
Rotate: 45° anticlockwise about (7, 3)

4. Translate: $\begin{pmatrix} 1 \\ 5 \end{pmatrix}$
Enlarge: –
Rotate: 45° clockwise about (8, 8)

What is computer animation?

An animation provides the viewer with an illusion of movement. A sequence of static images are displayed in quick succession. An animated object consists of a series of connected polygons, usually triangles. These triangles are transformed using translations, rotations, reflections or enlargements to show movement.

Group work (*continued*)

1. Convert the instructions on the right into arrows on a grid that extends from 0 to 12 in both the x and y directions.

2. What is the final co-ordinate of the top left corner of the arrow?

3. Use the wind arrow below to create a set of computer instructions.

   Hint: There is only one enlargement.

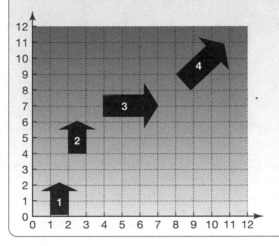

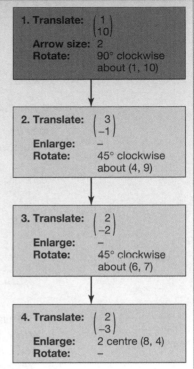

1. **Translate:** $\begin{pmatrix} 1 \\ 10 \end{pmatrix}$
   Arrow size: 2
   Rotate: 90° clockwise about (1, 10)

2. **Translate:** $\begin{pmatrix} 3 \\ -1 \end{pmatrix}$
   Enlarge: –
   Rotate: 45° clockwise about (4, 9)

3. **Translate:** $\begin{pmatrix} 2 \\ -2 \end{pmatrix}$
   Enlarge: –
   Rotate: 45° clockwise about (6, 7)

4. **Translate:** $\begin{pmatrix} 2 \\ -3 \end{pmatrix}$
   Enlarge: 2 centre (8, 4)
   Rotate: –

3.11 Bringing It All Together

Assignment questions

Round your answers to the nearest whole number unless the question specifies otherwise.

1. Does a round peg fit better in a square hole or a square peg in a round hole? In other words, in which of the two scenarios is the least space 'wasted'?

Round peg in square hole

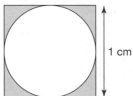

1 cm

Square peg in round hole

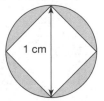

1 cm

   a. Calculate, to four decimal places, the red 'wasted' areas of both shapes.

   b. Work out the percentage of wastage in both cases.
      Hint: (area in colour ÷ area of larger shape) × 100.

   c. What is the answer to the initial question?

About cars

Hints and tips

1 m³ = 1 000 litres.

2. a. The radius of a car wheel is 32 cm.
     i. Calculate the circumference of the wheel.
     ii. What is the velocity of the car if the wheel rotates 300 times a minute? Give your answer in km per hour.
     iii. Work out (using your answer to a.i.) the number of times the wheel rotates every minute when travelling at 50 km per hour.

   b. A car's petrol tank is in the shape of a cuboid.

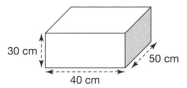

30 cm   50 cm

40 cm

     i. Calculate the volume of the tank.
     ii. Work out the capacity, in litres, of the tank.
     iii. If the fuel consumption of the car averages 8.4 litres per 100 km, how far could the car go on a full tank of petrol?

3. A RSPB (bird charity) worker sights a rare goose flying at an altitude of 130 m. He records its angle of elevation to be 27° and 1 minute later he records a second angle of elevation of 61°. During this time the bird flies in the same direction.

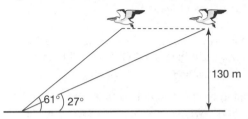

a. How far has the bird flown in the minute?
b. What is its speed in metres per second?
   Round your answer to two decimal places.
c. Convert this speed to miles per hour.

4. A person searching the web to buy a piece of land in Bulgaria came across this sketch:

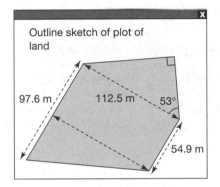

Outline sketch of plot of land

97.6 m   112.5 m   53°

54.9 m

She wanted to check the total perimeter and area of the plot of land.
What are they?

5. The forestry commission is spraying a field to control the bracken. They work to a strict set of instructions:
   • Start in the top left corner and work across the field.
   • When at the far edge move down 3 m and start spraying again.
   • Set the flow rate of the mixture from the knapsack to 2 ml per second.

Field to be sprayed at a walking pace of 2 m every 6 seconds.

Dilution of weed killer:
10 ml for every 1 litre of water.
Mixture held in a 7.2 litre knapsack.

66 m

40 m

a. Calculate the area to be sprayed.
b. What is the sprayer's speed in metres per minute?
c. How much weed killer has to be poured into the knapsack to obtain the correct dilution for 7 litres of water?
d. On completion of the task:
   i. how far will the sprayer have walked?
   ii. how long will it have taken him (in minutes)?
   iii. how much mixture will have been used?

Hints and tips

Use Pythagoras.

6. A person talking on the phone to a friend who lives 24 km due west of her saw a flash of lightning. Twenty one seconds later she heard the thunder. Seventy five seconds after she first saw lightning, she heard thunder over the phone.
Sound travels at approximately one third of a km per second.
Where was the lightning in relation to the two houses? (There are two possible answers.)

7. The table below shows the approximate oil consumption of three countries, together with their population size.
a. Copy and complete the table:

	Number of barrels used a day (million)	Population (millions)	Number of barrels used in a year (nearest million)	Volume of oil used a year (nearest million m³)	Height of column of oil (nearest km)	Volume of oil used per person per year (m³ to 1 d.p.)
UK	1.82	61				
China	6.53	1 300				
USA	20.73	300				

Hints and tips

Assume there are 365 days in a year.

1 barrel of oil: 0.16 m³

Oil column

b. The moon is approximately 380 000 km from the earth. Which of these columns reach the moon?

Note: All values are approximations.
The oil column has a base area of 1 m².

Examples of the golden ratio

You need look no further than your credit card.

The proportions of a dolphin's body.

The Parthenon in Athens is another example.

Assignment investigation – the golden ratio often denoted as φ (phi)

Since Renaissance times artists and architects have proportioned their work to approximate the golden ratio, believing this proportion to be aesthetically pleasing.

Here is a golden rectangle:

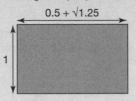

$0.5 + \sqrt{1.25}$

1

The units of the dimensions could be centimetres, metres, feet, inches etc.
It is the ratio of width to length that counts.

Tasks

1. The width of the rectangle above is 1 cm. Calculate its length to four decimal places.

2. Providing the width and length stay in the same proportion there are many dimensions for a golden rectangle.
    a. If the width is 3 m what is length?
    b. Are the dimensions of this book in the golden ratio?
    c. Are the dimensions of your cheque card in the golden ratio?
    Round your answers for **a.** to two decimal places.

3. Given the diagram:
    a.   i. Use Pythagoras to work out the radius of the circle.
        ii. Use this length to find the length of the large rectangle.
       iii. Is it golden?

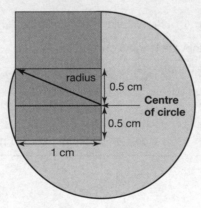

radius

0.5 cm

Centre of circle

0.5 cm

1 cm

b. Accurately copy the diagram but this time use dimensions of 10 cm instead of 1 cm and 5 cm instead of 0.5 cm.
    Start by:
    • drawing a square of dimensions 10 cm by 10 cm
    • finding the midpoint of the right vertical side – this is the centre of the circle
    • drawing a circle from this centre such that the circumference touches the two left corners of the square
    • extending the rectangle as shown in the diagram.

The triangulation method used when drawing scaled plans

Example

Below is a rough sketch of a plot of land the corners of which are labelled A, B and C, D and E.

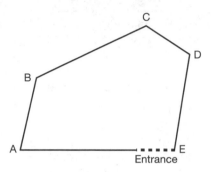

Using a suitable scale and the dimensions below, draw accurately the plot of land.

AE = 48 m   BE = 48 m
AB = 24 m   AC = 60 m
CE = 44 m   ED = 32 m
AD = 64 m

A scale of 1 cm to 4 m (1 : 400) will allow the diagram to fit nicely on an A4 sheet of paper.

Use this scale to obtain the lengths on the plan:

	AE	BE	AB	AC	CE	ED	AD
On the ground	48 m	48 m	24 m	60 m	44 m	32 m	64 m
On the plan	48 ÷ 4	48 ÷ 4	24 ÷ 4	60 ÷ 4	44 ÷ 4	32 ÷ 4	64 ÷ 4
	= **12 cm**	= **12 cm**	= **6 cm**	= **15 cm**	= **11 cm**	= **8 cm**	= **16 cm**

Split the shape into triangles with the same baseline, AE:

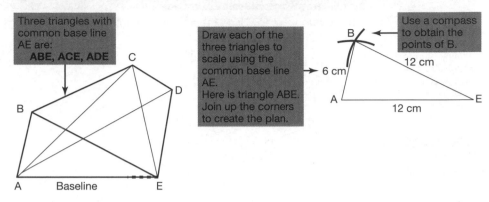

Three triangles with common base line AE are:
ABE, ACE, ADE

Draw each of the three triangles to scale using the common base line AE.
Here is triangle ABE. Join up the corners to create the plan.

Use a compass to obtain the points of B.

What is the area of the plot?

Triangulation

It is used in many walks of life. Forensic scientists use it to accurately map out the scene of a crime. Surveyors and garden designers use it to plot an area of land. For GPS to work the position of a point is required in 3D so the triangulation is also in 3D – a pyramid. Three satellites are used to map one point.

As the area is irregular it cannot be calculated using any one formula. It needs to be split into shapes that do possess an area formula. In this case, three triangles:

Area of any triangle: (base × height) ÷ 2

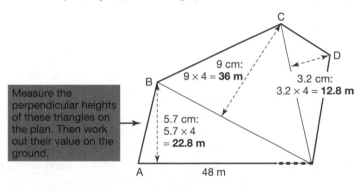

9 cm:
9 × 4 = **36 m**

3.2 cm:
3.2 × 4 = **12.8 m**

Measure the perpendicular heights of these triangles on the plan. Then work out their value on the ground.

5.7 cm:
5.7 × 4
= **22.8 m**

48 m

Area triangle ABE	48 × 22.8 ÷ 2 = 547.2 m²
Area triangle ACE	48 × 36 ÷ 2 = 864 m²
Area triangle CDE	44 × 12.8 ÷ 2 = 281.6 m²

Total area   **1 692.8 m²**

Track:
15 m long and
2.5 m wide
Outbuilding:
10 m by 10 m
Main building:
15 m by 15 m
Pond:
Diameter is 5 m

Mapping out

Triangulation:

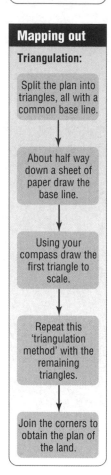

Split the plan into triangles, all with a common base line.

↓

About half way down a sheet of paper draw the base line.

↓

Using your compass draw the first triangle to scale.

↓

Repeat this 'triangulation method' with the remaining triangles.

↓

Join the corners to obtain the plan of the land.

Assignment investigation – The castaways

The group want to divide the area of land into various uses. To do this they decide a scale drawing is required.

Here is their rough sketch of part of the land, buildings, proposed track, vegetable plot and circular pond.

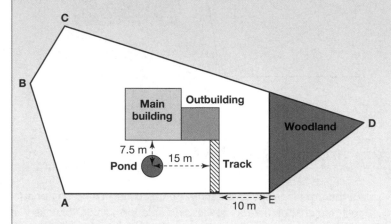

They have already taken some measurements:

AE = 50 m	AB = 30 m	BE = 65 m	AC = 45 m
CE = 70 m	AD = 75 m	DE = 30 m	

Tasks

If required, round your answer to two decimal places.

1. What is a suitable scale for the drawing?
2. Use this scale to calculate all the dimensions for the plan.
3. Use triangulation to accurately plot the outline of the land.
4. Accurately draw the track, outbuilding, main building and pond on your plan.
5. What is the area, on the ground, of the woodland?
6. a. What is the area of the pond?
   b. If it is to be 1.5 m deep, what volume of water will fill it?
7. The remaining area is to be left as grass.
   What is the size of this area?

U values

Brick wall: 0.2
Internal wall: 0.4
Concrete floor: 0.7
Ceiling: 0.2
Doors: 5
Windows
Single glazed: 4.3
Double glazed: 2.5

Plumbers Guide

Calculate the heat loss for each surface

Heat loss through surface:
Area x U value

↓

Total surface heat loss:

Add all the surface heat losses together.

↓

Heating requirements

Total heat loss x temperature difference
(answer in watts)

Investigation – working out the heating requirements of a room

When deciding on the size and number of radiators, a plumber needs to know:

- the maximum temperature difference between the inside and outside of a room
- the direct heat loss from the overall surface area of the room.

The heat loss is calculated by taking each surface in turn, calculating its overall area and multiplying by its 'U value'. U values indicate the heat flow through materials – the higher the figure, the higher the heat loss.

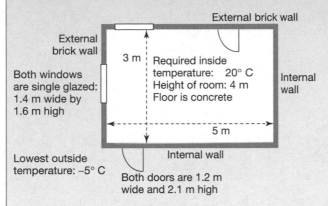

External brick wall

External brick wall

Both windows are single glazed:
1.4 m wide by 1.6 m high

3 m

Required inside temperature: 20° C
Height of room: 4 m
Floor is concrete

Internal wall

5 m

Internal wall

Lowest outside temperature: –5° C

Both doors are 1.2 m wide and 2.1 m high

1. Copy and complete the table, using the U values provided:

	Area m²	Heat loss
Both windows	2 × 1.4 × 1.6 = 4.48	4.48 × 4.3 = 19.264
Both doors		
Right internal wall		
Bottom internal wall		
Top external wall		
Left external wall		
The floor		
The ceiling		

2. What is the total heat loss?

3. Work out the room's heating requirements in watts.

4. Calculate how many radiators the room requires if each radiator produces 600 watts of heat.

5. The single-glazed windows were replaced with double-glazed ones (U value 0.6). How many radiators are now required?

4 Algebra

In this chapter you will learn:

✓ how to work with number sequences
✓ how to work with formulae
✓ how to solve linear, simultaneous and quadratic equations
✓ how to graph equations and interpret them
✓ how to solve inequalities

In this chapter you will need:

✓ a pencil
✓ ruler
✓ calculator
✓ graph paper

Introduction

Algebra is an Arabic word meaning 'bringing together broken parts.' This description still holds today. Algebra is still concerned with fitting together parts of a picture in order to see the whole.

Just what is the secret of happiness? Forget true love, loads of money, or a thrilling lifestyle, think algebra.

Work out your own happiness rating by answering the following four questions:

The questions should be answered on a scale of one to ten, where one is 'not at all' and ten is 'to a large extent'.

a. Are you outgoing, energetic, flexible and open to change? ☐

b. Do you have a positive outlook, bounce back quickly from setbacks and feel that you are in control of your life? ☐

▶

Algebra is the invisible nuts and bolts of modern society. It lies behind anything that involves computers, from Internet searches to text messages to computer gaming.

c. Are your basic life needs met, in relation to personal health, finance, safety, freedom of choice and sense of community? ☐

d. Can you call on the support of people close to you, immerse yourself in what you are doing, meet your expectations and engage in activities that give you a sense of purpose? ☐

Now put your scores into the formula:

Happiness = Answer to **a** + answer to **b** + five times answer to **c** + three times answer to **d**

Or the shorthand, algebraic version:

Happiness = $\mathbf{a} + \mathbf{b} + 5 \times \mathbf{c} + 3 \times \mathbf{d}$

4.1 Patterns in Numbers

New houses are to be built on one side of a street. The houses are to be either detached or semi-detached. Here are the architect's drawings of the possible arrangements when there are just three houses to be built:

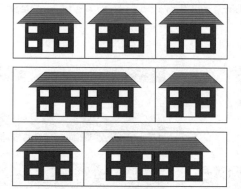

A pair of semis take up the same 'frontage' as two detached houses.
With three houses there are three possible ways the 'street' can be laid out.

The builders have planning permission to build up to ten houses, but as yet are unsure how many they can afford to build and how they will set them out on the 'street.'

Task

1. By drawing the 'street', work out the number of possible layouts for 1–6 houses. Copy and complete the table:

Number of houses	1	2	3	4	5	6
Number of layouts	1		3			

2. What is the pattern in the number of layouts? This number pattern is known as the **Fibonacci number sequence**.

3. Use this pattern to predict, without drawing, the number of possible layouts when building:
    a. seven houses
    b. eight houses
    c. nine houses
    d. ten houses.

Fibonacci and his furry friends

Suppose a newly-born pair of rabbits, one male, one female, are put in a rabbit-proof field. Amazingly, rabbits are able to mate at the age of one month and the pregnancy lasts just a month so at the end of its second month a female can produce another pair of rabbits.

The puzzle that Fibonacci posed was . . .

How many pairs of rabbits will there be in the field in one year?

Generating the Fibonacci series

For the sake of simplicity, Fibonacci assumed that the rabbits never die and the female **always** gives birth to one male and one female **every month** from the second month on and has no 'rest' months i.e. no sooner has she given birth, she becomes pregnant again.

 New born rabbits

 Mating rabbits

 Original pair of mature rabbits

Although this system does simplify nature, it can be adapted to predict the growth of populations.

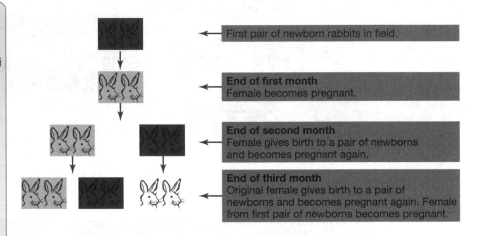

First pair of newborn rabbits in field.

End of first month
Female becomes pregnant.

End of second month
Female gives birth to a pair of newborns and becomes pregnant again.

End of third month
Original female gives birth to a pair of newborns and becomes pregnant again. Female from first pair of newborns becomes pregnant.

Task

a. Copy and continue this diagram for another three months.

b. Copy and complete this table:

Number of months	1	2	3	4	5	6
Number of rabbits	2	4	6			

c. Without drawing any more rabbits, predict how many rabbits there will be after twelve months?

Key term

Fibonacci
A set of numbers in which each number is the sum of the two preceding numbers.

Investigation 1 – Fibonacci in nature

Half way down a sheet of A4 graph paper:

a. Draw a 1 cm square.
b. Draw another one to the right of it.
c. Draw a 2 cm square below it.
d. Draw a 3 cm square to the left.
e. Draw a 5 cm square above it.
f. Draw two more squares in the same manner.
g. If drawn, what would be the lengths of the sides of the eighth and ninth squares?
h. Connect opposite corners of square 1 with a smooth curve.
i. Continue connecting corners, making sure all curves are connected smoothly.
j. What shape have you drawn?

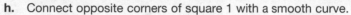

Investigation 2

1. Work out how this series of numbers is progressing and write down the next three top heavy fractions:

$$\frac{1}{1}, \quad \frac{2}{1}, \quad \frac{3}{2}, \quad \frac{5}{3}, \quad \frac{8}{5}, \cdots$$

2. Use your calculator to provide decimal answers (to two decimal places) to these divisions.
4. What seems to be happening?
5. Look back to page 349 and see if you can see a connection.

Investigation 3

The Fibonacci numbers can also be found in the rhythm of music and poetry. Use the Internet to investigate this.

Special
occasion
cake

Wedding
cake

Work it out

1. Ken, a cake maker, takes half a day to make a special occasion cake and a whole day to make a wedding cake. He is inundated with work and wants to sort out his diary. Looking at the first two days, the different ways Ken could arrange his work-load are:

There are five possible ways he could fill out two days of his diary.

How many possible ways could Ken fill out his diary if he was sorting out his baking for the next:
a. three days?
b. four days?
c. seven days?

2. Why is this tree obeying the Fibonacci series?

Hints and tips

Look at the branching of the tree.

In those desolate times before algebra. . . .

Key term

Formula
A shorthand way of writing a rule. Letters are often used to represent values.

In ancient times the taxmen collected taxes from crop farmers in the form of part of their harvest. They used tables to work out how much each farmer should pay:

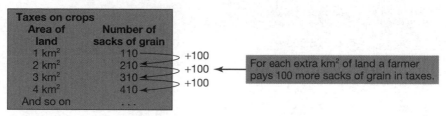

Taxes on crops

Area of land	Number of sacks of grain	
1 km²	110	+100
2 km²	210	+100
3 km²	310	+100
4 km²	410	
And so on	. . .	

For each extra km² of land a farmer pays 100 more sacks of grain in taxes.

1. What is the tax on a farmer who has 6 km² of land?

$410 + 100 + 100 = \textbf{610 sacks of grain}$

2. How can the tax man write a **formula** that can be applied to any area of land?

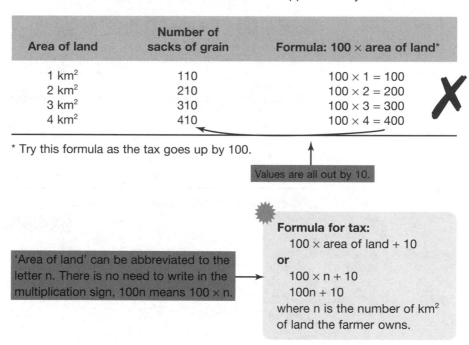

Area of land	Number of sacks of grain	Formula: 100 × area of land*
1 km²	110	100 × 1 = 100
2 km²	210	100 × 2 = 200
3 km²	310	100 × 3 = 300
4 km²	410	100 × 4 = 400

* Try this formula as the tax goes up by 100.

Values are all out by 10.

'Area of land' can be abbreviated to the letter n. There is no need to write in the multiplication sign, 100n means 100 × n.

Formula for tax:
$100 \times \text{area of land} + 10$
or
$100 \times n + 10$
$100n + 10$
where n is the number of km² of land the farmer owns.

3. Use your formula to work out the tax on a farmer who has 26 km² of land?

$100 \times 26 + 10 = \textbf{2 610 sacks of grain}$

Tax formulae today

This table shows the tax paid on four different salaries that are taxed at the basic rate:

> There is no tax paid on the first £5 000 earned.

Annual salary	Annual tax	
£5 000	£0.00	⟩ + £0.22
£5 001	£0.22	
£5 002	£0.44	⟩ + £0.22
£5 003	£0.66	⟩ + £0.22

Note: For each extra £1 in salary we pay £0.22 more in taxes.

1. What will a person earning £5 006 pay in taxes each year?

> $0.66 + 0.22 + 0.22 + 0.22 = **£1.32**$

This method is too laborious for bigger salaries.

2. What formula can the taxman use for any salary that is taxed at the basic rate?

Annual salary	Annual tax	Formula: 0.22 × salary*
£5 000	0	$0.22 \times 5\,000 = £1\,100.00$
£5 001	£0.22	$0.22 \times 5\,001 = £1\,100.22$
£5 002	£0.44	$0.22 \times 5\,002 = £1\,100.44$
£5 003	£0.66	$0.22 \times 5\,003 = £1\,100.66$

* Try this formula as the tax goes up by £0.22.

Values are all out by £1 100.

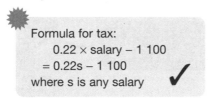

> Formula for tax:
> $0.22 \times \text{salary} - 1\,100$
> $= 0.22s - 1\,100$
> where s is any salary ✓

3. Use the formula to work out the tax on someone earning £25 000.

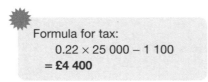

> Formula for tax:
> $0.22 \times 25\,000 - 1\,100$
> $= **£4\,400**$

> ### Work it out

In all these questions n is any positive whole number.

1. The table below shows the cost of staying at the San Marino hotel:

Number of nights	Cost
1	£80
2	£140
3	£200
4	£260

   a. Work through this flow chart:

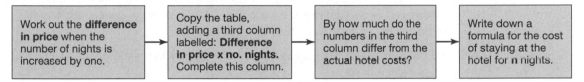

| Work out the **difference in price** when the number of nights is increased by one. | Copy the table, adding a third column labelled: **Difference in price x no. nights.** Complete this column. | By how much do the numbers in the third column differ from the actual hotel costs? | Write down a formula for the cost of staying at the hotel for n nights. |

   b. Use your formula to work out the cost of staying at the San Marino for:
      i.   ten nights
      ii. a fortnight.

2. This table shows how the price of a new two bedroomed house has changed over a period of four years:

Year	Price
1	£100 000
2	£115 000
3	£130 000
4	£145 000

   a. How much does the price of the house increase by each year?
   b. If this pattern continues, what will be the cost of the house in year 6?
   c. Copy the table and add an extra column that is labelled **price increase x year number**. Complete this column.
   d. Write down the general formula for the price of a new house after **n** years.
   e. Use this formula to work out the price of a house twelve years after the start of the survey.

3. An architect is designing a block of flats that are arranged in a U-shape.
   a. Copy and complete the table:

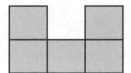

▶

Number of storeys	Number of flats
1	5
2	10
3	
4	

b. Add an extra column and label it with a suitable formula for the number of flats. Complete this column.

c. Write down the general formula for the number of flats when there are **n** storeys.

d. Use your formula to work out how many flats there are in a building that is 40 storeys high?

e. The architect decides to create a large foyer on the ground floor. This means there is only enough space for two flats. What now is the general formula for the number of flats when there are **n** storeys?

4. This diagram shows how a landscaper lays out paving slabs at the junction of four paths in a park:

The white and grey squares are slabs. The red squares represent lawn.

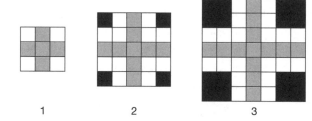

Level   1   2   3

a. Copy and complete the table:

Level (n)	Number of grey slabs	Number of white slabs	Total Number of slabs
1		5	49
2			
3			
4			
5			

b. Work out a general formula for the number of:
   i. grey slabs after **n** levels
   ii. white slabs after **n** levels
   iii. total number of slabs after **n** levels.

c. Use your formula to work out:
   i. the number of grey tiles in the twelfth level
   ii. the number of white tiles in the twentieth level
   iii. the total number of tiles in the hundredth level.

Hints and tips

Draw a table with three columns, the first being the number of days, the second the amount made on that day and the third, your attempt at the formula. The shop is open every day.

Key term

Number sequence
A set of numbers that are connected in some manner. Each number in the sequence is called a **term**.

5. A new shop opened for business on Monday morning. Each day the shop made £20 more than the previous day and this pattern continued for the first four weeks. On Monday the shop made £60. How much money did it make on:
   a. Friday?
   b. the following Monday?
   c. **n** days after the opening day?
   d. the last day of the four week period (use your general formula)?

6. Write down the next two terms in the following **number sequences**:
   a. 2, 6, 10, 14, ☐, ☐
   b. 2, 12, 22, 32, ☐, ☐
   c. 7, 15, 23, 31, ☐, ☐

7. Copy and complete the two grids, the first row of a has been done for you:

   a.

3	5	7	9	11	13
	9				
				32	37
		32			

   b.

4					
		15		23	
				51	

   There is a different number sequence in each row and column.
   Each term in each sequence goes up by a set amount.

For the next three questions n represents the position of a term within the sequence.

8. For the following number sequences:
   • write down the missing terms
   • work out the general formula for the **n**th term
   • use your formula to work out the value of the term in the 100th position.
   One has been done for you:

   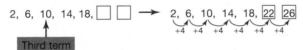

   2, 6, 10, 14, 18, ☐ ☐ → 2, 6, 10, 14, 18, 22 26
   +4 +4 +4 +4 +4 +4

   Third term

   Working out the formula for the nth term:
   Write out the first five terms of the number sequence as a table:

Position (n)	Value of the term	4 × n*
1	2	4 × 1 = 4
2	6	4 × 2 = 8
3	10	4 × 3 = 12
4	14	4 × 4 = 16
5	18	4 × 5 = 20

   * Try this formula as the sequence goes up by +4

   There is a difference of –2.

   Formula: **4n – 2**
   Value of term in 100th position:
   4 × 100 – 2 = 398

a. 3, 5, 7, ☐, ☐
b. 4, 7, 10, ☐, ☐
c. 9, 15, ☐, ☐, 33
d. 30, ☐, 50, ☐, 70
e. ☐, ☐, 16, 22, 28
f. 3, 10, 17, ☐, ☐

9. Write the first three terms of the formulae:
   a. $3n + 7$
   b. $5n - 4$

10. Write the third and sixth terms of the formulae:
    a. $6n + 3$
    b. $9n - 12$

11. What will be the difference between neighbouring numbers in the following sequences:
    a. $3n - 7$?
    b. $5n + 2$?

12. a. Use the diagram to work out the co-ordinates of the right angle in the:
       i. tenth triangle
       ii. hundredth triangle
       iii. n^{th} triangle.

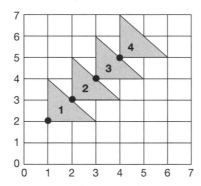

    b. Use the diagram to work out the co-ordinates of the circle in the:
       i. tenth diamond
       ii. hundredth diamond
       iii. n^{th} diamond.

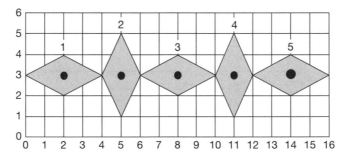

Hints and tips

All angles at the centre of a circle total 360°.

Investigation

A circle is completely divided into n sectors in such a way that the size of the angle of each sector is a term in a number sequence.
The first angle is 30° and the fourth is 66°.
Work out the rest of the angles.

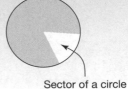

Sector of a circle

Special formulae – the family tree

The diagram shows the number of ancestors one person has when we go back four generations:

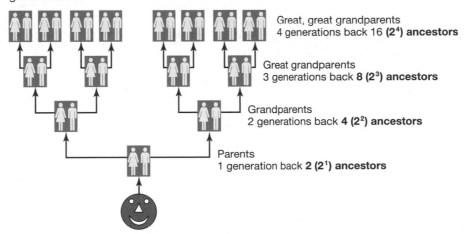

Great, great grandparents
4 generations back 16 (2^4) **ancestors**

Great grandparents
3 generations back **8 (2^3) ancestors**

Grandparents
2 generations back **4 (2^2) ancestors**

Parents
1 generation back **2 (2^1) ancestors**

Five generations back there are 2^5 ancestors and so on.
What is the formula for the number of ancestors **n** generations back?

2^n **ancestors, where n is the number of generations**

Example

Triangular numbers

Ann is participating in a radio quiz. She wins £1 if she answers the first question correctly, £2 if the second answer is correct, £3 if the third answer is correct and so on.

1. Ann answers the first four questions correctly, how much money does she take home?

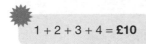
$1 + 2 + 3 + 4 =$ **£10**

2. Work out a general formula for the money Ann makes when she answers the first **n** questions correctly.

    The winnings can be shown diagrammatically:

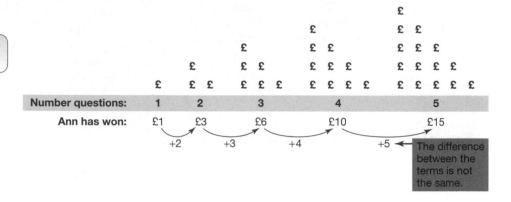

£: Ann has won a pound.

Supposing Ann won twice as much at each stage of the quiz, then this diagram can be drawn:

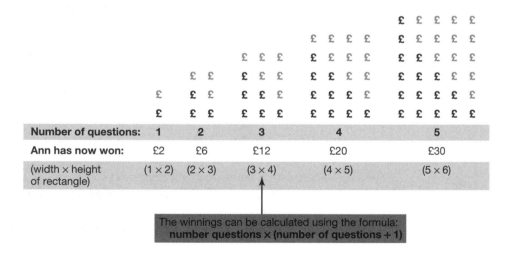

Number of questions:	1	2	3	4	5
Ann has now won:	£2	£6	£12	£20	£30
(width × height of rectangle)	(1 × 2)	(2 × 3)	(3 × 4)	(4 × 5)	(5 × 6)

The winnings can be calculated using the formula:
number questions × (number of questions + 1)

Key term

Triangular sequence
A set of numbers that obey the formula $\frac{1}{2}n(n+1)$ where n is any whole number.

Ann's winnings:

Half of number questions × (number of questions + 1)

$= \frac{1}{2} \times n \times (n+1)$

$= \frac{1}{2}$**n (n + 1)** where n is the number of questions answered correctly.

There is an implied multiplication here.

Work it out

1. a. Use the family tree formula to work out the number of ancestors:
   i.   10 generations back
   ii. 20 generations back.
b. How many years are there between you and:
   i.   three generations back?
   ii. ten generations back?
   iii. **n** generations back, where **n** is the number of generations.

> Assume there are 28 years between generations.

Square numbers

2. Here is a number sequence:

$$1, \quad 4, \quad 9, \quad 16, \quad 25, \ldots$$

a. What are the next two terms in the sequence?
b. Write down the general formula for the **n**th term in the sequence.
c. Use this formula to work out the value of the
   i.   tenth term
   ii. hundredth term.

3. Here is a number triangle:

```
            1    2
         3    4    5
       6   7   8   9
    10    11    12    13    14
   15   16   17   18   19   20
```

> **Hints and tips**
>
> Use triangular numbers.

a. What is the value of the first number (on the left hand side) in the two hundredth row?
b. How many numbers will be on this row?
c. What is the value of the last number on this row?

4. Investigate the following patterns and find a formula for the nth term.

> **Hints and tips**
>
> **(for a.)** It may help to double the number of dots to make a rectangle. Write the numbers in a table.

a.

b.

Hints and tips

Work out the sum of the numbers when there are just one, two, three numbers etc. and see if this provides a pattern.

Carl Gauss was a German child prodigy who in later life made many significant contributions to mathematics.

Hints and tips

Draw out a table with two columns, the first labelled number of years, the second number of customers.

5. As the story goes, when Carl Gauss was at school the teacher asked the whole class to work out the total of all the numbers up to one hundred. The children immediately took pencil to paper and set about busily adding up the numbers. When the teacher saw Gauss staring into space she thought he was daydreaming but no, he had already worked out the answer.

   See if you can match Gauss, the child genius, by using a formula to calculate the answer.

6. For a particular Internet provider, the number of its customers has doubled every year. In the first year there were 1 000 customers, how many will there be after:

   a. **n** years?

   b. ten years?

   c. 20 years?

4.2 Working with Formulae

The world would fall apart without formulae.

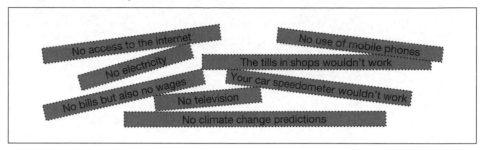

Example

d = 3   **e** = 2   f = −4

Work out:

a. 2**d**

$2 \times \mathbf{3} = \mathbf{6}$

There is an implied multiplication when:
- a number and letter are next to each other, e.g. $3n = 3 \times n$
- two letters are next to each other, e.g. $ab = a \times b$
- a letter or number is next to a bracket, e.g. $a(2 + b) = a \times (2 + b)$

b. **d** − f

$\mathbf{3} - (-4) = 3 + 4 = \mathbf{7}$

c. 3**e** + 7

$3 \times \mathbf{2} + 7 = 6 + 7 = \mathbf{13}$

d. 3f − 5**d**

$3 \times -4 - 5 \times \mathbf{3} = -12 - 15 = \mathbf{-27}$

e. 5(**de** − 4)

$5(\mathbf{3} \times \mathbf{2} - 4) = 5(6 - 4) = 5 \times 2 = \mathbf{10}$

First work out what is inside the bracket.

f. **def** ÷ 6

$\mathbf{3} \times \mathbf{2} \times -4 \div 6 = -24 \div 6 = \mathbf{-4}$

g. **d**^{2} + 3f^2

$\mathbf{3}^2 + 3 \times (-4)^2 = 9 + 3 \times 16 = 9 + 48 = \mathbf{57}$

Work it out

$a = 2$, $b = 3$, and $c = 4$
Work out the value of the following:

1. $2a + 3$ **2.** $3b + a$
3. a^2 **4.** $c^2 - 2b$
5. $3a + 2b$ **6.** ab
7. $a + b + c$ **8.** abc
9. $a^2 + b^2$ **10.** $bc - ac$

$p = 2$, $q = 4$, and $r = -2$
Work out the value of the following:

11. $2(p + 1)$ **12.** $3(q + 4)$
13. $4(2p + 3)$ **14.** $2(q^2 - p)$
15. $3(p + r^2)$ **16.** $2(r - q)$
17. $(p + q) \div 4$ **18.** $(3p^2 + q) \div 2$
19. $(4p + r) \div 2$ **20.** $(4q + 2) \div p$

21. Connect the formula with the correct expression; the first one has been done for you:

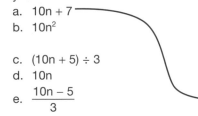

a. $10n + 7$ g. Ten times the square of a number.
b. $10n^2$ h. Ten times a number minus five, all divided by three.
c. $(10n + 5) \div 3$ i. Ten times a number.
d. $10n$ j. A number divided by ten.
e. $\dfrac{10n - 5}{3}$ k. Ten times a number plus seven.
f. $\dfrac{n}{10}$ l. Add five to ten times a number then divide the total by three.

22. i. Use these flow charts to work out the output number when 8 is the input number.
    ii. Write a formula for each flowchart
The first one has been done for you.

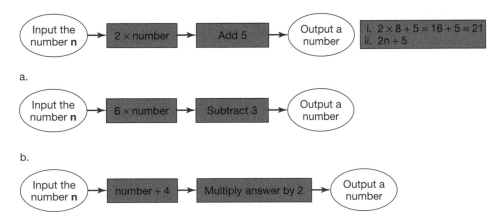

Hints and tips

When there is a multiplication or division at the end, use brackets in your formula.

c.

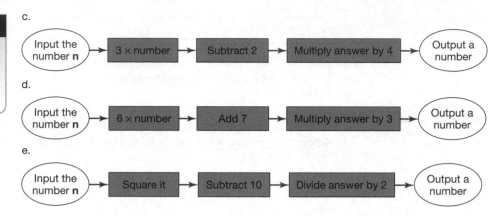

Input the number **n** → 3 × number → Subtract 2 → Multiply answer by 4 → Output a number

d.

Input the number **n** → 6 × number → Add 7 → Multiply answer by 3 → Output a number

e.

Input the number **n** → Square it → Subtract 10 → Divide answer by 2 → Output a number

Investigation

Substitute the numbers in the box for the letters in the expressions to make the largest possible value:

1. $a^2 - b^2$
2. $\dfrac{ab}{cd}$
3. $(a - b)(c + d)$
4. $ab + bc + cd + da$

10	1
5	0.1

Practical uses of formulae

If your BMI is:

- less than 18.4 you're underweight
- between 18.5 and 24.9 you're an ideal weight
- between 25 and 29.9 you're over the ideal weight
- over 30 you're obese.

The Body Mass Index (BMI) can be regarded as an indicator of whether you are a healthy weight for your height.

The BMI formula is:

weight ÷ (height × height)

or

w ÷ h²   w: weight in kilograms
           h: height in metres

What is the BMI for a person that weighs 65 kilograms and is 1.65 metres tall?

 BMI = $65 \div 1.65^2$ = **23.88** (ideal weight for their height)

On the calculator: 65 ÷ 1.65 x² =

Work it out

If required round your answers to one decimal place.

1. a. Work out the BMI for Rajiv who weighs 78 kilograms and is
        1.92 metres tall.
    b. Is Rajiv a healthy weight for his height?

> Stone = 14 pounds
> 1 foot = 12 inches

c. Sam only knows his measurements in imperial units. He is 12 stone
    4 pounds in weight and 5 foot 8 inches tall. He uses this formula to work
    out his BMI:

$$(w \div h^2) \times 698 \qquad \text{w: weight in pounds}$$
$$\text{h: height in inches}$$

Work out Sam's BMI.

d. Is Sam a healthy weight for his height?
e. Work out your own BMI (not to be marked).

2. Here are some formulae for changing from imperial units to metric:

Kilograms = 0.45**p**   **p**: weight in pounds
Centimetres = 2.54**n**   **n**: length in inches
Litres = 0.47**t**   **t**: number of pints

a. Work out the height in centimetres and weight in kilograms for:
    i.   Haroon who weighs 13 stone 13 pounds and is 5 foot 10 inches tall
    ii. Mandeep who weighs 11 stone 5 pounds and is 5 foot 7 inches tall.
b. It is recommended that we drink about 4 pints of liquid each day. What is this
    in litres?

Calorie consumption

> This formula is
> for a person who
> undertakes a
> little light activity
> each week.

3. To work out your ideal daily calorie requirement you can use the Harris–Benedict
    formula:

for men: 92 + 19**w** + 7**h** – 10**a**   **w**: weight in kilograms
for women: 998 + 14**w** + 3**h** – 7**a**   **h**: is height in centimetres
                                              a: is age

a. When working out the daily calorie requirement, is weight a bigger factor for
    women or men?
b. Use your answers from question 2 to work out the ideal calorie intake for:
    i.   Haroon, a 30 year old man.
    ii. Mandeep, a 25 year old woman.
c. Neither Haroon nor Mandeep are happy with their weights. Haroon wants
    to lose 1.5 pounds a week for the next ten weeks and Mandeep's target is
    1 pound a week for the same period. To work out their new daily calorie
    consumption, substitute this information, together with your answers in **b**
    into this formula:

new daily calorie = **c** – 500**n**   **c**: Harris–Benedict calorie requirement
consumption   **n**: planned weekly weight loss in pounds

d. If they stick to this diet, what will be Haroon's and Kate's weight, in stones and pounds, by the end of the ten weeks?

e. What do you think of the Harris-Benedict formula?

4. A company has a pay policy of increasing employee wages by 10% each year. This can be written as the formula:

New wages = $\mathbf{w}1.1^n$

w: wage in the first year of employment
n: number of years employed

Use this formula to work out the wages, rounded to the nearest pound, of:

a. an employee who has been with the company for five years and in their first year earned £17 000

b. an employee who has been with the company for ten years and in their first year earned £12 000.

5. While out walking near a sea cliff John dropped his glasses over the edge of the cliff. His wife could see they were unbroken (John could see very little). Being climbers, they had a 70 metre rope and climbing equipment in the boot of their car, but this was five miles away.

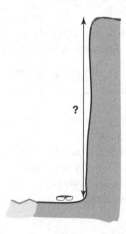

To work out if it was worth trekking back to the car John decided to estimate the height of the cliffs by dropping a stone from the cliff edge and timing how long it took to hit the beach. It took 4 seconds.

He then used this physics formula:

height = $5\mathbf{t}^2$ **t**: time, in seconds, for pebble to hit the beach; height is in metres.

Use the formula to work out if the rope is long enough for one of them to climb down to retrieve his glasses.

6. In 1898, A. E. Dolbear came up with a formula to work out the outside temperature, in Fahrenheit, based on the number of chirps a cricket makes each minute:

Temperature = $40 + \dfrac{\mathbf{N}}{4}$ **N**: number of cricket chirps per minute

▶

> Crickets, like all insects, are cold blooded. This means that as the temperature increases so does the cricket's metabolism and the speed at which it chirps.

a. Use the formula to work out the temperature when there are:
  i. 60 chirps a minute
  ii. 160 chirps a minute.
b. The formula for converting temperature in Fahrenheit to Centigrade is:

$$\text{Centigrade} = \frac{5}{9}(\mathbf{F} - 32) \qquad \mathbf{F}:\text{ Fahrenheit temperature}$$

Convert your two answers for **a.** to Centigrade.

7. A runner, Zac, trains at his local athletics club. Often he's restricted to certain tracks, this presents a problem when he's using the track for speed workouts as he's never quite sure how far he has run. He posted this question on a website dedicated to athletes:

'How can I calculate the exact distance for each lane around an oval track?'

Here is a reply from a running coach:

> 'This is a common question. You could simply pace each lane out but that's time consuming and fraught with errors or you could use my own personal formula that seems to work':
>
> Length of a complete circuit: $400 + 2\pi\mathbf{w}(\mathbf{n} - 1)$
> Where **w** is the width of each track and **n** is the lane number.
>
> 'This assumes the length of your inner lane is 400 m. Good luck'!

a. The coach did not specify whether the lane numbers are measured from the outside or inside. What do you think?
b. The track at Zac's athletics club has lane widths of 1.2 m. How far does Zac run when he completes a circuit in the fourth lane?
c. Zac wants to time his run over 400 m. When running in the seventh lane, how much of the circuit should he not run?

World War II

> By using this formula, it was estimated that the Germans produced 246 tanks per month between mid 1940 and mid 1942. At the same time, standard intelligence believed the number was far higher, at around 1 400. After the war, the Allies captured German production records. These revealed that the true number of tanks produced during this period was 245 per month!

8. In 1940, the Allies had very little idea of how many tanks the enemy was capable of producing in one year. Without this information, they were unsure whether any invasion of the continent on the Western front could succeed. However, Allied intelligence did possess one key piece of information – the serial numbers on captured tanks. They believed that the logically inclined Nazi regime would have numbered their tanks in order. Using this assumption, mathematicians were able to estimate the total number of tanks that had been produced at any given time with this formula:

$$\frac{(\mathbf{B} - 1)(\mathbf{N} + 1)}{\mathbf{N}} \qquad \begin{array}{l}\mathbf{B}:\text{ biggest serial number in the tanks captured}\\ \mathbf{N}:\text{ number of tanks captured}\end{array}$$

If five tanks were captured with serial numbers 30, 45, 92, 78, 21, how many tanks at that time had been produced?

Group work – investing early pays

After graduating, Dwaine and Kieran both start new jobs. This table shows the amounts Dwaine and Kieran save over the next thirty years:

	Kieran	Dwaine
First ten years	Saves nothing	Invests £1 000 each year
Next twenty years	Invests £1 000 each year	Stops investing. The money in his account accrues interest.

a. Copy this table and use the formulae below to complete it:

Amount saved after:	Kieran	Dwaine
Ten years	0	
Thirty years		

→ use the first formula where n = 10

→ use the second formula n = 20 and p is the answer from the first formula

↑ n = 20 in first formula

Round all your answers to the nearest pound.

b. Does Kieran have more in her account than Dwaine after 30 years?

c. At the end of sixty years, with Kieran continuing to invest £1 000 a year and Dwaine making no new savings what will be the amount each has saved?

'Formula' for working out the amount in the bank when a person invests the same amount each year for a set number of years.

$$a = 1 + r$$
$$\downarrow$$
$$b = a^n$$
$$\downarrow$$
$$c = b - 1$$
$$\downarrow$$
$$\text{Money now in account} = \frac{ac\mathbf{m}}{r}$$

The letters a, b and c are used as temporary totals.

m: money invested each year
r: interest rate as a decimal
n: number of years invested

'Formula' for working out the amount in the bank when a person leaves money in the bank to accumulate interest.

$$\text{Money now in account} = \mathbf{p}(1 + \mathbf{r})^n$$

p: initial amount of money put in the bank
r: interest rate as a decimal
n: number of years invested

Group work

Narveen is suing a manufacturing plant for discharging a highly toxic chemical into the river near where she grew up. As a child Narveen regularly swam in the river. Now she has cancer and believes she knows who is to blame for it.

Before the case went to court the owner of the company sent her this letter:

> Dear Madam
>
> After extensive research into this case, we have calculated that the amount of chemical we discharged into the river resulted in the river containing only 6.3 mg of the toxin per m³ of river water (I have enclosed our calculations on a separate sheet).
> This measure is well below the permissible exposure level of 7 mg per m³.
> In the light of this you may want to consider withdrawing from what could be a lengthy and expensive court case that you have no realistic chance of winning.
>
> Yours truly
>
> T. Poisonne

1 milligram (mg) is one thousandth of a gram.

T. Poisonne's calculations:

Concentration of chemical in river:
$$\frac{CD}{60R}$$

C: amount of chemical in one litre of water that goes into the river (**3 mg**)
D: amount of chemical solution being discharged into the river each minute (**50 litres**)
R: the flow rate of the river in (**0.4 m³ per second**)

This is Narveen's reply:

> Dear Sir
>
> I agree with your formula, however I disagree with your figures. You have used today's flow rate (R) for the river, not what it was thirty years ago when I was swimming in the river. Then the flow of the river was much slower, only 0.1m³ per second. This results in a much higher concentration of toxins.
> **You may want to reconsider the court case, especially as I am open to any reasonably fair out of court settlement.**
> Yours truly
>
> N. Gant

1. Use T. Poisonne's figures and formula to see if his calculation is correct.
2. Work out the concentration levels using Narveen's figures.
3. Should T. Poisonne be worried?

Creating formulae

For the crossing between Dover and Calais a ferry company charges £45 for a car and driver plus £15 for every extra passenger. Write this out as a formula.

Cost of ferry = 45 + 15n   n is the number of passengers

What is the cost of the crossing for a driver with three passengers in his car?

Cost of ferry = 45 + 15 × 3 = 45 + 45 = **£90**

Work it out

Callout charge: the charge made for turning up to a job.

1. Work out the formulae for the following situations:
   a. a plumber's callout charge is £35 and they then charges £15 per hour.
   b. a photographer charges £45 for expenses and then £30 per hour of the 'shoot'.
   c. a newspaper advertisement costs £12 plus £1.50 per word.

Hints and tips

Always state what the letter in the formula represents.

2. a. To work out an adult's shoe size, multiply the length of the foot, in inches, by 3 and subtract 24.
   Write this out as a formula.
   b. A person's foot is ten inches long, what is their shoe size?
   c. For what lengths of foot will the formula not work?

3. A clothes shop is to have a sale. All goods are to be reduced by 15%.
   a. Write out a formula describing the new price of an item in terms of its old price.
   b. Use your formula to work out the new price of a pair of jeans that were originally priced at £28.

4. In football, teams gain three points for winning and one for drawing.
   a. Write a formula for the total points gained by one team. Let **w** be the number of games won and **d** be the number of games drawn.
   b. Use your formula to work out the total points for
      i. Gadlock United
      ii. Burford Town.
   c. The two teams play twenty games in a season. Is it still possible for Burford Town to beat Gadlock United and if so how?

Gadlock United: won twelve games, lost two and drawn five.
Burford Town: won eight games, lost two and drawn six.

5. A small company owns one company car that is used by several members of staff for out of town meetings. The company accountant has estimated that the annual cost of the car is:

   £560 – a fixed cost that covers tax, insurance and general maintenance
   40p per mile for petrol

   a. Write a formula for the cost of the company car.
   b. The accountant has also estimated that if the company switches to using just public transport, the cost will be 50p a mile. Write a formula for this.
   c. Which method of transport is more economical when the annual staff travel is:
      i. 4 000 miles?
      ii. 10 000 miles?
      iii. 15 000 miles?

Hints and tips

Your formula will consist of two letters. one for the course work mark and the other for the exam mark. Both marks are out of 100.

6. For a degree in Health and Social Care, a student's overall result is split into:
   • course work, worth 40%
   • final exams, worth 60%
   a. Write out a formula for a student's final result.
   b. Teckler has gained 72% in her coursework and 52% in her final exams. What is her overall result?

7. A company plans to purchase some mobile phones for its employees. They anticipate that all phones will be used for over 800 minutes a month and some will be used for over 1 400 minutes a month. This flow chart shows the charges they will incur:

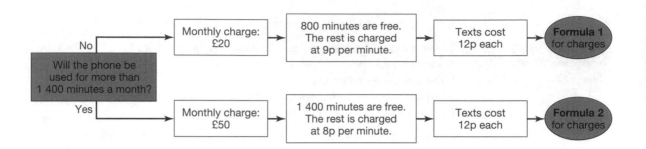

Let **p** be the number of minutes spent talking on the phone each month. Let **t** be the number of texts sent a month.

a. Write out two formulae for charges per month: one for a phone used for less than 1 400 minutes (Formula 1) and the other for over 1 400 minutes (Formula 2).

b. Use your Formula 1 to work out the cost of the phone for a month for an employee who:
   • spends 1 200 minutes talking on the phone
   • and sends 220 text messages.

c. Use your Formula 2 to work out the costs of the phone for a month for an employee who:
   • spends 1 800 minutes talking on the phone
   • and sends 300 text messages.

d. One month a 'Formula 2' user goes on holiday for two weeks and only uses the phone for 1 000 minutes and sends 180 text messages. What will be the cost for the month?

CASE STUDY

Using Maths at Work – Ian: project accountant

'I've recently been helping the Computing Department plan for a computer games room. This will be a room dedicated for the use of undergraduates on a new three year computer games programming course. The Department wants to purchase state of the art hardware and software to place the university at the forefront in this field. We have already worked together to get an idea of the costings. Here is what we've come up with:'

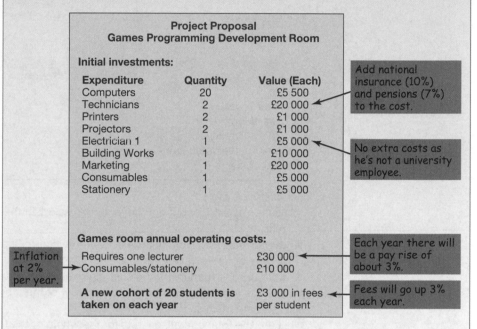

Project Proposal
Games Programming Development Room

Initial investments:

Expenditure	Quantity	Value (Each)
Computers	20	£5 500
Technicians	2	£20 000
Printers	2	£1 000
Projectors	2	£1 000
Electrician	1	£5 000
Building Works	1	£10 000
Marketing	1	£20 000
Consumables	1	£5 000
Stationery	1	£5 000

Add national insurance (10%) and pensions (7%) to the cost.

No extra costs as he's not a university employee.

Games room annual operating costs:

Requires one lecturer	£30 000
Consumables/stationery	£10 000

Each year there will be a pay rise of about 3%.

Inflation at 2% per year.

A new cohort of 20 students is taken on each year   £3 000 in fees per student

Fees will go up 3% each year.

As a general rule we predict there will be a drop out of three students each year, giving student numbers of:

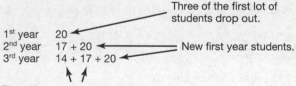

Three of the first lot of students drop out.

1st year	20
2nd year	17 + 20	New first year students.
3rd year	14 + 17 + 20

Three final year students and three second year students drop out.

My task here is to make sure the university sees a positive return on the investment after three years. I generally put these figures into a spreadsheet which requires the use of algebraic formulae. Here are some of the formulae I use on a regular basis:

1. New wages: $1.03s$ (s: previous year's salary)
2. Cost of an employee $1.17w$ (w: current year's salary)
   to the university:
3. Surplus: $F - (I + C)$ (F: fees, I: initial costs, C: operating costs)

▶

CASE STUDY (*continued*)

Tasks

Round all answers to the nearest pound.

Initial costs

1. a. Use formula **2** to work out the total cost of the two technicians.
    b. Work out the total initial costs.

Operating costs

2. a. Copy the table:

Operating costs	First year	Second year	Third year
Lecturer salary			
Cost of lecturer to the university			
Consumables/stationery			
Total costs			

 b. Complete the table:
     i.   use formula **1** to work out the lecturer's salary in the second and third year
     ii. use formula **2** to work out the cost of the lecturer's salary to the university for each year
     iii. work out the formula for the cost of consumables/stationery each year
     iv. use this formula to complete the next row of the table
     v.   complete the final row of the table.
 c. What are the total operating costs for the whole of the three year period?

Income from student fees

3. a. Copy this table and complete the 'Number of students' row:

	Year one	Year two	Year three
Number of students			
Fees for one student	£ 3 000		
Total fees			

 b. Write down the formula that can be used to work out current student fees. The formula should be in terms of the previous year's fees.
 c. Use your formula to complete the 'Fees for one student' row of the table.
 d. Complete the final row of the table.
 e. Over the three years, how much income has the project generated?

Surplus

4. Will the project make a surplus (use formula **3**) and if so, what is it?

4.3 Simplification of Algebraic Expressions

Maddie went shopping at the local market. At one stall she bought 2 apples and 5 oranges, at another she bought 3 apples, 1 orange and 2 bananas.

To summarise:

In her shopping bag she had 5 apples, 2 bananas and 6 oranges.

Just as the total number of apples or oranges are combined, so are the total number of a's or b's in an algebraic expression.

Lucky Lucy and Larry the lottery winners are reluctant to reveal their winnings

Last year we won **p** pounds three times.

And **q** pounds five times!

This year's been even better, already we've won **p** pounds five times.

Not forgetting the six times we've won **q** pounds and just last week we won another £25!

But we didn't keep it all to ourselves – our two sons each received £40.

And that's on top of the two **q** prizes we gave them both.

How much did sickeningly smug Lucy and Larry win over the two years?

Last year: 3p + 5q
This year: 5p + 6q + 25   +
Total: 8p + 11q + 25

All the p's can be combined as can the q's.

How much did they have left after giving some of the prize money to their two sons?

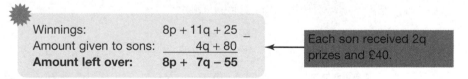

Winnings: 8p + 11q + 25
Amount given to sons: 4q + 80   –
Amount left over: 8p + 7q − 55

Each son received 2q prizes and £40.

Example

Simplify:

1. 3a + 2b + a + 4b

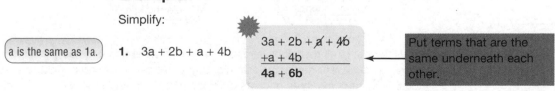

3a + 2b + a + 4b
+a + 4b
_____
4a + 6b

Put terms that are the same underneath each other.

▶

2. $4c + 3 - 5c - 2$

$4c + 3 - \cancel{5c} - \cancel{2}$
$-5c - 2$
$-c + 1$

> The sign before the number or expression moves with it.

3. $3dc + 5cd$

8dc or 8cd

> In the same way as 2×3 is equal 3×2 dc is the same as cd.

4. $3p^2 + 4p - 7p^2 + 2p$

$3p^2 + 4p - \cancel{7p^2} + \cancel{2p}$
$-7p^2 + 2p$
$-4p^2 + 6p$

5. $3mn^2 - 2mn + 5mn^2 - 6mn$

$3mn^2 - 2mn + \cancel{5mn^2} - \cancel{6mn}$
$+5mn^2 - 6mn$
$8mn^2 - 8mn$

Work it out

1. Tim and Brendan sell roses for Valentine's day:

	Tim sells	Brendan sells	Cost in pounds:	
White roses	10	5	One white rose	w
Red roses	6	7	One red rose	r
Bunch of roses	4	8	Bunch of roses	b

Write a simplified algebraic expression for the money they make from all the roses they sell.

2. Partners, Ron and Enid, both decide to go Christmas shopping during their lunchtime on the same day. Unfortunately, neither knew what the other was doing. Here are their shopping baskets:

Mince pies, each costing **m** pounds

Sherry, each costing **£8**

Port costing **£10**

Wine, each costing **w** pounds

Ron's shopping

Enid's shopping

> Ron and Enid bought the same mince pies and bottles of wine.

a. Write the cost of all their shopping as a simplified algebraic expression.

b. When they both returned home that night they decided they had bought too much. They returned three packets of mince pies, two bottles of wine and one bottle of sherry. How much have they spent Christmas shopping now?

3. Connect and combine together the same terms, one has been done for you:

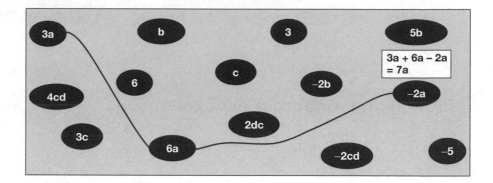

4. Simplify the following:
  a. $2x + 5y + 4x + 8y$
  b. $2p^2 + 2p + p^2 - p$
  c. $7a + 3b + 2a + 5b$
  d. $2pq + qp$
  e. $x + y + x + y$
  f. $3xy - 2y + 2yx - y$
  g. $3m + 2n + 4m - m$
  h. $3m^2 - 3m + 3m^2 - m$
  i. $2m - 3n + 2m - n$
  j. $4x^2 + 3x - 2x^2 + 5x$
  k. $6 + a + 3 - a$
  l. $10xy^2 + 3x + 3xy^2 - 2x$
  m. $x + 2x + 3y - 3x$
  n. $12x + 12 - 13x - 10$

5. Connect and combine together the same terms:

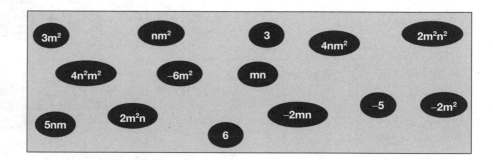

6. Copy and complete these algebraic bricks, the first one has been done for you:

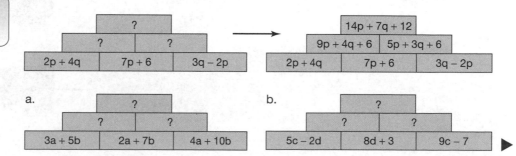

c.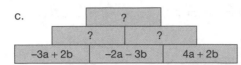

d.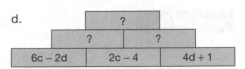

Multiplying algebraic expressions

Example

Simplify:

1. $5a \times 3a$

$(5 \times 3) \times (a \times a)$
$= \quad 15 \quad \times \quad a^2$
$= \mathbf{15a^2}$

Multiply the numbers separately from the letters and then combine the two.

2. $3 \times 4c \times 2d \times d$

$(3 \times 4 \times 2) \times (c \times d \times d)$
$= \quad\quad 24 \quad\quad \times \quad cd^2$
$= \mathbf{24cd^2}$

3. $3r^2 \times 5r^3$

$(3 \times 5) \times (r^2 \times r^3)$
$= \quad 15 \quad \times \quad r^5$
$= \mathbf{15r^5}$

When multiplying letters in index form the indices are added together.

4. $4a^2b^2 \times 6ab^3$

$(4 \times 6) \times (a^2 \times a) \times \mathbf{(b^2 \times b^3)}$
$= \quad 24 \quad \times \quad a^3 \quad \times \quad \mathbf{b^5}$
$= \mathbf{24a^3\,b^5}$

A letter on its own has an index of one, e.g. $a = a^1$.

5. $30pq \div 5p$

$\dfrac{\mathbf{30pq}}{\mathbf{5p}} = \dfrac{30 \times \cancel{p}q}{5 \quad \cancel{p}}$
$\qquad = 6 \times q$
$\qquad = \mathbf{6q}$

With division, the expression can be written as a fraction and then cancelled down.

6. $18v^5w^2 \div 9v^3w$

$\dfrac{\mathbf{18v^5w^2}}{\mathbf{9v^3w}} = \dfrac{18}{9} \times \dfrac{v^5}{v^3} \times \dfrac{w^2}{w}$
$\qquad\quad = 2 \times v^2 \times w$
$\qquad\quad = \mathbf{2v^2w}$

When dividing letters in index form the indices are subtracted.

Work it out

1. Simplify the following:
   a. $4m \times m$
   b. $2q^2 \times 6q^3$
   c. $3n \times 2n$
   d. $6r \times 2r^3$
   e. $4q \times 2p$
   f. $s^4 \times 7s^5$
   g. $5a \times 6b$
   h. $m \times m^2 \times m^3$
   i. $4m \times 2 \times n$
   j. $3n^2 \times n^2 \times 2n^2$
   k. $2b \times 3 \times 2b$
   l. $6ab \times 2ab$
   m. $3 \times b \times 2 \times a$
   n. $cd^2 \times c^2d$
   o. $2m \times 3 \times n \times 3$
   p. $2e^2f^2 \times 3ef$
   q. $3 \times 2a \times 6 \times a$
   r. $4gh^3 \times g^3h$
   s. $2p \times 5 \times 2$
   t. $3j^2k^4 \times 5j^3k^5$

2. Simplify the following:
   a. $32m \div 8m$
   b. $15p \div 3p \times 4p$
   c. $12q \div 4$
   d. $q^4 \div q^2$
   e. $24q \div 6q$
   f. $r^6 \div r^3$
   g. $18mn \div 9mn$
   h. $s^7 \div s$
   i. $30pq \div 5p$
   j. $10t^3 \div 2t^2$
   k. $12mn \div 4m$
   l. $12u^4 \div 6u$
   m. $8m^2 \div 4m$
   n. $8v^6 \div 2v^5$
   o. $15p^2 \div 3p$
   p. $20w^4 \div 20w^4$
   q. $24p \div 3p \times 4$
   r. $16x^5 \div 8x^6$
   s. $12m \div 4m \times 2$
   t. $24y^7 \div 6y^5$

Multiplying out brackets

Example

Multiply out the brackets and if possible simplify:

1. $5(2a + 4b) - 12a$

   $5(2a + 4b) - 12a$

   $= 10a + 20b - 12a$

   $\underline{- 12a}$

   $\mathbf{-2a + 20b}$

   5 is multiplied by each expression inside the bracket.

   The a's are combined.

2. $3(3c - 2d) + 4(5d - 2c)$

   $3(3c - 2d) + 4(5d - 2c)$

   $= 9c - 6d + 20d - 8c$

   $\underline{-8c + 20d}$

   $\mathbf{c + 14d}$

   Multiply out both brackets.

   Combine the like terms.

3. 2(3e + 4) − 3(5e − 6)

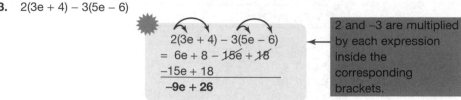

2(3e + 4) − 3(5e − 6)
= 6e + 8 − 15e + 18
−15e + 18
−9e + 26

2 and −3 are multiplied by each expression inside the corresponding brackets.

4. 2f(f + 2g) − 5f(4g − 2f)

2f(f + 2g) − 5f(4g − 2f)
= 2f² + 4fg − 20fg + 10f²
+10f² − 20fg
12f² − 16fg

Mapping out

Multiply out all brackets.

↓

Combine like terms.

Potential pitfalls

When multiplying out a bracket only the first expression is multiplied, e.g.:

4(2a + 3)
= 8a + 3

It should be:

8a + 12

When multiplying out a bracket the sign before the number outside the bracket is ignored, e.g.:

−3(2a − 3)
= 6a − 9

It should be:

−6a + 9

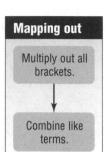

−3 × 2   −3 × −3

Work it out

1. Multiply out the brackets and simplify where possible:
   a. 3(2a + 4b)
   b. 4e + 4(8 + 3e) + 7
   c. 5(3c − 2d)
   d. 4c + 2(b − c) + 4b
   e. 4(3p − 2q + 5r)
   f. −3g − 1(2g − 4)
   g. 4(a + 2b) + 3a
   h. 3(v + 2w) + 4(3w + v)
   i. 7(3e + 4f) + 10e
   j. 10(m − n) − 6(m + n)
   k. 5(2 + g) − 8g
   l. 5(3 + 2q) − 4(2 − q)
   m. 2m + 3(3m + 2)
   n. 2(a − b) − 2(a + b)
   o. 8p − 2(4p + 2q)
   p. 7(3c − 2d) − 4(2c − 3d)
   q. 12 + 4(2a − 3)
   r. −2(5 − 2p) − 3(4p − 2)
   s. 3d − 2(d − 3c)
   t. 2(4 + 4e − 3f) + 3(7 − 2e + 5f)

2. Multiply out the brackets and simplify where possible:
   a. 3a(a + 4)
   b. 3h² + 2h(3 − 3h) + 10h
   c. 7b(2b − 2c)
   d. 2k(1 + 3k) + 3k(2k − 4)
   e. d(3e − 4d) + 5d²
   f. 9m(m − 1) − 3m(2m − 3)
   g. 5f(2g + 3f) − 3fg
   h. −3n(2n − 3m) − 5n(m − 4n)

3. Let **x** be any integer. Write down in terms of **x** the product of two consecutive integers. Multiply out any brackets.

Expand and simplify all the expressions.

4. a. Use the plan to work out the total area of garden in terms of **n**.
  b. Work out the total area of borders, in terms of **n**.
  c. A path of area $3n^2 - 6n$ is to be laid in the borders. How much border area will remain?

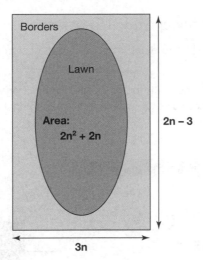

Group investigation

Each member of the group inputs their birth year to obtain their unique birth number.

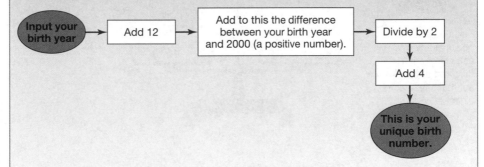

Hints and tips

Assume 2000 is bigger than the birth year.

1. What do you notice?
   Investigate what is happening.
2. Replace the birth year by the letter **n** and write the flow chart as an algebraic expression.
3. Simplify this expression.

4.4 Equations

Achieving the mythical work–life balance

This means different things to different people, but most people have about 16 waking hours to play with.

Agricola's work–life balance is to be at 'home' for half her working hours. She has not achieved this as she spends two more hours working (including travel) than she does at home.
How is her time split?

 Number of hours at home

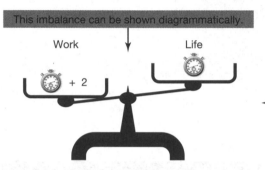

Work   Life

+ 2

This shows the situation but does not help us work out how much time Agricola spends at home or work. To do this we need the two sides of the scale to be equal.

This question can be solved by trial and error, but a far more direct approach is to use algebra.

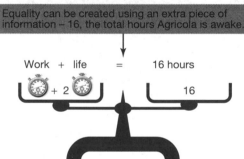

Equality can be created using an extra piece of information – 16, the total hours Agricola is awake.

Work + life   =   16 hours

+ 2   16

This can be written as an equation:
Work + life = 16
n + 2 + n = 16
2n + 2 = 16

Collect together the n's.
This mathematical sentence can be written in words:
Some number plus two makes 16.

2n = 14

Some number is 14 – two n's are 14.

n = 7

One n is 7

Number of hours at home: 7
Number of hours at work: 7 + 2 = 9

Let **n** be the number of hours at home.
Number of hours in the office:
n + 2

Clifford, a workaholic, spends three times more hours at work than he does at home. How is his time split?

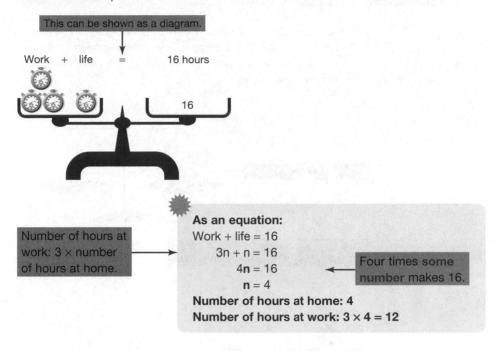

This can be shown as a diagram.

Work + life = 16 hours

16

Number of hours at work: 3 × number of hours at home.

As an equation:
Work + life = 16
3n + n = 16
4n = 16
n = 4
Number of hours at home: 4
Number of hours at work: 3 × 4 = 12

Four times **some number** makes 16.

Work it out

1. a. Naz is awake for 18 hours. She spends twice as much time at home as she does at work.
        i. Write this as an algebraic equation.
        ii. Work out how her time is split.
    b. Ken is awake for 17 hours. He spends three more hours at work than he does at home.
        i. Write this as an algebraic equation.
        ii. Work out how his time is split.

2. Write these sentences as algebraic equations and solve them:
    a. '**Some Number**' plus eight gives twelve.
    b. Four times '**Some Number**' gives twenty eight.
    c. Two times '**Some Number**' plus three gives eleven.
    d. Three times '**Some Number**' minus four gives fourteen.

3. Write these equations as sentences and solve them:
    a. $n + 6 = 15$
    b. $5n = 30$
    c. $2n - 5 = 7$
    d. $3n + 3 = 18$

Using rules to solve equations

When solving more complicated equations a set of rules can steer you to the solution.

There are two sets of kitchen weights, silver ones that have their weight in ounces clearly stamped on them and four black ones whose weights are unknown. The task is to use kitchen scales to work out the unknown weights, **a**, **b**, **c** and **d** and in so doing obtain some useful rules.

1.

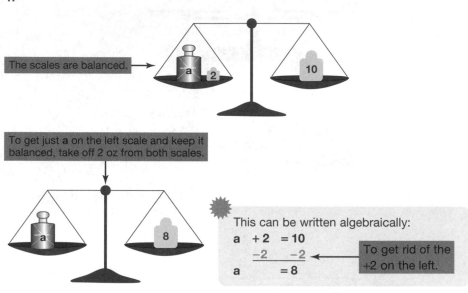

The scales are balanced.

To get just **a** on the left scale and keep it balanced, take off 2 oz from both scales.

This can be written algebraically:

$$a + 2 = 10$$
$$\underline{-2 \quad -2}$$
$$a \quad\quad = 8$$

To get rid of the +2 on the left.

2.

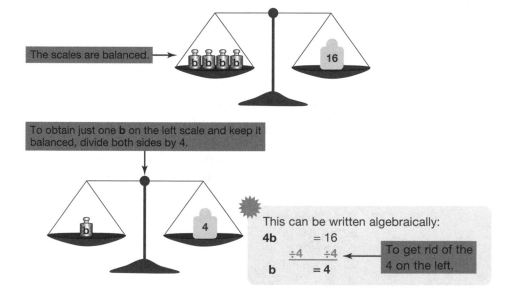

The scales are balanced.

To obtain just one **b** on the left scale and keep it balanced, divide both sides by 4.

This can be written algebraically:

$$4b \quad\quad = 16$$
$$\underline{\div 4 \quad \div 4}$$
$$b \quad\quad = 4$$

To get rid of the 4 on the left.

3.

To get just two **c** weights on the left scale but
maintain the balance, take off 3 off from both scales.

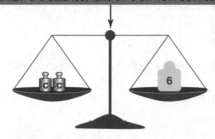

To obtain just one **c** on the left scale and keep the
balance, halve the weights on both sides.

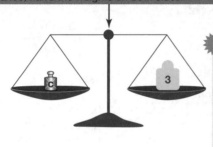

This can be written algebraically:

$$2c + 3 = 9$$
$$\underline{ -3 \quad\quad -3}$$
$$2c = 6$$
$$\underline{ \div 2 \quad\quad \div 2}$$
$$c = 3$$

To get rid of the
+3 on the left.

To get rid of the
2 on the left.

Key rules

To keep the
equation balanced,
always do the same
thing to both sides
of an equation.

When there are two
expressions on one
side of the equation
always get rid of
the number on its
own before getting
rid of the number
next to the letter.

Example

Solve

1. $3m - 7 = 8$

$$3m - 7 = 8$$
$$\underline{ +7 \quad +7}$$
$$3m = 15$$
$$\underline{ \div 3 \quad \div 3}$$
$$m = 5$$

Always eliminate any number that
is on its own (–7) and then get rid
of the number next to the letter (3).

2. $\dfrac{m}{4} = 7$

$$\frac{m}{\cancel{4}} \times \cancel{4} = 7 \times 4$$
$$m = 28$$

Multiplying both sides by four
leaves m alone on the left hand
side of the equation.

Work it out

1. Work out the size of these weights:

   a.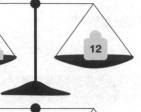

   b.

   c.

   d.

2. Solve these equations:
   a. $n + 2 = 7$ b. $m + 3 = 9$
   c. $p - 4 = 10$ d. $n + 7 = 12$
   e. $r - 7 = 2$

3. Solve these equations:
   a. $3a = 6$ b. $5b = 20$
   c. $\dfrac{a}{4} = 5$ d. $\dfrac{b}{3} = 2$
   e. $4b = 12$

4. Solve these equations:
   a. $2r + 7 = 11$ b. $5s + 3 = 18$
   c. $6t - 4 = 20$ d. $3v + 4 = 31$
   e. $2w - 6 = 8$ f. $7m - 3 = 25$
   g. $3z + 2 = 17$ h. $12 - x = 9$
   i. $4y - 5 = 19$ j. $10n + 7 = 62$

5. Copy these 'equation' walls and work out the value of n. The first one has been done for you:

   a.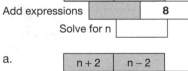

   b.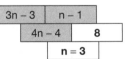

   c.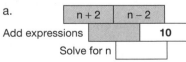

   d.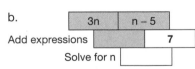
       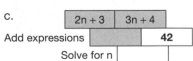
       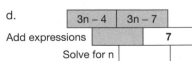

Example 1

Work out the size of the weights **d**.

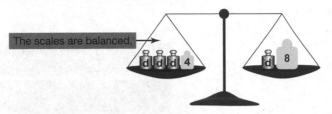

The scales are balanced.

To obtain **d**'s just on the left scale, take off a **d** weight from both sides.

To get rid of the 4oz weight on the left scale, take off 4oz from both sides.

To obtain just one **d** on the left scale halve the weights on both sides.

This can be written algebraically:

$$3d + 4 = d + 8$$
$$\underline{-d \qquad -d}$$
$$2d + 4 = \qquad 8$$

Get rid of the **d**'s on the side with the least number of them – the right.

$$\underline{-4 \qquad -4}$$
$$2d \qquad = 4$$

Get rid of the +4 on the left.

$$\underline{\div 2 \quad \div 2}$$
$$d \qquad = 2$$

Get rid of the 2 on the left.

Example 2

Solve:

1. $2p + 5 = 11 - p$

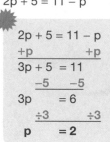

$$\begin{array}{lcl} 2p + 5 & = & 11 - p \\ +p & & +p \\ \hline 3p + 5 & = & 11 \\ -5 & & -5 \\ \hline 3p & = & 6 \\ \div 3 & & \div 3 \\ \hline \mathbf{p} & \mathbf{=} & \mathbf{2} \end{array}$$

- Get rid of the –p on the right as it is the side with the least number of p's.
- Get rid of +5 on the left side of the equation as this is the side for the algebraic expression.
- Get rid of the 3 on the left.

2. $24 - 5q = 3 + 2q$

$$\begin{array}{lcl} 24 - 5q & = & 3 + 2q \\ +5q & & +5q \\ \hline 24 & = & 3 + 7q \\ -3 & = & -3 \\ \hline 21 & = & 7q \\ \div 7 & & \div 7 \\ \hline 3 & = & q \\ & \mathbf{q = 3} & \end{array}$$

- Remove the q's on the left as there are less q's there than on the right (–5 is less than 2).
- Get rid of the 3 on the right as this is the side for the algebraic expression.
- Get rid of the 7 on the right.

3. $4(6 - 2r) = 8 + 5(2r - 4)$

$$\begin{array}{lcl} 4(6 - 2r) & = & 8 + 5(2r - 4) \\ 24 - 8r & = & 8 + 10r - 20 \\ 24 - 8r & = & 10r - 12 \\ +8r & & +8r \\ \hline 24 & = & 18r - 12 \\ 12 & = & +12 \\ \hline 36 & = & 18r \\ \div 18 & & \div 18 \\ \hline 2 & = & r \\ & \mathbf{r = 2} & \end{array}$$

- Multiply out the brackets.
- Combine the numbers on the right of the equation.
- Remove the r's from the left as there are less r's there than on the right (–8 is smaller than 10).
- Remove 12 from the right as this is the side for the algebraic expression.
- Get rid of the 18 on the right.

4. $\frac{2}{7}(2s - 4) = 5$

$$\begin{array}{lcl} \frac{2}{7}(2s - 4) \times 7 & = & 5 \times 7 \\ 2(2s - 4) & = & 35 \\ 4s - 8 & = & 35 \\ +8 & & +8 \\ \hline 4s & = & 43 \\ \div 4 & & \div 4 \\ \hline \mathbf{s} & \mathbf{=} & \mathbf{10.75} \end{array}$$

- Get rid of the fraction.
- Multiply out the brackets.
- Get rid of the –8 on the left.
- Get rid of the 4 on the left.

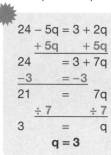

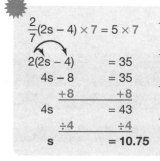

Mapping out

If there are any fractions, get rid of them by multiplying both sides by the denominator.

↓

Expand any brackets and if required, simplify the expression.

↓

- Get rid of the letters (e.g. 2p, −3p) from the side of the equation that contains the least number of letters.
- Get rid of the numbers (e.g. +3, −4) from the other side.

↓

To obtain just one letter, divide both sides by the number the letter is multiplied by.

Hints and tips

What you do to one side of an equation you must do to the other.

Annotate your work.

Work it out

1. Solve these equations:
   a. $3x = 20 - x$
   b. $5q = 12 - q$
   c. $2r = 15 - 3r$
   d. $5f - 9 = 2f$
   e. $3t = 32 - t$
   f. $4q = 12 - 2q$
   g. $4t + 2 = 17 - t$
   h. $12 - 2m = m$
   i. $3c + 2 = 10 - c$
   j. $4q + 3 = q + 6$
   k. $10 - 6n = 2 + 2n$
   l. $3a - 1 = a + 7$
   m. $6m - 1 = m + 9$
   n. $3d + 5 = 4d - 6$
   o. $8 - 3n = 12 - 5n$

2. Solve these equations:
   a. $2(3p + 4) = 32$
   b. $4(r - 1) = 12$
   c. $12 = 3(3q - 5)$
   d. $25 = 5(2q + 3)$
   e. $3(2z - 5) = z + 15$
   f. $m + 2(m + 1) = 14$
   g. $3(n + 5) + n = 23$
   h. $4(2w + 3) + 7 = 43$
   i. $2(3 - 2x) = 2(6 - x)$
   j. $5(x + 1) - 14 - 3(x - 1)$
   k. $3(4x - 1) - 3 = x + 16$
   l. $4x - 2(x + 4) = x + 1$
   m. $3(y + 1) + 2(y + 2) = 22$
   n. $5(a - 3) + 3(a + 2) = 7$
   o. $4n - 3(n - 10) = 3(2 + 3n)$

3. Ahmed has solved this equation correctly, but has missed out stages and has not annotated his work. Copy out his solution, adding in any missed stages and describe what is happening at each step.

$$3(n + 2) - 2(3n - 6) = 7n$$
$$-3n + 18 = 7n$$
$$18 = 10n$$
$$n = 1.8 \checkmark$$

4. Solve these equations, writing your answer in its simplest form:
   a. $7t = \dfrac{7}{3}$
   b. $\dfrac{5y}{2} = 2$
   c. $3 = \dfrac{12n}{5}$
   d. $\dfrac{3}{a} = 7$
   e. $\dfrac{500}{y} = 10$

5. Solve these equations:
   a. $\dfrac{1}{2}(m + 2) = 7$
   b. $\dfrac{2}{3}(n - 3) = 4$
   c. $\dfrac{2}{5}(n + 4) = 6$
   d. $\dfrac{3}{8}(n - 5) = 3$
   e. $\dfrac{2}{7}(2n + 3) = 4$
   f. $\dfrac{4}{9}(3n - 6) = 6$

Group investigation 1 – proving 1 = 2

Suppose n = 4.

Then
$$n + 4 = 4 + 4$$ ← Add 4 to both sides.
$$4 + n = 2 \times 4$$
$$4 + n - 2n = 2 \times 4 - 2n$$ ← Subtract 2n from both sides.
$$1(4 - n) = 2(4 - n)$$ ← Put the expressions in brackets.
$$\frac{1(4 - n)}{(4 - n)} = \frac{2(4 - n)}{(4 - n)}$$ ← Divide both sides by 4 – n.
$$1 = 2$$

Is this the case or is something wrong with the workings?

Investigate.

Group investigation 2

Put this flow chart into an equation to work out the input number if the output number is:

a. 3
b. 1

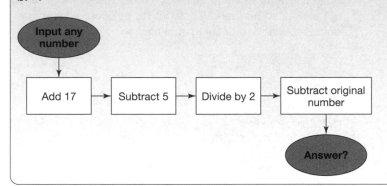

Practical uses of equations

Rob, the manager of a new gym, carried out a bit of market research before deciding on the pricing structure for his customers. He found that, on average, the other gyms in the area charged an annual membership fee of £30 plus £28 per month for the 'standard' package.

Hoping to encourage people to use his facilities, Rob decides to forgo the membership fee.

How much should Rob charge per month in order to make the same income as the other gyms for one year from one member?

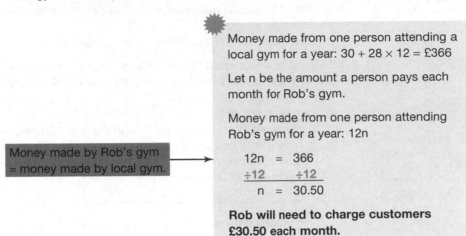

Money made from one person attending a local gym for a year: $30 + 28 \times 12 = £366$

Let n be the amount a person pays each month for Rob's gym.

Money made from one person attending Rob's gym for a year: $12n$

Money made by Rob's gym = money made by local gym.

$$12n = 366$$
$$\div 12 \qquad \div 12$$
$$n = 30.50$$

Rob will need to charge customers £30.50 each month.

Hints and tips

Let **n** be the width of the rectangle. Sketch the rectangle.

Work it out

1. The length of a rectangle is three times the width. If the total perimeter is 24 cm:
   a. what is the length and width?
   b. what is the area of the rectangle?

2. Write an equation for each of the diagrams and solve it for x.

   a.    b.   c.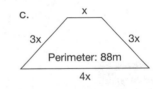

3. There are four angles at a point. The first is n degrees, the second is double this, the third is double the second and fourth is double the third.
   a. Write an equation using this information.
   b. Solve the equation and work out the size of all four angles.

Let **n** be the number of days.

4. A graduate in web design hires himself out at a rate of £125 a day plus a fixed charge of £70. A firm paid £695 for the designer's services.
   a. Form an equation using this information.
   b. Use the equation to work out how many days the firm hired the designer.

Let **n** be the number of employees.

5. An office manager purchases 470 memory sticks. This will give each employee 3 and there will be an extra 50 'spare'.
   a. Form an equation using this information.
   b. Use the equation to work out how many employees there are.

> Let **n** be the
> number of months.

6. Dale has £90 in his savings account and plans to add £40 each month. Oswald has £1 260 in his savings account and plans to spend £50 each month.
   a. Form an equation describing when they both have the same amount in the bank.
   b. Solve this equation.
   c. How much do they then have in their account?

7. Ellie has an unauthorised overdraft and her bank charges her £192 for this transgression and explains that their policy is to charge £42 for administrative costs plus £30 for each 'bounced' cheque.
   a. Create an equation using this information.
   b. Solve the equation to work out the number of Ellie's cheques that have bounced.

> Let **n** be the
> number of bounced
> cheques.

   c. In response to bad press publicity, the bank decides to change its charging structure. For the month following the changes the bank included this footnote in any customer correspondence:

> **Putting customers first**
>
> After listening to your views we have decided to forgo the administrative costs for an unauthorised overdraft.

   The bank did not mention that it has increased the charge for a bounced cheque to £44.
   How many bounced cheques will it take for a customer to be paying exactly the same as they did with the old charging structure?
   d. Would Ellie have been better off with this new charging structure?

8. A doctor can treat patients with the same disease with two different drugs, dyperin and thymoxine. Dyperin is three times more expensive than thymoxine. The doctor has a budget of £16 280 for the two drugs. He has seventeen patients taking thymoxine and nine dyperin. What are the costs of each drug if:
   a. he has spent all his budget?
   b. he is over-budget by £1 100?

Hints and tips

> Let **t** be the
> number of hours
> of the chase.
> Distance:
>   speed × time
> Form an equation.

9. For the Children In Need programme a marathon winner challenged a TV presenter to a chase. The presenter is given a six mile head start and jogged along at a speed of 6 miles per hour. The average speed of the marathon runner was 14 miles per hour.
   a. Create an equation using this formation.
   b. How long, in minutes, is it before the marathon runner catches the presenter?

Hints and tips

> Time:
>   distance ÷ speed

←———— 6 miles ————→

10. A motorbike and car were 165 miles apart when they set off at midday to meet each other. The car averaged 60 miles per hour whereas the bike went at a speed of 50 miles per hour.

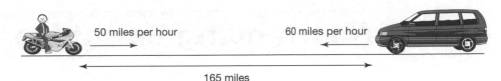

50 miles per hour   60 miles per hour

165 miles

a. Create an equation using this information.
b. How far had the biker travelled when they met?
c. What was the time?

11. At a works Christmas 'do' $\frac{1}{4}$ of the department didn't bother to turn up, $\frac{1}{2}$ of the department brought partners and another 20 people turned up (no one was quite sure where they came from). In total there were 120 people.
a. Use this information to form an equation.
b. Solve the equation and so work out the number of people in the department.

12. The Rhind papyrus has many mathematical problems. The Egyptians made little attempt to lighten things up as can be seen in this problem:

Problem 25: *A quantity and its half added together become 16. What is the quantity?*

Use an equation to solve this problem.

Paired work

Chris is organising a music festival and wants to work out the ticket price. Here is the conversation she has with her accountant.

At each of the three stages create an equation for **p**, the full price of a ticket and solve it.

4.5 Rearranging Formulae

This is when the **subject of a formula** is changed.

Make **d** the subject of the equation:

$$s = \frac{d}{t}$$

s: speed in miles per hour
d: distance in miles
t: time in hours

$$s \times t = \frac{d}{\cancel{t}} \times \cancel{t}$$

$$st = d \rightarrow d = st$$

Multiply both sides by **t**, to get rid of **t** on the right.

Example

Make **a** the subject of the following equations:

1. $b = \dfrac{3a}{7}$

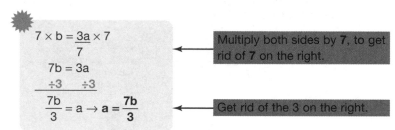

$$7 \times b = \frac{3a}{7} \times 7$$

$$7b = 3a$$

$$\underline{\div 3 \qquad \div 3}$$

$$\frac{7b}{3} = a \rightarrow a = \frac{7b}{3}$$

Multiply both sides by **7**, to get rid of **7** on the right.

Get rid of the 3 on the right.

$$b = 2a - 4$$

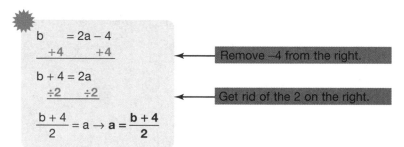

$$b \quad = 2a - 4$$

$$\underline{+4 \qquad\quad +4}$$

$$b + 4 = 2a$$

$$\underline{\div 2 \qquad \div 2}$$

$$\frac{b + 4}{2} = a \rightarrow a = \frac{b + 4}{2}$$

Remove −4 from the right.

Get rid of the 2 on the right.

2. b = 2(3a + 1)

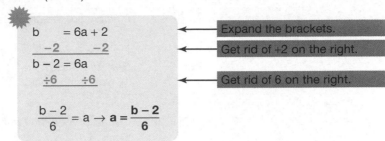

$$b = 6a + 2$$ ← Expand the brackets.

$$\underline{-2 \qquad -2}$$ ← Get rid of +2 on the right.

$$b - 2 = 6a$$

$$\div 6 \qquad \div 6$$ ← Get rid of 6 on the right.

$$\frac{b-2}{6} = a \rightarrow \mathbf{a = \frac{b-2}{6}}$$

3. $b = \frac{2}{3}(5a - 2)$

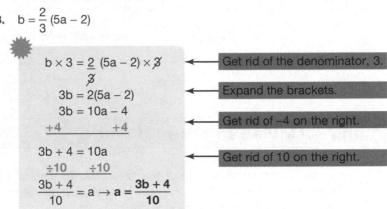

$$b \times 3 = \frac{2}{\cancel{3}}(5a - 2) \times \cancel{3}$$ ← Get rid of the denominator, 3.

$$3b = 2(5a - 2)$$ ← Expand the brackets.

$$3b = 10a - 4$$

$$\underline{+4 \qquad\qquad +4}$$ ← Get rid of −4 on the right.

$$3b + 4 = 10a$$ ← Get rid of 10 on the right.

$$\div 10 \qquad \div 10$$

$$\frac{3b+4}{10} = a \rightarrow \mathbf{a = \frac{3b+4}{10}}$$

Mapping out

If there is a fraction get rid of it by multiplying both sides by the denominator.

↓

If there are brackets expand them.

↓

If there is a number on its own (e.g. +3, −4) on the same side as the letter that is to be made subject, get rid of it.

↓

If there is a number attached to the letter to be made the subject, get rid of it.

Work it out

1. Make **x** the subject of the following formulae:

  a. $y = \frac{x}{5}$ b. $y = 3x$ c. $y = \frac{x}{2}$

  d. $y = \frac{2x}{7}$ e. $y = \frac{4x}{9}$ f. $y = \frac{5x}{11}$

  g. $y = wx$ h. $y = \frac{x}{w}$ i. $y = \frac{3w}{x}$

2. Make **m** the subject of the formulae:

  a. $n = m + 1$ b. $n = m - 3$ c. $n = 2m - 1$

  d. $n = 3m + 2$ e. $n = 4m - p$ f. $n = 2m + p$

3. Make **x** the subject of the formulae:

  a. $y = 2(x + 1)$ b. $y = 3(x - 1)$ c. $y = 2(x + 4)$

  d. $y = 4(x + 4)$ e. $y = 3(x - w)$ f. $y = 5(x + w)$

4. Make **q** the subject of the formulae:

  a. $p = \frac{3}{4}(q + 2)$ b. $p = \frac{4}{5}(q - 2)$ c. $p = \frac{5}{6}(q + 3)$

  d. $p = \frac{2}{7}(q - 3)$ e. $p = \frac{3}{5}(q - 3)$ f. $p = \frac{2}{3}(2 + q)$

  g. $p = \frac{5}{r}(2 + q)$ h. $p = \frac{3}{m}(q - 1)$ i. $p = \frac{4}{n}(n + q)$

5.   a.   What's wrong with this method for making **x** the subject of the formula?

$$y = \frac{3}{5}(4 + x) \rightarrow y = \frac{12 + 3x}{5}$$ *Multiply out the brackets.*

$$\downarrow$$

$$y - 12 = \frac{3x}{5}$$ *Get rid of the 12 on the right by subtracting 12 from both sides.*

$$\downarrow$$

$$5(y - 12) = 3x$$ *Get rid of 5 on the right by multiplying both sides by 5.*

$$\downarrow$$

$$x = \frac{5(y - 12)}{3}$$ *Divide both sides by 3.*

b.   Work out the correct answer.

Rearranging formulae in the real world

Tim has recently taken charge of the day to day running of a busy restaurant in the centre of a small market town. For now he is keeping the menu he inherited, but wants to make sure it can generate a good profit.

> Gross profit is the profit before general running costs such as wages, heating etc. have been deducted. Most restaurants aim to make a gross profit of between 60% and 70%.

A popular lunchtime choice is goat's cheese ciabatta for £3.20. Each ciabatta costs Tim:

Goats Cheese	65p
Ciabatta	40p
Tomato	15p
Butter	3p
Salad garnish	35p
Total	**£1.58**

The formula used to work out the percentage gross profit:

$$p = \frac{100}{c}(c - r)$$

c = cost to customer
r = cost to restaurant
p = percentage gross profit

What is the gross profit made from each ciabatta?

$$p = \frac{100}{3.20}(3.20 - 1.58) = \frac{100}{3.20} \times 1.62$$

$$= 51\%$$

Despite customers being charged more than double the cost of the food Tim is still not hitting the target profit of between 60% and 70%.

What Tim really needs to know is how much he should charge a customer in order to make a gross profit of between 60% and 70%.

Work out the formula to make a gross profit of 60%.

The profit formula needs to be rearranged to make **c**, the cost to a customer, the subject.

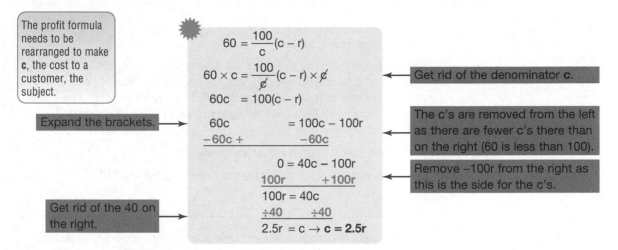

Get rid of the denominator **c**.

Expand the brackets.

The c's are removed from the left as there are fewer c's there than on the right (60 is less than 100).

Remove −100r from the right as this is the side for the c's.

Get rid of the 40 on the right.

$$60 = \frac{100}{c}(c - r)$$

$$60 \times c = \frac{100}{\cancel{c}}(c - r) \times \cancel{c}$$

$$60c = 100(c - r)$$

$$60c = 100c - 100r$$
$$-60c + \qquad -60c$$

$$0 = 40c - 100r$$
$$100r \qquad +100r$$
$$100r = 40c$$
$$\div 40 \qquad \div 40$$
$$2.5r = c \rightarrow \mathbf{c = 2.5r}$$

What should the restaurant charge for the goat's cheese ciabbatta to make 60% gross profit?

$$\mathbf{c} = 2.5 \times 1.58 = \mathbf{£3.95}$$

Work it out

1. Using the information about Tim's restaurant:
    a. Rearrange the percentage gross profit formula so that the restaurant can work out what to charge customers in order to make a 70% profit.
    b. What should Tim be charging customers for the goat's cheese ciabbata to make the gross profit of 70%?
    c. Carrot soup with roll costs Tim £1.26 to make. How much should he charge customers if he wants to make a gross profit of:
        i. 60%?
        ii. 70%?

2. Kellie has worked out her own formula for the gym:

    $$t = \frac{c}{10}$$
    c: calories burnt
    t: time, in minutes on treadmill

    a. Kellie ate a bar of chocolate containing 420 calories. How long will she need to go on the treadmill to burn off those calories?
    b. Rearrange the formula to make **c** its subject.
    c. Kellie went on the treadmill for twenty minutes. How many calories has she burnt?

3. Sam dreams of winning a cool million in the lottery. Being a person that likes to flesh out his dreams with detail, he wonders how much of this million he will need to invest to live comfortably for the rest of his life. He remembers this formula from his school days:

$$I = \frac{5P}{100}$$ I: interest made in a year
P: money invested

> This formula is for an interest rate of 5%.

   a. Rearrange the equation to make **P** the subject.
   b. Sam thinks he'll be able to live fairly comfortably on an interest **I** of £40 000. How much money, to the nearest pound, will he need to invest?
   c. How much money will Sam have left over from his million to spend on fast cars, holidays and the high life?

4. Hugh posted this question on a walker's website:

   'How can I work out how long it will take me to climb a mountain?'

   Here is the reply:

   > >To get a rough idea of the time it will take you to climb a mountain, multiply the miles walked by 20 and add 30 minutes for every 1 000 feet climbed.

   a. Write down a formula for the total time **t** in minutes, of a walk. The formula should combine the time taken to walk a distance of **d** miles and ascend **h** thousand feet.
   b. Hugh walked three miles in 120 minutes when climbing to the summit of a mountain.
      i. Rearrange the formula to make **h** its subject.
      ii. Work out the height climbed by Hugh.

5. The formula for converting Fahrenheit (F) temperatures to Centigrade (C) is:

$$C = \frac{5}{9}(F - 32)$$

   a. Rearrange the formula to make **F** its subject.
   b. Use this new formula to work out the temperature in Fahrenheit when:
      i. water freezes (0°C)
      ii. water boils (100°C).
   c. What is the temperature when the Fahrenheit and Centigrade reading are the same?

> Drugs administered by drip come in a solution. The nurse sets the drip to the correct amount to be given to a patient each hour.
>
> A microgram is a thousandth of a gram.
>
> The dosage is micrograms of the drug to be given to the patient each minute.

6. A patient with heart problems is prescribed the drug dopamine to provide additional pumping strength to his heart muscles. The drug is being administered intravenously by a drip. This is the formula nurses can use to work out the rate the drug should be given.

$$R = \frac{60VDW}{A}$$ R: rate of drip in millilitres per hour
V: volume of solution, in millilitres
A: amount of drug, in micrograms, contained in the solution
D: the dosage prescribed by the doctor
W: weight of patient in kilograms.

a. Rearrange the equation to make **D** its subject.

b. A senior nurse wants to check the dosage prescribed by the doctor. She sees the drip rate **R** has been set to 5.1 millilitres an hour. The volume of solution **V** is 500 millilitres and contains 800 000 micrograms **A** of dopamine. The patient weighs 68 kilograms.

    Work out what dosage **D** the doctor has prescribed.

> The winner averaged a speed of 9.8 m per a second throughout the race.

Hints and tips

Make t the subject of the formula for speed.

Speed of sound: 340 m per second

Investigation 1

1. In a 100 m race Frank comes second by 0.01 seconds. He notices the winner is wearing a particularly thick vest – probably 0.5 cm thick. Should Frank be concerned about this?
Investigate.

2. At the start of another race, the runner in lane one is 4 m from the starter with his starting gun whereas Frank, in lane eight, is 14 m away. The runner in lane one won the race by 0.01 seconds, Frank came second – should he feel unhappy?
Investigate.

Investigation 2 – the salary theorem

We all know that knowledge is power and time is money and some of you may also know the physics formula:

$$power = \frac{work}{time}$$

This can be written as:

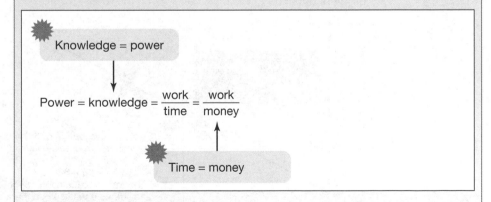

a. What does money equal in terms of work and knowledge?

b. What happens to money as knowledge gets smaller?

4.6 Straight Line Graphs and Their Equations

The traffic police in Northern Norway carried out a survey to see if there is a connection between the number of hours of darkness and the number of road accidents in their region.

Here is a computer generated scatter plot, with a line of best fit, of the results:

As the number of hours of darkness increases, so does the number of road accidents each week.

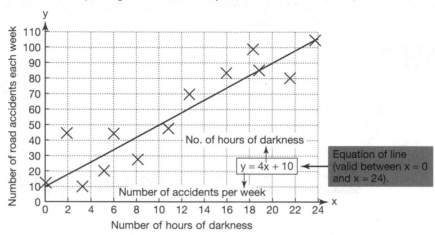

No. of hours of darkness

$y = 4x + 10$

Number of accidents per week

Equation of line (valid between x = 0 and x = 24).

How many accidents should the traffic police expect when there are:

a. 13 hours of darkness?
b. 24 hours of darkness?

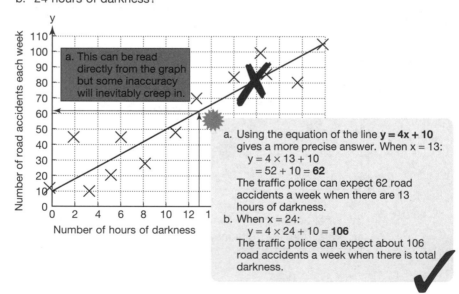

a. This can be read directly from the graph but some inaccuracy will inevitably creep in.

a. Using the equation of the line **y = 4x + 10** gives a more precise answer. When x = 13:
   $y = 4 \times 13 + 10$
   $= 52 + 10 = \mathbf{62}$
   The traffic police can expect 62 road accidents a week when there are 13 hours of darkness.

b. When x = 24:
   $y = 4 \times 24 + 10 = \mathbf{106}$
   The traffic police can expect about 106 road accidents a week when there is total darkness.

> ## Work it out

1. A similar survey was carried out in a second region and the two results were drawn on the same graph:

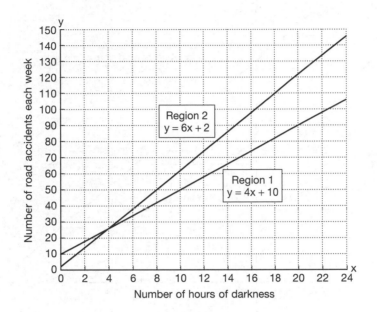

a. Use the equation of the line for the second region to work out how many accidents the traffic police can expect when there are:
    i. 13 hours of darkness
    ii. 24 hours of darkness.
b. When there are 24 hours of daylight, how many accidents can the traffic police expect in each region?
c. What is the connection between your answers to b. and the figures in the two equations?
d. In which region is the number of accidents more affected by the number of hours of darkness?

2. A survey was carried out concerning the cost of heating a home as the outside temperature changes. Here are the computer generated lines of best fit and their equations:

The two lines were produced after several hundred homes were surveyed for a whole year. The flats and houses in the survey were all less than five years old.

Hints and tips

Use a calculator to work out your answers.

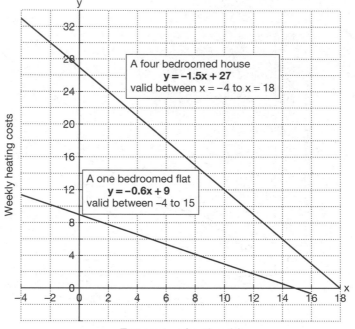

A four bedroomed house
$y = -1.5x + 27$
valid between $x = -4$ to $x = 18$

A one bedroomed flat
$y = -0.6x + 9$
valid between -4 to 15

Weekly heating costs

Temperature (centigrade)

a. In both equations what does:
    i.   y represent?
    ii. x represent?
b. At what temperatures does neither household pay any heating costs?
c. Use the equations of the lines to work out the heating costs for each household when the temperature is:
    i.   7° C
    ii. 0° C.
d. What is the connection between your answers to c.ii. and the figures in the equations of the lines?
e. What household bill is most affected by the temperature?

Getting the equation of a line

The equation can be split into two parts, the gradient and the intercept.

These mountains have different gradients:

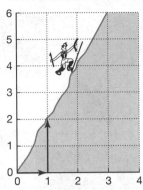 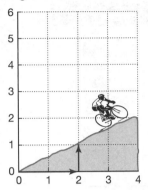 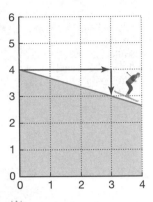

For every 1 m the climber goes along he ascends 2 m.
Gradient:
    increase in **y** ÷ increase in **x**
    = 2 ÷ 1 = **2**

For every 2 m the cyclist goes along he ascends 1 m.
Gradient:
    increase in **y** ÷ increase in **x**
    = 1 ÷ 2 = 0.5

For every 3 m the skier goes along he descends 1 m.
Gradient:
    decrease in **y** ÷ increase in **x**
    = −1 ÷ 3 = −0.33

The value is negative because the slope is downhill.

Example 1

Key terms

Gradient
The slope or rate of ascent/descent of a road, riverbed, line etc.

Increase/decrease in height ÷ horizontal distance

Intercept
Where a line cuts the y-axis.

Gradient: −1 ÷ 2
        = **−0.5**
Intercept: 5
y = −0.5x + 5

Gradient: 3 ÷ 1
        = **3**
Intercept: −4
y = 3x − 4

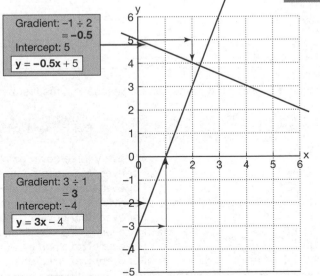

An equation of a straight line, in the form
y = mx + c where
• the gradient **m**, is the number next to the **x**
• the intercept, c, is the number on its own.

Example 2

Work out the equations of these lines:

The gradient of a straight line is the same along its whole length so you can find the gradient at any point. However, it is often easiest to draw a horizontal line to the right of the intercept.

a.

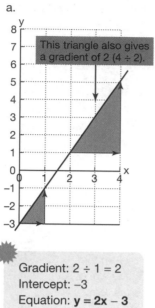

This triangle also gives a gradient of 2 (4 ÷ 2).

Gradient: 2 ÷ 1 = 2
Intercept: –3
Equation: **y = 2x – 3**

b.

With this line, if the horizontal line extends from the intercept by just one unit it is difficult to measure accurately the length of the vertical line.

To ensure the length of the vertical line is a whole number (5) extend the horizontal line by 2 units.

Gradient: –5 ÷ 2 = –2.5
Intercept: 6
Equation: **y = –2.5x + 6**

Work it out

Hints and tips

It may be helpful to sketch the description of the line, e.g. for every four along go up three:

Gradient: $\frac{3}{4}$ = 0.75

1. Connect the gradient with the correct description, the first has been done for you:

Gradient	Description
a. 11	i. For every three down go along one
b. –5	j. For every ten along go up six
c. –0.8	k. For every twelve up go along three
d. 2.5	l. For every one along go up 11
e. –3	m. For every four down go along five
f. 1.5	n. For every five up go along two
g. 4	o. For every two along go down ten
h. 0.6	p. For every two along go up three

2. Work out the gradients of these lines:

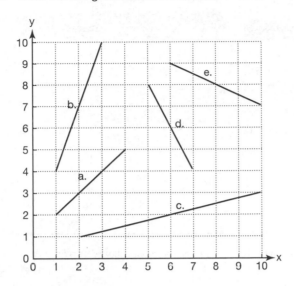

3. Work out the gradients of the lines connected by the points:
    a. (2, 3) and (1, 6)
    b. (0, 2) and (4, 10)
    c. (3, 5) and (11, 7)
    d. (6, 1) and (4, 9)

4. Without measuring, match the lines up with the gradients.

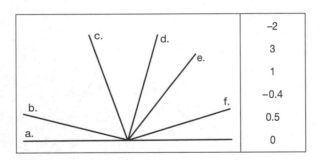

5. On graph paper accurately draw lines with the following gradients:
    a. 2   b. 3
    c. 2.5   d. −0.5

> Think of the equation of the line as the line's address – it tells you exactly where the line should be placed on a grid.

6. Copy and complete this table:

Equation of line	Gradient	Intercept
$y = 3x - 2$		
$y = 6x + 5$		
$y = 10x$		
$y = -2x + 0.4$		
$y = 5$		
$y = 0.5x + 0.3$		
$y = 1 + 2x$		
	3	7
	-2	0
	-0.2	3
	0	4
	-5	-5

7. Write an equation of a line that is parallel to the line:
   a. $y = -3x + 4$
   b. $y = 6$

8. Write an equation of a line that has the same intercept as the line:
   a. $y = -2x - 3$
   b. $y = 4x$

9. Write down the gradients and intercepts of the two lines drawn by the traffic police in northern Norway.

10. For the following lines, work out:
    i.   the gradient
    ii. the intercept
    iii. the equation of the line.

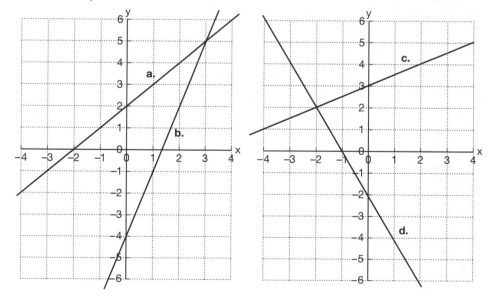

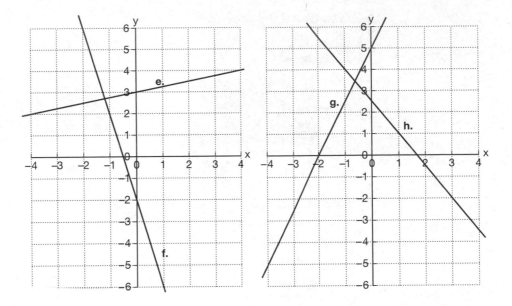

Drawing straight lines

To draw a straight line you need to know the position of at least two points.

1. Draw the line $y = 3x - 5$.

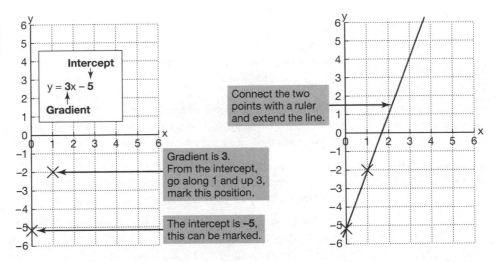

Intercept
$y = 3x - 5$
Gradient

Connect the two points with a ruler and extend the line.

Gradient is **3**. From the intercept, go along 1 and up 3, mark this position.

The intercept is **–5**, this can be marked.

2.   Draw the line $y = -0.4x + 6$.

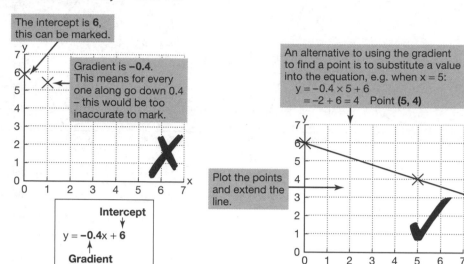

The intercept is **6**, this can be marked.

Gradient is **–0.4**. This means for every one along go down 0.4 – this would be too inaccurate to mark.

An alternative to using the gradient to find a point is to substitute a value into the equation, e.g. when $x = 5$:
$y = -0.4 \times 5 + 6$
$\quad = -2 + 6 = 4$ Point **(5, 4)**

Plot the points and extend the line.

Intercept
↓
$y = \mathbf{-0.4}x + \mathbf{6}$
↑
Gradient

Hints and tips

You may want to draw two or three lines on the same grid.

Always mark the intercept on the grid.

When the gradient is not a whole number it may be easier to substitute a value of x into the equation, e.g. find the value of y when $x = 4$.

Work it out

1.   Plot the following lines on a grid that extends from -4 to 4 in the x direction and -15 to 15 in the y direction:

   a. $y = 2x + 1$ b. $y = 3x + 7$

   c. $y = x - 4$ d. $y = -0.5x + 10$

   e. $y = -x - 12$ f. $y = -8$

   h. $x = 3$.

2.   a.   On a grid that extends from 0 to 8 in the x direction and -5 to 5 in the y direction, draw the lines connecting the co-ordinates:

      i.   (6, 3) and (3, 0)

      ii.   (1, 3) and (3, -1).

   b.   Work out the gradients of both lines.

   c.   Write down the intercepts by extending both the lines to the y-axis.

   d.   What are the equations of the two lines?

Hints and tips

(Q. 4) To find two points on each line substitute a value into each equation, e.g. find the value of y when $x = 0$ and find the value of x when $y = 0$.

3.   Work out the equation of the line that:

   a.   passes through the point (2, 4) and the intercept is 2

   b.   passes through the point (3, 1) and has a gradient of -2.

4.   Plot the following lines on a grid that extends from 0 to 8 in the x direction and -5 to 5 in the y direction:

   a. $2x + 3y = 6$

   b. $x + 2y = 8$

   c. $2x - y = 3$

> Call out charge is the charge made before doing any work.

5. This graph shows the call out charges Sean the electrician makes.

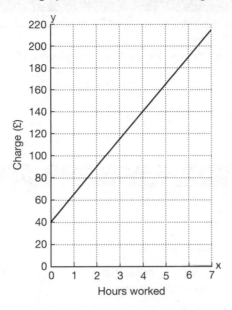

a. What is the gradient and intercept of the line?

b. Write down the equation of the line.

c. What is Sean's call out charge?

d. What is Sean's hourly rate?

e. Sean is thinking of doing away with his call out charge but charging £35 an hour.
Copy the graph and line and draw this new method of charging as a line on the graph.

f. Most of Sean's jobs tend to last three hours or less. Will he be financially better off using this second method of charging?

Hints and tips

Let **x** represent the time in hours (from 0 to 2 hours). Let **y** represents the distance in miles (from −2 to 5).

6. Mandeep and Jasmin are going for a walk. Mandeep leaves at midday and walks at a speed of 2 miles an hour. Jasmin is delayed by 30 minutes, but sets off running at a speed of 4 miles an hour.

a. Draw their progress as two lines on a grid.

b. What does the gradient of each line represent?

c. When does Jasmin catch up to Mandeep?

d. Write the equation of the two lines that describes Mandeep's and Jasmin's progress.

Investigation 1

1. By drawing a series of lines on a grid, investigate the gradients of lines that are at right angles to a line.
2. Use your conclusions to work out the gradient of a line that is perpendicular to the lines:
   a. $y = 2x + 3$
   b. $y = -4x - 2$
   c. $y = 0.2x + 3$

Investigation 2

The equations of two lines are:

$y = ax + b$ and $y = cx + d$

where a, b, c and d are any number.

What can you say about a, b, c and/or d if:
1. the two lines have the same intercept?
2. the two lines are parallel?
3. the two lines are perpendicular?
4. the first line never crosses the x-axis?

4.7 Simultaneous Equations

Key term

Simultaneous equations
A pair of equations each with two unknowns. These unknowns have the same values in both equations.

Three office clerks cost a construction company £27 an hour.

How much is each clerk paid per hour?

There is just one solution to this 'pictorial equation'.

An office clerk is paid: $\dfrac{27}{3} = $ **£9 an hour**

One day there are three managers and two manual workers on the building site. This costs the company £76 per hour:

There are hundreds of solutions to this 'pictorial equation'.

Task

Work out two possible combinations of the managers and workers hourly rate that fits this information.

To get the exact rates of pay we need more information

On another day there are three managers and one worker on the building site. This costs the company £68 pound a hour:

These two 'pictorial equations' can be subtracted:

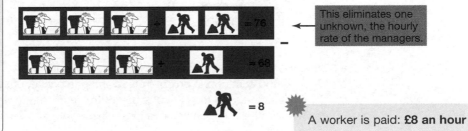

This eliminates one unknown, the hourly rate of the managers.

 $ = 8$

A worker is paid: **£8 an hour**

Algebraically:
The hourly pay for:
• a manager is **m**
• a worker is **w**

Two equations can be formed and subtracted:

$$\begin{array}{r} 3m + 2w = 76 \\ 3m + w = 68 \\ \hline w = 8 \end{array}$$

Substituting this value back into the first equation:

$$3m + 2 \times 8 = 76$$
$$3m + 16 = 76$$
$$\underline{ -16 \quad -16}$$
$$3m = 60$$
$$m = 60 \div 3 = \mathbf{20}$$

Using this information in the first 'pictorial equation':

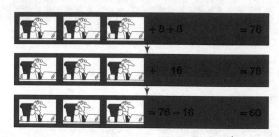

A manager is paid: 60 ÷ 3 = **£20 an hour**

Work it out

1. A Christmas gift box containing luxury soaps and bath oils is sold in two sizes:

    £6.00

    £5.00

    a. Write this information out as two pictorial equations.
    b. By subtracting these equations, work out the cost of one bar of soap and one bottle of bath oil.

2. A Christmas coffee hamper contains packets of real coffee and small boxes of Belgium truffles.

    £15.50

    £13.50

    a. Write this information out as two pictorial equations.
    b. Work out the cost of one box of truffles and one packet of coffee.
    c. Using the letters **t** for the cost of a box of truffles and **c** for the cost of a packet of coffee, create two equations. Check your answers to b. by solving these equations algebraically.

Solving simultaneous equations algebraically

Solve the simultaneous equations:

1. $3x + 4y = 25$ (1)
$3x + 2y = 17$ (2)

Label the equations (1) and (2).
The next step is to eliminate one of the unknowns – this will be x as there are the same number of x's in both equations.

$$3x + 4y = 25$$
$$3x + 2y = 17$$
$$2y = 8$$
$$\mathbf{y = 4}$$

(2) minus (1)
Do the subtraction this way round so as to give a positive number of y's.

$$3x + 4 \times 4 = 25$$
$$3x + 16 = 25$$
$$\underline{-16 \quad -16}$$
$$3x = 9$$
$$\mathbf{x = 3}$$

The value for **y** is substituted into equation **(1)**.
It could have equally been substituted into equations **(2)**.

Get rid of the 16 on the left.

2. $5x - 3y = 5$ (1)
$2x + 3y = 23$ (2)

As there is a 3y in both equations the y's will be eliminated.

$$5x - 3y = 5$$
$$2x + 3y = 23$$
$$3x - 6y = 28 \quad \textsf{✗}$$

(1) minus (2)
The y's are not eliminated because the sign before the 3y is different in each equation – adding the two equations will get rid of the y's.

$$5x - 3y = 5$$
$$2x + 3y = 23$$
$$7x = 28$$
$$\mathbf{x = 4} \quad \textsf{✓}$$

(1) plus (2)

$$2 \times 4 + 3y = 23$$
$$8 + 3y = 23$$
$$\underline{-8 \qquad -8}$$
$$3y = 15$$
$$\mathbf{y = 5} \quad \textsf{✓}$$

The value for **x** is substituted into equation **(2)**.
It could have been substituted into equation **(1)** but the workings may be a bit harder with negative values.

Get rid of the 8 on the left.

A practical example

Karen, the new manager of a 'video' rental shop, was sent this report from head office:

Profits made at Warrenstone Store

Week ending	No. DVDs rented	No. DVDs sold	Profit
12/07/08	120	80	£144
19/07/08	170	80	£164
. . .	. . .	. . .	. . .

Keen to maximise profits, she decided to work out how much the shop makes from selling one DVD and renting one to customers.

Hints and tips

Before creating the equations it may help to write the information in words, e.g.: *The profit from renting 120 DVDs and the profit from selling 80 DVDs makes a total profit of £144.*

x is the profit made from renting out one DVD
y is the profit made from selling a DVD

← Give the two unknowns letters.

$120x + 80y = 144$ (1)
$170x + 80y = 164$ (2)

← Use the information in the report to create two simultaneous equations.

$$170x + 80y = 164$$
$$\underline{120x + 80y = 144}\,{}^{-}$$
$$50x = 20$$
$$x = 20 \div 50 = \mathbf{0.40}$$

← **(2) minus (1)**
This eliminates the y's and produces an equation with a positive number of x's. This equation is then solved.

Potential pitfall

(1) minus (2):
$120x + 80y = 144$
$\underline{170x + 80y = 164}\,{}^{-}$
$-50x = -20$
This can be solved, but gives you a bit of extra work.

$$120 \times 0.4 + 80y = 144$$
$$48 + 80y = 144$$
$$\underline{-48 -48}$$
$$80y = 96$$
$$y = 96 \div 80 = \mathbf{1.20}$$

← Substitute the value of **x** into equation **(1)** and solve for y.

Each DVD rented out makes a profit of £0.40 and each DVD sold makes a profit of £1.20 – Karen plans to increase the price of renting out a DVD.

Work it out

1. Solve the following simultaneous equations:
   a. $2x + 3y = 8$
   $2x + 2y = 6$
   b. $x + 2y = 7$
   $x + y = 5$
   c. $3x + y = 6$
   $2x + y = 1$
   d. $4x + 3y = 11$
   $3x + 3y = 9$
   e. $3x + 4y = 27$
   $3x + 2y = 21$
   f. $3x + 4y = 10$
   $5x + 4y = 14$
   g. $3x + 2y = 15$
   $7x + 2y = 35$
   h. $4x + 2y = 10$
   $4x + 5y = 7$

2. Solve the following simultaneous equations:
   a. $x - y = 5$
   $x + y = 7$
   b. $x + y = 5$
   $2x - y = 4$
   c. $2x - 3y = 11$
   $2x - 5y = 9$
   d. $x - y = 4$
   $2x + y = 11$
   e. $5x - 2y = 19$
   $7x - 2y = 29$
   f. $4x + 5y = 42$
   $11x - 5y = 3$
   g. $5x - 2y = 7$
   $4x + 2y = 20$
   h. $2x - 3y = 6$
   $5x - 3y = -3$

3. Here is Agrícola's marked solution to the two simultaneous equations $3x - 2y = 9$ and $5x - 2y = 23$:

   $3x - 2y = 9$
   $5x - 2y = 23$ (add the equations to eliminate 2y)
   $8x = 32$
   $x = 4$ ✗

   $3 \times 4 - 2y = 9$ (substitute x into the first equation)
   $12 - 2y = 9$ ($21 -$ something $= 9$)   I really like the annotation you've used, but you've made a mistake early on that has affected both your answers.
   $2y = 3$
   $y = \frac{3}{2} = 1.5$ ✗

   a. What mistake is the tutor referring to in her comment?
   b. What are the correct values of x and y?

4. A rugby team has played 12 matches and won 20 points. They have drawn **d** matches, won **w** matches and, to date, not lost a single match.
   a. Use this information to write down two simultaneous equations.
   b. Solve these equations in order to work out the number of matches the team has drawn and won.

> Wood is often dealt with in volume of timber rather than number of trees.

5. The Forestry Commission wants to fell 2 100 m³ of pine trees and 2 700 m³ of fir trees across two forests. This table provides information on the trees in the forest:

	Volume of pine trees per hectare	Volume of fir trees per hectare
High Tarn forest	150 m³	150 m³
Lower Skiddaw forest	160 m³	240 m³

x is the total number of hectares felled in High Tarn forest.
y is the total number of hectares felled in Lower Skiddaw forest.

a. Use the information in the table to create two simultaneous equations.
b. Solve these equations in order to work out the total number of hectares to be felled in each forest.

More simultaneous equations

Solve the following simultaneous equations:

$2x + 5y = 29$ (1)
$4x + 3y = 23$ (2)

Neither unknowns have the same number before them so adding or subtracting will not eliminate an unknown.

$4x + 10y = 58$ (3)

2 × (1)   (all values in the equation are multiplied by 2) This gives a **4x** which occurs in equation **(2)**.

$$\begin{array}{r} 4x + 10y = 58 \\ \underline{4x + 3y = 23} \\ 7y = 35 \\ \mathbf{y = 5} \end{array}$$

(3) minus (2)

$$\begin{array}{r} 2x + 5 \times 5 = 29 \\ 2x + 25 = 29 \\ \underline{-25 -25} \\ 2x = 4 \\ \mathbf{x = 2} \end{array}$$

Substitute the value of y into **equation (1)**.

Work it out

1. Solve the following simultaneous equations:

    a. $3x + y = 7$
        $5x + 2y = 12$

    b. $2x + y = 11$
        $x + 3y = 18$

    c. $2x + 5y = 24$
        $6x + 3y = 24$

    d. $3x + y = 23$
        $5x + 4y = 50$

    e. $5x - y = 1$
        $7x + 2y = 15$

    f. $8x + 3y = 45$
        $3x - y = 2$

    g. $3x - 2y = 7$
        $5x - 4y = 11$

    h. $7x - 4y = 3$
        $3x - y = 7$

2. This is a question from a pub quiz:

    > Three pizzas and two portions of potato wedges cost £9.50
    > Six pizzas and five portions of potato wedges cost £20.
    > How many pizzas can I get with £32?

    a. Use the information in the first two sentences to create two simultaneous equations.
    b. Solve the equations.
    c. Answer the quiz question.

Hints and tips

For the quarter:
let **r** be the cost of one radiator
let **c** be the cost of one convection heater.

3. The manager of an office plans to reduce the winter heating bills.
    - Last year they used five radiators and four convection heaters. The quarterly bill came to £275.
    - This year when just two radiators were used and one convection heater (and a lot of woolly jumpers) the bill was slashed to £95 for the same quarter.

    a. Use this information to write down two simultaneous equations.
    b. Solve the equations and so work out the cost of each radiator and convection heater.
    c. After receiving legwarmers from his staff at Christmas and overhearing talk of frostbite, the manager decides to use three radiators and two convection heaters next winter. What will be the fuel bill?

4. Just before cashing up, shopkeeper Sarah received this e-mail from the police:

    > **Watch out – counterfeit one pound coins are being circulated in the area**
    > The coins can be recognised by their shine – they are slightly duller than real ones and they are not as heavy.

    Unfortunately, the police did not mention the weight of a real or fake coin.
    Sarah separated out the coins in her till and to her dismay found she had eight normal coins but three dull ones. The weight of these 11 coins was 63 g. ▶

Sarah phoned her son who also ran a shop on the other side of town and asked him to do the same. He had ten normal and nine fake coins that in total weighed 105 g.

a. Use this information to form two simultaneous equations.

b. Solve the equations in order to work out the weight of a real and counterfeit coin.

5. A hotelier placed an advertisement in the paper:

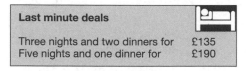

Last minute deals	
Three nights and two dinners for	£135
Five nights and one dinner for	£190

a. Create two simultaneous equations using this information.

b. Solve these equations in order to work out the cost of staying a night in the hotel and eating dinner at the hotel.

6. Here is Bill's confession to the group leader of the 'PoundLess Club', a club set up for people wanting to lose weight:

a. Use the information provided by Bill and the club leader to create two simultaneous equations.

b. Solve the equations to calculate the calories of each treat.

c. What should Bill give up?

Solving simultaneous equations graphically

To draw a straight line at least two points on the line need to be known.

Solve these simultaneous equations graphically:

$3x - y = 1$ (1)
$2y - 3x = 4$ (2)

Rearrange the two equations to make y the subject.

(1) $3x - y = 1$

$$\underline{+y \qquad +y}$$
$3x \qquad = 1 + y$
$$\underline{-1 \quad -1}$$
$3x - 1 = \qquad y$
$y = 3x - 1$

(2) $2y - 3x = 4$

$$\underline{+3x \qquad +3x}$$
$2y \qquad = 4 + 3x$
$$\underline{\div 2 \qquad \div 2}$$
$$y = \frac{3x + 4}{2}$$

Work out the co-ordinates of two points on each line.

$x = 0 \quad y = 3 \times 0 - 1 = -1$ **(0, -1)**
$x = 4 \quad y = 3 \times 4 - 1 = 11$ **(4, 11)**

$x = 0 \quad y = \dfrac{3 \times 0 + 4}{2} = \dfrac{4}{2}$ **(0, 2)**

$x = 4 \quad y = \dfrac{3 \times 4 + 4}{2} = \dfrac{16}{2} = 8$ **(4, 8)**

Mark the co-ordinates on a grid and draw the two lines.

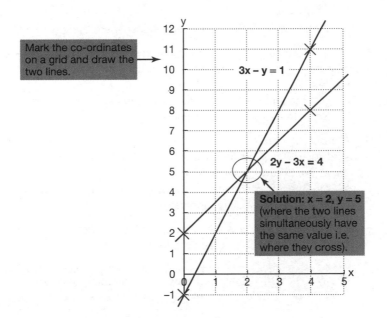

$3x - y = 1$

$2y - 3x = 4$

Solution: x = 2, y = 5 (where the two lines simultaneously have the same value i.e. where they cross).

Work it out

1. Graphically solve the following simultaneous equations:
   a. $y = x + 3$
      $y = 3x - 3$
   b. $y = 2x$
      $y = -x + 3$
   c. $3x - y = 2$
      $y - x = 4$
   d. $4x - y = 2$
      $y + x = 3$
   e. $2y - 3x = 6$
      $2y - x = 10$
   f. $5x - 2y = -2$
      $2y \times x = 10$

2. Graphically solve the following simultaneous equations:
   a. $y - 2x = 2$ Draw a grid from x = –3 to x = 3
      $2y - 3x = 4$ and y = –3 to y = 4

   b. $x - y = 2$ Draw a grid from x = 0 to x = 6
      $y + 3x = 2$ and y = –4 to y = 4

   c. $2y - x = 2$ Draw a grid from x = 0 to x = 6
      $2y + x = 6$ and y = 0 to y = 4

3. a. Why is there no solution to the following equations:
      $y = 2x + 5$
      $y = 2x - 5$?
   b. Write down another pair of equations where there is no solution.

4. Mark is returning from a holiday in France. He is bringing back a total of 20 bottles of wine and beer. He has four times the number of beer bottles as he has wine bottles.
   a. Use the information to create two simultaneous equations.
   b. Solve the equations graphically.

5. A group of work colleagues club together to buy concert tickets as a leaving present for a fellow worker. If they each contribute £5 they are £4 short and if they each give £6 they have £4 spare.
   a. Use the information to create two simultaneous equations.
   b. Solve the equations graphically.

6. On top of his regular wages Gavin, a telesales worker, makes a commission. Here are the commissions he receives for two days:

	Car insurance sales	Home insurance sales	Total commission
Monday	3	1	£18
Tuesday	2	2	£16

   For obvious reasons, Gavin is keen to find out which sales give the most commission.
   a. Use the information in the table to create two simultaneous equations.
   b. Solve the equations graphically.
   c. Which sales should Gavin push?

7. This graph describes the journey of two cars:
    a. Explain in words what is happening.
    b. What are the speeds of the two vehicles?
    c. What are the two equations of the lines?
    d. When do the two cars meet?

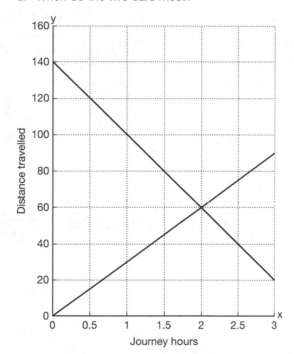

Kim's overheads include stall rental, the cost of a juicer, glasses, kitchen implements etc.

Costs (y):
    overheads
        +
cost of a smoothie
    multiplied by
    number of
smoothies sold (x)

Income (y):
price of a smoothie
    multiplied by
number smoothies
    sold (x)

8. Kim has set up a market stall selling smoothies. Her initial overheads are £270 and each smoothie she sells costs her on average, £0.60. Kim sells each smoothie at the flat rate of £2.40.
    a. Write down two equations, one for costs and one for income.
    b. Draw these two equations on a grid.
    c. What does the point where the two lines cross represent?
    d. How many smoothies has Kate sold at the point where the two lines cross?

4.8 Inequalities

Here are some age restrictions that can be written as **inequalities**:

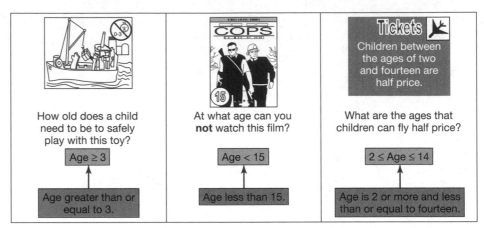

Work it out

1. Here some vehicle restrictions

All restrictions are the maximum allowable value.

Write the inequality for:
a. the speed you can drive
b. the vehicle height in metres, that is not permissible
c. the permitted weight of a vehicle
d. the times you are allowed to park.

2. Write these sentences as inequalities:
a. No more than nine people are allowed in the lift.
b. The maximum weight of baggage for a aeroplane luggage hold is 25 kg.
c. Only people who are over 130 cm tall and below 200 cm tall are allowed on the fair ride.

3. Write these inequalities as sentences:
   a. 20 minutes < time
   b. Number of people ≥ 10
   c. 5 ≤ age ≤ 16

Inequalities on the number line

The inequality x ≤ 4 can be shown on the number line as:

The solid circle shows that x can equal 4.

The inequality −2 ≤ x < 3 can be shown on the number line as:

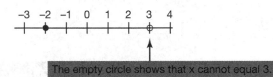

The empty circle shows that x cannot equal 3.

If the **or** is replaced by **and** the inequality would be a nonsense – you can't have x both less than 0 and greater than 15.

The inequality x < 0 **or** x > 15 can be shown on the number line as:

```
 -10 -5   0   5  10  15  20  25
  +---+---ϕ---+---+---ϕ---+---+
```

Work it out

1. On a number line draw the inequalities:
   a. x > 4   b. x ≤ −2
   c. x ≥ −3   d. 1 ≤ x ≤ 4
   e. −5 < x < −2   f. −1 < x and 3 ≥ x
   g. x > 2 or x < −1

2. In terms of x, write the inequalities shown on the number line:

   a.
   ```
    0   1   2   3   4   5   6
    +---+---●---+---+---+---+
   ```

   b.
   ```
   -6  -5  -4  -3  -2  -1   0
    +---+---+---+---+---ϕ---+
   ```

   c.
   ```
    4   5   6   7   8   9  10  11
    +---ϕ---+---+---+---+---●---+
   ```

▶

d.   -7 -6 -5 -4 -3 -2 -1

e.   0   1   2   3   4   5   6

f.   -20 -10 0 10 20 30 40

3. x is a number such that $0 < x < 1$. Provide two possible values of x.

4. x is a number such that $x > -2$ and $x \le 3$. List the possible values of x when x is:
   a. an integer
   b. a natural number.

5. y is a whole number such that $8 \le y < 15$. List the possible values of y when y is:
   a. a prime number
   b. a number divisible by three.

6. Given that $-6 \le x \le 4$ and $-5 \le y \le 3$, write down:
   a. the largest possible value of x^2
   b. the largest possible value of xy
   c. the smallest possible value of xy
   d. the smallest possible value of y^2.

Investigation

1. Which of these inequalities cannot be true:
   a. $20 < x < 30$ b. $30 < x > 40$
   c. $10 > x > 20$ d. $0 < x < 10$
   e. $-10 > x > 10$ f. $20 < x > -10$?

2. Which one of these inequalities describes the whole of the number line?
   a. $x < 5$ and $x > 10$ b. $x < 10$ and $x > 5$
   c. $x < 10$ or $x > 5$ d. $x < 5$ or $x > 10$?

Solving inequalities

Solve the inequality $3x - 5 > 7$.

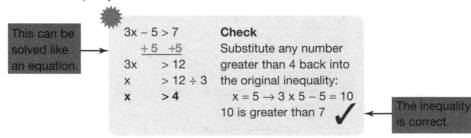

This can be solved like an equation.

$$3x - 5 > 7$$
$$\underline{+5 \quad +5}$$
$$3x \qquad > 12$$
$$x \qquad > 12 \div 3$$
$$x \qquad > 4$$

Check
Substitute any number greater than 4 back into the original inequality:
   $x = 5 \rightarrow 3 \times 5 - 5 = 10$
10 is greater than 7 ✓

The inequality is correct.

Exception to the key rule

Key rule

Figures on either side of an inequality can be rearranged by adding, subtracting, multiplying or dividing both sides by the same positive number.

Multiplying or dividing both sides of an inequality by a negative number.
Multiply both sides of this inequality by −3:

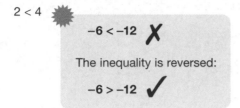

$2 < 4$

$-6 < -12$ ✗

The inequality is reversed:

$-6 > -12$ ✓

Example 1

Solve the inequality: $-4x < 16$

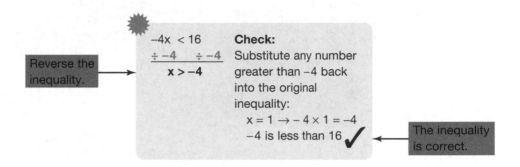

Reverse the inequality.

$-4x < 16$
$\div -4 \quad \div -4$
$x > -4$

Check:
Substitute any number greater than −4 back into the original inequality:
$x = 1 \rightarrow -4 \times 1 = -4$
−4 is less than 16 ✓

The inequality is correct.

Example 2

Working with a double inequalities

Solve the inequality $19 \leq 3x + 2 \leq 25$

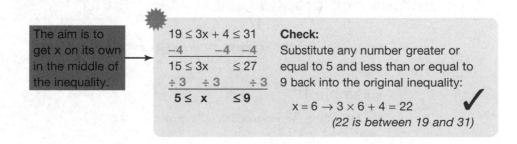

The aim is to get x on its own in the middle of the inequality.

$19 \leq 3x + 4 \leq 31$
$\underline{-4 \qquad -4 \quad -4}$
$15 \leq 3x \qquad \leq 27$
$\div 3 \quad \div 3 \qquad \div 3$
$5 \leq \ x \qquad \leq 9$

Check:
Substitute any number greater or equal to 5 and less than or equal to 9 back into the original inequality:

$x = 6 \rightarrow 3 \times 6 + 4 = 22$ ✓
(22 is between 19 and 31)

Work it out

1. Solve these inequalities:
   a. $2x > 8$
   b. $14 - 5x \geq 4$
   c. $3x \leq 15$
   d. $5 \leq 17 - 3x$
   e. $x - 5 < 3$
   f. $-2x > 10$
   g. $2x - 3 \geq 5$
   h. $-3x < -9$
   i. $7x + 2 > 16$
   j. $-x + 2 < 7$
   k. $17 < 3x + 2$
   l. $-3x - 5 > 7$
   m. $7 - x > 4$
   n. $-7x > 14$
   o. $3 + 2x < 1$
   p. $13 < -4x - 3$

2. Solve these inequalities:
   a. $2x + 3 > x + 7$
   b. $3x - 7 \leq 7 + 2x$
   c. $2(x - 3) < 2$
   d. $4(x - 2) > 2x + 6$
   e. $5(x + 1) < 3x - 7$
   f. $-8x + 1 > 3(x - 7)$

3. Solve these inequalities:
   a. $3 < x + 2 < 7$
   b. $0 \leq x - 3 < 5$
   c. $4 \geq 2x \geq -6$
   d. $20 \geq x - 10 \geq 10$
   e. $9 < 2x - 1 < 11$
   f. $17 \leq 3x + 2 < 26$

4. What is wrong with this solution:

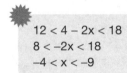

$12 < 4 - 2x < 18$
$8 < -2x < 18$
$-4 < x < -9$

Investigation

What whole numbers satisfy all three inequalities?

$0 < x + 3 < 7$
$9 > x + 7 > 3$
$-4 < x - 2 < 6$

Inequalities and graphs

Inequalities with two unknowns can be represented graphically.

Example 1

Represent the two inequalities graphically:
   $1 < x \leq 4$ and $0 \leq y < 5$

Dashed line: points on the line are not valid.
Unbroken line: points on the line are valid.

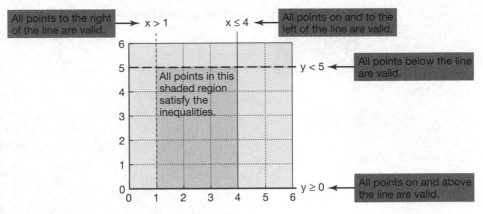

All points to the right of the line are valid. → $x > 1$

$x \le 4$ ← All points on and to the left of the line are valid.

All points in this shaded region satisfy the inequalities.

$y < 5$ ← All points below the line are valid.

$y \ge 0$ ← All points on and above the line are valid.

State two points that satisfy the inequalities.

 (4, 3) and **(2, 4)**

Does the point (1, 2) satisfy the inequalities?

No – the point lies on a dashed line.

Example 2

Graph the three inequalities:
   $x \ge 1$, $2y - x \ge 2$ and $y < -x + 7$
To do this the three lines **x = 1**, **2y − x = 2** and **y = −x + 7** are plotted on a grid:

To plot a sloping line the co-ordinates of two points on it are worked out, plotted on a grid and joined together by a straight line.

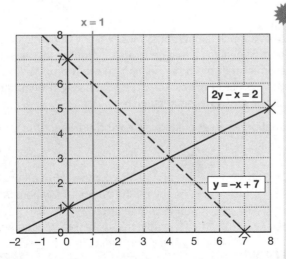

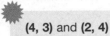 x = 1

2y − x = 2

y = −x + 7

Make y the subject of the equation:

2y − x = 2

$$\begin{array}{r} +x \quad\quad +x \\ 2y \quad = 2 + x \end{array}$$

$$y \quad = \frac{2 + x}{2}$$

Work out two points on the line:

x = 0	x = 8
$y = \dfrac{2}{2}$	$y = \dfrac{2 + 8}{2}$
y = 1	y = 5
(0, 1)	**(8, 5)**

Work out two points on the line **y = −x + 7:**

x = 0	x = 7
y = 7	y = −7 + 7
	y = 0
(0, 7)	**(7, 0)**

▶

Now the region that satisfies all three inequalities is shaded:

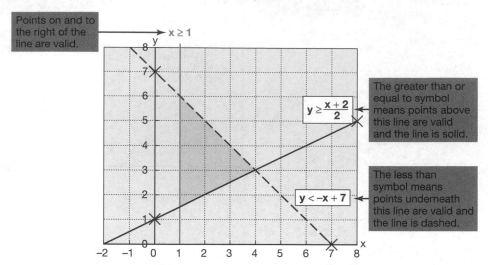

State two sets of co-ordinates that fit the three inequalities:

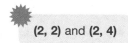

(2, 2) and (2, 4)

Example 3

Profit here means the money made after all overheads are paid.

Alan, the owner of a small restaurant, cooks two set Christmas meals. Customers can choose either a traditional meal that generates a profit of £3 per serving or a vegetarian option that makes a profit of £5 per serving. In the run up to Christmas, Alan's target is to make a daily profit in excess of £150. Each day he has time to prepare up to 50 traditional dishes and 35 vegetarian dishes.

Write this information as a set of inequalities and graph them.

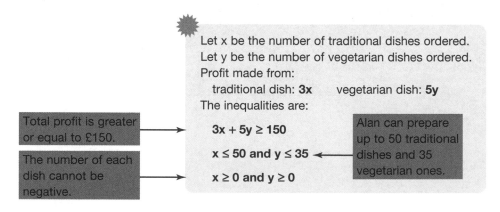

Let x be the number of traditional dishes ordered.
Let y be the number of vegetarian dishes ordered.
Profit made from:
    traditional dish: **3x**   vegetarian dish: **5y**
The inequalities are:

Total profit is greater or equal to £150.

$$3x + 5y \geq 150$$

Alan can prepare up to 50 traditional dishes and 35 vegetarian ones.

$$x \leq 50 \text{ and } y \leq 35$$

The number of each dish cannot be negative.

$$x \geq 0 \text{ and } y \geq 0$$

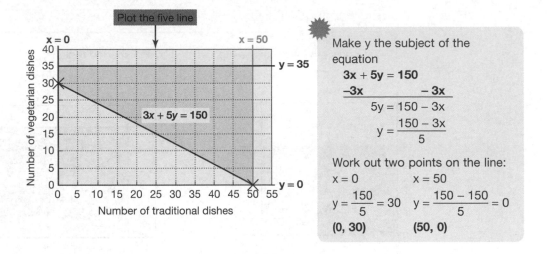

Plot the five line

Make y the subject of the equation

$$3x + 5y = 150$$
$$\underline{-3x \qquad\qquad -3x}$$
$$5y = 150 - 3x$$
$$y = \frac{150 - 3x}{5}$$

Work out two points on the line:

x = 0   x = 50

$$y = \frac{150}{5} = 30 \quad y = \frac{150 - 150}{5} = 0$$

(0, 30)   **(50, 0)**

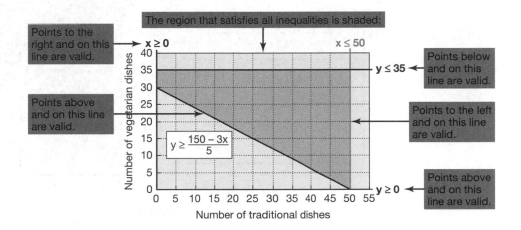

One day Alan sells 35 traditional dishes and 25 vegetarian dishes. Does this meet his target?

Yes, x = 35 and y = 25 is a point within the shaded area.

What is the maximum profit Alan can make in one day?

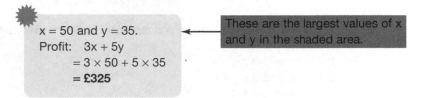

x = 50 and y = 35.
Profit: 3x + 5y
      = 3 × 50 + 5 × 35
      = **£325**

These are the largest values of x and y in the shaded area.

Work it out

1. Write down the inequalities represented by the shaded regions:

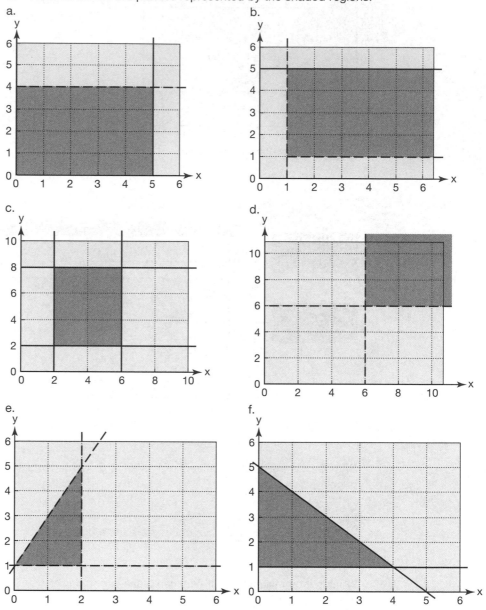

a.

b.

c.

d.

e.

f.

2. On a grid draw and shade the region represented by the inequalities:

a. $x \geq 3$ and $y \geq 2$

b. $0 \leq x \leq 6$ and $0 \leq y < 6$

c. $2 \leq x \leq 8$ and $3 \leq y \leq 6$

d. $x \leq 4$ and $1 \leq y \leq 6$

3. On a grid, draw and shade the region represented by the inequalities:
   a. $x > y$ and $0 \leq y \leq 8$
   b. $y > 2x$ and $0 \leq y < 9$
   c. $y < x + 4$, $y \geq 0$ and $1 \leq x \leq 5$
   d. $y \geq 2x - 3$, $x \geq 0$ and $0 \leq y \leq 5$
   e. $y - 0.5x > 1$ and $x \geq 0$ and $y < -x + 10$
   f. $y \geq 2$ and $y \leq 2x + 1$ and $2y + x < 16$

> x is the number of men in the cells.
> y is the number of women in the cells.

4. A police station has enough cells to lock up eight men and five women. Show this as a shaded region on a grid.

> x is the number of hot drinks sold.
> y is the number of brownies given away.
> **Break even:**
> profit − loss = 0

5. Steve, the owner of a coffee shop, is running a promotional offer on chocolate brownies. By doing this he hopes to attract more customers who will buy a hot drink to go with the brownie.
   For every brownie Steve gives away he loses 12p, for every hot drink he sells he makes a profit of 60p. He aims to, at the very worst, break even.
   a. Write down the break-even inequality.
   b. Write down two more inequalities that describe this information.
   c. Draw these inequalities as a shaded region on a grid.
   d. One day he gave away 160 brownies and sold 30 hot drinks. Did Steve break even?

> x is the number of minutes on the rowing machine.
> y is the number of minutes on the running machine.

6. Using just the rowing and running machines, a top athlete works out in the gym for up to 60 minutes a day. On the rowing machine he burns 25 calories a minute and on the running machine 30 calories a minute. His target is to burn over 1 500 calories in the whole session.
   a. Write down the inequality for time spent on the machines.
   b. Write down the inequality for calories burnt.
   c. Write down two more inequalities that describe this information.
   d. Show these inequalities as a shaded region on a grid.
   e. In one session the athlete spent 30 minutes on each machine. Has he met his target?
   f. What is the maximum number of calories he can burn? How many minutes has he spent on each machine to do this?

> Let x be the number of football games.
> Let y be the number of war games.

Hints and tips

Write all your inequalities in pence and minutes.

7. Derek, a pub landlord, has just bought a new games console that plays either a football or a war game. Both games last ten minutes. Derek makes a profit of £2.00 each time a customer plays on the football game and £2.60 for each go on the war game. Derek aims to make a daily profit of at least £52. He is open for just six hours a day.
   a. Write an inequality for the profit.
   b. Write an inequality for the time available for the games to be used.
   c. Write two more inequalities describing the situation.
   d. Draw these inequalities as a shaded region on a grid.
   e. What is the maximum profit Derek can make in one day?

All about university fees

8. At one university, the fee for a Psychology course is £3 000 for EU citizens and £14 000 for 'overseas' residents. The university aims to generate at least £420 000 from Psychology student fees, but the course cannot take more than 80 students in total.

    a. Write down the four inequalities that describe this information.
    b. Draw these inequalities as a shaded region on a grid.
    c. One year there are 45 EU and 35 overseas candidates who successfully apply for the course. Does this meet the course criteria?
    d. i. What is the maximum amount of money the university can generate from the Psychology course?
        ii. How many EU and overseas students would be on the course?
    e. The Psychology course consists of a mixture of tutorials and formal lectures. The tutorials last an hour and the lectures two hours. Each student attends no more than 16 hours a week. The student should have no more than ten sessions in total in a week.
        i. Write down the four inequalities that describe this information.
        ii. Draw these inequalities as a shaded region on another grid.
        iii. A student is timetabled for four tutorials and seven lectures. Does this meet the criteria?

Investigation

Investigate the two inequalities $x + y < 3$ and $y - 2x > 4$ by drawing them as lines on a grid.
What are your conclusions?

4.9 Drawing Curves

Curves are not only aesthetically pleasing but can be used to mathematically describe a situation.

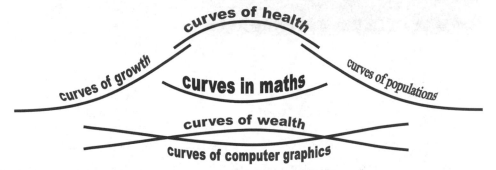

The mathematics of the spread of infectious diseases

Diseases are an everyday part of our lives. They range from the common cold, with generally minor symptoms, to swine flu or AIDs, diseases which can have fatal consequences. Over the years, mathematicians have worked on modelling the spread of these diseases in order to predict and prepare for future outbreaks.

This example is a simplified model of the spread of measles.

The equation is only valid between $x = 1$ and $x = 35$.

In a highly populated city, packed full of citizens who are not vaccinated against measles, there is an outbreak. Every day a record is kept of the number of new cases. Here is a computer generated 'curve of best fit' and its equation describing the spread of the disease:

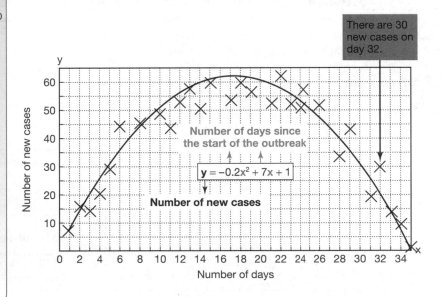

There are 30 new cases on day 32.

Number of days since the start of the outbreak

$$y = -0.2x^2 + 7x + 1$$

Number of new cases

1. How many new cases should a health authority expect if there was a similar outbreak after:
  i.   6 days?
  ii. 21 days?

These figures can be keyed directly into your calculator:

It is more accurate to use the equation of the line, $y = -0.2x^2 + 7x + 1$, rather than reading a value off the graph.

1. $x = 6$
$y = -0.2 \times 6^2 + 7 \times 6 + 1$
$\quad = 35.8$
After 6 days there will be about **36** new cases.

$x = 21$
$y = -0.2 \times 21^2 + 7 \times 21 + 1$
$\quad = 59.8$
After 21 days there will be about **60** new cases.

2. Comment on the chart.

2. The measles outbreak lasted 35 days, peaking between the 17th and 18th days when there were about 62 new cases. After this there was a steady decline in the number of new cases, presumably as most people had already been infected or were resistant to the virus.

The plague is still with us today and some scientists anticipate there will be more outbreaks of this disease as the climate gets warmer and wetter. There is also the real threat that the virus could be used in bioterrorism.

The equation is valid between $x = 4$ and $x = 30$.

Task

The computer generated curve and its equation describes the rate of deaths in a city in India at the turn of the century from the spread of the bubonic plague.
a. Use the equation of the curve to work out how many deaths there were after:
  i.   12 days
  ii. 24 days.
b. Comment on the chart.

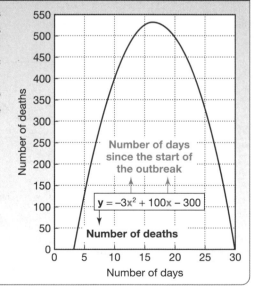

Plotting curves

When plotting straight lines, we only really need to know the position of two points that can be joined using a ruler:

But with curves it's different. The more points there are, the more accurately the curve can be drawn.
Computer generated curves will use literally thousands of points in order to draw a smooth curve:

Example

1. Plot the curve $y = x^2 - 4x$ from $x = 0$ to $x = 6$.
   The y value of each of the six points between $x = 0$ and $x = 6$ is calculated:

x	0	1	2	3	4	5	6
$y = x^2$ $-4x$	0^2 -4×0	1^2 -4×1	2^2 -4×2	3^2 -4×3	4^2 -4×4	5^2 -4×5	6^2 -4×6
y	0	−3	−4	−3	0	5	12

This is the point (1, −3)

With curves there are often repeats in the y values.

These figures can be keyed directly into your calculator:

6 x^2 − 4 x 6 =

These points can now be plotted on a grid:

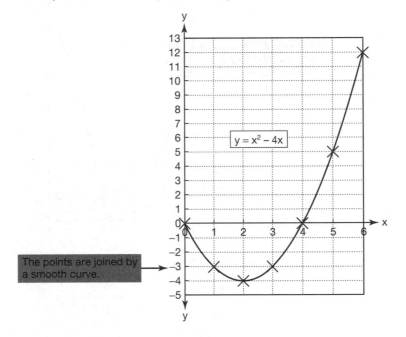

$y = x^2 - 4x$

The points are joined by a smooth curve.

Key fact

The x within an equation of a straight line is always to the power of 1, e.g.
$y = 3x + 1$
The equation of a curve must contain an x that is not a power of 1, e.g.
$y = 2x^2 + 5x$

2. Plot the curve $\mathbf{y} = -x^2 + 3x + 3$ between x = –2 and x = 4.
   The co-ordinates of points on the curve are calculated:

x	–2	–1	0	1	2	3	4
$\mathbf{y} = -x^2$ $+3\mathbf{x}$ $+3$	$-(-2)^2$ $+3 \times -2$ $+3$	$-(-1)^2$ $+3 \times -1$ $+3$	$-(0)^2$ $+3 \times 0$ $+3$	$-(1)^2$ $+3 \times 1$ $+3$	$-(2)^2$ $+3 \times 2$ $+3$	$-(3)^2$ $+3 \times 3$ $+3$	$-(3)^2$ $+3 \times 4$ $+3$
y	–7	–1	3	5	5	3	–1

These figures can be keyed directly into your calculator:

— (— 2) x² + 3 x — 2 + 3 =

This is the point (**4, –1**).

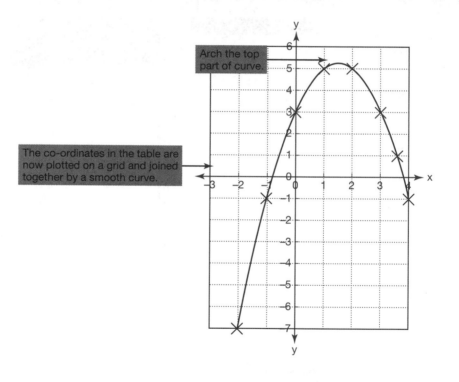

Arch the top part of curve.

The co-ordinates in the table are now plotted on a grid and joined together by a smooth curve.

3. Plot the curve $y = \frac{4}{x}$ from $x = 0.5$ to $x = 6$.

Here x = 0.5 has been added in order to get a better feel for the shape of the curve.

x	0.5	1	2	3	4	5	6
$y = \frac{4}{x}$	$\frac{4}{0.5}$	$\frac{4}{1}$	$\frac{4}{2}$	$\frac{4}{3}$	$\frac{4}{4}$	$\frac{4}{5}$	$\frac{4}{6}$
y	8	4	2	1.33	1	0.8	0.67

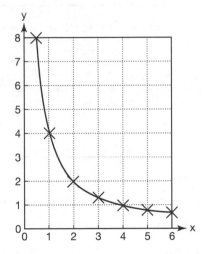

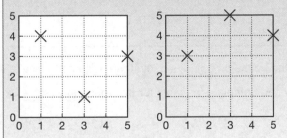

Investigation – paired work

Copy these grids:

1. Join the points up to create curves.
2. Compare your curves with your partner's.
    What do you notice?
    What conclusions can you make?

Key term

Quadratic curve/parabola
Curves where the highest power of x is two. They all have the same basic 'U' shape and have one line of symmetry. Here are four quadratic curves:

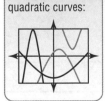

Work it out

1. If plotted, which of the following equations would not produce a curve:
    a. $y = x^3 + 4$
    b. $y = 2x - 1$
    c. $y = 10$
    d. $y^2 = x$
    e. $y = \frac{1}{x}$
    f. $y = x^2 + 3x + 4$

2. a. Copy and complete the table for the equation $y = x^2 - 3x$.

x	0	1	2	3	4	5
$y = x^2$ $-3x$		1^2 -3×1			4^2 -3×4	
y		-2	-2			10

b. Plot the points on a grid and join them together to make a smooth curve.

3. a. Copy and complete the table for the equation $y = x^2 + 2x$.

x	-3	-2	-1	0	1	2
$y = x^2$ $+2x$	$(-3)^2$ $+2 \times -3$				1^2 $+2 \times 1$	
y	3	0		0		

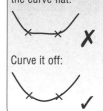

Potential pitfall

You make the top or the bottom of the curve flat:

Curve it off:

b. Plot the points on a grid and join them together to make a smooth curve.

4. a. Copy and complete the table for the equation $y = x^2 - 4x + 3$.

x	0	1	2	3	4	5
$y = x^2$ $-4x$ $+3$			2^2 -4×2 $+3$		4^2 -4×4 $+3$	
y	3		-1			8

b. Plot the points on a grid and join them together to make a smooth curve.

5. a. Copy and complete the table for the equation $y = x^2 - 2x - 4$.

x	-2	-1	0	1	2	3
$y = x^2$ $-2x$ -4	$(-2)^2$ -2×-2 -4					3^2 -2×3 -4
y	4			-5	-4	

b. Plot the points on a grid and join them together to make a smooth curve.

6. a. Copy and complete the table for the equation $y = -x^2 + 5x - 6$.

x	0	1	2	3	4	5
$y = -x^2$ $+5x$ -6			$-(2)^2$ $+5 \times 2$ -6			$-(5)^2$ $+5 \times 5$ -6
y		-2	0		-2	

b. Plot the points on a grid and join them together to make a smooth curve.

7. Dale has plotted this curve which looks nice but is incorrect.
   a. Work out what Dale has done wrong.
   b. Draw the correct curve for the equation.

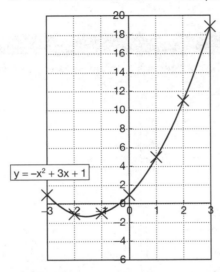

$y = -x^2 + 3x + 1$

8. Plot the curves:
   a. $y = x^2 - 5x + 4$ From x = 0 to x = 5
   b. $y = x^2 - 7x + 10$ From x = 0 to x = 5
   c. $y = x^2 + 2x - 3$ From x = -3 to x = 2
   d. $y = x^2 - x - 7$ From x = -3 to x = 3

9. a. On the same grid, plot the two graphs $y = x^2$ and $y = -x^2$ from x = -3 to x = 3.
   b. Now add the two lines $y = x^2 + 2$ and $y = -x^2 + 2$ from x = -3 to x = 3.
   c. Without working out the co-ordinates sketch the two lines $y = x^2 - 4$ and $y = -x^2 + 4$.

10. Plot the two curves $y = \sin x$ and $y = \cos x$ on the same grid (from x = 0° to x = 180°, increasing in 30° steps).

11. a. Copy the curve from Example 3, but this time extend the x-axis back to -6 and the y-axis down to -8.
   b. Work out the values of y for the same equation, $y = \frac{4}{x}$, from x = -0.5 to x = -6 (seven points).

c. Plot these values on the grid.

d. Why has the point when x = 0 not been included?

e. Describe the shape of the curves.

12. Plot the curve of the triangular number sequence, $y = 0.5x(x + 1)$ from $x = 0$ to $x = 10$, increasing in twos (i.e., find the y values when $x = 0$, $x = 2$, $x = 4$, etc.).

Hints and tips

There is an x^3 button on most calculators.

13. a. Plot the curve $y = x^3$ from $x = -3$ to $x = +3$

b. On the same grid plot the curve $y = x^3 + 2$

c. Without working out the exact co-ordinates sketch the graph of:

    i. $y = x^3 + 5$

    ii. $y = x^3 - 5$.

14. a. Draw a grid extending in the x-axis from -3 to $+3$ and the y-axis from -35 to $+35$.

b. On the grid plot the three curves
$y = -x^3$, $y = -x^3 + 2x$, $y = -x^3 - 2x$.

Hints and tips

A multiplication is required.

Investigation 1

Use the equation of the coloured curve to investigate the equations of the other four curves.

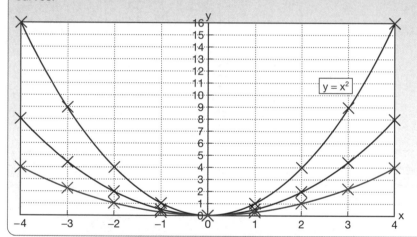

Investigation 2

Work out the equations of these two lines:

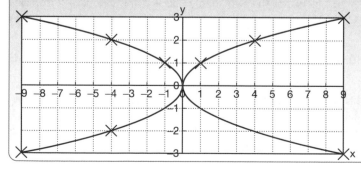

More practical uses of curves

The equation works for up to ten years after a person has first been diagnosed with breast cancer.

Here is an equation describing an approximate survival rate for breast cancer:

Number of years since a person was first diagnosed

$$y = 0.17x^2 - 4.2x + 100$$

Percentage of people diagnosed that are still surviving

This equation can be plotted on a grid.
Here is a table of co-ordinates of six points:

x	0	2	4	6	8	10
$y = 0.17x^2$ $-4.2x$ $+100$	0.17×0^2 -4.2×0 $+100$	0.17×2^2 -4.2×2 $+100$	0.17×4^2 -4.2×4 $+100$	0.17×6^2 -4.2×6 $+100$	0.17×8^2 -4.2×8 $+100$	0.17×10^2 -4.2×10 $+100$
y	100	92	86	81	77	75

These statistics for breast cancer (and prostate cancer) are hypothetical. In reality a lot more points are plotted, but this is not practical here.

Plot the points on a grid and join them together with a smooth curve.

75% of people who contract breast cancer are alive after ten years.

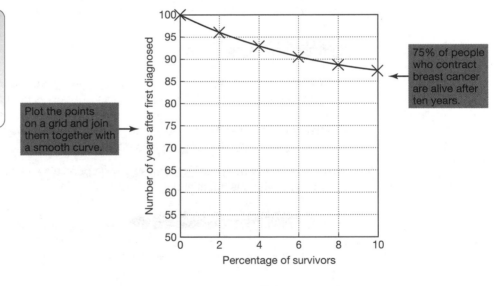

Work it out

> Drawing curves is a useful way of visually comparing the survival rates of the two cancers.

1. a. Copy the curve for breast cancer survival rates.
    b. The equation governing the survival rate for prostate cancer is:

    $$y = 0.24x^2 - 6.9x + 100 \qquad \text{Holds true up to } x = 10$$

    Create a table similar to the one in the example and work out the survival rates for prostate cancer.
    c. Plot a curve of the co-ordinates on the same grid as the curve for breast cancer.
    d. What percentage of prostrate cancer victims are alive after:
        i. five years?
        ii. ten years?
    e. Comment on the two curves.

2. On a small remote island far away, the ruling party is concerned about the growing prison population. They currently have capacity for 70 prisoners. The governor has been given two equations predicting the likely growth in the prison population:

> The equations are reliable for up to six years.

Number of years from today

(1) $y = 3x^2 + 52$ (High prediction for the increase in prison population)
(2) $y = x^2 + 52$ (Low prediction for the increase in prison population)

Predicted number of prisoner

    a. Not being a mathematician, these equations meant nothing to him. He asked one of his advisors to plot the equations as two curves on the same grid – do this for him.
    b. After how many years will they run out of prison cells? Give two answers, one using equation **(1)**, the other equation **(2)**.

3. A careers advisory body carried out a survey on people's earnings after graduation and came up with this equation:

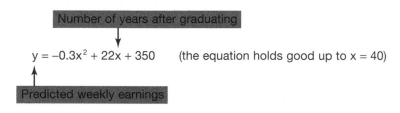

Number of years after graduating

$$y = -0.3x^2 + 22x + 350 \qquad \text{(the equation holds good up to } x = 40)$$

Predicted weekly earnings

> Start at x = 0 and increase in fives to x = 40.

    a. Plot the graph of this equation.
    b. How much can a graduate expect to earn:
        i. immediately after graduating (i.e. x = 0)?
        ii. 40 years after graduating?
    c. Do you think the careers advisory board have got it right?

The mathematics of networking

4. In life there are lots of networks, social networks, electronic networks on the web, networks of work colleagues and so on.

    A mathematician has come up with this equation that describes how the number of vistors to a few websites grow at a phenomenal rate whereas others languish in obscurity:

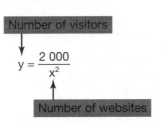

Number of visitors

$$y = \frac{2\ 000}{x^2}$$

Number of websites

> This type of curve can be applied to many situations. For instance, at a party you are more likely to speak to someone who looks sociable than someone who doesn't. So his/her network grows whereas many others make few contacts.
> It can also describe why the rich, wlth lots of investment opportunities, just keep on getting richer whereas the poor, with nothing to invest, remain poor.

    a. Copy and complete the table:

x	5	10	20	30	40
$y = \dfrac{2\ 000}{x^2}$	$\dfrac{2\ 000}{(5^2)}$				
y	80				

    b. Draw a curve of the co-ordinates.
    c. Comment on the curve.

5. A particular bacteria grows at a rate governed by the equation:

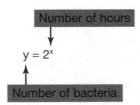

Number of hours

$$y = 2^x$$

Number of bacteria

    a. Plot this growth on a grid between $x = 0$ and $x = 6$.
    b. What is happening to the number of bacteria each hour?

4.10 Quadratic Equations

At a National Union of Teachers' meeting it was declared that the **quadratic equation** was dead, it had no role to play in modern maths apart from inflicting cruel torture on unsuspecting students.

Was anyone bothered by this, did anyone come to its defence?

Well yes, the quadratic equation was defended passionately not only in the newspapers but on the radio and even in the Houses of Parliament, more used to discussing weighty issues concerning the state of our nation.

One MP stated that putting aside quadratic equations is like telling us to ignore 400 years of intellectual, scientific and technological development. These equations underpin modern life, and have a wide range of applications, from sports technology to watching TV, to saving our lives.

Solving quadratic equations algebraically

Before you can solve these equations you must be able to multiply out brackets and factorise algebraic expressions.

Example
Multiplying out brackets

Multiply out these brackets:

1.

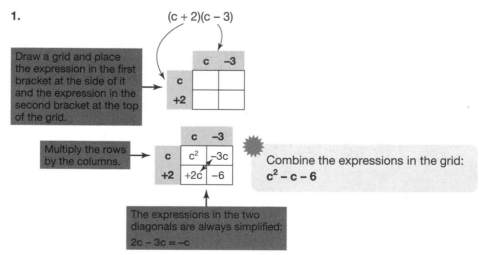

2. $(2d - 5)^2$

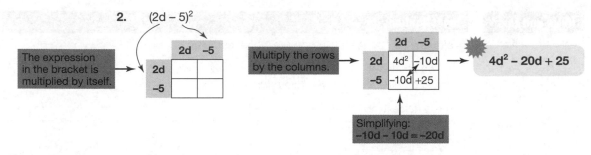

3. $(3e - 2)(2e + 7) - 2e(e + 3)$

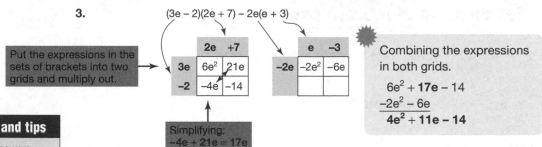

Work it out

1.   Multiply out the following brackets:

a. $(c + 2)(c + 3)$ b. $(d + 4)(d + 1)$

c. $(e + 5)(e + 3)$ d. $(f + 2)(f + 6)$

e. $(g + 3)(g - 2)$ f. $(h - 2)(h - 3)$

g. $(j - 1)(j - 5)$ h. $(k - 4)(k + 4)$

i. $(m + 3)(m - 3)$ j. $(n - 3)(n - 6)$

2.   Multiply out the following brackets:

a. $(2c + 1)(c + 2)$ b. $(d + 2)(3d + 3)$

c. $(3e + 1)(2e + 4)$ d. $(4f + 1)(f + 3)$

e. $(1 + 3g)(1 + 2g)$ f. $(3h + 3)(3h - 3)$

g. $(5j - 2)(2j - 3)$ h. $(3 - 2k)(1 + 4k)$

i. $(3m + 2)(4 - 3m)$ j. $(4 - 3n)(3n - 5)$

3.   Multiply out the following brackets:

a. $(c + 1)^2$ b. $(d - 7)^2$

c. $(2e + 3)^2$ d. $(3f - 5)^2$

4.   Write the following expressions as simply as possible:

a. $(3m + 2)(m - 2) + 6m$ b. $(3 + 5n)(2n - 3) + 4n^2$

c. $(2r + 1)(2r - 1) + 4r$ d. $(3 + 5s)^2 + 4$

e. $(3t + 2)^2 - 6t$ f. $(2u + 1)(3u - 2) - 4u^2 + 5u$

g. $(3v - 2)^2 - 3(v^2 + 2)$ h. $(3w + 2)(2w - 1) - w(w + 3)$

Hints and tips

Let n be the first number, n + 1 be the second and so on.

Investigation

Take any four consecutive positive whole numbers.

'The square of the first added to the square of the last is always bigger than the sum of the squares of the two middle numbers.'

True or false. Investigate.

Factorising algebraic expressions

Finding the highest common factor of an algebraic expression works in the same way as finding one when dealing with just numbers – the factor, whether a number or letter, must divide into all terms in the expression.

This is the reverse of multiplying out brackets.

Example 1

Find the highest common factor of the expressions:

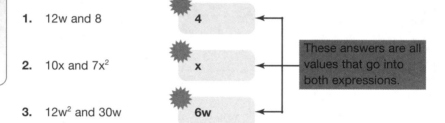

1. 12w and 8   **4**

2. 10x and $7x^2$ **x**

These answers are all values that go into both expressions.

3. $12w^2$ and 30w   **6w**

Example 2

Key term

Factorising an expression
The highest common factor of an expression is multiplied by what is left of the expression after this factor has been removed from each term.

Factorise the following:

1. 10a + 15   ← 5 goes into both terms.

  5(2a + 3)

2. 8b + 12 – 20c   ← 4 goes into all three terms.

  4(2b + 3 – 5c)

3. $d^2 – 6d$ ← d goes into both terms.

  d(d – 6)

4. $27e^2 – 6e$ ← 3e goes into both terms.

  3e(9e – 2)

Work it out

1. Find the highest common factor of the expressions:
   a. 12 and 16
   b. 12v and 16v
   c. 40 and 16w
   d. 72x and $60x^2$
   e. $3y^2$ and $4y^2$
   f. $36z^2$ and 42z

2. Factorise the following:
   a. 3m + 6
   b. 8 + 12n
   c. 10p − 25
   d. 8p + 20q
   e. 16q + 12qr
   f. 6r + 9s − 15
   g. 30s − 25 + 15t
   h. 120t − 80u − 160

3. Factorise the following:
   a. $m^2 − m$
   b. $n^2 + 4n$
   c. $p^2 − 5p$
   d. $6q^2 + 6q$
   e. $6r^2 + 9r$
   f. $25s^2 − 10s$
   g. $33t + 22t^2$
   h. $50m^2 + 30m$

More factorising

When multiplying out two brackets:

$$(a + \mathbf{4})(a + \mathbf{2}) = a^2 + 2a + 4a + 8$$
$$= a^2 + \mathbf{6}a + \mathbf{8}$$

This number is always the product of the two numbers in the bracket: **4 × 2**.

This number is always the sum of the two numbers in the bracket: **4 + 2**.

These two facts can be used when factorising quadratics:

1. $e^2 + 7e + 10$

The sum of the two unknown numbers is 7.

The product of the two unknown numbers is 10.

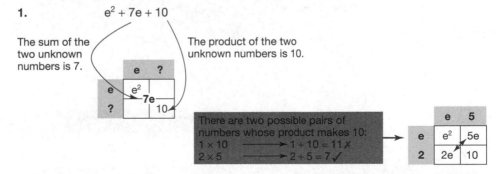

There are two possible pairs of numbers whose product makes 10:
1 × 10 ⟶ 1 + 10 = 11 ✗
2 × 5 ⟶ 2 + 5 = 7 ✓

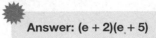

Answer: (e + 2)(e + 5)

2.

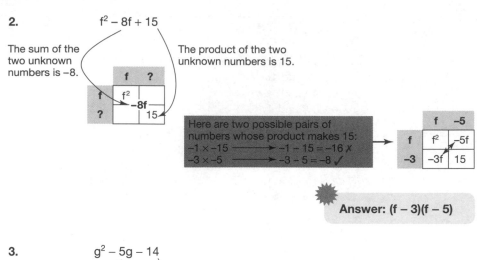

$f^2 - 8f + 15$

The sum of the two unknown numbers is –8.

The product of the two unknown numbers is 15.

	f	?
f	f^2	–8f
?		15

Here are two possible pairs of numbers whose product makes 15:
–1 × –15 ⟶ –1 – 15 = –16 ✗
–3 × –5 ⟶ –3 – 5 = –8 ✓

	f	–5
f	f^2	–5f
–3	–3f	15

Answer: (f – 3)(f – 5)

3.

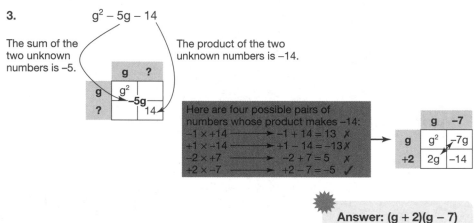

$g^2 - 5g - 14$

The sum of the two unknown numbers is –5.

The product of the two unknown numbers is –14.

	g	?
g	g^2	–5g
?		14

Here are four possible pairs of numbers whose product makes –14:
–1 × +14 ⟶ –1 + 14 = 13 ✗
+1 × –14 ⟶ +1 – 14 = –13 ✗
–2 × +7 ⟶ –2 + 7 = 5 ✗
+2 × –7 ⟶ +2 – 7 = –5 ✓

	g	–7
g	g^2	–7g
+2	2g	–14

Answer: (g + 2)(g – 7)

4.

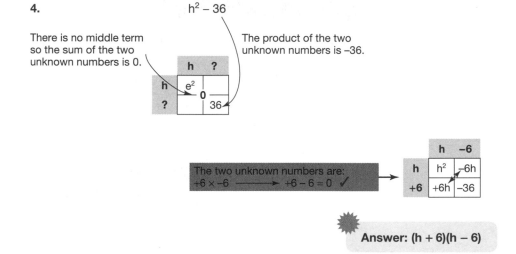

$h^2 - 36$

There is no middle term so the sum of the two unknown numbers is 0.

The product of the two unknown numbers is –36.

	h	?
h	e^2	0
?		36

The two unknown numbers are:
+6 × –6 ⟶ +6 – 6 = 0 ✓

	h	–6
h	h^2	–6h
+6	+6h	–36

Answer: (h + 6)(h – 6)

5.

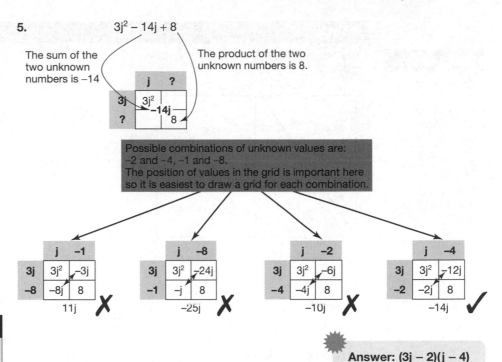

$3j^2 - 14j + 8$

The sum of the two unknown numbers is −14

The product of the two unknown numbers is 8.

Possible combinations of unknown values are:
−2 and −4, −1 and −8.
The position of values in the grid is important here so it is easiest to draw a grid for each combination.

Answer: (3j − 2)(j − 4)

Work it out

1. Factorise the following:
   a. $x^2 + 6x + 5$
   b. $x^2 + 9x + 14$
   c. $x^2 + 6x + 8$
   d. $x^2 + 11x + 18$
   e. $x^2 + 7x + 12$
   f. $x^2 + 13x + 12$

2. Factorise the following:
   a. $x^2 + 15x + 36$
   b. $x^2 + x - 6$
   c. $x^2 - 6x + 8$
   d. $x^2 - x - 6$
   e. $x^2 - x - 20$
   f. $x^2 + 2x - 8$
   g. $x^2 + 11x + 30$
   h. $x^2 - 4x - 21$
   i. $x^2 + x - 20$
   j. $x^2 + 8x + 15$
   k. $x^2 + 8x + 16$
   l. $x^2 - 9x + 14$

3. Factorise the following:
   a. $x^2 - 1$
   b. $x^2 - 25$
   c. $x^2 - 49$
   d. $x^2 - 100$

4. Factorise the following:
   a. $2x^2 + 5x + 3$
   b. $2x^2 + 11x + 12$
   c. $3x^2 + 11x + 6$
   d. $3x^2 - 10x - 8$
   e. $2x^2 - 13x + 15$
   f. $3x^2 + 12x - 15$
   g. $5x^2 - 32x + 12$
   h. $10x^2 - 40$

Investigation

The two red lines have the same gradient.
Show that $c = b + a$.

You will need to combine your knowledge of working out gradients with factorising the difference of two square numbers (look back at your answers to question 3).

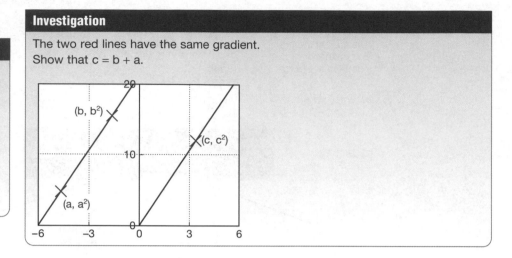

Solving quadratic equations

Solve:

1. $x^2 + 9x + 20 = 0$

First factorise the expression:
The product of the numbers is 20 and they must combine together to make 9: **5 and 4**

	x	4
x	f^2	4x
5	5x	20

(with **9x** marked between f^2 and 4x)

$(x + 5)(x + 4) = 0$
$x + 5 = 0$ or $x + 4 = 0$
$x = -5$ or $x = -4$

Then solve the equation.

The product of two values is zero. This means at least one of the brackets equals zero.

2. $x^2 - 2x - 35 = 0$

First factorise the expression.
The product of the numbers is −35 and they must combine together to make −2: **−7 and 5**

	x	5
x	f^2	5x
−7	−7x	−35

(with **−2x** marked between f^2 and 5x)

$(x - 7)(x + 5) = 0$
$x - 7 = 0$ or $x + 5 = 0$
$x = 7$ or $x = -5$

3. The square of Scott's age 12 years ago is the same as the age he will be in 78 years time. His age is in double figures. How old is Scott?

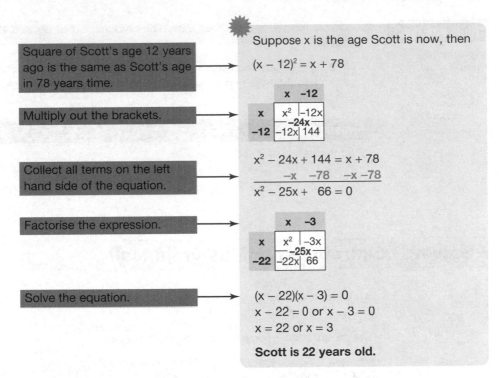

Square of Scott's age 12 years ago is the same as Scott's age in 78 years time.

Suppose x is the age Scott is now, then

$(x - 12)^2 = x + 78$

Multiply out the brackets.

Collect all terms on the left hand side of the equation.

$x^2 - 24x + 144 = x + 78$

$\underline{-x \quad -78 \quad -x -78}$

$x^2 - 25x + \ 66 = 0$

Factorise the expression.

Solve the equation.

$(x - 22)(x - 3) = 0$

$x - 22 = 0 \text{ or } x - 3 = 0$

$x = 22 \text{ or } x = 3$

Scott is 22 years old.

Work it out

Hints and tips

Check your answers by substituting them back into the equations.

1. Solve these equations:
   a. $(x - 2)(x - 3) = 0$
   b. $(x - 5)(x - 4) = 0$
   c. $(x + 1)(x - 6) = 0$
   d. $(x + 4)(x + 7) = 0$
   e. $x(x - 6) = 0$
   f. $(2x - 3)(x + 10) = 0$

2. Solve these equations:
   a. $x^2 + 3x + 2 = 0$
   b. $x^2 + 8x + 7 = 0$
   c. $x^2 + 10x + 24 = 0$
   d. $x^2 + 13x + 36 = 0$
   e. $x^2 - 16x + 15 = 0$
   f. $x^2 + 5x - 24 = 0$
   g. $x^2 - 3x - 40 = 0$
   h. $x^2 - 7x + 6 = 0$
   i. $x^2 + 19x + 18 = 0$
   j. $x^2 + x - 6 = 0$

Hints and tips

Rearrange the equation so the right hand side is equal to zero.

3. Solve these equations:
   a. $x^2 - 6x = 0$
   b. $x^2 + 2x = 15$
   c. $x^2 - 25 = 0$
   d. $x^2 - 6x = 27$
   e. $x^2 + x = 30$
   f. $x^2 - 10x = -25$
   g. $x^2 = 100$
   h. $x^2 = 15x - 50$

4. A field with an area of 70 m^2 is to be fenced. The length of the field is 3 m longer than the width. Work out the length of the perimeter to be fenced.

5. When a book is opened the product of the two page numbers is 110. Work out the page numbers.

Hints and tips

Let **x** be the length of the hypotenuse. Use Pythagoras' Theorem.

6. Lisa is two years older than Sam. The product of their ages is 483. What are their ages?

7. In a right-angled triangle, one side is 4 cm less than the hypotenuse, the other is 2 cm less than the hypotenuse. What are the lengths of all three sides?

Investigation

Find the values of x in the equation:

$$2^{x^2-8x+12} = 1$$

Solving quadratic equations graphically

By plotting the curve $y = x^2 - 8x + 12$ from $x = 0$ to $x = 7$ solve the equation $x^2 - 8x + 12 = 0$.

The co-ordinates of seven points on the curve are:

x	0	1	2	3	4	5	6	7
$y = x^2$	$(0)^2$	$(1)^2$	$(2)^2$	$(3)^2$	$(4)^2$	$(5)^2$	$(6)^2$	$(7)^2$
$-8x$	-8×0	-8×1	-8×2	-8×3	-8×4	-8×5	-8×6	-8×7
$+12$	$+12$	$+12$	$+12$	$+12$	$+12$	$+12$	$+12$	$+12$
y	12	5	0	–3	–4	–3	0	5

These points are now plotted on a grid and joined together by a smooth curve.

All along the x-axis y = 0, so the points where the curve cuts the x-axis give the solution to the equation.

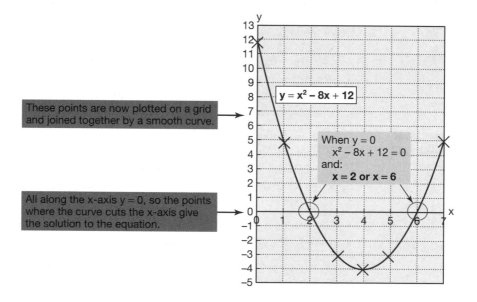

$y = x^2 - 8x + 12$

When y = 0
$x^2 - 8x + 12 = 0$
and:
x = 2 or x = 6

Mapping it out

Draw a table. The first row contains values of x ranging from the smallest to the largest integer value given in the question.

↓

Use your calculator to work out the position of y for each x value.

↓

Plot these co-ordinates on a grid and connect them with a smooth curve.

↓

The solution is the value of x when the curve cuts the x-axis.

Hints and tips

Think about how the equation of the curve can be factorised.

Work it out

1. Solve these equations graphically:

   a. $x^2 - 5x + 4 = 0$ Draw a grid from $x = 0$ to $x = 5$ and $y = -3$ to $y = 5$

   b. $x^2 - 7x + 10 = 0$ Draw a grid from $x = 0$ to $x = 6$ and $y = -4$ to $y = 10$

   c. $x^2 - 8x + 7 = 0$ Draw a grid from $x = 0$ to $x = 8$ and $y = -10$ to $y = 10$

   d. $x^2 - 3x = 0$ Draw a grid from $x = -1$ to $x = 4$ and $y = -5$ to $y = 5$

   e. $x^2 - 2x - 3 = 0$ Draw a grid from $x = 1$ to $x = 4$ and $y = -5$ to $y = 6$

   f. $x^2 - x - 6 = 0$ Draw a grid from $x = -3$ to $x = 4$ and $y = -7$ to $y = 7$

Investigation 1

What do the two lines $y = \dfrac{x^2 - 6x + 8}{x - 2}$ and $y = x - 4$ have in common? Investigate.

Investigation 2

Work out the equation of this curve:

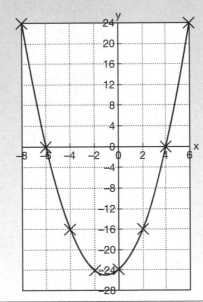

4.11 Bringing It All Together

Job description:

Dave is part of a small team investigating serious vehicle collisions. He is called out to about two hundred accidents each year. At the scene, he collects evidence which he takes back to the office to interpret mathematically. The reports he writes are often used as evidence in court.

What Dave says:

'This is a job that combines my interest in cars and motorbikes with my enjoyment of problem solving. At the scene of a collision we always take witness statements but often these people are in a state of shock and can say things that are obviously incorrect, like the car was coming from the right instead of the left. The maths is there as an impartial witness. The equations I use are like chapters in a book, each telling part of the story of how the collision occurred.'

CASE STUDY

Using Maths at Work – Dave: forensic collision investigator

Usually a crash is the combination of a number of factors such as poor visibility, excessive speed, momentary lapses in concentration or the influence of alcohol or drugs.

One case I've just gathered evidence for is an incident where a driver hit a pedestrian causing the pedestrian's death. The driver could now be facing charges of Causing Death by Dangerous Driving or Careless Driving with sentences of up to fourteen years.

This is an outline plan of the scene:

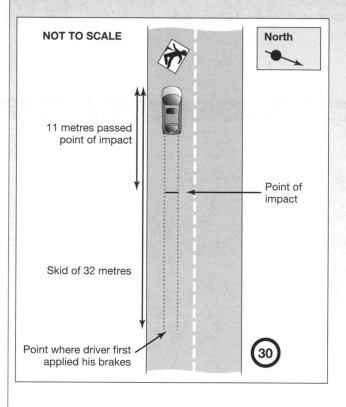

NOT TO SCALE

North

11 metres passed point of impact

Point of impact

Skid of 32 metres

Point where driver first applied his brakes

30

The coefficient of friction measures how easily tyres slide over the tarmac on the road. Each road will have its own coefficient. An icy road will have a lower coefficient than a road in normal conditions.

Hints and tips

1 mile = 1 609.34 m
When a square is the subject of an equation, take the square root of both sides of the equation, e.g.
$a^2 = 3bc$

$a = \sqrt{3bc}$

'We always use the lowest value of μ as this works in the driver's favour as it slightly reduces his speed.

CASE STUDY (*continued*)

The road was immediately blocked off and fellow officers and myself spent several hours meticulously recording the details of the collision.

Eye witnesses were interviewed, a video recording was made of the scene and the whole area was surveyed electronically.

The tyres of the car involved in the collision were checked and found to be in good order as were the brakes.

Once all the evidence had been gathered I performed two test skids using my own car. This is to obtain the coefficient of friction (μ), for the section of road where the crash occurred, under the same weather conditions.

Driving at a speed of 35 mph I pressed down heavily on the brakes to force them to lock. Here are the distances it took the car to come to rest.

Test 1:   S = 19 m
Test 2:   S = 18.6 m

The formula for the coefficient of friction (μ) is:

(1) $\mu = \dfrac{2u^2}{19.62 \times S}$ **u** is the speed of the car, in metres per second
S is the distance of the skid in metres

Between the two tests there is always a slight difference for the value of μ. We are able to allow up to a 10% difference or tolerance, otherwise the tests are repeated.

To obtain the tolerance, this formula is used:

(2)   Percentage difference $= \dfrac{\mu \text{ (test 2)} - \mu \text{ (test 1)}}{\mu \text{ (test 2)}} \times 100$

Task 1
Round all your answers to two decimal places.

1. Change the speed Dave was driving just before he applied the brakes to metres per second.
2. Use formula **(1)** to work out μ for both tests. Give your answers to two decimal places.
3. Use formula **(2)** to check if the tests are within tolerance.
4. The coefficient can now be used to work out the speed of the car during the collision.
   Rearrange formula **(1)** to make **u** the subject of the equation. **u** in this case represents the speed of the car just after impact, **S** is the length of the skid between the point of impact and the position of the car when it came to rest.
5. Use your formula from question 4 to work out the speed of the car, **u**, just after the point of impact.
6. Convert your answer to question 5 from metres per second to miles per hour.
7. Was the driver breaking the speed limit at this stage of the collision?

This formula is used whenever a vehicle has not come to rest but the speed has changed.

CASE STUDY (*continued*)

We now work out the driver's speed when he applied the brakes. We can use this formula:

(3) $u = \sqrt{v^2 + 19.62\mu S}$ ◄——

u is the speed of the car, in metres per second, at the start of the skid

S is the length of the skid from its start to the point of impact

v is the speed, in metres per second, just before the point of impact

Task 2

1. Work out the speed of the car, in metres per second, just before the point of impact.
2. Work out the distance of the skid to the point of impact.
3. Use formula **(3)** and your answers to questions 1 and 2 to work out the speed of the car when the driver first applied the brakes.
4. Convert your answer to question 3 to miles per hour.
5. Was he within the speed limit?

The question now to be asked is would the collision have happened if the car had been going at 30 mph – just within the speed limit?

Task 3

1. Convert 30 mph into metres per second.
2. Rearrange formula **(1)** to make **S** the subject of the equation.
3. Use your answer to question **1** in the formula in question **2** to work out how long, in metres, it would take the car to come to rest.
4. Would the car have hit the pedestrian if it had been travelling at 30 mph?

A car hitting a bike

Another incident involved a car hitting the back of a stationary motorbike near roadworks; the biker was seriously injured. After recording the data and solving some equations we discovered the driver had been going at a speed of 13.5 metres per second just before impact and the coefficient of friction, μ, was 0.6. Here is an outline plan of the crash:

When a car hits a person we can assume its speed is **reduced** by 0.4 metres per second.

CASE STUDY (*continued*)

NOT TO SCALE

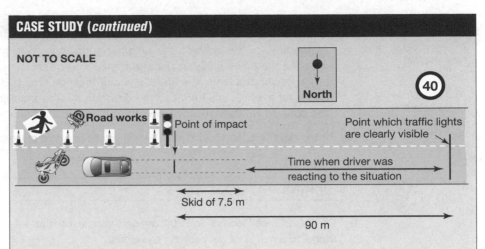

Skid of 7.5 m

90 m

Task 4

1. At this point I asked a trainee investigator to work out the speed of the car in mph, when the driver applied the brakes. Here are his workings:

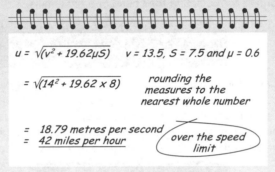

> In this job there are no marks for method, the answer **must** be correct.

$u = \sqrt{(v^2 + 19.62\mu S)}$ $v = 13.5$, $S = 7.5$ and $\mu = 0.6$

$= \sqrt{(14^2 + 19.62 \times 8)}$ *rounding the measures to the nearest whole number*

$= 18.79$ metres per second
$= 42$ miles per hour   *over the speed limit*

He has made some errors that could have had serious repercussions.

a. Can you spot them?
b. What was his speed in
    i.   metres per second
    ii. miles per hour?

2. Had the driver been breaking the speed limit of 40 mph?

3. Reaction time is the time between first seeing a situation and reacting to it. This can be calculated using the formula:

(4) $t = \dfrac{d}{v}$ ◄── **d** distance driven before applying the brakes
v is the average speed of the car just before he applied the brakes

> Most people's reaction time is between 1 and 3 seconds.

a. Assuming the driver saw the lights when they were clearly visible, how far did he travel before he applied his brakes?
b. Use formula **(4)** to work out how many seconds it took the driver, after he had seen the bike, to apply the brakes. This is his reaction time.

CASE STUDY (*continued*)

4. At the time of the collision the weather conditions were good. Further tests revealed the driver was not under the influence of any drugs nor did he have any eyesight problems. His unusually long reaction time had us scratching our heads for a while until I noticed the direction he was travelling and the time of the collision (8.30am in early November). Can you figure out what happened?

5. If the driver's speed had been 30 mph would he have collided with the bike?

Assignment questions

1. On the 26th of December 2004 an earthquake off the west coast of Indonesia triggered a series of devastating tsunamis.

    Unfortunately, there were no early warning systems for tsunamis in the Indian Ocean. This meant that people were largely unaware of the approaching tsunami and had no time to escape the vulnerable coastline to the safety of higher ground. The formula for detecting the speed of a tsunami is:

$$V = \sqrt{9.8D}$$ ◄— **V**: speed of tsunami, in metres per second

D: depth of ocean floor, in metres, at the epicentre of the earthquake (6 000 m)

a. Change the formula for **V** to one that will work out the speed in kilometres per hour.

b. Use your formula in a, to obtain the speed of the tsunami in kilometres per hour. Round your answer to the nearest whole number.

c. The time taken for the wave to move a certain distance is given by the formula:

$$T = \frac{d}{V}$$ ◄— **T**: time in hours

d: distance in km, **V**: speed of tsunami, in km per hour

Use the formula to work out the time it took, in hours and minutes, for the tsunami to arrive at the following places:

	Distance from epicentre of earthquake
Indonesian coast	120 km
Thailand	600 km
Sri Lanka	1 700 km

d. If there had been wave sensors in place to detect potential tsunamis would the people living in the three places have had enough time to react?

2. Lisa is organising a rugby match. The tickets have been priced at £12 and £8 and all 600 tickets are now sold. The number of cheaper tickets sold is three times more than the number of expensive ones.

    a. Write down two formulae using this information.

    b. Solve the simultaneous equations algebraically.

  c. How much income has been generated from the match?
  d. Lisa is unhappy with the amount of money made from the tickets. For the next match she stipulates that the tickets should generate at least £6 000 in income. Create four inequalities and plot them on a grid.
  e. What combination of tickets will give Lisa the largest income?

3. Ejaz is thinking of buying the car in this advertisement. He will probably pay for the car in monthly instalments.

R: interest rate
A: amount loaned
n: total number of payments over the five year period.

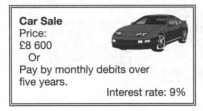

Car Sale
Price:
£8 600
   Or
Pay by monthly debits over five years.
                    Interest rate: 9%

To work out the monthly debits the sellers uses this flowchart:

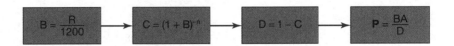

$$B = \frac{R}{1200} \quad \rightarrow \quad C = (1 + B)^{-n} \quad \rightarrow \quad D = 1 - C \quad \rightarrow \quad P = \frac{BA}{D}$$

  a. Use the flow chart to calculate to four decimal places:
    i. B, C, D and n
    ii. P, the monthly payments.
  b. If he uses this method of paying rather than paying £8 600 up front, how much more will the car cost him?
  c. Ejaz is interested in some other cars. He can afford to pay back £200 (**P**) a month, but wants to know how much this translates to in terms of the price of a car. Rearrange the final formula in the flow chart to make **A** the subject.
  d. Use your answers for a.i. to work out how much he can afford to spend on a car. Round your answer to the nearest pound.

4. In an adrenalin packed all-action film, there is a car chase where the heroes successfully jump across a deep cavern. Here is a diagram of the situation:

Speed: 145 km an hour

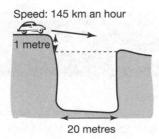

1 metre

20 metres

The horizontal movement is treated separately from the vertical one.

▶

a. Use this flow chart to see if this is a work of fiction or could the heroes have mathematically done it?

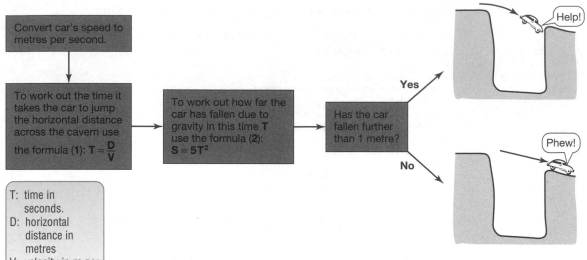

T: time in seconds.
D: horizontal distance in metres
V: velocity in m per second
S: vertical distance in metres

This is the minimum speed of the car that ensures it will jump the ravine safely.

b. Rearrange the formula (**2**) to make **T** its subject.
c. Use your formula in b, to work out the time taken for the car to fall one metre.
d. Rearrange the formula (**1**) to make **V** its subject.
e. Work out using answers c and d, the speed of the car that would cause it to fall exactly one metre when successfully jumping the cavern, in:
   i. metres per second
   ii. kilometres per hour, to the nearest 10 km
   iii. miles per hour (1 kilometre = 0.62 miles), to the nearest mile.
f. In the film *Tomorrow Never Dies*, Pierce Brosnan jumps at a speed of 30 km per hour across two buildings that are 15 m apart and the second is 1.5 m below the first. Is this possible?

5. Mislo, the marketing manager of a bank, wants to demonstrate visually how one of their savings account's compares to a competitor's. He asks an accountant to produce a graph of two curves, one showing how £1 000 grows over ten years if invested at their interest rate of 10%, the other showing how it would grow in a comparable account with 4% interest rate.
The accountant uses this formula:

$$S = A(1 + 0.01R)^n$$

A: initial investment
R: interest rate
n: number of years money is kept in the account
S: the money accrued in the account

Hints and tips

Horizontal axis: number of years the money is invested.
Vertical axis: money accrued in the account. Start the vertical scale at £1 000.

a. Plot the two curves for Mislo.
b. How much more money will an investor have after ten years if they had put their £1 000 into the bank's account rather than a typical other account?

Answer Section

Chapter 1: Number Work

1.1 Place Value

Work it out, page 3

1. a. 600
   b. 6 000
   c. 6 000 000
   d. 6
   e. 600 000
   f. 600 000

2. a. 5 430, 0345
   b. 9 771, 1779

3. a. 4
   b. 7

4. a. 3
   b. 5

5. 732 690

6. 7 401 350

7. a. 23 054
   b. 540 989
   c. 1 905 393
   d. 7 349 200

8. a. 40
   b. 56 478
   c. 63 725
   d. It all rests on the final level – the other levels are of no consequence.
   e. There are many answers.

9. a. 37 326
   b. 13 564
   c. 6 541
   d. drawing

10. a. $12 + 3 + 4 - 5 = 14$
    b. $123 + 45 = 168$
    c. $12 + 3 + 45 = 60$

Work it out, page 7

1. a. two hundred and thirty six
   b. eighty nine
   c. twenty three thousand and ninety
   d. four million five hundred and six thousand, eight hundred and twenty

2. a. 37
   b. 534
   c. 42 583
   d. 7 307 999

3. a. one hundred and seventeen
   b. 68
   c. one thousand two hundred and eighty
   d. fourteen thousand and seventy three
   e. 578 207
   f. three million two hundred and nine thousand, three hundred and sixty two
   g. 7 580
   h. 53 408
   i. 53 408

4. The amount in words is 120 300, not 12 300

Investigation, page 8

1. 4 and 33; 5 and 10; 1032; 6 and 203; 2 202; 320 000

2. ꝍnnꝍll ꝍꝍꝍꝍ ƚꝍꝍꝍⅠⅠⅠⅠⅠⅠⅠⅠ

3. The position of a symbol within a number is not important – there can be a lot of repeats of each symbol.

Work it out, page 9

1. a. 5 000   b. 300
   c. 450 000   d. 234 000

2. a. 100   b. 80
   c. 100   d. 540

3. a. 60   b. 72
   c. 432   d. 430

4. a. 10   b. 80
   c. 100   d. 730 000

1.2 Number Types

Work it out, page 13

1. 257

2. Could be: 3 and 5; 11 and 13; 17 and 19; 29 and 31

3. 24, 25, 26, 27 and 28

4. a. 1, 2, 3, 6, 9, 18
   b. 1, 2, 4, 8, 16, 32
   c. 1, 2, 4, 5, 8, 10, 20, 40
   d. 1, 2, 3, 4, 6, 8, 9, 12, 18, 24, 36, 72

5. a. 6
   b. 12
   c. 16, 18 amongst others

6. a. $2 \times 2 \times 2 \times 3$
   b. $7 \times 2 \times 3$
   c. $5 \times 5 \times 2$
   d. $2 \times 3 \times 11$

7. a. 6   b. 36
   c. 9   d. 15

8. a. 9, 18, 27, 36
   b. 24

9. a. fourth multiple of 8
   b. sixth multiple of 12

10. a. 20, 30, 35
    b. 35, 56, 63

11. a. 35
    b. 99

12. a. 12   b. 21
    c. 24   d. 18
    e. 60   f. 90
    g. 72   h. 240

13. 1 and 25

14. a. 36
    b. 5 and 4

15. 3 P.M.

16. 55 minutes

17. 1 hour, 44 minutes

18. Possible solution:

	Number greater than 10	Factor of 60	Multiple of 3	Prime number
Factor of 36	18	4	9	3
Multiple of 5	25	30	90	5
Odd number	13	15	33	7
Even number	16	10	42	2

Investigation 1, page 15

A prime number can't have a factor of 3.

Game for two people, page 15

It is not fair – there is likely to be more even numbers than odd because an odd multiplied by an even always results in an even number.

Investigation 2, page 15

Task 1

a. 23×31

b. 47×51

1.3 Fractions

Group task, page 16

One week

Work it out, page 19

1. a. $\frac{3}{4}$ b. $\frac{1}{6}$

    c. $\frac{5}{6}$ d. $\frac{4}{9}$

    e. 1 f. $\frac{5}{9}$

    g. $\frac{1}{2}$ h. $\frac{4}{5}$

2. a. $\frac{2}{9}$ b. $\frac{5}{6}$

    c. $\frac{4}{5}$ d. $\frac{3}{8}$

    e. $\frac{1}{2}$

3. There are various answers.

4. Answer b

5. The shape has not been evenly divided.

6. a. $\frac{1}{12}$ b. $\frac{1}{3}$

    c. $\frac{1}{2}$ d. $\frac{1}{4}$

7.
    a. $\overset{\times 5}{\frac{3}{4}} = \underset{\times 5}{\frac{15}{20}}$ b. $\overset{\times 3}{\frac{6}{10}} = \underset{\times 3}{\frac{18}{30}}$

    c. $\overset{\times 6}{\frac{2}{5}} = \underset{\times 6}{\frac{12}{30}}$ d. $\overset{\div 5}{\frac{20}{45}} = \underset{\div 5}{\frac{4}{9}}$

    e. $\overset{\times 4}{\frac{3}{4}} = \underset{\times 4}{\frac{12}{16}}$ f. $\overset{\div 5}{\frac{20}{25}} = \underset{\div 5}{\frac{4}{5}}$

g. $\overset{\div 3 \quad \div 4}{\frac{24}{36} = \frac{8}{12} = \frac{2}{3}}$
$\underset{\div 3 \quad \div 4}{}$

h. $\overset{\div 2 \quad \div 3}{\frac{12}{42} = \frac{6}{21} = \frac{2}{7}}$
$\underset{\div 2 \quad \div 3}{}$

i. $\overset{\div 9 \quad \div 2}{\frac{18}{36} = \frac{2}{4} = \frac{1}{2}}$
$\underset{\div 9 \quad \div 2}{}$

8. $\frac{5}{6} = \frac{30}{36} = \frac{20}{24}$

    $\frac{2}{7} = \frac{6}{21} = \frac{10}{35}$

    $\frac{2}{3} = \frac{8}{12}$

    $\frac{9}{15} = \frac{3}{5} = \frac{21}{35}$

9. There are several answers, including: a. $\frac{2}{6}, \frac{3}{9}$; b. $\frac{4}{10}, \frac{6}{15}$; c. $\frac{6}{14}, \frac{9}{21}$.

10. a. $\frac{1}{2}$ b. $\frac{2}{3}$

    c. $\frac{3}{5}$ d. $\frac{3}{4}$

    e. $\frac{2}{3}$ f. $\frac{3}{4}$

    g. $\frac{2}{3}$ h. $\frac{3}{4}$

    i. $\frac{4}{5}$

11. a. $\frac{5}{16}$

    b. $\frac{1}{4}$

    c. $\frac{7}{16}$

12. a. $\frac{1}{3}, 1, \frac{3}{4}, \frac{2}{3}, \frac{1}{2}$

    b. $\frac{13}{20}$

13. $1, \frac{3}{4}, \frac{1}{2}, \frac{1}{3}, \frac{1}{4}, \frac{1}{12}$

14. a. $\frac{9}{10}$ b. $\frac{19}{30}$

    c. $\frac{31}{50}$ d. $\frac{7}{12}$

15. a. $\frac{3}{8}$ b. $\frac{1}{2}$

    c. $\frac{1}{4}$ d. $\frac{1}{8}$

16. football fans

17. one fifth
    one quarter
    two thirds
    half
    nine tenths
    one sixth

Group investigation, page 23

1. $\frac{32}{64}$ or $\frac{23}{46}$

2. a. +2
   b. +7
   c. +19

Work it out, page 24

1. a. $\frac{9}{5}$ b. $\frac{11}{8}$
   c. $\frac{17}{7}$ d. $\frac{7}{2}$
   e. $\frac{27}{11}$ f. $\frac{34}{7}$

2. a. $1\frac{5}{7}$ b. $2\frac{4}{9}$
   c. $1\frac{4}{5}$ d. 3
   e. $1\frac{11}{12}$ f. $4\frac{3}{8}$

Work it out, page 27

1. a. $\frac{5}{7}$ b. $\frac{5}{9}$
   c. $\frac{2}{5}$ d. 1
   e. $\frac{1}{2}$ f. $\frac{3}{8}$
   g. $\frac{9}{10}$ h. $\frac{13}{15}$
   i. $1\frac{3}{20}$ j. $1\frac{7}{18}$

2. a. $\frac{4}{11}$ b. $\frac{5}{17}$
   c. $\frac{1}{4}$ d. $\frac{11}{18}$
   e. $\frac{1}{28}$ f. $\frac{16}{33}$
   g. $\frac{7}{30}$ h. $\frac{7}{20}$

3. a. $2\frac{3}{10}$ b. $2\frac{3}{4}$
   c. $4\frac{1}{2}$ d. $1\frac{20}{21}$
   e. $2\frac{7}{15}$ f. $1\frac{7}{24}$
   g. $5\frac{1}{8}$ h. $4\frac{1}{12}$

4. a. $\frac{3}{20}$
   b. $\frac{7}{24}$

5. $\frac{21}{64}$

6. 96 days

7.

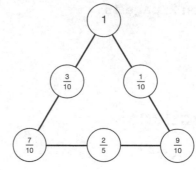

8.

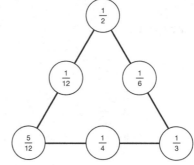

9. a. (i) $\frac{1}{2}$ and $\frac{1}{4}$
      (ii) $\frac{3}{8}$ and $\frac{1}{8}$
   b. (i) $\frac{1}{2}$
      (ii) $\frac{3}{8}$
   c. $\frac{1}{16}$ and $\frac{3}{16}$
   d. There are many different answers.
   e. (i) 2
      (ii) $\frac{3}{4}$

10. 46

Investigation 1, page 29

1. to avoid negative fractions

2. a. $\frac{2}{2} + 2$
   b. $999 + \frac{9}{9}$

Investigation 2, page 29

1. $\frac{1}{2} + \frac{1}{3} + \frac{1}{6}$

2. $\frac{1}{2} + \frac{1}{6}, \frac{1}{3} + \frac{1}{15}, \frac{1}{4} + \frac{1}{28}$

   Denominator in first fraction increases by one, denominator in second fraction is obtained by multiplying denominator in original fraction by denominator in first fraction.

$\frac{2}{9} = \frac{1}{5} + \frac{1}{45}$, $\frac{2}{11} = \frac{1}{6} + \frac{1}{66}$

3. Each person gets $\frac{1}{2}$ plus $\frac{1}{7}$.

Work it out, page 31

1. a. $\frac{10}{21}$ b. $\frac{1}{24}$
    c. $\frac{2}{7}$ d. $\frac{1}{12}$
    e. $\frac{1}{6}$ f. $\frac{1}{9}$
    g. $\frac{1}{12}$ h. $\frac{3}{4}$
    i. $\frac{15}{28}$

2. a. $\frac{7}{8}$ b. $\frac{5}{9}$
    c. $\frac{2}{15}$ d. $1\frac{7}{8}$
    e. $2\frac{14}{15}$ f. $4\frac{1}{5}$
    g. 6   h. 8
    i. $8\frac{3}{4}$

3. a. $\frac{7}{12}$ b. $1\frac{2}{5}$
    c. $1\frac{1}{3}$ d. $\frac{1}{2}$
    e. $1\frac{1}{2}$ f. $\frac{2}{3}$
    g. $5\frac{2}{3}$ h. $1\frac{3}{7}$
    i. $5\frac{1}{9}$

4. a. $1\frac{4}{5}$ b. $\frac{1}{6}$
    c. 2   d. $1\frac{1}{10}$
    e. $1\frac{3}{7}$ f. $\frac{15}{22}$
    g. $2\frac{11}{32}$ h. $2\frac{1}{2}$
    i. $\frac{20}{27}$

5. a. (i)   £405 million
        (ii) £270 million
        (iii) £135 million
    b. 300
    c. 480
    d. 120

6. a. £3.36
    b. 32 g
    c. 92 p

7. a. (i) $\frac{1}{2}$
        (ii) $\frac{3}{25}$
    b. (i) 22 500 000 hectares
        (ii) 2 880 000 hectares

8. a. $\frac{1}{4}$
    b. $\frac{3}{20}$

9. a and c

Investigations, page 34

1. a and b – yes

2. four times

1.4 Working with Numbers After the Decimal Point

Work it out, page 37

1. a. 1.8   b. 3.63
    c. 8.36   d. 11.2
    e. 2.66   f. 0.04

2. a. $\frac{7}{10}$ b. $\frac{7}{1\,000}$
    c. $\frac{7}{1\,000}$ d. $\frac{7}{100}$

3.

4. a. $\frac{9}{10}$ b. $\frac{13}{20}$
    c. $\frac{2}{25}$ d. $\frac{13}{125}$
    e. $\frac{1}{40}$ f. $\frac{1}{200}$

5. a. 0.8   b. 0.55
    c. 0.015   d. 0.005
    e. 0.64   f. 0.75
    g. 0.045   h. 0.04

6. a. 0.3   b. 0.01
    c. 0.089   d. 0.707

7. a. 0.037, 0.073, 0.307, 0.703
    b. 0.010, 0.011, 0.101, 0.11
    c. 0.09, 0.099, 0.909, 0.99

8. a. 0.8 cm
    b. 15 cm
    c. 1.7 cm

9. a and d

Work it out, page 39

1. a. 560   b. 40
    c. 920   d. 15
    e. 16 200   f. 2 070

2. a. 10 000   b. 8
    c. 100   d. 0.054
    e. 0.005   f. 0.0066

3. a. 0.06   b. 0.72
    c. 0.32   d. 0.043

4. a. 100   b. 0.08
    c. 100   d. 73 000
    e. 0.2   f. 310

5. a. × 10   b. × 100
    c. ÷ 1 000   d. × 100
    e. × 10   f. × 1 or ÷ 1

Paired work, page 40

1.

×	10	100	1 000
0.003	0.03	0.3	3
5.62	56.2	562	5 620
0.04	0.4	4	40

÷	10	100	1 000
15	1.5	0.15	0.015
2.3	0.23	0.023	0.0023
278	27.8	2.78	0.278

2. Tables

Investigation, page 40

1. multiplying by 0.01

2. dividing by 0.01

3. dividing by 0.01

Work it out, page 41

1. a. (i) 12.5 hours
        (ii) 3 hours
    b. £5.42

2. a. £917.20
    b. £10 089.20

3. £1.12

4. loaf = 93 p; jam = £1.75;
    coffee = £4.10

5. £52

6. a. £22.50
    b. £35.70
    c. £18.40
    d. 13.20

7. a. £2.70
    b. 21

8. a. £6 666.40
    b. £106 662.40

9. a. £29.94
    b. £57.90
    c. £18.30

10. a.

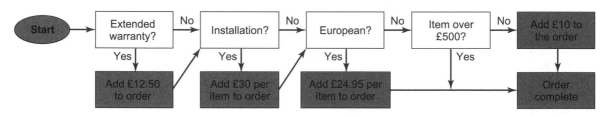

    b. £317.45
    c. installation and extended warranty

Investigation, page 43

Dan has spent £90 whereas Greg has only spent £60. Dan should receive £40 and Greg £10.

1.5a Approximations

Group work, page 44

There are various answers.

Work it out, page 45

1. a. 90   b. 200
    c. 2 380   d. 6 000
    e. 45 000

2. There are various answers.

Group work, page 46

There are various answers. Tom's final answer should be 2 000.

Work it out, page 47

1. a. 380   b. 2 300
    c. 87 200   d. 43 000
    e. 240 000   f. 1 000

2.

	Nearest 100	Nearest 1 000	Nearest 10 000	Nearest 100 000	Nearest 1 000 000
2 456 231	2 456 200	2 456 000	2 460 000	2 500 000	2 000 000
14 281 340	14 281 300	14 281 000	14 280 000	14 300 000	14 000 000

3. a. 100   b. 10
    c. 100   d. 10 000
    e. 100 000   f. 10
    g. 10 or 100

4. (1) 710
    (2) 6 000
    (3) answer is correct
    (4) 1 100
    (5) 11 000
    (6) 3 100

5. a. 550, 649   b. 595, 604
    c. 7 500, 8 499 d. 135 000, 144 999

6. a. 38 000
    b. (i) £17 750
       (ii) £61 922

Group work – errors in rounding, page 48

1. £62 000

2. £67 000

3. £62 000

4. £5 000; 0

1.5b Rounding to Decimal Places

Work it out, page 49

1. a. 5.6   b. 0.3
    c. 23.55   d. 0.003
    e. 1.000   f. 0.1

2.

	To zero decimal places	To 1 decimal place	To 2 decimal places	To 3 decimal places
19.8946	20	19.9	19.89	19.895
0.03039	0	0.0	0.03	0.030
0.98989	1	1.0	0.99	0.990

3. a. 0.55, 0.64
    b. 0.550, 0.649
    c. 0.005, 0.014

4. 7.29

5. a. 19.1
    b. 0.016
    c. 5.22
    d. 15.30

6. a. 31.07
    b. 1 p

7. £18.88

8. a. 10
    b. 21

9. a. £18.30
    b. £17.61
    c. yes

Work it out, page 52

1. a. 300   b. 3 430
    c. 3.5   d. 1.02
    e. 0.011   f. 1
    g. 0.00007   h. 10

2.

	To 1 significant figure	To 2 significant figures	To 3 significant figures
21 876	20 000	22 000	21 900
409 622	400 000	410 000	410 000
32.456	30	32	32.5
1.0028	1	1.0	1.00
0.004567	0.005	0.0046	0.00457

3. 9 995 or 9 996 or 9 997 or 9 998 or 9 999

4. a. 0.4, 0.37
    b. 0.05, 0.053

5. a and 2 – 4 significant figures
    b and 1 – 2 significant figures
    c and 5 – 3 significant figures
    d and 4 – 1 significant figure
    e and 3 – 5 significant figures

6. a. 23 500, 24 499
    b. 445 000 000, 454 999 999
    c. 2 hours, 30 minutes; 3 hours, 29 minutes

Group work, page 53

1. 1 sig fig – £3 000

2. 1 sig fig – 3 million

3. 1 sig fig – 500 litres

4. 1 significant figure (or nearest hour) – 70 hours

5. 1 significant figure – 35 bottles

6. 2 significant figures – 44 000

1.6 Estimation

Work it out, page 55

1. a. £40
    b. 25 kg
    c. £300
    d. 40 km

2. (1) a, b, d and e
    (2) b and e

3. a and 3; b and 4; c and 5; d and 1; e and 2

4. a. 552
    b. 3
    c. 24 192

5. a. £7
    b. £11
    c. £13

6. $400

7. £8 000

8. £600 000

9. 23 lbs

10. a. no – 5 500 miles
    b. (i)   3 hours
        (ii) 20 litres
        (iii) £20
    c. (i)   100 000 000
        (ii) 500 million tonnes
        (iii) 480 million tonnes

11. a. 6 000 minutes
    b. 5 000 minutes
    c. 100 and 83 hours

12. a. (i)   256 000 hours
        (ii) over estimated
        (iii) 12 800 days, 32 years
    b. (i)   400 000 minutes
        (ii) 6 667 hours
        (iii) 333 days
    These answers may vary. It depends how you estimated.

1.7 Negative Numbers

Work it out, page 59

1. 3, 1, −4

2. a. −3 b. 3
   c. −2 d. 2
   e. −2 f. 2

3. E to A and C to F

4. −8, −7, −6, −5, −4, −2, 0, 1, 8, 10

Work it out, page 60

1. a. 2 b. −7
   c. −2 d. 3

2. a. 4 b. −4
   c. −1 d. −1
   e. 0 f. −6
   g. −9 h. −7

3. a. −1 b. 10
   c. 4 d. −3
   e. −5 f. 3

4. a. 5 b. 0
   c. −12 d. −3
   e. −6 f. −6

5. a. −8 b. −2
   c. +2 d. −3
   e. −1 f. −2

6. a. 8 b. 2
   c. 4 d. 5
   e. 0 f. 5

7. a. 5 b. −5
   c. −10 d. 2
   e. −3

8. a.

	Number goals for (scored)	Number goals against (conceded)	Goal difference
Oker Utd	6	7	**−1**
Darley Town	6	**8**	−2
Rowsley Utd	4	8	−4
Tansley	**4**	9	−5

   b. Oker Utd.

9. a.

   b.

10.

11. a. −7° C
    b. On Saturday the temperature dropped by 3° C. On Sunday, there was an increase of 5° C. On Monday the temperature dropped by 2° C and on Tuesday there was an increase of 1° C.
    c. −6° C

12. a. (i) −£449
       (ii) £561
       (iii) −£77
    b. £191

Group investigation, page 63

a. −20
b. 6

Work it out, page 64

1. a. −1   b. −10
    c. −6   d. −7
    e. −8   f. −3
    g. 9   h. 0

2. a. | −2 | 0 | −2 | −2 | b. | −4 | −1 | −5 | −6 |

    c. | −1 | −4 | −5 | −9 | d. | 7 | −4 | 3 | −1 |

    e. | 2 | −4 | −2 | −6 | f. | −5 | 4 | −1 | 3 |

3. a. −£850
    b. £650

Group work, page 65

−2	15	−4
1	3	5
10	−9	8

−3	0	−3
−2	−2	−2
−1	−4	−1

−2	−3	−7
−9	−4	1
−1	−5	−6

Work it out, page 66

1. a. −14   b. −4
    c. 49   d. −8
    e. −1   f. 4
    g. −30   h. 30
    i. −6   j. −4
    k. 16   l. 24
    m. −16   n. −5

2. a. | −1 | −3 | 3 | −9 | b. | −5 | −2 | 10 | −20 |

    c. | 1 | −7 | −7 | 49 | d. | −3 | 5 | −15 | −75 |

3. a.

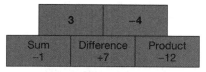

    b.

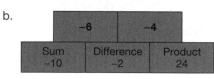

c.

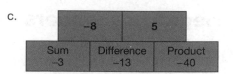

d.

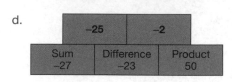

4. a. (i) −8° C
        (ii) −17° C
    b. 10 A.M.

5. a.

	Correct answers	Incorrect answers	No answer	Total points
Sam	4	8	1	**−5**
Haroon	**2**	7	0	−8
George	5	**6**	3	0

    b. George

6. a. April and May
    b. (i) −£3 000
        (ii) −£4 000
    c. −£1 200
    d. 15 months

7. a. 800, 1 400
    b. 1 050, 650
    c. 5 more minutes
    d. The Alliance

Group work, page 69

a.

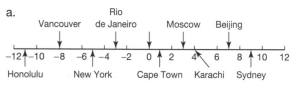

b. 12 hours
c. 6 hours
d. Honolulu and Beijing
e. Rio de Janeiro
f. Beijing

g.

	Flight time	Departure time (local)	Arrival time (local)
Karachi to New York	22 hours	Wed. 10:00 A.M.	Wed. 11:00 A.M.
London to Karachi	10 hours	Wed. 6:00 A.M.	**Wed. 8 P.M.**
London to Vancouver	10 hours	**Wed. 7 P.M.**	Wed. 9:00 P.M.
London to Honolulu	20 hours	**Wed. 4 A.M.**	Wed. 1:00 P.M.
Sydney to Moscow	24 hours	Wed. 10:00 A.M.	**Thurs. 4 A.M.**
Beijing to New York	**8 hours**	Wed. 9:00 A.M.	Wed. 5:00 A.M.

1.8 Priorities in Arithmetic

Work it out, page 71

1. a. 17 b. 9
   c. −7 d. 11
   e. 31 f. 27
   g. 96 h. 9
   i. 19 j. 8
   k. 15 l. 33
   m. 16 n. 8

2. a. 7 b. 1
   c. 43 d. 6
   e. 13

3. a. 78
   b. −78

4. a. $(5 + 3) \times 2 - 6 = 10$
   b. $(7 - 3) \times 4 + 1 \times 2 = 18$

5. a. £170 b. 161 minutes
   c. 146 lbs d. £160
   e. 4.7 hours

Investigation, page 72

There are various answers.

Work it out, page 74

1. a. 1 b. 5
   c. 2 d. 4
   e. 22 f. 25
   g. 3 h. 18

2. a. 6 b. 11
   c. 3 d. 1
   e. 5 f. 2
   g. 18 h. 9

3. a and 3, 17 b and 4, 33
   c and 1, 8 d and 2, 67
   e and 5, 3

1.9 Percentages

Work it out, page 78

1. a. Grey 20% 0.2 $\frac{1}{5}$
      Red 32% 0.32 $\frac{8}{25}$
      White 48% 0.48 $\frac{12}{25}$
   b. Grey 36% 0.36 $\frac{9}{25}$
      Red 24% 0.24 $\frac{6}{25}$
      White 40% 0.4 $\frac{2}{5}$

2. b and v; c and p; d and u; e and r; f and q; g and s

3. a. $\frac{1}{4}, \frac{3}{10}$, 31%, 0.315, 32%
   b. $\frac{4}{5}$, 0.82, 0.84, $\frac{17}{20}$, 86%

4. 0.85, $\frac{17}{20}$

5. a. (i) 0.165
      (ii) $\frac{33}{200}$
   b. 15%

Investigation 1, page 78

There are various answers.

Investigation 2, page 78

There should be separate diagrams for males and females.

Investigation 3, page 78

No. 40% is the same as $\frac{2}{5}$ – one would expect this fraction for two days.

Work it out, page 80

1. a. 50% b. 62.2%
   c. 44.3% d. 4%
   e. 30% f. 100%

2. a. 68%
    b. 32%

3. a. 82.2%
    b. 17.8%

4. IT

5. a. males 84.9%, females 14.3%
    b. 23.4%
    c. your survey.

6.

	1970	2008
Total percentage of people with no natural teeth	38%	10%
Percentage of people older than 65 with no natural teeth	80%	35%
Percentage of people less than 65 with no natural teeth	31.1%	5.9%

7.

Crisps	High
Cheddar cheese	High
Natural yoghurt	Medium
Pizza	Medium
Crunchy nut cornflakes	Medium

Investigation, page 81

45%

Work it out, page 82

1. a. £30   b. 22.5 m
    c. 2.8 kg   d. 8.75 km
    e. £2

2. a. 32.8 km   b. £99
    c. 175.2 g   d. £7.44
    e. $4.20

3. 18 hours

4. 2nd beer

Group work, page 83

1. Poland has a relatively small population with a high percentage whereas USSR had a large population with a smaller percentage.

2. Number of casualties:
    USSR: 21 million
    China: 11 million
    Poland: 7 million
    Germany: 6 million
    UK: 0.4 million

Group investigation, page 83

Overall success rate Zylon: 68.3%; Binderin: 66.7%.

Work it out, page 85

1. a. 250 m
    b. £232.40
    c. 49 kg
    d. £15.47
    e. £131.60
    f. 531.25 g

2. £41 141.88

3. a. £15 900
    b. £61 480

4. £592.80

5. £165 600

6. a. 16.67%   b. 60%
    c. 25%   d. 11.11%
    e. 29.17%   f. 10.64%

7. 17.14%

8. yes: 2008

9. £28.80

10. a. 160 kg   b. £120
    c. £200   d. 50 km

11. £175

12. 8 000

13. 75 kg

Group investigation, page 86

A. 60%
B. 24%
C. 42%
D. 41%
E. 22%
F. 20%

Group investigation, page 86

1. no – values are different for each percentage

2. no – 10% of different values

3. no – measuring different values

Group work, page 87

1. c

2. —

3. 200% trebles the cost.

Case study tasks, page 88

1. 31.7%

2. 3 725

3. 0.06%

4. a. 390 b. 1 082

5. 177.4%

6. a. 39.2%
    b. 1.6%
    c. 11.5%

7. a. 47.2% b. 64.2%

8. The testing for the infection and the treatment of infected women.

Case study tasks, page 89

1. 5 784

2.

	Percentage of births
Normal vaginal delivery	50%
Emergency caesarean	13%
Elective caesarean	7%
Assisted birth (e.g. forceps or ventouse)	15%
Induced	15%

3. In most cases the hospital has to intervene less, e.g. fewer induced births, fewer elective caesareans and fewer assisted births but more normal deliveries.

1.10 Ratios

Work it out, page 90

1. a. 5 : 4
    b. 2 : 1
    c. 3 : 1

2. a. 1 : 2 b. 2 : 3
    c. 5 : 7 d. 1 : 3
    e. 1 : 4 f. 2 : 3 : 4
    g. 1 : 5 : 3 h. 4 : 2 : 5

3. b and r; c and p; d and v; e and s; f and q; g and t

4. a. 4 : 1 b. 1 : 3
    c. 4 : 3 d. 1 : 3
    e. 23 : 26

5. a. 30 b. 9
    c. 35 d. 9
    e. 100 f. 20

6. 1 : 1

7. a. 1 : 8
    b. 8
    c. 14 400

8. a. 2 : 27
    b. 13.5

9. a. £6.50
    b. Yes

10. a. 12 : 16 : 7
    b. 12

11. a. 2 : 17
    b. 8.5
    c. 41
    d. Bermuda: 1 person; Burma: 147 people; UK: 2 people

Work it out, page 93

1. a. £12, £8 b. £35, £25
    c. 9 kg, 15 kg d. 40 km, 48 km
    e. £80, £240 f. £4, £8, £16
    g. 6 kg, 12 kg, 18 kg h. £25, £15, £10

2. a. 2 400 g
    b. 600 g

3. a. 2 : 1 : 3
    b. (i) £12, £6, £18
        (ii) £100, £50, £150
        (iii) £40 160, £20 080, £60 240
    c. £451, £225.50

4. a. 30
    b. 10
    c. 5

5. a. 21 months
    b. 6 months

6. a. 320   b. 800
    c. 120 000   d. 192 000

7. a. 2
    b. (i) 12
        (ii) 96
    c. 10
    d. 21
    e. (i) 816
        (ii) 102

8. a. 1 : 3
    b. 75

9. a. 4 : 1
    b. 6

10. a. 6 : 3 : 10 : 2
    b. 66 cl vodka, 110 cl cranberry juice,
        22 cl lime
    d. 231 cl

11. a. £20   b. £45
    c. £21   d. 5 : 2
    e. no

Group work 1, page 95

Answer 3.

Group work 2, page 95

16

Group work 3, page 95

1. 1 tin A, 2 tins B
2. 2 tins A, 1 tin B

Group work 4, page 96

1. 1 : 2

2. 4 : 11

3. 6 : 19

4. 3.2

1.11 The Power of Numbers

Investigation, page 98

The indices are multiplied together.

Work it out, page 98

1. a. 5^2 b. 7^4
    c. 3^5 d. 4^1

2. a. 9   b. 16
    c. 256   d. 81
    e. 1 000   f. 1
    g. 64   h. 81

3. a. 2^7 b. 7^{11}
    c. 8^9 d. 5^3
    e. 3^9 f. 6^{16}
    g. 0.2^{13} h. 11^{13}

4. a. $2^3 \times 3^2$ b. $5^4 \times 4^4$
    c. $8^4 \times 9^2$ d. $7^2 \times 3^3 \times 2^4$

5. a. 9^3 b. 3^4
    c. 15^1 d. 6^7
    e. 2^5 f. 10^6
    g. 14^{-2} h. 21^{10}
    i. 7^{12} j. 8^5

6. a. 5^{12} b. 6^{10}
    c. 7^{20} d. 11^{48}
    e. 2^{26} f. 3^3
    g. 7^{22} h. 4^8

7. Corrections a: 6^3, c: 8^3, d: 2^8 and g: 4^{15}

8. a. | 4^5 | 4^6 | **4^{11}** | **4^{17}** |

    b. | **2^4** | **2^3** | 2^7 | 2^{10} |

c. | **5⁶** | 5⁷ | 5¹³ | **5²⁰** |

d. | 8⁴ | **8⁴** | **8⁸** | 8¹² |

9. a. cube of 3
    b. square of 15

10. 16, 25, 36

11. 8, 64 and 125

12. 8 and 4

Work it out, page 100

1. a. $\frac{1}{8}$ b. $\frac{1}{9}$
    c. $\frac{1}{64}$ d. $\frac{1}{32}$

2. a. 3^{-3} b. 5^{-5}
    c. 4^4 d. 2^{-9}
    e. 5^{-6} f. 7^{-2}
    g. 2^{-4} h. 5^2
    i. 6^{-7} j. 3^5
    k. 5^0 l. 4^{-1}

3. a.
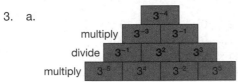

    b.
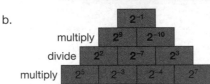

    c.
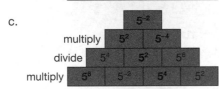

    d.
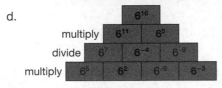

Investigation, page 101

There are various answers.

Work it out, page 101

1. a. 5   b. 6
    c. 9   d. 17
    e. 4.36   f. 1.96
    g. 2.18   h. 2.77

2. a. 10.24   b. 1.17
    c. 14 616.27   d. 136.82

3. a. 2 916.39   b. 13 710.31
    c. 27.70   d. 0.29
    e. 0.10   f. 357.54
    g. 44.93   h. 487.75

4. a and 4; b and 1; c and 6; d and 5; e and 3;
    f and 2

5. a and c

Work it out, page 103

1. a.

	Minimum growth	Maximum growth
Five years	1 611	2 488
Ten years	2 594	6 192

    b. 877, 3 598

2. a. (i)   36   b. 4, 32, 1 024
        (ii) 7 776
        (iii) 60 466 176

3. a. 2 960 acres
    b. 888 acres
    c. 197 acres

4. a.

	Cat	Horse	African elephant	Human
Lifespan (years)	13	38	74	25

    b. For all animals apart from humans.
    c. No

5. a. £2 140
    b. £2 850
    c. £3 934

6. a. 64
    b. 1 073 741 824

7. a. (i)   9
        (ii) 10
        (iii) 23
        (iv) 62
    b. 15
    c. (i)   1 1 1
        (ii) 1 1 0 0
        (iii) 1 0 0 0 0
        (iv) 1 0 0 1 0 1

8. a. 1 024
    b. 1 048 576
    c. 1 073 741 824

9. a. 586 megabytes
    b. 4 096 megabytes
    c. 3 510 megabytes

10. a. 4.88 megabytes
    b. (i) 9 766 megabytes
        (ii) 10 gigabytes
    c. No

Investigation, page 106

1. a. £363   b. £88 572

2. Maths looks good but the business idea not so good.

1.12 Scientific Notation

Work it out, page 110

1. a, e, f and g

2. a. 470   b. 13 800
    c. 99 000   d. 230 900
    e. 8 700   f. 15
    g. 373.2   h. 89 352 000
    i. 80.242   j. 600.4

3. a. 0.0047   b. 0.0138
    c. 0.06406   d. 0.000023
    e. 0.00092   f. 0.00015
    g. 0.465   h. 0.008905
    i. 0.0203   j. 0.06

4. a. 2.34×10^2 b. 1.29×10^4
    c. 7.5×10^6 d. 5.74×10^1
    e. 4.5×10^3 f. 3.76×10^6

g. 9.9×10^0 h. 1.021×10^1
i. 1.1×10^0 j. 1×10^9

5. a. 2.3×10^{-2} b. 9.93×10^{-3}
    c. 5.7×10^{-3} d. 1.4×10^{-1}
    e. 9.2×10^{-2} f. 3.04×10^{-4}
    g. 1×10^{-5} h. 5.7×10^{-6}

6. 5.58×10^2; 1.64×10^3; 1.25×10^4;
    3.62×10^4;

7. c, d, e, f and g

Investigation, page 111

1. 9 600

2. a. 43 000
    b. 670 000

Work it out, page 112

1. a. 8×10^5 b. 6×10^7
    c. 1.5×10^8 d. 2.8×10^9
    e. 9×10^2 f. 3×10^{-6}
    g. 4×10^2 h. 3×10^5

2. a. 5.2×10^8 b. 3.5×10^7
    c. 3.1×10^7 d. 2.4×10^5
    e. 4.4×10^2 f. 6.9×10^{10}
    g. 4.5×10^3 h. 1.4×10^6

3. a. 5×10^5 b. 2×10^{100}
    c. 8.8×10^{13} d. 1×10^9
    e. 1×10^{15} f. 1×10^{112}

4. £22 131

5. 2.71×10^9 km

6. a. 2.0×10^{-7} mm
    b. 1.0×10^{24}

7. a. 2.9×10^7
    b. (i) 2×10^{16} m
        (ii) 5×10^8
    c. 1.5×10^9 d. 2.7×10^5
    e. 1×10^6 f. 1.4×10^8

8. a. 15 656   b. 43 years

9. a. 1.2×10^9
    b. 4.2×10^8
    c. North America and the Middle East

1.13 Co-ordinates

Work it out, page 116

1. b: (1.5, 0); c: (–1, –3); d: (1, –3)

2. a. (4, 7), (2, 3)
    b. (6, 1), (5, 2)

3. a. (0, 4), (3, 0), (4, 2), (6, 1), (8, 3)
    b. 7
    c. (i)

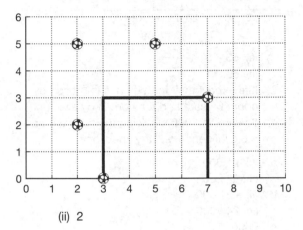

    (ii) 2

4. a.

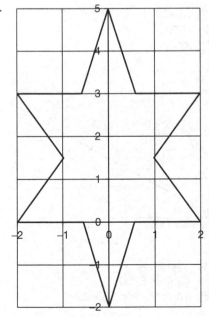

    b. Star

5. (–3, –2), (–3, –4), (–6, –4), (–6, –6), (4, –6),
    (4, –4), (3, –4), (3, 0), (6, 0), (6, 1.5) finish

6. a. (3, 6)
    b. (11, 4)
    c. (2, 3)
    d. (–6, –4)

1.14 Interpretation and Plotting of Graphs

Group work, page 119

No units on either axis, the vertical axis could finish at 5 000, the horizontal scale is not correct.

Work it out, page 119

1. a. number of visitors to a fun fair
    b. hormones present in blood
    c. temperature
    d. speed of car
    e. thickness of ice
    f. temperature

2. a. 1 800 km
    b. 6 minutes
    c. 400 metres per minute
    d. 1 400 m
    e.

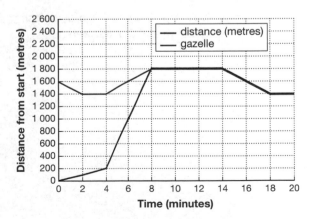

    f. killed by cheetah and dragged away

3. a. 10 hours
    b. chart

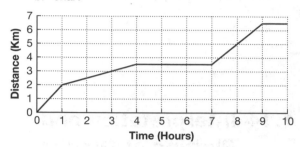

    c. (i) 6.5 km
        (ii) 0.65 km per hour
        (iii) 5 km

4. a.

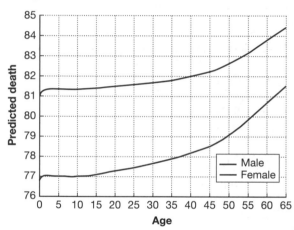

    b. (i) 81.5
        (ii) 82
    c. Women live longer than men, the difference is 4 years at birth and 3 at 65 years.

d.

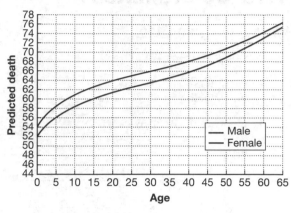

e. (i) 63, 65
    (ii) 69, 71
f. Life expectancy for men has improved by about 6 years and for women by about 8 years. In 1900 surviving the first year had a big influence on life expecancy.

5. a. (i) £1 000
        (ii) £2 200
    b. (i) £21 000
        (ii) £47 000
    c. £500

6. a. (i) £2 400
        (ii) £500
    b. £27 000
    c.

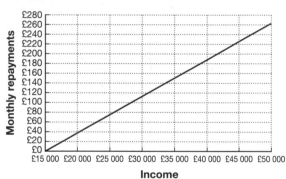

    d. (i) £120, £80
        (ii) £1 440, £960
        (iii) 10 years and 16 years

7. a.

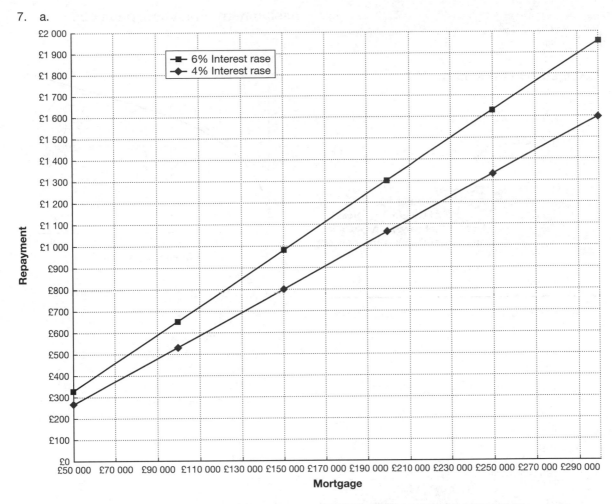

b. (i) £900
    (ii) £1 100
c. £90 000 at 6% or £110 000 at 4%
d. £150

Investigation, page 124

1 and e; 2 and a; 3 and c; 4 and f; 5 and d; 6 and b

1.15 Bringing It All Together

Case study tasks, page 125

1. 275%
2. 21.7%, 15.8%, 19.0%
3. a.

	Referred to another service	Person declined our service	Other reason, e.g. moved out of area
January	3	12	5
February	3	6	3
March	6	7	3

b. (i) 25%
    (ii) 52.1%
    (iii) 22.9%

Case study tasks, page 127

1. a. (i) $\frac{1}{80}$
    (ii) $\frac{1}{50}$
  b. 1%, 2%
  c. a mental illness
  d.

	Not happy	Number of people not happy and poor	Not happy and mentally ill
UK	2 400 000	610 000	970 00
Local population	3 200	800	1 300

e. Because you can be unhappy without being poor or mentally ill.

2. a. 8 080 000
  b. 10 600

3. a. 76%   b. 24%
  c. 10%   d. 15%

4. a. 159
  b. 106

5. a. £25 000 millions
  b.

	Percentage of total costs
Time off work or not working (including cost of carer)	68.0%
GP time	3.6%
Mental health trusts	19.6%
Drugs	3.2%
Social services	5.6%

c. 2%

Assignment questions, page 126

1. a.

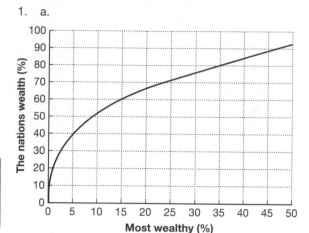

b. (i) 35%
    (ii) 60%
    (iii) 7%

2. a. (i) £18 900, £20 500
    (ii) £21 879, £22 000
  b. It depends how long Matt intends to work for the company – five years or less then he should chose the second option, otherwise the first option will be the best financial choice.

3. a. 35 miles   b. £6
  c. 10 kg   d. £30

4. £3 000

5. a. 18 000
  b. 7

6. 9 : 1

7. a. flour: 12 oz, lard and butter: 3 oz, salt: 0.75 of a teaspoon, water: 4.5 tablespoons
  b. 4

8. a. all inclusive: £1 968.13; full board: £1 572.12; bed and breakfast: £1 679.15; internet option: £1 446.50
  b. The internet option.

9. a.

	Tonnes today	Tonnes in 1990	Change in emissions (%)	Tonnes per square kilometre (today)	Population
United States	6 000 million	5 000 million	Increase 20%	6.2×10^2	300 million
United Kingdom	560 million	590 million	Decrease 5%	2.3×10^3	62 million
Pakistan	130 million	71 million	Increase 83%	1.6×10^2	163 million
Trinidad and Tobago	33 million	17 million	Increase 94%	6.3×10^3	1 million

b. Trinidad and Tobago.
c. (i) 260 000 000 tonnes
(ii) 170 000 000 tonnes
(iii) 130 000 000 tonnes

10. a. (i) £6 000
(ii) £4 000
b. 2 500 miles
c. (i) £8 000
(ii) 53%
d. 50 000 miles

11.

2	3	4	6		1	7	2	8
6	6		4	6	4		4	2
3		3		0		6		4
	3	2	0		3	6	2	
8		4		3		6		8
5	8		2	4	6		1	1
2	0	0	0		4	9	0	0

12. a. 5 450 should be 6 050, 56% should be 36%, one fiftieth should be one fifth.
b. (i) 28%
(ii) 14%

Investigation, page 131

They are both correct.

Group work 1, page 132

a. 248 days
b. 1 000 kg
c. (i) 248 000 kg
(ii) 9 920 kg
(iii) 9 225.6 kg

Group work 2, page 133

1. £118.80

2. $\frac{1}{4}$

3. £192

4. $1\frac{11}{16}$

5. 111 000 square metres

6. AE£2 538

7. a. a graph

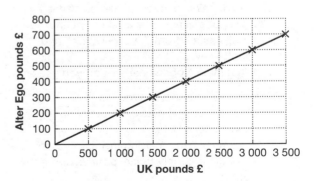

b. £500
c. £308

Chapter 2: Collecting, Recording and Analysing Data

2.1 Statistics Today

Task, page 135

There are many possible answers.

Discussion, page 137

There are many possible answers.

Group tasks, page 138

There are many possible answers.

Paired work, page 140

1. These are possible answers:
    a. Who would you vote for if an election was called tomorrow – then list the three main candidates and provide the extra options 'other' and 'wouldn't vote'.
    b. Have you eaten in a restaurant in the last two weeks?
    c. Do you think education is failing our children?
    d. Do you think children should be banned from pubs? Then give a list of options: 'at all times', 'from 7 P.M. onwards', and 'don't know'.
    e. What mobile phone network do you use?

2. Reasons for the answers may vary:
    a. Biased – people outside of pet shops are likely to keep pets.
    b. Biased – when receiving their certificates students are likely to feel positive about the course.
    c. Unbiased – collected by nurses and doctors.
    d. Biased – Monday morning is unlikely to be representative of the rest of the week.
    e. Unbiased – collected by the police.

Group task 1, page 141

There are many possible answers.

Group task 2, page 141

There are many possible answers.

Work it out, page 142

1. a. There are many possible answers.
    b. (i) What do you like most about your mobile phone? Then provide a list of options.
        (ii) Easier to do maths on the answer.

2. a. It's a customer satisfaction questionnaire.
    b. The questions are all open.
    c. The questions could remain the same but each should have a list of options that people could choose from.

2.2 Charting Data

Task, page 143

a. discrete
b. continuous
c. continuous, but can be treated as discrete
d. discrete
e. discrete
f. discrete
g. continuous
h. discrete

Work it out, page 149

1. a. incorrect   b. correct
    c. incorrect   d. correct
    e. incorrect   f. incorrect

2. a. 0 or 2   b. 0, 2 or 8
    c. 10, 8 or 2   d. 0 or 2
    e. 2 and 0   f. 0

3. a. | 2 | < | 6 | > | 3 | < | 10 | < | 20 |

   b. | 110 | < | 120 | > | 52 | > | 40 | < | 100 |

   c. | 2 | < | 3 | < | 8 | < | 3 | < | 1 |

4. a. 64

   b. discrete

   c.

Chart showing how people answered the question:
'If, in the middle of the night, you awoke to the sound of strange noises coming from downstairs. What would you do?.'

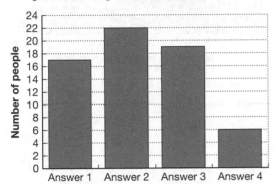

Key:
Answer 1: Hide under the duvet in the hope that the noise would go away.
Answer 2: Use your mobile to phone the police.
Answer 3: Wake up somebody else in the house and let them deal with it.
Answer 4: Go downstairs armed with your bedside table lamp.

   d. other

   e. There are many possible answers.

   f. There are many possible answers.

5. a. 30

   b. discrete

   c.

	Number of people
Nokia	3
Samsung	7
Siemens	7
Motorola	9
Sony Eriksson	4

   d.

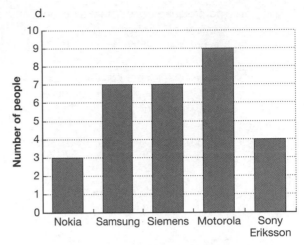

6. a. 30

   b. discrete

   c. **Chart showing who people thought made Britain great**

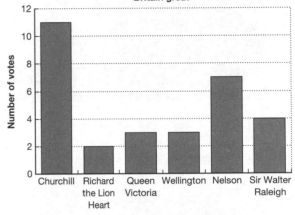

7. a. **Chart showing the number of votes cast in four elections**

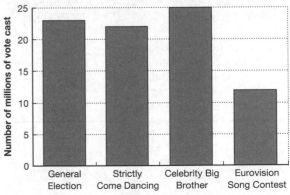

   b. There are many possible answers.

8. a. (i)   The grouping does not take account of fractions of numbers.
        (ii) It is not clear which group 5, 10, 15 etc. goes.
        (iii) The groups are not equal.
        (iv) There is no group for the numbers 10, 20, 30, etc. to go in.
        (v)   Good
        (vi) The large groupings may mean some of the detail is lost.

    c.

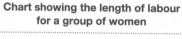

Chart showing the length of labour for a group of women

    d. There are many possible answers.

9. a. 32
    b. discrete
    c. Table.

Number of celebrities named	Number of people
0 < number of celebrities ≤ 10	12
10 < number of celebrities ≤ 20	8
20 < number of celebrities ≤ 30	7
30 < number of celebrities ≤ 40	3
40 < number of celebrities ≤ 50	2

    d.

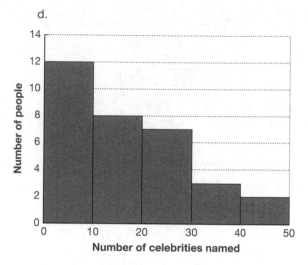

    e. Your conclusions.

10. a. 50
    b. continuous
    c.

Amount spent on text books (£)	Number of students
0 < £ ≤ 10	5
10 < £ ≤ 20	10
20 < £ ≤ 30	10
30 < £ ≤ 40	12
40 < £ ≤ 50	6
50 < £ ≤ 60	5
60 < £ ≤ 70	2

    d.

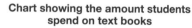
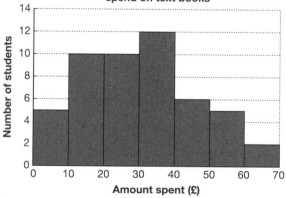

Chart showing the amount students spend on text books

11. a. 60

b.

Time spent in front of a computer screen (hours)	Number of employees
0 < hours ≤ 5	3
5 < hours ≤ 10	5
10 < hours ≤ 15	7
15 < hours ≤ 20	11
20 < hours ≤ 25	10
25 < hours ≤ 30	16
30 < hours ≤ 35	8

c.

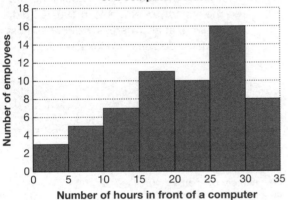

Chart showing the amount of time employees of a web design company spend in front of a computer screen

d. There are many possible answers.

Investigation, page 153

a. 40

b.

Number of Days	Number of people
0–10	9
11–20	14
21–30	8
31–40	4
41–50	3
51–60	2

Project, page 153

There are many possible answers.

2.3 Frequency Polygons

Work it out, page 156

1. a.

Average life expectancy of the world population and the population of Botswana

b. There could be several answers to this question including deaths from AIDS has decreased life expectancy in Botswana.

2. a.

Chart showing the average distance a person is from a rat

b. 2004 and 2005

c. Answers will vary.

3. a. and e.

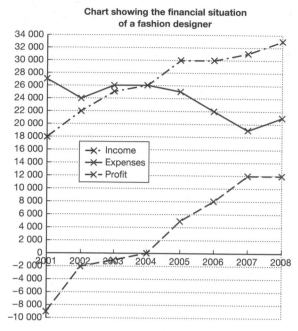

Chart showing the financial situation of a fashion designer

b. 2004

c. 2005

d. 2007 and 2008

4. a. (i)

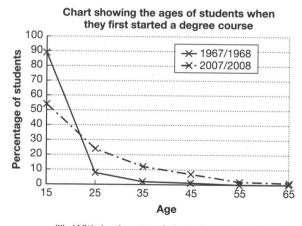

Chart showing the ages of students when they first started a degree course

(ii) With both sets of data the majority of students are under 20 years of age but in 2007/2008 the majority is smaller and there is more variety in age. In 1967/68 there are no students over the age of 50 whereas in 2007/2008 there is a small percentage.

b. (i)

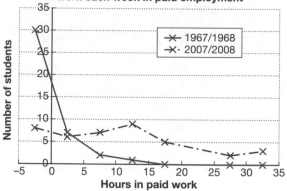

Chart showing the number of hours students work each week in paid employment

(ii) A lot more students work in 2007/2008 compared to 1967/68, with some students working the equivalent of a full time job. The majority of students in 1967/68 did not work at all, whereas in 2007/08 most students do some work each week.

5. a. (i)

Number of spam e-mails per week	e-shoppers	People who rarely e-shop
0 < number of spams ≤ 10	0	27
10 < number of spams ≤ 20	1	9
20 < number of spams ≤ 30	2	3
30 < number of spams ≤ 40	2	1
40 < number of spams ≤ 50	6	0
50 < number of spams ≤ 60	7	0
60 < number of spams ≤ 70	8	0
70 < number of spams ≤ 80	5	0
80 < number of spams ≤ 90	5	0
90 < number of spams ≤ 100	4	0

(ii) **Chart showing the number of spam e-mails received by two types of shoppers**

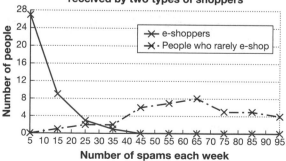

(iii) People who shop on the internet are likely to receive more spam e-mails.

b. (i)

Number of web words	Number of people
0 < number of words ≤ 5	3
5 < number of words ≤ 10	5
10 < number of words ≤ 15	6
15 < number of words ≤ 20	7
20 < number of words ≤ 25	9

(ii)

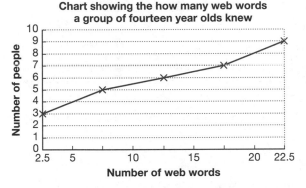

(iii) There are many possible answers.

Investigation 1, page 159

1. 30
2. a.

Number of times eat out	Number of people: UK	Number of people: USA
None	14	3
0 < number times eat out ≤ 4	9	4
4 < number times eat out ≤ 8	4	7
8 < number times eat out ≤ 12	2	11
12 < number times eat out ≤ 16	1	2
16 < number times eat out ≤ 20	0	3

b. For the first 'group' – none.
c. Answers will vary.

Investigation 2, page 160

1. Points are not connected with straight lines. The points are not in the middle of the group.

2.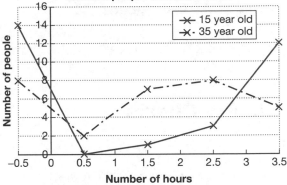

3. More 15 year olds do no exercise each week compared to 35 year olds, however there are more 15 year olds who spend over 3 hours exercising compared to 35 year olds.

2.4 Pictograms

Work it out, page 162

1. a. 3.5 billion tons
   b. 5.5 billion tons
   c. 16.5 billion

2. Possible answer:
   Casino Royale ★★★★★
   Click ★★★
   The Reef ★
   The Queen ★★★★★

3. Possible answer:

Ratings (out of 10: 10 being excellent, 0 being never again)	
Location	☺ ☺ ☺ ☺ ☾
Food	☺ ☺ ☺
Room	☺ ☺
Facilities	☺ ☺ ☺ ☾

2.5 Drawing Angles

Paired work: Task 1, page 165

Answers will vary.

Paired work: Task 3, page 165

a. 78°, acute
b. 122°, obtuse
c. 157°, obtuse
d. 285°, reflex
e. 12°, acute
f. 243°, reflex

2.6 Pie Charts

Work it out, page 167

1 **The amount of time a student studies**

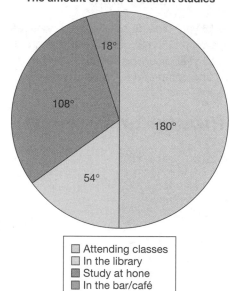

Legend:
- Attending classes
- In the library
- Study at hone
- In the bar/café

2. a. **How a 'typical' person spends their day**

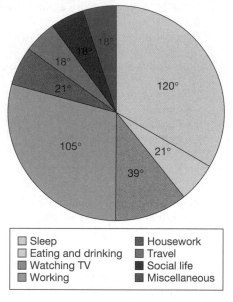

Legend:
- Sleep
- Eating and drinking
- Watching TV
- Working
- Housework
- Travel
- Social life
- Miscellaneous

b. Yes all we do is eat, sleep, work and watch telly!
c. There are many possible answers.
d. There are many possible answers.

3. a. **Type of goal scored in a premiership football matches**

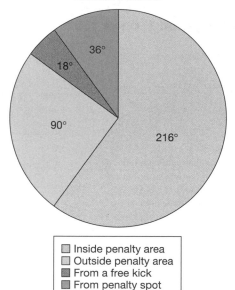

Legend:
- Inside penalty area
- Outside penalty area
- From a free kick
- From penalty spot

b.

How TV football is shared out

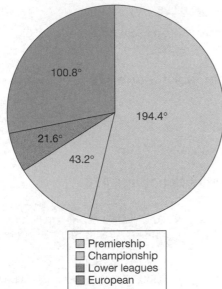

☐ Premiership
☐ Championship
■ Lower leagues
■ European

b.

A carbon footprint

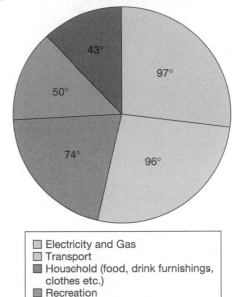

☐ Electricity and Gas
☐ Transport
■ Household (food, drink furnishings,
   clothes etc.)
■ Recreation
■ Share of public health services
   (health, education, defence)

c. The second chart, not as busy as the first.
You're able to quickly see how the 'carbon
footprint' is shared out amongst the
categories.

Work it out, page 171

1. a. Yes: 19
   No, but only tell your closest friend/relative:
   51
   No and tell everyone about your luck: 20
   b. 144
   c. There are many possible answers.

4. a.

A carbon footprint

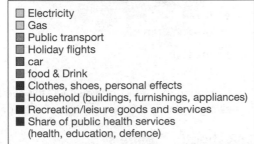
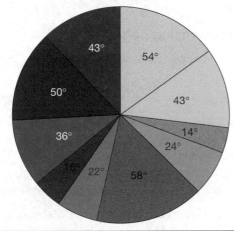

☐ Electricity
☐ Gas
■ Public transport
■ Holiday flights
■ car
■ food & Drink
■ Clothes, shoes, personal effects
■ Household (buildings, furnishings, appliances)
■ Recreation/leisure goods and services
■ Share of public health services
   (health, education, defence)

2. a. Food and non-alcoholic drinks: 34.4
   Fuel and power: 25.6
   Travel costs: 4.72
   Clothing, footware and personal effects: 12.8
   Housing: 13.3
   Leisure: 9.2
   b. There are many possible answers.

3. a. Computer   42
      TV   12
      Mobile phone: 84
      DVD   6
   b. There are many possible answers.

Task, page 173

a.

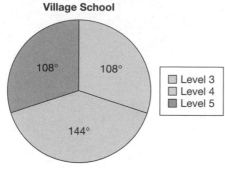

Village School

108° | 108°

144°

Level 3
Level 4
Level 5

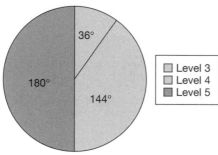

Large School

36°

180° | 144°

Level 3
Level 4
Level 5

b. As the overall pupil numbers are small in the village school a small change can look quite dramatic.
c. A chart that deals with raw figures such as a frequency polygon (the results for the two years could go on the same chart for each school.)

2.7 Averages

Work it out, page 175

1. mean: 4.4; median: 4; mode: 3; range: 4

2. mean: 10; median: 10; mode: 11; range:7

3. mean: 18; median: 17; mode: 17; range:19

4. mean: 6; median: 5; no mode; range:14

5. mean: 5; median: 5; mode: 4 and 6; range: 10

6. mean: 11; median: 10.7; no mode; range: 5.4

7. mean: 4; median: 3.8; no mode; range: 7.8

8. mean: 11 991; median: 12 003; mode: 12 032; range: 133

9. mean: 0.0575; median: 0.0275; mode: 0.04; range: 0.298

10. mean: 8.8; median: 2.53; mode: 2.53; range: 24.95

Group tasks, page 176

1. 1

2. 4.75

3. £1 064

Investigation, page 176

	Total sales	Total items	Average sales
Bob	£640	11	£58.18
Azim	£540	9	£60.00

Azim could be regarded as the better salesman as his average is higher, however Bob's total sales is higher.

Group tasks, page 178

1. There are many possible answers.

2. a.

	Mean	Median	Mode	Range
East Midlands	12	12	11,12	3
South East	12	10	12	35

b. There are a variety of possible answers.

3. a. mean: £11.50; median: £7.50; mode: £8; range: £50.
   b. mean
   c. median or mode

4. a. median
   b. median

5. As student results improve so will the average – all students cannot achieve above average.

Investigation, page 178

a. 20
b. mean: 1.2; median: 1; mode: 1; range: 3

c.

Number of goals scored	Number of matches
0	6
1	7
2	4
3	3

d. investigation.

Work it out, page 180

1. a. 27
   b. mean: 4; median: 4; mode 5; range 4
   c. There are a variety of possible answers.

2. a. 50
   b. mean: 3.96; median: 5; mode: 5; range: 6
   c. There are a variety of possible answers.

3. a. 52
   b. mean: 6.02; median: 6; mode: 6; range: 6
   c. There are a variety of possible answers.

4. a. 734 600
   b. mean: £25.49; median: £10; mode: £10; range: £2 482 366
   c. mean: £10.40; median: £5; mode: £5; range: £249 995
   d. How many people who won nothing.

Work it out, page 183

1. a. 300
   b. £12 933.33
   c. £8,000 < debt ≤ £12,000

2. a. 340
   b. 27.94
   c. 25 < age ≤ 30
   d. There are many possible answers.

3. a. Mean for families with young children: 4
   Mean for eighteen to twenty year olds: 13.7
   b. Modal group for families with young children: 0 < times ≤ 5
   Modal group for eighteen to twenty year olds: 10 < times ≤ 15
   c. There are many possible answers.

4. a. 30
   b. 30 < time (minutes) ≤ 60

c.

Time (minutes) to get to work	Number of people
0 < time ≤ 30	8
30 < time ≤ 60	12
60 < time ≤ 90	7
90 < time ≤ 120	3

d. 50 minutes

2.8 Cumulative Frequency Charts

Work it out, page 189

The median and quartiles are all approximations.

1. a. 100
   b.

Weight (g)	Number of boxes	Cumulative frequency
720 < weight ≤ 730	8	8
730 < weight ≤ 740	21	29
740 < weight ≤ 750	27	56
750 < weight ≤ 760	24	80
760 < weight ≤ 770	14	94
770 < weight ≤ 780	4	98
780 < weight ≤ 790	2	100

c.

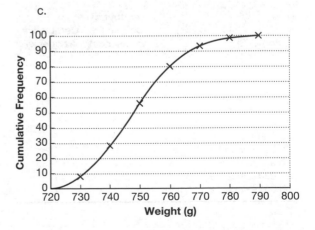

d. 748 g
e. 758 g, 739 g
f. 19 g
g. 30

2. a.

House price (thousands £)	Number of houses	Cumulative frequency
50 < price ≤ 100	50	50
100 < price ≤ 150	280	330
150 < price ≤ 200	250	580
200 < price ≤ 250	150	730
250 < price ≤ 300	70	800

b.

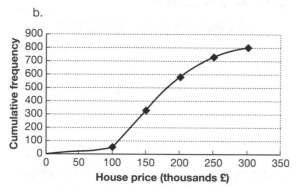

c. (i) £164 000
    (ii) £126 000, £205 000
    (iii) £79 000
d. 140
e. 160

3. a. 120
    b.

Income (£)	Number of people (in thousands)	Cumulative frequency
0 < income ≤ 10 000	9	9
10 000 < income ≤ 20 000	25	34
20 000 < income ≤ 30 000	30	64
30 000 < income ≤ 40 000	21	85
40 000 < income ≤ 50 000	18	103
50 000 < income ≤ 60 000	7	110
60 000 < income ≤ 70 000	6	116
70 000 < income ≤ 80 000	2	118
80 000 < income ≤ 90 000	1	119
90 000 < income ≤ 100 000	1	120

c.

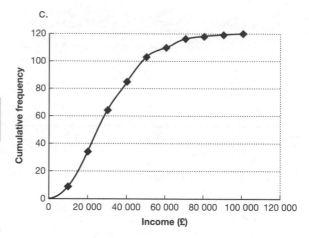

d. (i) £28 000
    (ii) £42 000, £18 000
    (iii) £24 000
e. £56 000 or more, 12
f. 7

4. a. 40
    b. and c.

Time spent on the Internet (hours)	Number of people	Cumulative frequency
0 < time ≤ 1	8	8
1 < time ≤ 2	11	19
2 < time ≤ 3	5	24
3 < time ≤ 4	9	33
4 < time ≤ 5	4	37
5 < time ≤ 6	0	37
6 < time ≤ 7	2	39
7 < time ≤ 8	1	40

d.

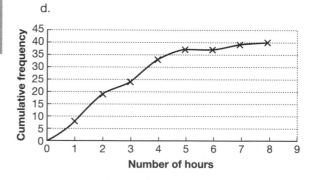

e.   (i) 3.2 hours
(ii) 4.7 hours, 2.2 hours
(iii) 2.5 hours
f.   There are various answers.

5.   a. 120
b. nurses
c. English literature: 3.5; nursing: 6.1
d. English literature: 68; nursing: 24
e. English literature: 12; nursing: 24

6.   a. 1 200 in each survey
b.

Marks (%)	No. of students 2007	No. of students 2008	Cumulative frequency 2007	Cumulative frequency 2008
0 < mark ≤ 10	5	120	5	120
10 < mark ≤ 20	15	160	20	280
20 < mark ≤ 30	30	200	50	480
30 < mark ≤ 40	55	220	105	700
40 < mark ≤ 50	105	150	210	850
50 < mark ≤ 60	140	140	350	990
60 < mark ≤ 70	160	90	510	1 080
70 < mark ≤ 80	240	80	750	1 160
80 < mark ≤ 90	260	30	1 010	1 190
90 < mark ≤ 100	190	10	1 200	1 200

c.

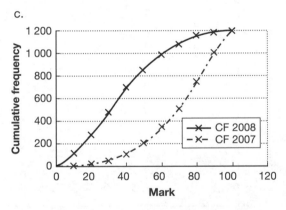

d.

	2007	2008
Fail	100	700
Pass	250	290
Merit	400	170
Distinction	450	40

e. The 2007 was too easy.
f.   (i) 300

(ii)

	2007	2008
Fail	56 and below	21 and below
Pass	57–74	22–35
Merit	75–86	36–53
Distinction	Above 86	Above 53

Group task, page 192

No units on either axis, the curve should join the origin, no title and the points are in the middle, not the end of each group.

2.9 Scatter Plots

Group work, page 196

1.   There is zero correlation and so there should be no line of best fit.
2.   The line is not positioned correctly.
3.   People have arguments about things other than money.

Work it out, page 197

1.   a. age   b. number of people
c. either   d. use of internet
e. weight   f. either

2.   a and b:

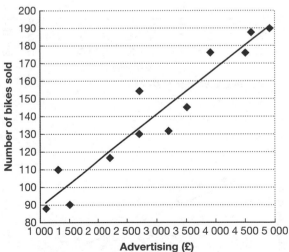

c. positive correlation
d.   (i) 110
(ii) 178

3. a and b:

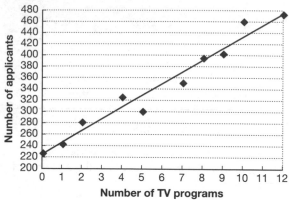

Number of TV programs

c. positive correlation
d. (i) 287
   (ii) can't say.

4. a and b:

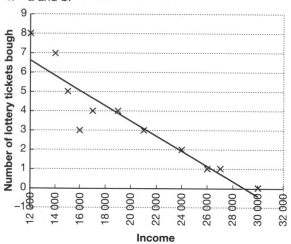

Income

c. negative correlation
d. (i) 3
   (ii) Can't say.

5. a and b:

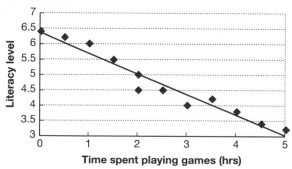

Time spent playing games (hrs)

c. negative correlation
d. (i) 4
   (ii) Can't say.

6. a and b:

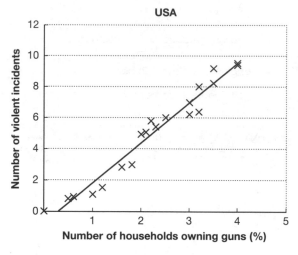

Number of households owning guns (%)

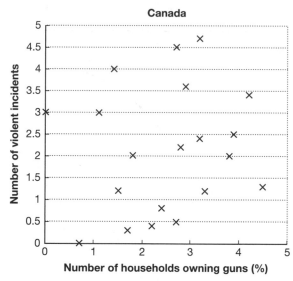

Number of households owning guns (%)

c. positive and zero correlations
d. (i) 4
   (ii) can't say
e. There are many possible answers.

Group investigation and group discussion, page 200

There are many possible answers.

2.10 Probability

Group tasks 1 and 2, page 202

There are various answers.

Work it out, page 203

1. a. $\frac{1}{6}$

    b. $\frac{1}{2}$

2. a. $\frac{1}{2}$

    b. $\frac{3}{13}$

    c. $\frac{1}{52}$

3. a. $\frac{1}{16}$

    b. $\frac{7}{16}$

    c. $\frac{1}{4}$

    d. $\frac{3}{14}$

Work it out, page 204

1. a.

	1	2	3	4	5	6
1	2	3	4	5	6	7
2	3	4	5	6	7	8
3	4	5	6	7	8	9
4	5	6	7	8	9	10
5	6	7	8	9	10	11
6	7	8	9	10	11	12

    b. Second players: there are more possible outcomes for totals 7, 8 and 9.

2. a.

Wessington	Wessington	Wessington	N. Darley	N. Darley	N. Darley	Oker Utd	Oker Utd	Oker Utd	Wensley	Wensley	Wensley
N. Darley	Oker Utd	Wensley	Wessington	Oker Utd	Wensley	Wessington	N. Darley	Wensley	Wessington	N. Darley	Oker Utd

    b. $\frac{1}{12}$

    c. $\frac{1}{2}$

3. a.

George	Wine	Wine	Wine	Beer	Lager	Lager	Lager	Beer	Beer
Harry	Wine	Beer	Lager	Wine	Wine	Lager	Beer	Lager	Beer

    b. (i) $\frac{1}{9}$

       (ii) $\frac{2}{9}$

4. a.

1	1	1	1	2	2	2	2	3	3	3	3	4	4	4	4	5	5	5	5
2	3	4	5	1	3	4	5	1	2	4	5	1	2	3	5	1	2	3	4

    b. $\frac{1}{10}$

Work it out, page 206

1. 0.9

2. 0.35

3. a. $\frac{12}{25}$ b. $\frac{117}{250}$

4. a. $\frac{7}{10}$ b. only 10 people in survey

5. a. $\frac{3}{200}$ b. $\frac{3}{800}$

    c. $\frac{1}{250}$

6. a. $\frac{23}{5\,000}$ b. $\frac{1}{100}$

Discussion, page 208

1. leave

2. no

3. –

Work it out, page 209

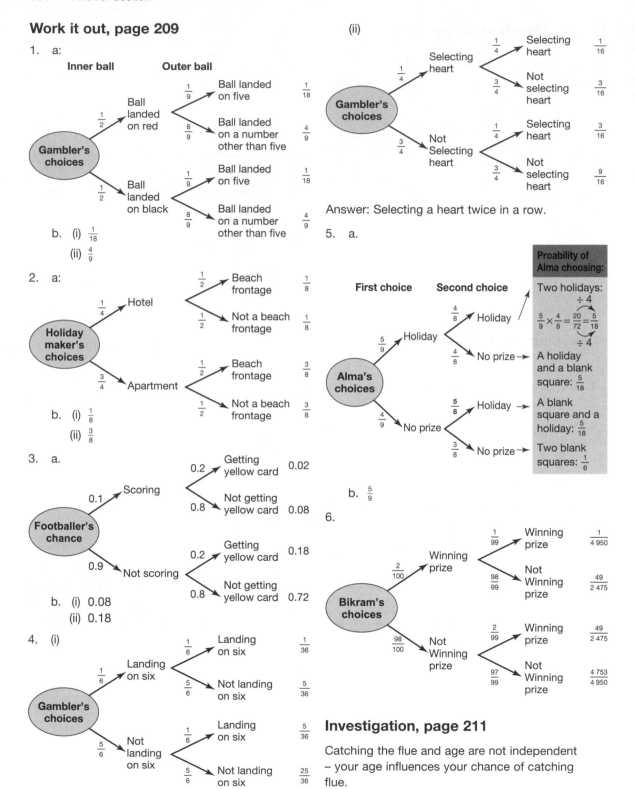

1. a:

    | Inner ball | Outer ball |

    Gambler's choices

    $\frac{1}{2}$ Ball landed on red
    $\frac{1}{9}$ Ball landed on five — $\frac{1}{18}$
    $\frac{8}{9}$ Ball landed on a number other than five — $\frac{4}{9}$

    $\frac{1}{2}$ Ball landed on black
    $\frac{1}{9}$ Ball landed on five — $\frac{1}{18}$
    $\frac{8}{9}$ Ball landed on a number other than five — $\frac{4}{9}$

    b. (i) $\frac{1}{18}$
        (ii) $\frac{4}{9}$

2. a:

    Holiday maker's choices

    $\frac{1}{4}$ Hotel
    $\frac{1}{2}$ Beach frontage — $\frac{1}{8}$
    $\frac{1}{2}$ Not a beach frontage — $\frac{1}{8}$

    $\frac{3}{4}$ Apartment
    $\frac{1}{2}$ Beach frontage — $\frac{3}{8}$
    $\frac{1}{2}$ Not a beach frontage — $\frac{3}{8}$

    b. (i) $\frac{1}{8}$
        (ii) $\frac{3}{8}$

3. a.

    Footballer's chance

    0.1 Scoring
    0.2 Getting yellow card — 0.02
    0.8 Not getting yellow card — 0.08

    0.9 Not scoring
    0.2 Getting yellow card — 0.18
    0.8 Not getting yellow card — 0.72

    b. (i) 0.08
        (ii) 0.18

4. (i)

    Gambler's choices

    $\frac{1}{6}$ Landing on six
    $\frac{1}{6}$ Landing on six — $\frac{1}{36}$
    $\frac{5}{6}$ Not landing on six — $\frac{5}{36}$

    $\frac{5}{6}$ Not landing on six
    $\frac{1}{6}$ Landing on six — $\frac{5}{36}$
    $\frac{5}{6}$ Not landing on six — $\frac{25}{36}$

(ii)

Gambler's choices

$\frac{1}{4}$ Selecting heart
$\frac{1}{4}$ Selecting heart — $\frac{1}{16}$
$\frac{3}{4}$ Not selecting heart — $\frac{3}{16}$

$\frac{3}{4}$ Not Selecting heart
$\frac{1}{4}$ Selecting heart — $\frac{3}{16}$
$\frac{3}{4}$ Not selecting heart — $\frac{9}{16}$

Answer: Selecting a heart twice in a row.

5. a.

    | First choice | Second choice | Proability of Alma choosing: |

    Alma's choices

    $\frac{5}{9}$ Holiday
    $\frac{4}{8}$ Holiday
    $\frac{4}{8}$ No prize

    $\frac{4}{9}$ No prize
    $\frac{5}{8}$ Holiday
    $\frac{3}{8}$ No prize

    Two holidays:
    $\div 4$
    $\frac{5}{9} \times \frac{4}{8} = \frac{20}{72} = \frac{5}{18}$
    $\div 4$

    A holiday and a blank square: $\frac{5}{18}$

    A blank square and a holiday: $\frac{5}{18}$

    Two blank squares: $\frac{1}{6}$

    b. $\frac{5}{9}$

6.

    Bikram's choices

    $\frac{2}{100}$ Winning prize
    $\frac{1}{99}$ Winning prize — $\frac{1}{4\,950}$
    $\frac{98}{99}$ Not Winning prize — $\frac{49}{2\,475}$

    $\frac{98}{100}$ Not Winning prize
    $\frac{2}{99}$ Winning prize — $\frac{49}{2\,475}$
    $\frac{97}{99}$ Not Winning prize — $\frac{4\,753}{4\,950}$

Investigation, page 211

Catching the flue and age are not independent – your age influences your chance of catching flue.

2.11 Misleading Charts

Work it out, page 213

1. a. (i) The vertical scale is just between 4% and 5%.
        (ii)

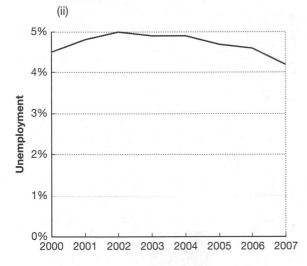

    b. No scale up the vertical axis.

2. Does up to £100 include 0? Even if it doesn't the majority of wins could be just £5. The group needs to be split, i.e. number of winners between 0–20, 21–30 etc.

3. No units, e.g. vitamins in vegetables is it measuring grams or kilograms?

4. (i) The bar for Cloudhoppers is wider than the others making it very eye catching. Other competitors in the market for cheap flights?
    (ii) A pie chart would be a better chart.

5. a. People have ticked more than one option.
    b. It looks like people have ticked just one option.

c.

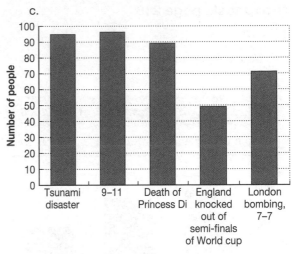

2.12 Bringing It All Together

Group task, page 217

1. There are many possible answers.

2. 330

3. a: possible measures

	Mean	Median	Mode	Range
Question 1			Once a week	
Question 2a.	3.3	4	4	5 points
Question 2b.	3.9	4	4	5

    b: possible chart

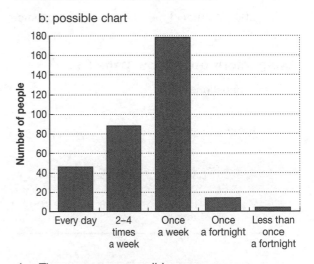

4. There are many possible answers.

Group task, page 218

1. –37

2. Wadhurst, Cottenham

3.

	Mean 2007	Mean 2008
All four universities	198.25	189

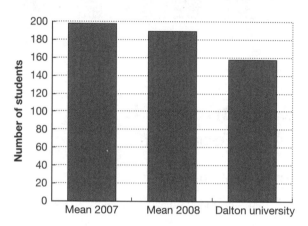

4. a. They've gone down by 22.
   b.

	Mean 2007	Mean 2008
All four universities	21	17.25

   c. 2007: 1 student more; 2008: 17.25 students less

Assignment questions, page 218

1. open questions

2. a. continuous
   b. Kiruna, Sweden
   c.

	London	Kiruna	Nairobi
Mean	12.29	12.78	12.10
Range	8.8	24	0

d.

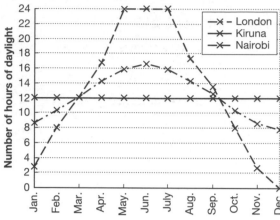

3. a. £19 300
   b. £15 000 < salary ≤ £20 000
   c.

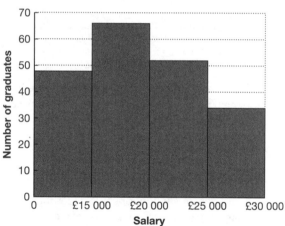

4. a.

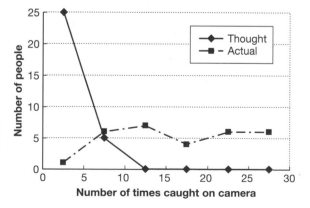

b.

	Thought	Actual
Mean	3.066667	17.3
Range	9	28
Mode	2	14
Median	2.5	17.5

5. a. mean = 5.8; range = 11
    b. 3
    c. and e.

Number of days customers wait	Number of customers	Cumulative frequency
0 < days ≤ 3	13	13
3 < days ≤ 6	16	29
6 < days ≤ 9	15	44
9 < days ≤ 12	6	50

d.

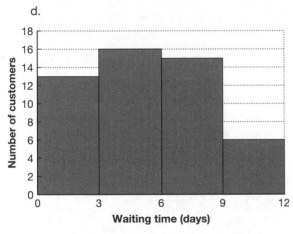

f.

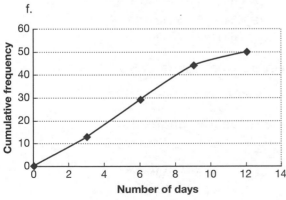

g. (i) 5.5 days – just outside the target
    (ii) 3.3 (no) and 8 days (yes)

6. a. and b.

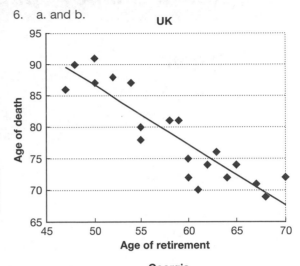

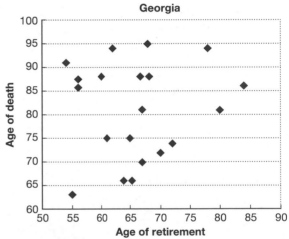

c. UK: negative correlation; Georgia: no correlation
d. (i) 85
    (ii) 62
e.

	UK		Georgia	
Mean	58.4	78.7	65.95	81
Range	23	22	30	32

f. The figures are too varied.
g. There are many possible answers.
h. There are many possible answers.

Chapter 3: Shape, Space and Measurement

3.1 Polygons

Work it out, page 225

D and E

Group work, page 226

There are many possible answers.

Task, page 226

a. none
b. none
c. vertical
d. horizontal and vertical
e. none
f. vertical

Group investigation, page 227

a. 3
b. 4
c. 6

Work it out, page 228

1. a. 1   b. 7
    c. 3   d. 6
    e. 1   f. 1

2. There are many possible answers.

Investigation, page 228

a. 2
b. 1
c. 5
d. infinity

Work it out, page 229

1. a. 4
    b. none
    c. 3

2. a. A and E, B and D, C and F
    b. The lines are parallel.

Investigation, page 229

a., b., c. and e.

Work it out, page 230

1. a. scalene
    b. isosceles

2. none

3. a. There are many possible answers.
    b. There are many possible answers.
    c. All sides 5cm long.

Work it out, page 232

1. a. rhombus
    b. rectangle

2. No lines of symmetry, order of rotational symmetry: 2, 2 pairs of parallel lines, opposite angles and sides equal, diagonals bisect each other.

3. H

4. a and d

5. a. 30 cm
    b. 40 cm
    c. 20 cm
    d. 40 cm, 20 cm and 20 cm
    e. 20 cm and 40 cm

Group work, page 233

There are many possible answers.

Investigation, page 233

1. 25

3.2 Angles

Group investigation, page 234

Opposite angles are always equal.

Work it out, page 235

a = 57°   b = 146°
c = 96°   d = 52°
e = 128°   f = 64°
g = 45°   h = 44°
j = 68°

Work it out, page 236

1.

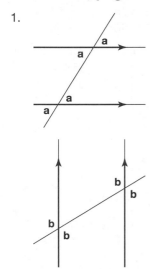

2. a = 59°   b = 121°
    c = 143°   d = 37°
    e = 119°   f = 42°
    g = 106°   h = 92°
    j = 78°   k = 145°
    m = 118°   n = 104°
    p = 122°   q = 117°
    r = 100°

3. 128° and 57°

Work it out, page 238

1. a = 60°   b = 27°
    c = 43°   d = 60°

e = 36°   f = 48°
g = 39°

2. 65° and 65° or 50° and 80°

3. a = 30°
    b = 120°
    c = 60°
    d = 30°
    e = 60°

Group work, page 238

1. a = 59°
2. b = 51°
    c = 73°

Investigation 1, page 239

a = 8°
b = 8°

Investigation 2, page 239

1. 7°

2. 25 714 miles

Work it out, page 239

1. a = 49°
    b = 49°
    c = 38°

2. 140° and 30°, 120° and 50°, 85° and 85°

Investigation, page 241

1. a. 120°
    b. 135°

2. a. and c.

Number of sides	3	4	5	6	7	8
Number of triangles	1	2	3	4	5	6
Size of each ange	60	90	108	120	128.6	135

b. The number of triangles is 2 less than the number of sides.
d. (i) 18
    (ii) 162°

3.

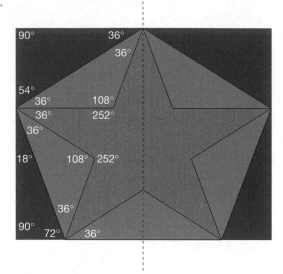

3.3 Drawing Shapes

Work it out, 242

1.   90°, 37°, 53°

2.   60°

3.   2.9 cm

4.   108°

5.   a.   kite
     b.   regular octagon

Investigation, page 243

1.   yes
2.   3D cubes

3.4 Bearings

Work it out, page 244

1.

Direction	Bearing
North west	315°
South west	225°
North east	045°
West	270°
East	090°
South east	135°
South	180°

2.   A   150°   B   228°
     C   025°   D   346°

3.   (not accurate)

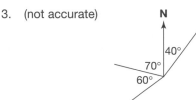

4.   a = 168°; b = 123°; c = 69°

5.   Scale drawing

6.   a.   196°, 270°, 225°
          Not measuring clockwise from the north.
     b.   230°

Paired work, page 246

1.   scale drawing

2.   pentagon

3.   see figure below.

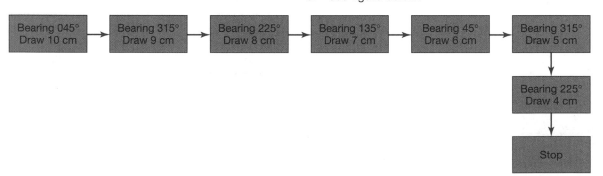

4. a. scale drawing
    b. scale drawing
    c. yes

3.5 Units of Measure and Compound Measures

Group work, page 248

There are many different answers.

Group discussion, page 249

There are many different answers.

Paired work, page 250

	Imperial	Metric
Distance	1 mile	1.61 km
	1 yard	0.92 m
	1 inch	2.56 cm
Weight	1 pound (lb)	0.45 kg
	1 ounce (oz)	28.57 g
Capacity	1 pint (pt)	0.57 litre
	1 gallon	4.55 litre

Work it out, page 251

1. a. 0.9 kg
    b. 179.2 cm
    c. 66.6 kg

2. a. 1 foot and 10 inches
    b. 0.56 m
    c. –

3. **Acceleration:** 0 to 96.6 kmph in ten seconds
    Fuel economy: 9.6 km per litre (urban)
    Engine Size: 2 litres
    Fuel capacity: 63.7 litres

125.92 cm

448 cm

4. Metric – the number is smaller.

5. 3

6. 48.3 kmph, 46.1 m

7. a. the first
    b. a pint of beer
    c. cheddar

8. a. 6
    b. second person

Work it out, page 253

1. a.

Kilometre $\xrightarrow{\times 1\,000}$ Metres
$\div 1\,000$

Metre $\xrightarrow{\times 100}$ Centimetres
$\div 100$

Centimetre $\xrightarrow{\times 10}$ Millimetres
$\div 10$

b.

Tonne $\xrightarrow{\times 1\,000}$ Kilograms
$\div 1\,000$

kilogram $\xrightarrow{\times 1\,000}$ grams
$\div 1\,000$

litre $\xrightarrow{\times 100}$ centilitres
$\div 100$

centilitre $\xrightarrow{\times 10}$ millilitres
$\div 10$

day $\xrightarrow{\times 24}$ hours
$\div 24$

hour $\xrightarrow{\times 60}$ minutes
$\div 60$

minute $\xrightarrow{\times 60}$ seconds
$\div 60$

2. a. 12 000 m   b. 400 m
   c. 2 m   d. 540 m
   e. 0.24 m   f. 70 m

3. a. 16 kg   b. 0.57 kg
   c. 2 000 kg   d. 0.025 kg
   e. 500 kg   f. 2.4 kg

4. a. 0.33 l   b. 0.25 l
   c. 6.34 l   d. 0.024 l
   e. 0.012 l   f. 0.000067 l

5. a. 90 seconds
   b. 8 436 seconds
   c. 5.25 hours
   d. 10.83 seconds

6. a. 4 minutes
   b. 0.5 mm
   c. 66.5 kg

7. a. Ten 500 ml cartons, twenty 25 cl bottles, there are many other ways.
   b. Three 200 g and one 150 g packets, five 150 g packets, there are many other ways.

8. a. £3 600
   b. £60

Work it out, page 255

1.

Speed (mph)	Distance	Time (in hours and minutes)
40	80 miles	2 hours
66.7	100 miles	1 hour 30 minutes
40	12 miles	15 minutes
36	108 miles	3 hours
60	140 miles	2 hours 20 minutes
50	125 miles	2 hours 30 minutes
60	100miles	1 hour 40 minutes

2. a. (i) first section
      (ii) 38.7 miles per hour
   b. 50
   c. 30 minutes
   d. 888.9 km

3. a. Liverpool captain
   b. half a second

4. a. 1.8° C per hour.
   b. 63.7 words per minute
   c. 30 000 000 litres

5. a. (i) 0.5 lbs per week
      (ii) 2 150 calories
   b. 28.8 lbs

6. a. 2.6 km
   b. 7.5 calories per minute
   c. Laura
   d. Ashley: 6.5 km, 225 calories / Laura: 5.3 km, 309.4 calories

7. a. 3:06 P.M.
   b. 11:06 A.M.

3.6 Similar Shapes

Work it out, page 259

1. a. 2   b. 3
   c. not similar   d. 0.4
   e. not similar

2. a. 3, 13 cm and 21 cm
   b. 0.5, 8 cm and 3.5 cm
   c. 1.5, 6 cm
   d. 2.5, 5 cm, 2 cm and 15 cm, 17.5 cm
   e. 4, 10 cm, 9.5 cm and 12 cm

Investigation, page 261

The two triangles have equal angles.

Group work, page 261

True: 1, 5 and 6.

Investigation, page 261

1. a.   b.

2. 1 400 000 km

Work it out, page 262

1. The monitor will fit.

2. a. 36 inches
   b. Body proportions are not always similar.

3. 24.96 m

3.7 Scale Drawings and Models

Work it out, page 265

1. a. 1 : 500   b. 1 : 300 000
   c. 1 000 : 1   d. 1 : 7 200
   e. 1 : 10

2. a. 1 cm to 3 m
   b. 1 cm to 10 cm
   c. 1 cm to 50 m

3. a. 1 m   b. 100 m
   c. 0.5 cm   d. 1.5 m
   e. 1.2 mm

4. a. 30 cm   b. 10 cm
   c. 15 cm   d. 4 cm
   e. 32 cm

5. True: a and c

6. Scale 1 cm to 4 km or 1 : 400 000,
   (*scale drawing*)

7. a. (i) 2 km
      (ii) 24 cm
   b. (i) 1 : 2 200 000, 1 : 900 000
      (ii) All answers are approximations.

Route planner	Distance	Time (minutes)	Predicted speed
Derby–Lichfield	59 km	44	80 kmph
Lichfield–Bromsgrove	62 km	58	64 kmph
Bromsgrove–Bristol	98 km	59	96 kmph

      (iii) 115 minutes

8. a. Everything is too big.
   b. 1 cm to 1 m or 1 : 100
   c. (i) 1.4 m
      (ii) 80 cm
      (iii) 7.4 m, 3.7 m

Investigation, page 268

A scale drawing – some areas get sprayed by both machines and other areas don't get any fertiliser.

3.8a Area, Perimeter and Volume

Work it out, page 271

1. a. 80 cm^2, 36 cm
   b. 48 m^2, 28 m
   c. 156 cm^2, 50 cm
   d. 9.1 m^2, 12.2 m

2. a. 3 cm
   b. 3 cm

3. a. (i) 33 m^2, 47 m
      (ii) 33 m^2, 47 m
      (iii) 33 m^2, 47.5 m
   b. All the areas are the same.
   c. iii

4. a. 98.5 m, 186.5 m, 172.5 m
   b. Layout 1

Group work, page 272

1. Add the total length to the total width and multiply by two.

2. No – area is a multiplication whereas perimeter is an addition.

3. 6 m by 6 m

Work it out, page 273

1.

Conversion	Method
m² to cm²	multiply by 10 000
cm² to m²	divide by 10 000
km² to m²	multiply by 1 000 0000
m² to km²	divide by 1 000 0000

2. a.

Length	Width	Area in cm²	Area in m²
12 m	15 m	1 800 000	180
27 cm	28 cm	756	000.0756

b.

Length	Width	Area in m²	Area in km²
3 km	12 km	36 000 000	36
0.02 km	1.34 km	26 800	0.0268

3.   22 600 m²; 3 975 m²

Work it out, page 275

1.   30 cm²

2.   84 m²

3.   24 m²

4.   50 cm²

5.   176 m²

6.   130.5 cm²

7.   266 m²

8.   504 cm²

9.   Yes: a and b

Work it out, page 277

1.   a.   (i)   No division by 2 of the area of the triangles.
          (ii) 2 175 m²
          (iii) no

b.   (i)   120 m²
       (ii) 3 120
c.   (i)   Second end wall not to be rendered, not deducted area for windows.
       (ii) 128 m²

2.   9 091

3.   a.   (i)   140 m
          (ii) 7 200 m²
     b.   (i)   30 m
          (ii) 180 m
     c.   (i)   600 m²
          (ii) 142 m
          (iii) 12
     d.   There are many possible answers.

Paired work, page 279

1.   3

2.   a.   36 cm
     b.   24 cm
     c.   45 cm

3.   a.   3.14
     b.   3.14159265

Work it out, page 281

1.   18.85 cm, 28.27 cm²

2.   31.42 m, 78.54 m²

3.   47.12 cm, 176.71 cm²

4.   25.71 cm, 39.27 cm²

5.   10.05 m, 8.04 m²

6.   25.00 cm, 38.48 cm²

7.   41.14 m, 112.81 m²

8.   34.28 cm, 52.57 cm²

9.   no

10.

	Earth	Sun	Jupiter	Mars
Radius (km)	6 378	695 500	71 495	3 397
Circumference	40 074	4 369 955	449 216	21 344

Work it out, page 284

1. 160

2. yes

3. 6 546.02 m²

4. a. 36.95 m²
    b. 32

5. 53.66 m

Investigation, page 285

A circle.

3.8b Three-dimensional Shapes and Their Nets

Work it out, page 287

1. triangle
2.

	Sliced horizontally	Sliced vertically	Sliced at an angle from end to end
Cylinder	circle	rectangle	–
Cube	square	square	rectangle
Cuboid	rectangle	rectangle	rectangle
Triangular prism	rectangle	triangle	triangle

3. edges: 8; faces: 5; vertices: 5

4. a. cylinder
    b. triangular prism

5. a. 3 cm by 3 cm by 3 cm
    b.

Number faces painted	0	1	2	3	4
Number cubes	1	6	12	8	0

There are eight cubes each with three painted faces.

Investigation, page 288

	Vertices	Faces	Edges
Cube	8	6	12
Triangular pyramid	4	4	6
Square pyramid	5	5	8
Triangular prism	6	5	9
Pentagonal prism	10	7	15

vertices + faces = edges + 2

Group work, page 289

b, d and f

Work it out, page 289

1. a. triangular pyramid
    b. cylinder
    c. pentagonal pyramid

2. There are many different answers.

3. There are many different answers.

4. a and d

5.

6. a. and b.
    (i)

    (ii)

    (iv)

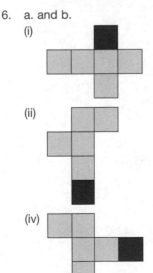

Group investigation, page 291

10

3.8c Volume and Surface Area

Work it out, page 293

1. 300 m^3, 280 m^2

2. 960 cm^3, 656 cm^2

3. 192.61 cm^3, 257.82 cm^2

Work it out, page 295

1. 3534.3 cm^3, 1295.9 cm^2

2. 72 mm^3, 156 mm^2

3. 3 000 cm^3, 1 860 cm^2

4. 615.8 m^3, 329.9 m^2

5. 504 m^3, 408 m^2

6. 1 008 cm^3, 688 cm^2

Work it out, page 297

1. a. 98 cm^3
   b. 3 640 cm^2

2. a. the second
   b. 12 cm
   c. the first glass

3. a. 210 cm^3
   b. 3 cm
   c. the second

4. a. 192 000 litres
   b. 20 hours
   c. There are many answers

5. a. (i) 22 m^3
      (ii) 20.11 m^3
      (iii) no
   b. (i) 14.98 m^3
      (ii) 24.98 m^3
      (iii) 2.67 m
      (iv) 138 days

6. a. 86 364 m^3
   b. (i) 340 014 316 m^2
      (ii) 340 km^2

Investigation 1, page 299

All stacked on top of each other to create a 8 cm high stack.

Investigation 2, page 300

1. 82 m

2. 89 m

Case study: Tasks, page 301

1. 110

2. 31

3. 1.29 m^3

4. a. 399.90 m^3 b. £9 997.50

5. 1.17

6. a. 234
   b. 98.04 m^3
   c £2 451

7. a. 25 m
   b. (i) 38 750 m^2
      (ii) 3.88 hectares

8. a. 695
   b. 111 trees per hectare

3.9a Right-angled Triangles and Their Special Properties

Investigation, page 302

Part 1

	Length a	Length b	Length c	Area square A $a \times a = a^2$	Area square B $b \times b = b^2$	Area square C $c \times c = c^2$
Triangle 1	3 cm	4 cm	5 cm	9	16	25
Triangle 2	5 cm	12 cm	13 cm	25	144	169
Triangle 3	7 cm	24 cm	25 cm	49	576	625
Triangle 4			There are many possible answers.			

Part 5   area A + area B = area C or $a^2 + b^2 = c^2$

Investigation, page 304

1. no

2. a. 13 m^2
   b. 9.4 m^2

3. a. yes
   b. any shape with a different height to the base length

Work it out, page 305

1. 5.48 m, 4.24 m, 3.46 m

2. 5.29 cm, 3.32 cm, 4.12 cm

3. The triangle does not contain a right angle.

Work it out, page 307

1. 15.23 cm

2. 10.30 m

3. 3.39 cm

4. 9.36 cm

5. 20.26 m

6. 6.66 m

Work it out, page 308

1. 16 m

2. 11.55 cm

3. 14.24 cm

4. 17.41 cm

5. 11.19 m

6. 6.57 m

Investigation, page 308

1. There are many possible answers including:
   5, 12, 13; 7, 24, 25; 9, 40, 41; 11, 60, 61 and 13, 84, 85

2. a. This arrangement of rope guarantees a right angle.

   b. There are many possible answers.

3. a. Draw the arms of a right angle of lengths:
      (i)   5 cm and 3 cm
      (ii) 3 cm and 3 cm
      (iii) 6 cm and 2 cm
   b. There are many possible answers.

Work it out, page 309

1. a. 113.06 km
   b. 18.90 km
   c. 195.98 m

2. a. 28.84 km
   b. no

3. yes

4. a. (i) not square rooted the answers, the felt is only 1.8 m wide so they will need to double up any final dimension
      (ii) 11.12 m
   b. (i) 1 is correct
      (ii) 25 cm, 4.42 m

5. a. 1 850 feet
   b. 715.89 feet

6. a. no, the lorry can only take poles up to 6.83 m
   b. 6.42 m

Investigation, page 312

a. c–g: $\sqrt{4}$, $\sqrt{5}$, $\sqrt{6}$, $\sqrt{7}$, $\sqrt{8}$

b. (i) $\sqrt{11}$

   (ii) $\sqrt{101}$

c. a construction

3.9b Right-angled Triangles and Trigonmetry

Work it out, page 313

1.

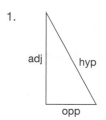

2.

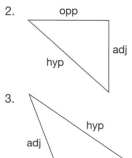

3.

Group task, page 313

Your answers should approximately equal the ones in this table:

	Length side a	Length side b	Length side c	a ÷ b opposite ÷ adjacent	a ÷ c opposite ÷ hypotenuse	b ÷ c adjacent ÷ hypotenuse
30°		There are many		0.577	0.5	0.866
45°		possible lengths		1	0.707	0.707
50°				1.192	0.766	0.643
60°				1.732	0.866	0.5

Investigation, page 315

1. There are many possible answers.

2. There are many possible answers.

3. Your answers should equal the answers in the example.

4. Your answers should equal the answers in the example.

Investigation, page 316

1. a. 0.625
   b. 0.64

2. There are many possible answers.

3. a. 4 cm
   b. 4.5 cm

4. Yes, they are.

Group work, page 317

1. a. 43°   b. 29°
   c. 28°   d. 44°

2. –

Work it out, page 319

1. 12.14 cm

2. 8.04 cm

3. 2.66 m

4. 9.42 cm

5. 14.28 m

6. 19.02 m

7. 54.10 cm

8. 11.04 cm

9. 11.96 cm

10. 12.82 m

11. 10.06 cm

12. 18.71 m

Work it out, page 321

1. 50.2°

2. 30.0°

3. 66.6°

4. 38.9°

5. 37.9°

6. 52.8°

7. 37.7°

8. 37.2°

Work it out, page 323

1. 826 km

2. 38 km

3. a. wood required: 190 × 2 = 380 cm (horizontal timber); 2 × 80 × sin 32 = 85 cm (two supporting struts); 190 × tan 32 = 119 cm (vertical timber); 2 × 190 ÷ cos 32 = 448 cm (two long sloping pieces of timber)
   b. 1 032 cm
   c. no
   d. There are many possible answers. The easiest is to reduce the size of the angle.

4. 18.6°

5. 84.5°

6. 69.4°

7. a. a = 5.7°; b = 10.1°
   b. 7.9°

Investigation, page 325

a. 38.7°
b. 30°
c. 90°

Task, page 326

1. –

2. –

3. stain 1: 17 cm; stain 2: 10 cm; stain 3: 13 cm

4. stain 1: 84.0°; stain 2: 86.5°; stain 3: 85.4°

5. stain 1: 162 cm; stain 2: 163 cm; stain 3: 162 cm

6. between 162 cm and 163 cm

3.10 Transformations

Task, page 328

2. a. $\begin{pmatrix} 5 \\ 7 \end{pmatrix}$ b. $\begin{pmatrix} 7 \\ 0 \end{pmatrix}$

Work it out, 329

1. A to F $\begin{pmatrix} 8 \\ -5 \end{pmatrix}$; B to G $\begin{pmatrix} -4 \\ -9 \end{pmatrix}$; C to H $\begin{pmatrix} 1 \\ 8 \end{pmatrix}$;

   D to E $\begin{pmatrix} 4 \\ -2 \end{pmatrix}$

2. a. $\begin{pmatrix} 2 \\ 3 \end{pmatrix}$ b. $\begin{pmatrix} -6 \\ 0 \end{pmatrix}$

   c. $\begin{pmatrix} -3 \\ -4 \end{pmatrix}$ d. $\begin{pmatrix} 2 \\ -6 \end{pmatrix}$

   e. $\begin{pmatrix} -2 \\ -3 \end{pmatrix}$, $\begin{pmatrix} 6 \\ 0 \end{pmatrix}$, $\begin{pmatrix} 3 \\ 4 \end{pmatrix}$, $\begin{pmatrix} -2 \\ 6 \end{pmatrix}$

3. a. (3, 4), (6, 4), (4, 6)
   b. (–1, 1), (2, 1), (0, 3)
   c. (0, –4), (3, –4), (1, –2)

4. a. (2, 6), (6, 6), (4, 4), (3, 4)
   b. (0, –1), (4, –1), (2, –3), (1, –3)
   c. (–5, 1), (–1, 1), (–3, –1), (–4, –1)

Investigation, page 330

Add the co-ordinates to the translation

a. (3, 6), (4, 8), (8, 3)
b. (–1, 7), (0, 9), (4, 4)

Work it out, page 333

1. b, d and g

2.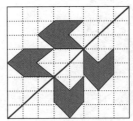
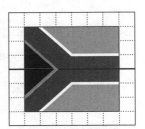

3. a. (−2, 3), (−1, 1), (−4, 1)
    b. (−1, 6), (1, 4), (−1, 3)
    c. (1, −1), (4, −1), (2, −3)

4.

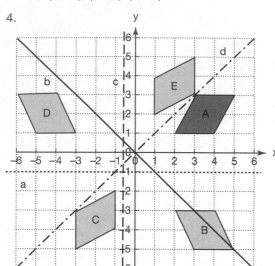

5. a. (4, 3) (3, 2) (3, 1) (6, 1) (6, 2)
    b. (4, 2) (5, 4) (1, 4)
    c. (2, 5) (4, 5) (4, 3) (2, 1)

Group investigation 1, page 334

1. There are many possible answers.

2. There are many possible answers.

3. The values of the x and y co-ordinates are reversed.

4. (1, 2) (2, 5) (4, 6) (5, 3)

Group investigation 2, page 335

Both 1 and 2 are incorrect.

Paired work, page 335

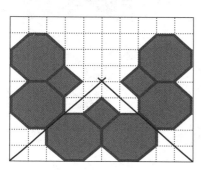

Work it out, page 338

1. a.

    b.

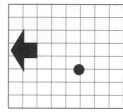

    c.

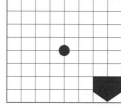

2.

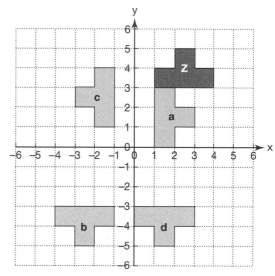

3. a. (0, 3)
    b. (0, 0)
    c. (4, 0)

Investigation, page 339

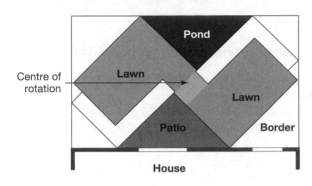

Group work, 339

1. See figure below.

2. See figure below.

3. a. See figure below.
   b. There are many other pairs of mirror lines.
   c. No

4. There are many other pairs (see figure).

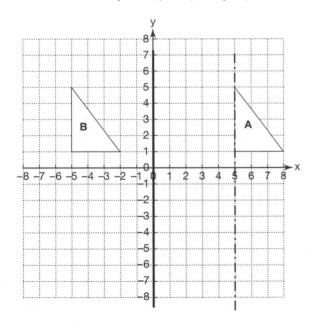

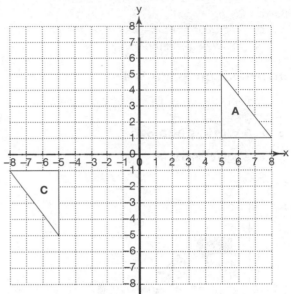

Work it out, page 341

1. a. (4, 0) scale factor 3
   b. (9, 4) scale factor 2
   c. (0, 2) scale factor 2
   d. (7, 4) scale factor 3

2.

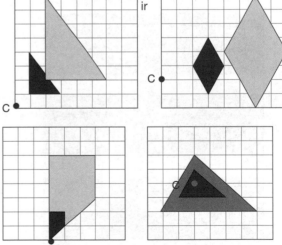

4. The point where the air is blown into the balloon.

5. a. 2   b. top right
   c. (4, 5)   d. (1.5, 2.5) (9, 2.5) (9, 9) (1.5, 9)

6. a. 2
    b. One quarter of the way down the page and half way along the page

Investigation, page 344

d. Multiply the co-ordinates by the scale factor.

Group work, page 345

1. See figure below.

2. (6, 4)

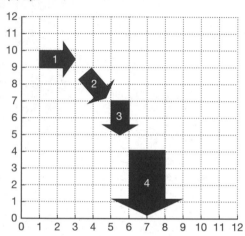

3. There are other possible answers.

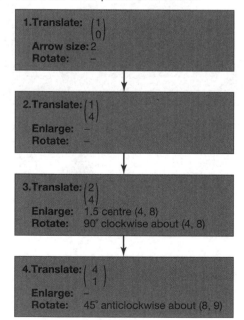

3.11 Bringing It All Together

Assignment questions, page 346

1. a. 0.2146 cm^2, 0.2854 cm^2
    b. 21%, 36%
    c. round peg fits better in the square hole

2. a. (i) 201 cm
        (ii) 36 kmph
        (iii) 415
    b. (i) 60 000 cm^3
        (ii) 60 litres
        (iii) 714 km

3. a. 183 m
    b. 3 metres per second
    c. 7 miles per hour

4. 430 m and 11 620 m^2

5. a. 2 640 m^2
    b. 20 metres per minute
    c. 70 ml
    d. (i) 920 m
        (ii) 46 minutes
        (iii) 5 520 ml

6. 7 km due north or south of the person's house.

7. a.

	Number of barrels used a day (million)	Population (millions)	Number of barrels used in a year (nearest million)	Volume of oil used a year (nearest million m³)	Height of column of oil (nearest km)	Volume of oil used per person (m³ to 1 d.p.)
UK	1.82	61	664	106	106 000	1.7
China	6.53	1 300	2 383	381	381 000	0.3
USA	20.73	300	7 566	1 211	1 211 000	4.0

   b. yes: China and USA

Assignment investigation, Tasks, page 349

1. 1.6180 cm

2. a. 4.85 cm
   b. No

3. a. (i) 1.118 cm
      (ii) 1.6180
      (iii) yes
   b. scale drawing (no associated questions)

Assignment investigation, Tasks, page 352

1. 1 : 500, 1 : 400 or 1 : 300

2. using the scale 1 : 500, AE = 10 cm, AB = 6 cm, BE = 13 cm AC = 9 cm, CE = 14 cm, AD = 15 cm and DE = 6 cm

3. a plan

4. a plan

5. 225 m² (approximately)

6. a. 19.6 m²
   b. 29.5 m³

7. 1 613 m² (approximately)

Investigation, page 353

1.

	Area m²	Heat loss
Both windows	4.48	19.264
Both doors	5.04	25.2
Right internal wall	12	4.8
Bottom internal wall	17.48	6.992
Top external wall	15.24	3.048
Left external wall	9.76	1.952
The floor	15	10.5
The ceiling	15	3

2. 74.756

3. 1 868.9 watts

4. 3

5. 2

Chapter 4: Algebra

4.1 Patterns in Numbers

Task, page 357

1.

Number of houses	1	2	3	4	5	6
Number of layouts	1	2	3	5	8	13

2. Each number is the sum of the previous two numbers.

3. a. 21 b. 34
   c. 55 d. 89

Task, page 358

a. diagram
b.

Number of months	1	2	3	4	5	6
Number of rabbits	2	4	6	10	16	26

c. 466

Investigation 1, page 359

1–9:

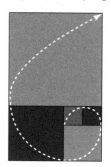

10. Spiral.

Investigation 2, page 359

1. $\frac{13}{8}, \frac{21}{13}, \frac{34}{21}$

2. 1, 2, 1.5, 1.67, 1.6, 1.63, 1.62, 1.62

3. The divisions are tending towards 1.62.

4. This is the number in the golden ratio.

Investigation 3, page 359

There are many possible answers.

Work it out, page 360

1. a. 8
   b. 13
   c. 55

2. The branching is obeying the series.

Work it out, page 363

1. a. $60n + 20$
   b. (i) £620
      (ii) £860

2. a. £15 000
   b. £175 000
   c. £15 000, £30 000, £45 000, £60 000
   d. $15\,000n + 85\,000$
   e. £265 000

3. a. and b.

Number of storeys	Number of flats	5 × number of storeys
1	5	5
2	10	10
3	15	15
4	20	20

c. $5n$

d. 200

e. $5n - 3$

4. a.

Row number (n)	No. of grey slabs	No. of white slabs	Total no. of tiles
1	5	4	9
2	9	12	21
3	13	20	33
4	17	28	45
5	21	36	57

b. (i) $4n + 1$

   (ii) $8n - 4$

   (iii) $12n - 3$

c. (i) 49

   (ii) 156

   (iii) 1197

5. a. 140   b. £200

  c. $20n + 40$ d. £600

6. a. 18, 22

  b. 42, 52

  c. 39, 47

7. a.

3	5	7	9	11	13
6	9	12	15	18	21
9	13	17	21	25	29
12	17	22	27	32	37
15	21	27	33	39	45
18	25	32	39	46	53

b.

1	3	5	7	9	11
4	7	10	13	16	19
7	11	15	19	23	27
10	15	20	25	30	35
13	19	25	31	37	43
16	23	30	37	44	51

8. a. 9, 11, $2n + 1$, 201

  b. 13, 16, $3n + 1$, 301

  c. 21, 27, $6n + 1$, 603

  d. 40, 60, $10n + 20$, 1 020

  e. 4, 10, $6n - 2$, 598

  f. 24, 31, $7n - 4$, 696

9. a. 10, 13, 16

  b. 1, 6, 11

10. a. 21, 39

   b. 15, 42

11. a. 3

   b. 5

12. a. (i) (10, 11)   b. (i) (29, 3)

     (ii) (100, 101)   (ii) (299, 3)

     (iii) $(n, n + 1)$ (iii) $(3n - 1, 3)$

Investigation, page 367

$30°, 42°, 54°, 66°, 78°, 90°$

Work it out, page 369

1. a. (i) 1 024

    (ii) 1 048 576

  b. (i) 84

    (ii) 280

    (iii) $28n$

2. a. 36, 49

  b. n^2

  c. (i) 100

    (ii) 10 000

3. a. 20 100

  b. 201

  c. 20 300

4. a. $(n + 1)(n + 2)/2$

  b. $(n + 2)^2$

5. 5 050

6. a. $1\,000 \times 2^n$

  b. 1 024 000

  c. 1 048 576 000

4.2 Working with Formulae

Work it out, page 372

1. 7

2. 11

3. 4

4. 10

5. 12

6. 6

7. 9

8. 24

9. 13

10. 4

11. 6

12. 24

13. 28

14. 28

15. 18

16. −12

17. 1.5

18. 8

19. 3

20. 9

21. b and g; c and l; d and i; e and h; f and j

22. a. 45, 6n − 3   b. 24, 2(n + 4)
    c. 88, 4(3n − 2)   d. 165, 3(6n + 7)
    e. 27, $(n^2 − 10)/2$

Investigation, page 373

1. 99.99

2. 500

3. 59.4

4. 60.6

Work it out, page 374

1. a. 21.2   b. yes
   c. 26.0   d. no

2. a. (i) 87.8 kg, 177.8 cm
      (ii) 71.6 kg, 170.2 cm
   b. 1.9 litres

3. a. men
   b. (i) 2 704.8 calories
      (ii) 2 336 calories
   c. 1 954.8 calories and 1 836 calories
   d. 12 stone 12 pounds and 10 stone 9 pounds

4. a. £27 379
   b. £31 125

5. 10 m short

6. a. (i) 55° F
      (ii) 80° F
   b. 13° C and 27° C

7. a. inside
   b. 422.6 m
   c. 45.2 m

8. 109.2

Group work, page 377

a.

Amount saved after:	Kieran	Dwaine
Ten years	0	£15 645
Thirty years	£49 423	£72 921

b. No
c. Kiernan: £619 672, Dwaine: £733 776

Group work, page 378

1. correct

2. 25 mg

3. yes

Work it out, page 379

1. a. 35 + 15n
   b. 45 + 30n
   c. 12 + 1.5w

2. a. 3n − 24
   b. 6
   c. When the length of foot is 8 inches or less.

3. a. p − 0.15p or 0.85p
   b. £23.80

4. a. $3w + d$
    b. (i) 41
        (ii) 30
    c. If it wins all its games and Gadlock Utd. lose all theirs.

5. a. $560 + 0.4m$
    b. $0.5\ m$
    c. (i)   public transport
        (ii) company car
        (iii) company car

6. a. $0.4n + 0.6e$
    b. 60%

7. a. $20 + 0.09(p - 800) + 0.12t$ for $m \geq 800$
        $50 + 0.08(p - 1\,400) + 0.12t$ for $m \geq 1\,400$
    b. £82.40
    c. £118
    d. £71.60

Case study: Tasks, page 382

1. a. £46 800
    b. £99 300

2. a. and b.

Operating costs	First year	Second year	Third year
Lecturer salary	£30 000	£30 900	£31 827
Cost to the university	£35 100	£36 153	£37 238
Consumables/ stationery	£10 000	£10 200	£10 404
Total costs	£45 100	£46 353	£47 642

   c. £139 095

3. a., c. and d.

	Year one	Year two	Year three
Number of students	20	37	51
Fees for one student	£ 3 000	£3 090	£3 183
Total fees	£60 000	£114 330	£162 333

   b. new fees = $1.03F$ (F: old fees)
   e. £336 663

4. £98 268

4.3 Simplification of Algebraic Expressions

Work it out, 384

1. $15w + 13r + 12b$

2. a. $6m + 10w + 26$
    b. $3m + 8w + 18$

3. a. $4cd$, $2dc$, $-2cd$
        $3c$, c
        6, 3, -5
        b, $5b$, $-2b$
    b. $4cd$
        $4c$
        4
        $4b$

4. a. $6x + 13y$ b. $3p^2 + p$
    c. $9a + 8b$ d. $3pq$
    e. $2y + 2x$ f. $5xy - 3y$
    g. $6m + 2n$ h. $6m^2 - 4m$
    i. $4m - 4n$ j. $2x^2 + 8x$
    k. 9 l. $13xy^2 + x$
    m. $3y$ n. $-x + 2$

5. $-5m^2 + 6m^2n^2 + 4mn + 7nm^2 + 4$

6. a.

	11a + 29b	
5a + 12b		6a + 17b
3a + 5b	2a + 7b	4a + 10b

    b.

	14c + 14d − 1	
5c + 6d + 3		8d + 9c − 4
5c − 2d	8d + 3	9c − 7

    c.

	−3a − 2b	
−5a − b		2a − b
−3a + 2b	−2a − 3b	4a + 2b

    d.

	10c + 6d − 7	
8c + 2d − 4		2c + 4d − 3
6c − 2d	2c − 4	4d + 1

Work it out, page 387

1. a. $4m^2$
    b. $12q^5$
    c. $6n^2$
    d. $12r^4$
    e. $8pq$
    f. $7s^9$
    g. $30ab$
    h. m^6
    i. $8mn$
    j. $6n^6$
    k. $12b^2$
    l. $12a^2b^2$
    m. $6ab$
    n. c^3d^3
    o. $18mn$
    p. $6e^3f^3$
    q. $36a^2$
    r. $4g^4h^4$
    s. $20p$
    t. $15j^5k^9$

2. a. 4
    b. $20p$
    c. $3q$
    d. q^2
    e. 4
    f. r^3
    g. 2
    h. s^6
    i. $6q$
    j. $5t$
    k. $3n$
    l. $2u^3$
    m. $2m$
    n. $4v$
    o. $5p$
    p. 1
    q. 32
    r. $2x^{-1}$ or $2/x$
    s. 6
    t. $4y^2$

Work it out, page 388

1. a. $6a + 12b$
    b. $16e + 39$
    c. $15c - 10d$
    d. $2c + 6b$
    e. $12p - 8q + 20r$
    f. $-5g + 4$
    g. $7a + 8b$
    h. $7v + 18w$
    i. $31e + 28f$
    j. $4m - 16n$
    k. $10 - 3g$
    l. $7 + 14q$
    m. $11m + 6$
    n. $-4b$
    o. $-4q$
    p. $13c - 2d$
    q. $8a$
    r. $-4 - 8p$
    s. $d + 6c$
    t. $29 + 2e + 9f$

2. a. $3a^2 + 12$
    b. $-3h^2 + 16h$
    c. $14b^2 - 14bc$
    d. $-10k + 12k^2$
    e. $3de + d^2$
    f. $3m^2$
    g. $15f^2 + 72fg$
    h. $14n^2 + 4mn$

3. $x(x + 1) = x^2 + x$

4. a. $6n^2 - 9n$
    b. $4n^2 - 11n$
    c. $n^2 - 5n$

Group investigation, page 389

1. Always the same answer: 1 010

2. $(n + 12 + 2\,000 - n)/2 + 4$

3. 1 010

4.4 Equations

Work it out, page 391

1. a. (i) $2n + n = 18$
        (ii) work 6 hours, home 12 hours
    b. (i) $n + n + 3 = 17$
        (ii) work 10 hours, home 7 hours

2. a. $n + 8 = 12, n = 4$
    b. $4n = 28, n = 7$
    c. $2n + 3 = 11, n = 4$
    d. $3n - 4 = 14, n = 6$

3. a. some number plus six gives 15, 9
    b. five times some number gives thirty, 6
    c. two times some number minus five gives 7, 6
    d. three times some number + three is 18, 5

Work it out, page 394

1. a. 8
    b. 6
    c. 4
    d. 2

2. a. 5
    b. 6
    c. 14
    d. 5
    e. 9

3. a. 2
    b. 4
    c. 20
    d. 6
    e. 3

4. a. 2
    b. 3
    c. 4
    d. 9
    e. 7
    f. 4
    g. 5
    h. 3
    i. 6
    j. 5.5

5. a. 5
    b. 3
    c. 7
    d. 3

Work it out, page 397

1. a. 5
    b. 2
    c. 7
    d. 3
    e. 8
    f. 2

g. 3

h. 4

i. 2

j. 1

k. 1

l. 4

m. 2

n. 11

o. 2

2. a. 4

b. 4

c. 3

d. 1

e. 6

f. 4

g. 2

h. 3

i. −3

j. 3

k. 2

l. 9

m. 3

n. 2

o. 3

3. $3n + 6 − 6n + 12 = 7n$ (expand the brackets)

$−3n + 18 = 7n$ (simplify the expression)

$\quad + 3n \quad\quad + 3n$ (get rid of 3n on left)

$18 = 10n$

$÷10 ÷10$ (get rid of 10 on right)

$1.8 = n$

4. a. $\frac{1}{3}$

b. $\frac{4}{5}$

c. $1\frac{1}{4}$

d. $\frac{3}{7}$

e. 50

5. a. 12

b. 9

c. 11

d. 13

e. 5.5

f. 6.5

Group investigation 1, page 398

Cannot divide by zero.

Group investigation 2, page 398

a. 6

b. 10

Work it out, page 399

1. a. 3 cm and 9 cm

b. 27 cm²

2. a. 30

b. 60

c. 8

3. a. $15n = 360$

b. 24°, 48°, 96°, 192°

4. a. $70 + 125n = 695$

b. five days

5. a. $3n + 50 = 470$

b. 140

6. a. $90 + 40n = 1\,260 − 50n$

b. 13

c. £610

7. a. $42 + 30n = 92$ b. 5

c. 3   d. No

8. a. £370, £1 110

b. £395, £1 185

9. a. $6t + 6 = 14t$

b. 45 minutes

10. a. $\dfrac{d}{50} = \dfrac{165 − d}{60}$ or $50t + 60t = 165$

b. 75 miles

b. 1.30 P.M.

11. a. $\frac{5n}{4} + 20 = 120$

b. 80

12. $10\frac{2}{3}$

Paired work, page 401

$2\,000n = 10\,000$, $n = £5$

$2\,000n − 800 − 1\,400 = 10\,000$, $n = £6.10$

$1\,500n + 500n/2 − 800 − 1\,400 = 10\,000$, $n = £6.97$

4.5 Rearranging Formulae

Work it out, 403

1. a. $5y$

b. $\dfrac{y}{3}$

c. $2y$

d. $\dfrac{7y}{2}$

e. $\dfrac{9y}{4}$

f. $\dfrac{11y}{5}$

g. $\dfrac{y}{w}$

h. wy

i. $\dfrac{3w}{y}$

2. a. $n - 1$ b. $n + 3$

    c. $\dfrac{n + 1}{2}$ d. $\dfrac{n - 2}{3}$

    e. $\dfrac{n + p}{4}$ f. $\dfrac{n - p}{2}$

3. a. $\dfrac{y - 2}{2}$ b. $\dfrac{y + 3}{3}$

    c. $\dfrac{y - 8}{2}$ d. $\dfrac{y - 16}{4}$

    e. $\dfrac{y + 3w}{3}$ f. $\dfrac{y - 5w}{5}$

4. a. $\dfrac{4p - 6}{3}$ b. $\dfrac{5p + 8}{4}$

    c. $\dfrac{6p - 15}{5}$ d. $\dfrac{7p + 6}{2}$

    e. $\dfrac{5p + 9}{3}$ f. $\dfrac{3p - 4}{2}$

    g. $\dfrac{pr - 10}{5}$ h. $\dfrac{pm + 3}{3}$

    i. $\dfrac{pn - 4n}{4}$

5. a. Second stage is incorrect, 12 is not a whole number but one that is divided by 5

    b. $\dfrac{5y - 12}{3}$

Work it out, page 405

1. a. $c = \dfrac{10r}{3}$
    b. £5.27
    c. (i) £3.15
        (ii) £4.20

2. a. 42 minutes
    b. $c = 10t$
    c. 200 calories

3. a. $P = 20l$
    b. £800 000
    c. £200 000

4. a. $t = 20d + 30h$
    b. (i) $\dfrac{t - 20d}{30}$
        (ii) 2 000 ft

5. a. $F = \dfrac{9C + 160}{5}$

    b. (i) 32° F
        (ii) 212° F
    c. −40°

6. a. $D = \dfrac{RA}{60VW}$
    b. 2 mg

Investigation 1, page 407

1. no

2. yes

Investigation 2, page 407

a. money = work/knowledge
b. it gets bigger

4.6 Straight Line Graphs and Their Equations

Work it out, page 409

1. a. (i) 80
        (ii) 14.6
    b. 10 and 2
    c. They are the values of y when the line cuts the y-axis.
    d. region 2

2. a. (i) weekly heating costs
        (ii) temperature (centigrade)
    b. 15° C and 18° C
    c. (i) £4.80, £16.50
        (ii) £9, £27
    d. They are the values of y when the line cuts the y-axis.
    e. A four bedroom house.

Work it out, page 412

1. b and o; c and m; d and n; e and i; f and p; g and k; h and j

2. a: 1   b: 3
    c: 0.25   d: −2
    e: −0.5

3. a. −3   b. 2
    c. 0.25   d. −4

4.   a: 0   b: −0.4
     c: −2   d: 3
     e: 1   f: 0.5

5.

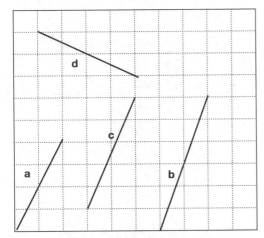

6.

Equation of line	Gradient	Intercept
$y = 3x - 2$	3	−2
$y = 6x + 5$	6	5
$y = 10x$	10	0
$y = -2x + 0.4$	−2	0.4
$y = 5$	0	5
$y = 0.5x + 0.3$	0.5	0.3
$y = 1 + 2x$	2	1
$y = 3x + 7$	3	7
$y = -2x$	−2	0
$y = -0.2x + 3$	−0.2	3
$y = -4$	0	4
$y = -5x - 5$	−5	−5

7.   a. $y = -3x$ (amongst many others)
     b. $y = 2$ (amongst many others)

8.   a. $y = 3x - 2$ (amongst many others)
     b. $y = 3x$ (amongst many others)

9.   gradients: 4 and 6; intercept: 10 and 2

10. a. (i)   1
         (ii) 2
         (iii) $y = x + 2$
     b. (i)   3
         (ii) −4
         (iii) $y = 3x - 4$
     c. (i)   0.5
         (ii) 3
         (iii) $y = 0.5x + 3$

     d. (i)   −2
         (ii) −2
         (iii) $y = -2x - 2$
     e. (i)   0.25
         (ii) 3
         (iii) $y = 0.25x + 3$
     f. (i)   −4
         (ii) −2
         (iii) $y = -4x - 2$
     g. (i)   5
         (ii) 2.5
         (iii) $y = 2.5x + 3$
     h. (i)   −1.5
         (ii) 2.5
         (iii) $y = -1.5 \times 2.5$

Work it out, page 416

1.

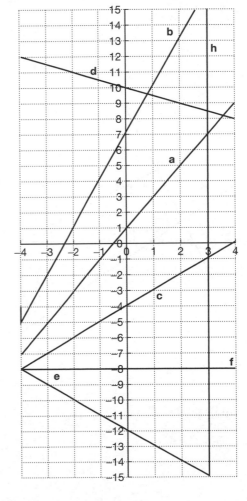

2. a.

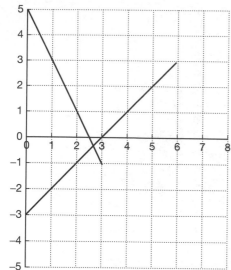

   b. gradients: 1, –2
   c. intercept: –3, 5
   d. equations: $y = x - 3$, $y = -2x + 5$

3. a. $y = x + 2$
   b. $y = -2x + 7$

4.

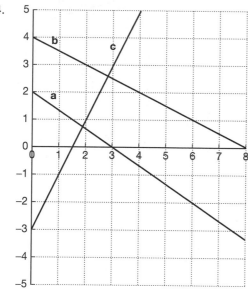

5. a. gradient: 25; intercept: 40
   b. $y = 25x + 40$
   c. £50
   d. ££25

e.

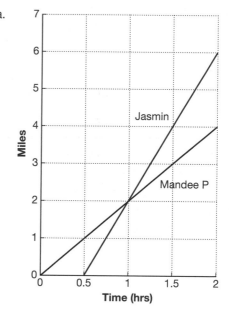

f. no
g. for jobs longer than 4 hours

6. a.

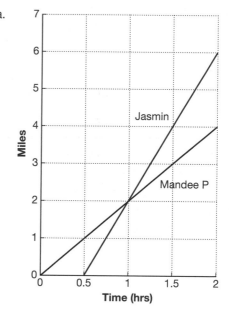

   b. the miles covered each hour
   c. 1 P.M.
   d. $y = 2x$, $y = 4x - 2$

Investigation 1, page 418

1. Gradient at right angles to a line has a gradient of −1 ÷ the gradient of the line.

2. a. −0.5
   b. 0.25
   c. −5

Investigation 2, page 418

1. $b = d$

2. $a = c$

3. $a = \frac{-1}{c}$

4. $a = 0$ and $b \neq 0$

4.7 Simultaneous Equations

Work it out, page 420

1. a. −
   b. soap, 50 p, oil £1.50

2. a. −
   b. truffles: £1; coffee: £2.50
   c. $8t + 3c = 15.50$; $6t + 3c = 13.50$

Work it out, page 423

1. a. 1, 2   b. 3, 2
   c. 5, −9   d. 2, 1
   e. 5, 3   f. 2, 1
   g. 5, 0   h. 3, −1

2. a. 6, 1   b. 3, 2
   c. 7, 1   d. 5, 1
   e. 5, 3   f. 3, 6
   g. 3, 4   h. −3, −4

3. a. Adding the equations does not eliminate the y's.
   b. 7, 6

4. a. $w + d = 12$, $3w + d = 20$
   b. $w = 4$, $d = 8$

5. a. $150x + 160y = 2\,100$, $150x + 240y = 2\,700$
   b. High Tarn: 7.5 hectares
      Lower Skiddaw: 6 hectares

Work it out, page 425

1. a. 2, 1   b. 3, 5
   c. 2, 4   d. 6, 5
   e. 1, 4   f. 3, 7
   g. 3, 1   h. 5, 8

2. a. $3p + 2w = 9.50$, $6p + 5w = 20$
   b. pizza: £2.50, wedges £1
   c. 12

3. a. $5r + 4c = 275$, $2r + c = 95$
   b. radiator: £35, convection: £25
   c. £155

4. a. $8n + 3c = 63$, $10n + 9c = 105$
   b. real: 6 g, fake: 5 g

5. a. $3n + 2d = 135$, $5n + d = 190$
   b. night: £35, dinner: £15

6. a. $14d + 10c = 6\,500$, $7d + 12c = 5\,350$
   b. chocolate bar: 300 calories, doughnut: 250 calories

Work it out, page 428

1. a.

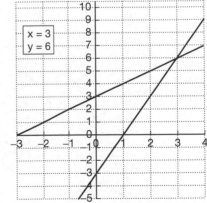

b.

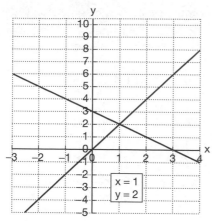

x = 1
y = 2

e.

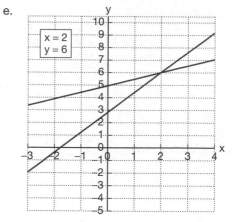

x = 2
y = 6

c.

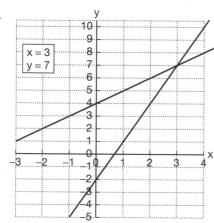

x = 3
y = 7

f.

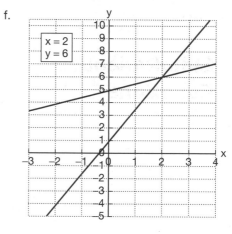

x = 2
y = 6

d.

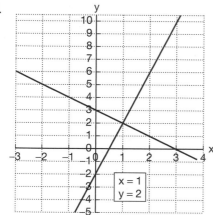

x = 1
y = 2

2. a.

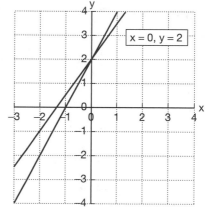

x = 0, y = 2

b.
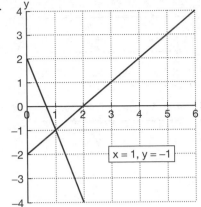

x = 1, y = −1

c.
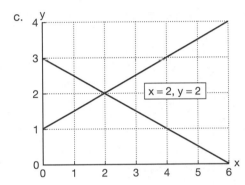

x = 2, y = 2

3. a. The two lines are parallel.
    b. There are many possible answers.

4. a. y = 4x, x + y = 20
    b.
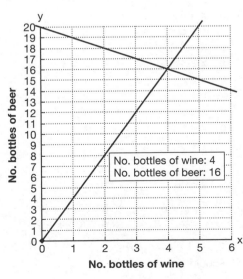

No. bottles of wine: 4
No. bottles of beer: 16

5. a. y = 5x + 4, y = 6x − 4
    b.
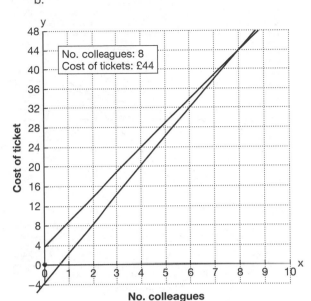

No. colleagues: 8
Cost of tickets: £44

6. a. 3x + y = 18, 2x + 2y = 16
    b.
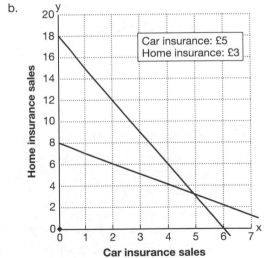

Car insurance: £5
Home insurance: £3

    c. car insurance

7. a. Cars are initially 140 km apart but are travelling towards each other.
    b. 40 kmph and 30 kmph
    c. y = −40x + 140; y = 30x
    d. After two hours.

8. a. $y = 270 + 0.6x$, $y = 2.4x$
    b.

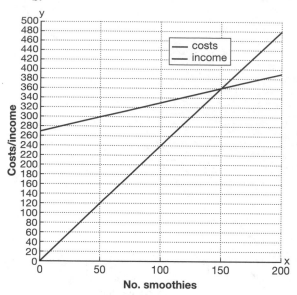

    c. income = costs
    d. 150

4.8 Inequalities

Work it out, page 430

1. a. speed ≤ 40
    b. height ≤ 4.1 m
    c. weight ≤ 7.5 T
    d. 6 A.M. $\leq$ parking ≤ 11 P.M.

2. a. no. people ≤ 9
    b. baggage ≤ 25 kg
    c. $130 <$ height < 200

3. a. time greater than 20 minutes
    b. number of people greater or equal to 10
    c. age between and including 5 and 16 years
    d. height between 130 cm and 200 cm

Work it out, page 431

1 a. 0 1 2 3 4 5 6

    b. −6 −5 −4 −3 −2 −1 0

c. −5 −4 −3 −2 −1 0 1

d. 0 1 2 3 4 5 6

e. −6 −5 −4 −3 −2 −1 0

f. −2 −1 0 1 2 3 4

g. −2 −1 0 1 2 3 4

2. a. $x \geq 2$ b. $x < -1$
    c. $5 < x \leq 10$ d. $-5 \leq x \leq 3$
    e. $x < 2$ or $x > 4$ f. $x \leq -10$ or $x > 20$

3. 0.2, 0.5 amongst others

4. a. −1, 0, 1, 2, 3
    b. 1, 2, 3

5. a. 11, 13
    b. 9, 12

6. a. 36   b. 30
    c. −20   d. 0

Investigation, page 432

1. c and e

2. c

Work it out, page 434

1. a. $x > 4$ b. $x \leq 2$
    c. $x \leq 5$ d. $x \leq 4$
    e. $x < 8$ f. $x < -5$
    g. $x \geq 4$ h. $x > 3$
    i. $x > 2$ j. $x > -5$
    k. $x > 5$ l. $x < -4$
    m. $x < 3$ n. $x < -2$
    o. $x < -1$ p. $x < -4$

2. a. $x > 4$ b. $x \leq 14$
    c. $x < 4$ d. $x > 7$
    e. $x < -6$ f. $x < 2$

3. a. $1 < x < 5$ b. $3 \leq x < 8$
    c. $2 \geq x \geq -3$ d. $30 \geq x \geq 20$
    e. $5 < x < 6$ f. $5 \leq x < 8$

4. Should be $-4 > x > -9$

Investigation, page 434

−1, 0, 1

Work it out, page 438

1. a. $0 \le x \le 5$ and $0 \le y < 4$
    b. $x > 1$ and $1 < y \le 5$
    c. $2 \le x \le 6$ and $2 \le y \le 8$
    d. $x > 6$ and $y > 6$
    e. $x < 2$, $y > 1$ and $y < 2x + 1$
    f. $y \ge 1$, $x \ge 0$ and $y \le -x + 5$

2. a.

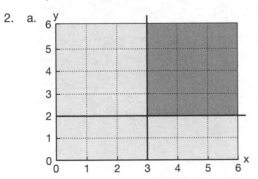

    b.

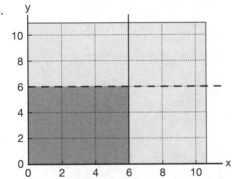

    c.

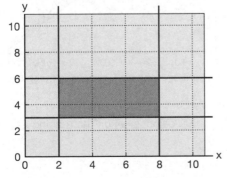

    d.

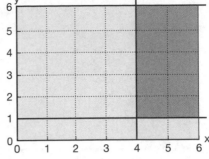

3. a.

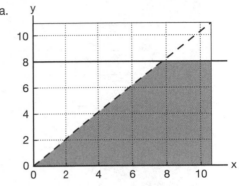

    b.

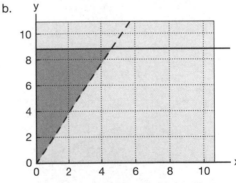

    c.

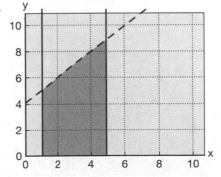

d.

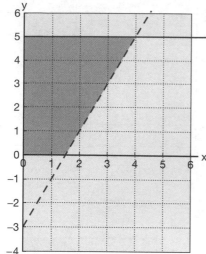

e.

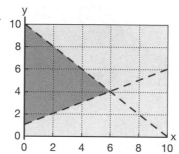

f.

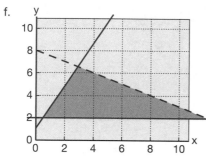

4.

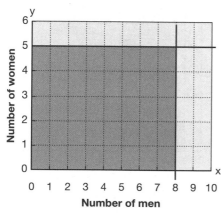

5.   a. $60x - 12y \geq 0$
   b. $x \geq 0, y \geq 0$
   c.

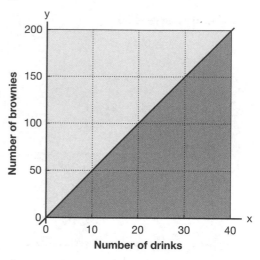

   d.   no

6.   a. $x + y \leq 60$
   b. $25x + 30y > 1\ 500$
   c. $x \geq 0, y \geq 0$
   d.

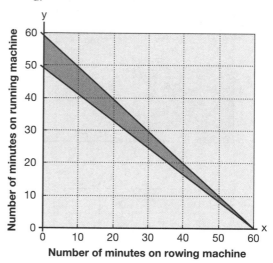

   e.   yes
   f.   1 800 calories, all on the running machine

7. a. $200x + 260y \geq 5\,200$
    b. $10x + 10y \leq 360$
    c. $x \geq 0,\ y \geq 0$
    d.

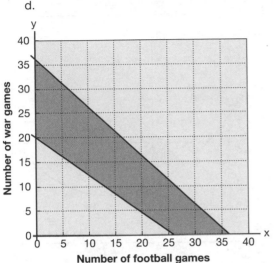

Number of football games

    e. £93.60

10. a. $3\,000y + 14\,000x \geq 420\,000,\ x + y \leq 80,$
     $x \geq 0,\ y \geq 0$
     b.

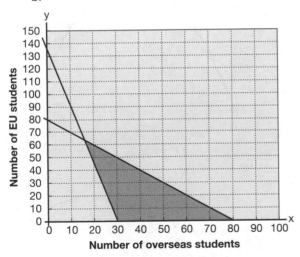

Number of overseas students

    c. yes
    d. (i) £1 120 000
        (ii) 0 EU and 80 overseas

e. (i) $x + 2y \leq 16,\ x + y \leq 10,\ x \geq 0,\ y \geq 0$
    (ii)

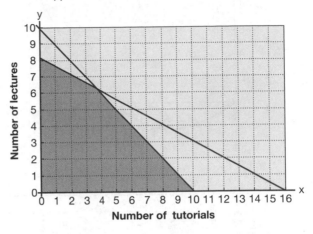

Number of tutorials

    (iii) no

Investigation, page 440

The inequalities are impossible.

4.9 Drawing Curves

Task, page 442

1. a. (i) 468
        (ii) 372
    b. –

Work it out, page 445

1. b and c

2. a.

x	0	1	2	3	4	5
y	0	−2	−2	0	4	10

b.

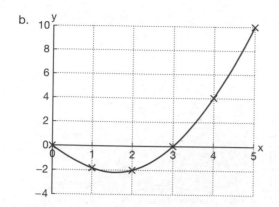

3. a.

x	-3	-2	-1	0	1	2
y	3	0	-1	0	3	8

b.

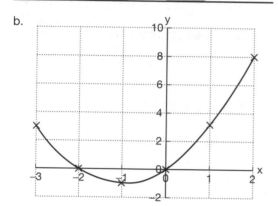

4. a.

x	0	1	2	3	4	5
y	3	0	-1	0	3	8

b.

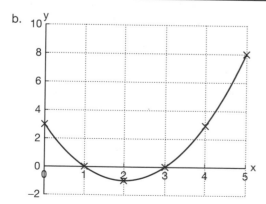

5. a.

x	-2	-1	0	1	2	3
y	4	-1	-4	-5	-4	-1

b.

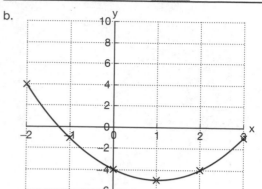

6. a.

x	0	1	2	3	4	5
y	-6	-2	0	0	-2	-6

b.

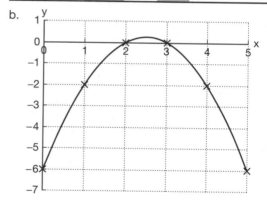

7. a. Not included the minus in the calculations
        for y.

b.

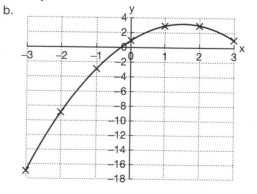